HOW CRIMINAL LAW WORKS

How Criminal Law Works

A Conceptual and Practical Guide

Samuel H. Pillsbury

PROFESSOR OF LAW AND WILLIAM M. RAINS FELLOW
LOYOLA LAW SCHOOL LOS ANGELES

CAROLINA ACADEMIC PRESS
Durham, North Carolina

Library of Congress Cataloging-in-Publication Data

Pillsbury, Samuel H.
How criminal law works : a conceptual and practical guide / Samuel H. Pillsbury.
p. cm.
ISBN 978-1-59460-631-1 (alk. paper)
1. Criminal law--United States. I. Title.
KF9219.P55 2009
345.73--dc22
2009025574

Carolina Academic Press
700 Kent Street
Durham, North Carolina 27701
Telephone (919) 489-7486
Fax (919) 493-5668
www.cap-press.com

Printed in the United States of America
2017 Printing

For my students,
past, present and future

CONTENTS

Introduction to Part Five • Defenses

LIST OF SIDEBARS

PREFACE

Criminal law looks easy. But it isn't.

Criminal law is certainly familiar. Basic concepts of crime inform a huge amount of popular culture: consider all the movies, television shows, books, magazine and newspaper articles about crime. Criminal law also uses ordinary ideas about blame, such as the difference between an accidental and an intentional harm. Blaming people—and excusing them—is basic to human society. Nothing new there.

If there is a hard part to criminal law, it would seem to be proof. Figuring out who did what, that's the usual challenge for television crime fighters. But that's not the central challenge of criminal law.

This book is about the hard part of criminal law, which is analyzing facts according to particular rules of criminal liability. To do this badly is easy. To do it well requires great care and considerable learning.

This book comes out of many years of teaching criminal law in law school, but also from my work as a prosecutor and before that, a newspaper reporter covering courts. It also comes from a personal commitment to improve our understanding of this most basic form of responsibility. Here we know less than we think we do and our ignorance can have serious consequences.

To introduce the methods and aim of this book, I begin with what I see as the four basic challenges of learning American criminal law: the challenges of analysis, of the familiar, of many rules, and of consistency. After detailing each and how the book addresses it, I note the limits of the book, consider its audience, and give a quick overview of the chapters to follow.

The Challenges of Criminal Law

The Challenge of Analysis

Students of law, whether in law school or other settings, often believe that learning the law means absorbing all available information about rules and rule distinctions. The more knowledge about rules the better. This neglects the critical skill emphasized in law school and important for anyone concerned with the law: the ability to *use* rules to analyze facts. Rules provide the means to a legal answer; they are not themselves the answer.

In learning to be a carpenter, you have to learn about the tools and materials of the trade. You need an introduction to 2 x 4's (a standard measurement of lumber), saws, hammers and nails, just for starters. But the most important learning comes with practice, with actual sawing, fitting and hammering. Similarly, substantive criminal law can be seen as a set of tools to be used by police officers, prosecutors, defense attorneys, judges, juries and others to reach reliable and just decisions about individual criminal responsibility. While the law's ideal is to resolve disputes by legal rules alone, the rules do nothing without human interpreters. Knowledge of rules is necessary, but not sufficient.

This book seeks to explain how criminal law *works*, not just what it says.

The Challenge of the Familiar

"Everyone Can Recognize When Someone Has Committed a Crime." This quote from Pope John Paul II appeared on a sign borne by a protester outside a meeting of Catholic bishops discussing child molestation charges against the clergy.[1] It states an important truth about criminal law. We can all recognize basic forms of criminality and make basic responsibility judgments. Virtually all adults—and most children—grasp the wrongness of stealing, defrauding, raping, robbing, murdering, as well as the need to punish such deeds. In the United States, the connection between popular understandings of criminal responsibility and criminal law is especially close, because all criminal offenses are defined by legislation approved by elected representatives and cases that go to trial are generally resolved by lay persons acting as jurors.

Most adults also learn a lot about crime and criminal justice by cultural osmosis. Crime suffuses popular culture: crime stories feature prominently in the news media and are a staple of movies, television dramas, and novels. Sometimes it just seems everywhere.

But the very familiarity of the subject, the very ease with which most of us reach preliminary judgments about criminal blame or excuse, represents the single greatest obstacle to legal understanding. This is because learning how to do criminal law analysis often requires altering established thought and speech habits; it requires unlearning old ways as much as it does learning new ones.

---

1. Michael Lobdell, Conservatives and Liberals Are Unified by Church Sex Scandal, Los Angeles Times, June 14, 2002, at A39.

Sound criminal law analysis demands a precision in expression beyond that required for ordinary conversation. Key words may be familiar, such as intentional or accidental, or archaic such as malicious, wanton or willful. But in any case, standard dictionary definitions will not suffice. Key legal terms have special *legal* meanings which must be learned and respected.

Criminal law analysis requires equal rigor at the conceptual level. Students must attend to distinctions in responsibility that make substantive criminal law analysis closer in both method and content to moral philosophy than to fields such as psychology or sociology which might seem to speak more directly about criminal behavior. (In fact, the latter fields do have more to say about criminal *behavior*, understanding why individuals offend; they have less to say, however, about criminal *responsibility*, determining who should be punished for crime.)

Unfortunately, the language and analysis skills needed here often conflict in some ways with existing knowledge and abilities. Learning here often requires changing ingrained habits of speech and thought. As a result, the experience of learning criminal law can be like someone telling you how to walk, a most annoying experience if you have not had any trouble walking since you were toddler. But just as an athlete or musician may have to unlearn old ways to take their game or musicianship to a higher level, so students of criminal law must sometimes—temporarily—regress to simpler, more deliberate modes of thought and speech to build the skills needed for sound legal analysis.

This book seeks to meet the challenge of the familiar primarily by the careful use of language. All critical legal terms are specifically defined and then illustrated by example. Linguistic traps—places where ordinary language meaning may confuse legal analysis—are pointed out.

The book also seeks to, where possible, reconcile common intuitions about responsibility with criminal law doctrine. As we will see, a great deal of criminal law involves finding a legal home for intuitive notions about responsibility. Learning about the law includes learning how to shape intuitions about blame and excuse into arguments about particular doctrines of criminal law.

The Challenge of Different Rules

Another challenge facing the student of American criminal law is its variety. In a nation with 52 independent criminal jurisdictions—the 50 states, the federal courts and military justice, it's hard to say what is the criminal law of the nation.

In order to give students the tools to learn the criminal law of different jurisdictions, teachers must concentrate on the basic principles of law which inform the codes and decisions of nearly all American jurisdictions. These are usually grouped under two general headings: the Model Penal Code and the common law. These provide a broad, but as we will quickly see, quite inadequate description of the sources of American law.

The Model Penal Code (MPC) is not the law of any particular jurisdiction, but a proposed criminal code that has proven influential both in practice and in the academy. During the 1950s a group of prominent lawyers, judges and academics in the American Law Institute created the MPC in hopes of reforming criminal law generally. A number of states, especially in the eastern half of the United States adopted many aspects of the MPC. Other states have adopted selected provisions, while a number of states have ignored it entirely. For law students, the importance of the MPC goes beyond its pattern of adoption, however. It provides a relatively clear and uniform method for tackling a variety of criminal law problems, especially mens rea, that makes it an important learning tool even for those who will practice in nonMPC jurisdictions.

The MPC is normally contrasted with the "common law." Unfortunately, what is meant by the common law is often unclear—except that it involves rules and concepts that predate the MPC. Classically speaking, the common law of crimes is the set of felonies, misdemeanors and their defenses established by English judges in decisions rendered prior to the nineteenth century. The standard source for this common law was William Blackstone's *Commentaries on the Criminal Law of England*, published in the second half of the 18th century. When used in the modern academy, however, the common law usually carries a more expansive meaning, referring to traditional Anglo-American principles and doctrines of criminal liability. Thus when an American court refers to the "common law view of provocation," the court may actually be referring to a modern manslaughter statute whose basic structure hails back to 18th century doctrine.

The reality is that many rules of American criminal law originate neither in traditional common law nor the MPC. For example, the rule of first-degree premeditated murder comes from Pennsylvania legislation enacted in the last decade of the 18th century and then adopted by many other states during the first half of the 19th century. It was never adopted in England and was not included in the MPC. Therefore, strictly speaking, premeditation is neither a common law nor an MPC rule. The point is that while the MPC and common law labels help distinguish some rule types, the terms do not cover many important features of the American criminal law landscape. In this, as in many other respects, American criminal law resists neat categorization.

This book seeks to meet the challenge of different rules by developing uniform terminology and methods. Instead of covering all the important rules of criminal law, the focus here is on setting out a few essential doctrines and explaining how analysis under those doctrines should be conducted. Emphasis is placed on identifying the right questions to ask, in the right sequence.

The Challenge of Consistency

In order to make sense of the many terms and rules that comprise the American criminal law, we need organizing principles. We need to see the *system* behind the mass of different criminal law doctrines. Ideally, each doctrine should fit into a larger legal system in the same way pieces of colored glass fit together to form the image in a stained-glass window.

A systematic approach to criminal law is also critical to justice. We measure justice in criminal law not just by a particular case outcome, but by the outcomes of all cases subject to the law. A just legal system treats like cases alike; conversely, it recognizes distinctions between truly different cases. The key is determining what differences between cases should carry legal weight and which should not. Differences in the severity of harm done or the culpability of the actor are among the most important differences which the criminal law should measure. An assault that causes grave injury generally merits greater punishment than one that produces minor injury; a deliberate wounding of another is considered more serious than recklessly causing injury. Meanwhile other differences, such as race, economic or social status, should almost never have legal significance.

Despite the importance of a systematic approach, the two main institutional actors in criminal law—legislators and courts—frequently take an essentially ad hoc approach to solving criminal problems. For reasons detailed in Chapter 1, legislators and courts tend to concentrate their efforts on the best resolution of the day's most pressing responsibility problems, paying less attention to whether the terminology or reasoning employed coheres with other areas of criminal law.

Variations in terminology often cause confusion. A legislature or a court may use words such as "intent" or "intentional," in quite different ways according to context, yet never note the disparity.

Similar inconsistencies can be found in analytic method. For example, we generally expect that a mens rea term such as "knowingly" will modify the word or words that follow it, especially if those words describe something critical to the wrongdoing involved. This principle suggests that the words "knowingly and unlawfully," in a criminal statute mean that the defendant must know that his conduct violated the criminal law. And in the context of *some* criminal offenses, this interpretation will be correct. Yet the same phrase appearing in another criminal statute may be interpreted differently because, as a court may say, ignorance of the law is no excuse. Under this principle, even though "knowingly" immediately precedes "unlawfully" in the statute, the defendant may be convicted even if he did not realize that his conduct was unlawful.

This book addresses the challenge of consistency primarily by the careful, consistent use of terminology. As mentioned before, critical terms are always defined and then employed in the same fashion in later discussions. But we also need a uniform *structure* for analyzing criminal law issues, a consistent way of approaching problems. In this book I provide such a structure in what I call the liability formula, introduced in Chapter 3. The formula helps organize criminal law analysis by placing criminal law doctrines into a few general categories. The formula sets out a sequence for analyzing issues according to category and so provides a series of basic questions to address all the major criminal law issues in a case. The formula also provides a way of understanding the relationship between different doctrines.

Finally, the book seeks to elucidate deeper continuities in the criminal law by frequent discussion of the values that inform doctrinal rules. A common failing of both courts and commentators is to assume that formal rule definitions provide all the guidance needed to resolve criminal cases. But policy considerations often shape the interpretation and application of rules. Where a rule produces inconsistent results in apparently similar cases, it is often because the rule involves competing policies, whose conflict must be worked out on a case-by-case basis.

Paying attention to policy helps us understand doctrine better. Making value conflicts explicit also eases the emotional resistance to learning that many students experience when they encounter a rule with which they disagree, something almost inevitable in this deeply normative field.

What the Book Is Not

I need to be clear about what this book is not. It is not, in any sense, a definitive work on U.S. criminal law. Many important categories of offenses go unexplored here, among them assault, theft, fraud and drug crimes. The coverage of defenses is similarly limited, excluding such important doctrines as necessity, duress and law enforcement. And even for those doctrinal areas that are covered, many rule variations are not detailed. These coverage limitations are made to preserve space for careful explanation of key terms and analytic concepts. Nor is the work heavily footnoted. Source notes are kept to a minimum and skew towards the MPC which is a national resource and California, which is my home state. For those interested in more complete coverage of criminal law rules and authorities, there are other books that do an excellent job of this.[2]

I must also confess a personal agenda. This book presents how *I* think criminal law issues should be stated and how I think they should be analyzed. In this regard, part of my aim is to improve the craft of criminal law analysis in the United States. In the discussion of doctrine, I favor certain terms and methods over others, including some widely used in the law. For example, here in California, courts rely heavily on the distinction between general and specific intent offenses. General and specific intent are analytic concepts that I and many other commentators find confusing and unhelpful. As a result, I use these terms as little as possible.

Some will object that this does not present the criminal law as it is today. And there is some truth to this. But I believe that students should learn good law before bad, meaning that a grounding in coherent analysis should take precedence over coverage of all terminologies and analytic techniques. Still, readers must beware. Other sources, including judicial opinions, will sometimes present criminal law controversies in different terms and in a different manner than I will here and the difference between their framing and mine will sometimes prove confusing. It cannot be helped.

These caveats should make clear that this book should not be used as a substitute for basic legal research in resolving particular criminal law issues. Just as reading a review is not the same as seeing the movie or reading the book, so reading a work of legal commentary—including this one—cannot substitute for basic case and statutory research.

Intended Audience

Finally, a word about who this book is for. I began writing this book for my own students: first semester, first-year law students studying criminal law. While I believed, and still believe, that studying appellate cases is critical to legal learning, I realized—after many years of teaching (some of us professors are slow learners) that students have a totally legitimate need for a secondary text on the law that explains basic principles accurately. I decided that if I was going to warn my students away from other works that I believed unhelpful or misleading, then I needed to supply an alternative. And so I have done.

---

2. See Joshua Dressler, *Understanding Criminal Law* (5th ed. 2009); Wayne LaFave, *Criminal Law* (4th ed. 2003).

My hope is that this book will be useful to many others besides law students, however. These may include students of criminal justice at the undergraduate or graduate level, practicing lawyers, journalists, and anyone else with a serious interest in the subject. While books intended for the legal market do not often reach lay audiences, and while there has traditionally been a nearly impermeable divide between the teaching of criminal law in law school and in criminal justice programs, these facts of current life are neither necessary nor healthy.

In truth, most first-year law students enter the classroom with the same prior knowledge of criminal law as most undergraduates. As a result, a book that does not presume prior familiarity with legal terms should work for students both in and out of the legal academy. The reader will be the final judge, of course.

Just one preliminary caution for criminal justice students: as detailed in Chapter 1, this is a book about substantive criminal law, not criminal procedure. Thus it covers rules about guilt, not rules for criminal investigation or adjudication.

A Brief Overview

Part One provides the basic context, structure and principles for an examination of American criminal law. In Chapter 1, after introducing basic criminal law institutions and related fields of law, we look at basic features of criminal adjudication. Principles of punishment and responsibility are introduced in Chapter 2. Chapter 3 sets out an essential structure for analyzing criminal doctrines in what is called the liability formula. The challenges of proof and persuasion, particularly rules about the burden of proof, are covered in Chapter 4.

Part Two introduces the single most important part of criminal law, the concept of mens rea, also sometimes called criminal intent. In its chapters we examine the most common forms of mens rea, their application to facts, their functioning in criminal statutes, and special problems in mens rea involving factual and legal mistakes.

In Part Three we turn to some basic crimes of violence: murder, manslaughter and rape.

Part Four covers inchoate liability, meaning criminal liability that does not depend on proof of a particular concrete harm. This includes liability for attempts at crime, for acting as an accomplice to another's offense and liability for conspiracy.

In Part Five, affirmative defenses are discussed, notably self-defense and insanity. Defense arguments related to intoxication are also covered.

Samuel H. Pillsbury
Los Angeles, 2009

ACKNOWLEDGMENTS

Many people helped in the writing of this book. For research assistance, my particular thanks go to Paula Mitchell, Julie Engel, George Kivork, Cassandra Hooks, Leila Orr, Brittany Whitman, Dorian Jackson, Nicole Pereira and Natalie Pifer.

How Criminal Law Works

Introduction to Part One

Basic Principles

With a big subject, it's always hard to know where to begin. It's a question of perspective. The big-budget Hollywood crime picture often opens with a tracking shot from a helicopter providing long swooping views of the glittering city at night, presented to a pulsing beat. But soon we are on the street, watching the action begin. While we're not making a movie here, initially we must also establish the big picture, the view from above, before getting down to life on the (doctrinal) streets.

Intellectually it makes sense to start with the big picture, with the relationship of criminal law to other fields of law such as evidence and criminal procedure, by introducing the primary institutional and individual actors in criminal law, and with the basic principles that inform criminal doctrine. This is the work of chapters 1 and 2.

We then move to ground level in Chapter 3, introducing the liability formula, which sets the essential structure for criminal law analysis. Chapter 4 presents the basics of proof and persuasion, matters of great controversy and consequence in criminal litigation, though not often front and center in the study of criminal law.

CHAPTER 1

Introducing Criminal Law

Time to meet the criminal law, up close and personal. Exactly what is the criminal law and where does it come from? How is it different from other kinds of law involved in criminal cases? Who are the key players in the formation, interpretation, and application of criminal law? What are the basic roles of legislatures and appellate courts, trial judges, juries, prosecutors and defense attorneys in criminal cases? Answering these questions will be the work of this chapter.

Here we will cover a great deal of criminal justice territory in a relatively short space. The point is to provide basic context for the criminal law explorations that follow. Readers who want to cut to the criminal law chase, so to speak, may skim what follows or skip it entirely, but I would urge an eventual return to this material, because it will help with many aspects of criminal justice that otherwise may seem puzzling.

Criminal Law and its Legal Relatives

Criminal law—or substantive criminal law as it is more precisely denominated—is the set of rules that determine what conduct may be punished by the state. It consists of the definitions of criminal offenses, the law governing defenses to criminal charges, and the minimum and maximum penalties for the offense. In sum, criminal law is the set of formal rules that tell us whether or not a defendant should be found guilty of a particular offense on a particular set of facts—and how much a person might be punished for the offense. Typical matters of substantive criminal law include issues of criminalization, such as whether use of marijuana for medicinal purposes or assisted suicide are criminal offenses; issues concerning degree of liability such as whether an intentional killing should be classified as murder or manslaughter; and basic liability questions, such whether a killing was justified because committed in self-defense.

American criminal law comes in two basic forms: statutes and case decisions. Statutes result from the passage of legislation by majority vote of the legislative body of the jurisdiction, usually with the concurrence of the executive authority (Governor or President). Case decisions are the published opinions of appellate courts that record the court's decision to affirm or reverse a decision at the trial level, as well as the reasoning behind that decision. In criminal law, case decisions are normally based on pre-existing statutes, but even so, appellate courts have significant authority of their own to shape the criminal law.

Meet the Relatives: Criminal Procedure, Evidence Law and Sentencing Law

Soon we will introduce the roles of criminal law decision makers and advocates but before we do, we need to situate criminal law in the larger field of law, and to introduce the criminal law's legal relations: criminal procedure, evidence law and sentencing law. For this, an example will help.

Anna was walking home from work on a darkening winter afternoon, listening to music on her headphones, when coming around a corner she suddenly found herself a few feet away from a large disheveled African American man. The man yelled at her: "Give me your money!" Anna, who is a slightly built Korean American woman of 26, was terrified and gave the man her wallet from her purse. He took the cash out of the purse, handed it back to her and disappeared.

Still shaking from the encounter, Anna went into a nearby store where she called the police. Based on her description, the police arrest Harry, a drifter who had recently taken up residence in the neighborhood. Found in his pocket is cash matching the amounts taken from Anna's wallet. In response to police questioning, Harry says that he got the money "from some lady who gave it to me." Police show Anna, photographs of six African American men. She identifies one of them — Harry — as the man who yelled at her.

Harry is charged with robbery.

Using this case as an example, we can start to distinguish between issues of criminal law, criminal procedure, evidence law, and sentencing law.

Criminal Procedure

The most commonly litigated issues in criminal cases involve criminal procedure, not criminal law. Rules of criminal procedure govern how police and prosecutors handle the investigation of crime and how lawyers, judges and juries handle the adjudication process in court.

What kinds of criminal procedure issues might be involved in Harry's case? The police questioning of Harry and the statement they obtain from him may implicate his Fifth Amendment right against self-incrimination, especially as established under the *Miranda* case.[1] The use of photographs to identify Harry will be subject to constitutional rights of due process to prevent unnecessarily suggestive procedures. These rights may be important here as cross-racial eyewitness identifications are especially unreliable. As the case goes forward, issues of criminal procedure may be implicated in the appointment of counsel and the selection of a jury, to name a few more possibilities.

Unlike criminal law which is primarily statutory, much of modern criminal procedure is constitutional; in its most important aspects it is often a matter of federal constitutional law. As a result, the United States Supreme Court's decisions— such as the *Miranda* decision—are preeminent with respect to many aspects of procedure. Such rulings set a national minimum for procedural rights in all American criminal courts—but only a minimum. Jurisdictions also establish criminal procedure rules by statute. For example, most jurisdictions have their own statutory rules concerning the setting of bail and the exchange of information between prosecution and defense attorneys, known as discovery.[2]

Rules of criminal procedure are frequently enforced by exclusionary rules, rules that mandate the exclusion of evidence at trial. Thus if the police interrogation of Harry violated the *Miranda* decision, the trial court might order the exclusion of his statements from the prosecution's case. Similarly, if the

---

1. 384 U.S. 436 (1966).

2. An additional source of procedural rights is state constitutions. Every state in the union has its own constitution, separate from the federal constitution, which potentially gives state courts independent authority to articulate procedural rights. This source of authority has become increasingly important in recent years as the United States Supreme Court has become more conservative in its view of federal rights. This means that state courts may apply *state* constitutional rights that are more expansive than *federal* constitutional rights, even when the respective constitutional provisions are identically worded. Thus, in Oregon, a police investigative practice may be deemed an unreasonable search or seizure under the state constitution even though the same practice constitutes a lawful search or seizure under the federal constitution. For example, see State v. Caraher, 553 P.2d 942 (Oregon 1982), in which the Oregon Supreme Court decision held that the state's constitutional prohibition on unreasonable searches and seizures operated differently with respect to searches incident to arrest than did the fourth amendment to the federal Constitution, as interpreted by the United States Supreme Court in United States v. Robinson, 414 U.S. 218 (1973).

prosecution fails to turn over to the defense evidence required under the rules of discovery, the prosecution may be prevented from presenting certain testimony at trial.

The operation of exclusionary rules makes criminal procedure decisions inherently controversial. Often courts must resolve a tension between powerful competing values: the importance of convicting the guilty and the importance of requiring the government to respect constitutional limits on the exercise of power.

Evidence Law

The law of evidence determines what testimony and physical evidence may be presented in court and how this evidence should be evaluated by the decision maker. In criminal cases, evidence law overlaps considerably with both substantive criminal law and criminal procedure, making them hard to distinguish for the new student. Criminal law will influence evidence questions by determining the relevance and therefore admissibility of certain kinds of evidence, including expert testimony. Constitutional rules of criminal procedure may also override otherwise applicable statutory rules of evidence.

An example of a common evidence law issue is the admission of prior bad act evidence. Prior bad acts include past crimes or other bad acts of the defendant that increase the likelihood that the defendant committed the charged offense. If, for example, Harry has a prior conviction for robbery, that fact, if communicated to the jury, would likely help the prosecution's case. But it also might lead to injustice. The danger with prior bad act testimony is that the decision maker will overvalue this evidence and will convict Harry based not on the current case but on his past. As a result, evidence law generally restricts prior bad act evidence to certain narrow uses, such as showing that the distinctive method used by the robber in the present case matches that of past robberies committed by the defendant. This limitation is designed to ensure that there is a strong evidentiary link between past conduct and present charges.

Sentencing Law

Until the advent of determinate sentencing in the 1970s and 1980s, there was very little *law* of sentencing in the United States. Judges had broad discretion to decide on sentence, limited primarily by the statutory maximum for the offense of conviction. Appeals focusing on sentencing decisions were rare, and almost always unsuccessful, except for those involving capital punishment. Again with the exception of capital cases, the critical *legal* decision for sentencing purposes was determining the crime of conviction. Under determinate sentencing, judicial decisions on sentencing are governed by statutes or legal guidelines. Such schemes vary widely in their structure and in how much they regulate judicial sentencing. The more that the scheme seeks to direct sentencing, the more sentencing law is needed.

A big sentencing law issue in recent years has involved distinguishing those matters that must be resolved at trial, subject to the constitutional right to a jury trial, and those that can be resolved at a sentencing hearing by a judge, subject to different rules of evidence and procedure than would apply at trial.[3]

To give an example of the kind of sentencing law issue that might arise in Harry's case, many jurisdictions provide for penalty enhancements for prior convictions or for committing a crime of violence. Attorneys in Harry's case might argue about whether any such enhancement would apply to the case and if so, whether the enhancement is discretionary, a matter for judicial determination according to the facts of the case; or mandatory, meaning that it is required by law.

Harry and the Criminal Law

But what might criminal law have to say about Harry's case?

Here an important issue is the definition of robbery, and particularly the definition of force required for robbery. Robbery is traditionally defined as the taking and carrying away of the personal property of another by force or threat of force. Harry may claim here that he did nothing more than ask Anna for money, albeit in a loud tone of voice. He was panhandling, nothing more. He did not use violence, he did not display a weapon and he did not make any overt threat. He did not demonstrate any purpose to threaten Anna with physical harm. Anna could simply have refused his request and walked away. In sum, Harry may claim that the entire prosecution case rests on a misunderstanding: she was scared of him for no good reason.

Assuming that there is credible evidence to support Harry's version of events, then a critical criminal law issue will involve the jury instruction on the force and threat element of robbery. The defense will insist that the instruction clearly inform the jury that the prosecution must prove beyond a reasonable

---

3. See United States v. Booker, 543 U.S. 220 (2005).

doubt that Harry acted with the purpose to threaten Anna in order to be guilty of robbery. It would not be enough to prove that she felt threatened.

Criminal Law Makers and Shapers: Legislatures and Appellate Courts

In the Anglo American tradition, a core principle of criminal law is that of *legality*, captured in the Latin phrase of *nullum crimen sine lege, nulla poena sine lege*, literally meaning, no crime without law, no punishment without law. This principle raises a critical question: Who creates the law? Who has authority to define criminality?

In early modern England (roughly 1500–1700), common law judges defined basic criminality. Judges set out definitions of basic felonies and misdemeanors which juries then applied to the facts presented at trial. While giving appointed judges rather than elected officials the power to define crime may disturb modern notions of democracy, at the time it represented a significant civil liberties achievement. It meant that the king could not unilaterally—and after-the-fact—establish criminal prohibitions or impose punishments. It meant that the criminal justice system had a measure of independence from the political desires of the monarch.

In the early years of the United States, most American jurisdictions drew heavily on English precedents in creating their own criminal law. But there was one important structural difference: legislatures became the primary source of criminal law. Today in the federal system and in most states, criminal charges must be based upon a criminal statute previously enacted by the jurisdiction's legislature.[4]

Although legislators have the first word in deciding what is criminal in the United States, courts have the last word on who is found guilty. Only courts can decide how criminal legislation applies to particular cases. The most important tribunals for determining the meaning of criminal law are the appellate courts, courts that decide appeals from trial court decisions. The highest appellate court of the jurisdiction has authority to decide the meaning of the jurisdiction's criminal statutes. Thus, a case of grand theft brought in Los Angeles Superior Court, a state trial court, will be governed by decisions of the

---

4. A few states recognize at least some common law crimes from English law. See Fla. Stat. sec. 775.01.

California Supreme Court, California's highest state court,[5] interpreting the state's grand theft statute.[6]

Legislatures

In the contemporary United States, a foundational assumption of our criminal justice system is that the people's elected representatives, state and federal, will determine the basic prohibitions of criminal law, state and federal. If the legislation proves unwise, courts may draw attention to its flaws and may interpret it narrowly, but with the exception of a few rarely-invoked constitutional limitations discussed later, courts may not overrule legislative choices about what to punish and how.

The legislature's role in criminal law is especially important in the United States, because ours is a heterogeneous society committed to diversity in culture, race, religion and much more. This means that we rely more heavily on criminal law to define basic community norms than do nations with more homogeneous populations and cultures. Americans accept, and even celebrate, the extent to which we disagree on many basic issues, but as to the criminal law we brook no disagreement. Criminal prohibitions represent nonnegotiable rules for all citizens, setting the essential terms for our coexistence.[7]

The Drafting of Criminal Legislation

The bulk of criminal law in the United States is found in thick criminal codes, compilations of statutes enacted by state legislatures with the consent of the state's chief executive, the governor. Criminal legislation at the federal level is enacted by Congress subject to Presidential approval. Cities and towns may also enact criminal ordinances.

---

5. In most states, the highest court is called the state's supreme court. Terminology does vary, however. In New York State, for example, trial courts are denominated supreme courts and the highest appellate court is the New York Court of Appeals.

6. Matters of state criminal law are rarely addressed by the United States Supreme Court because these rarely raise the kind of federal constitutional issues that demand the Court's attention. The Court does play an important role in federal criminal law, however, because it is the highest authority on the interpretation of statutes enacted by the federal Congress. Its interpretation of federal statutes may also influence state courts in their readings of similar state statutes.

7. Those who argue for cultural defenses in criminal law would strongly disagree with me here. E.g., Alison Dundes Rentein, *The Cultural Defense* (2004).

Now a word about the drafting of criminal statutes. It's not always a pretty picture. While many legislators are lawyers, a legal education by itself does not make one a good statutory draftsman. And many statutes are drafted by someone other than their legislative sponsor. Statutes may be written by legislative staffers, government agencies, advocacy groups or even interested lay persons. The language of a proposed statute may change during the legislative process to accommodate varying political interests. Ambiguity may even be deliberately created to win additional votes for passage.

Legislatures generally enact criminal prohibitions and penalty measures to address specific problems. The most recent set of broad scale criminal reforms focusing on offense definitions came in response to the promulgation of the Model Penal Code in 1960. In more recent years, legislative efforts at criminal law reform have centered on sentencing rather than the definition of crimes. Many jurisdictions, including the federal government, have changed their sentencing laws to restrict the discretion of judges and increase uniformity in sentencing.

Appellate Courts

Given that legislatures set basic criminal justice policy through the enactment of specific statutes and that courts must follow these statutes in presiding over criminal cases, the role of the courts in shaping the criminal law would seem quite limited. Yet courts, especially appellate courts, have considerable say over criminal law. Even carefully drafted statutes leave important questions to be resolved by judges—and many criminal statutes are not well drafted. Legislatures set the basic rules of criminal law, but many rule details are left to the courts, and here, as elsewhere in the law, the action is often in the details.

Understanding Case Precedent: The Holding of a Case

The key to understanding the role of appellate courts in shaping the criminal law of the United States is the concept of case precedent. Unlike many European civil law systems, where appellate court decisions resolve only the case before the court, published decisions by American appellate courts stand as legal precedents for subsequent criminal cases. Such appellate decisions represent rulings of law that must be followed by lower courts within the jurisdiction, at least to the extent that the ruling applies to the case at hand. For example, if the Minnesota Supreme Court holds that, under state law, criminal conspiracy requires proof of an overt act in furtherance of the conspiracy, then this requirement will apply to all subsequent prosecutions for conspiracy under

Minnesota state law. This requirement will remain in force unless the Minnesota legislature enacts a statute expressly to the contrary, or the Minnesota Supreme Court subsequently decides that it made a mistake and overturns its own precedent.

Not all criminal cases create legal precedents; indeed, only a tiny fraction of criminal cases attain this status. There are a number of prerequisites to a case decision becoming a legal precedent. First we need an appellate decision, because only appellate courts have the authority to establish a precedent for trial courts. Appeals normally require a previous trial and conviction.[8] Finally, the appellate court decision will not be precedential unless the court decides that the issues presented are sufficiently important for the decision to be published.

An appellate court decision represents a binding precedent on lower courts only to the extent that its *holding*—its resolution of the particular issue or issues presented—applies to future cases.[9] The holding of an appellate decision is the court's answer to the legal question or questions presented by the appeal.[10] The holding of the case must be distinguished from *dicta*. Dicta is any discussion in the judicial decision not absolutely necessary to the court's ruling. This may include background discussion of the law and legal theories. It may include some of the most compelling prose and clearest explanation of relevant principles of law and responsibility. It may also provide the best in-

---

8. In most jurisdictions, procedural rules limit the ability of defendants to appeal rulings made prior to trial. Guilty pleas generally may not be appealed on issues involving substantive criminal law. Trials that end in not guilty verdicts (acquittals) may not be appealed at all because of double jeopardy.

9. This raises a troublesome feature of the Anglo-American case method: the time it takes for the legal system to finally resolve certain interpretive and especially constitutional issues. For example, in 1994, California enacted a new statute which effectively revived the statute of limitations for many child abuse cases. Defendants charged with offenses pursuant to this statute immediately complained that it violated the ex post facto clause of the Constitution. A number of lower courts considered the issue, generally ruling against defendants, but the issue was not definitively resolved until 2003, when a conviction obtained under the new statute was finally reviewed on appeal by the United States Supreme Court. The Court held the law to be unconstitutional. Stogner v. California 539 U.S. 607 (2003). As a result, hundreds of cases against alleged child abusers, at all stages of investigation, prosecution, and punishment, were overturned. Obviously this decision making process was not the most efficient we could imagine; it disrupted the lives of alleged perpetrators and victims in traumatic fashion and wasted significant law enforcement, lawyer and judicial resources.

10. The lawyers on an appeal devote a great deal of effort to resolving what legal questions are properly before the court. The final decision on what questions are presented is the appellate court's.

dicator of future decisions of the appellate court. For all these reasons, dicta often attracts the attention of lay readers. This is what gets underlined and highlighted. But – statements in a decision that are dicta *are not binding* on lower courts. They do not represent rulings of law. Because the difference between holding and dicta is both important and not immediately obvious, we need to take a moment to explore it in more detail.

Also critical to the holding of an appellate decision is the procedural posture of the appeal. The procedural posture, or procedural history as it is sometimes called, helps define the legal question which the appellate court must answer. It may also determine what facts will be considered in the appeal. We can illustrate these concepts with an example.

> Defendant is charged with sexual assault. At trial the female complainant (the alleged victim) testifies that the defendant used physical force to coerce her into sexual intercourse. She states that she loudly protested against his advances. The defendant testifies that he had sex with the complainant, but with her consent. He maintains that she did not verbally or physically resist his advances.
>
> Defense counsel asks the trial court to instruct the jury on the doctrine of reasonable mistake. The defense counsel argues that the defendant may have been mistaken concerning the woman's consent, and that if this mistake was reasonable, defendant cannot be convicted. The judge refuses the request, however, stating there is not enough evidence to support the argument. The judge states that since the defendant did not testify that he was or might have been mistaken, the jury should not be instructed on this possibility.
>
> The defendant is convicted and now appeals. The appellate court must decide whether the trial court erred in refusing to instruct on mistake.
>
> In this case, if the defense wins the appeal, exactly what will that resolve?

The appeal in this case probably will *not* turn on whether the appellate court agrees with the jury verdict. For reasons discussed further below, appellate courts are reluctant to second-guess fact finders on questions of credibility: who to believe. Instead, the appellate court will likely focus on whether the trial judge made the correct legal decision in refusing to instruct the jury on the law of mistake. The appellate court will try to resolve this legal issue *without* taking on the jury's role of deciding whether to believe the complainant or the defendant. The court will do this by engaging in a form of hypothetical reasoning.

IF the jury believed the defendant, would the law support the defendant's mistake argument? To put this in more legal language, the court asks, *viewing the facts presented at trial in the light most favorable to the defendant,* might a properly instructed jury have acquitted the defendant of sexual assault because of reasonable mistake? If the answer to this question is yes, then the appellate court will reverse the conviction. In most instances, the case will be sent back to the trial court for possible retrial, this time with a proper jury instruction.

But the important question for the student of criminal law, is what this appellate decision stands for. For what point is this case a *precedent?* It all depends on the case holding, what the court actually decided.

Assume that the appellate court stated in its decision that the trial court's refusal to instruct was wrong because a mistake argument can be based on consideration of all of the evidence in the case; it doesn't have to be explicitly presented in the defendant's testimony. In other words, the defendant does not have to say that he was mistaken if there is other evidence suggesting that he was. Such a decision will stand as a precedent for when juries must be *instructed* concerning mistake in sexual assault cases. The decision will *not* be a precedent for when a mistake claim will succeed, however. Remember, the appellate court ruling rests on a hypothetical view of the defendant's credibility: the court considered the facts in the light most favorable to the defendant. At retrial, the jury may find the prosecution's witnesses more credible and again return a verdict of guilty.

This case tells us something about when a mistake instruction should be given in a rape case. If other cases present a similar fact pattern on mistake, then we know that the instruction must be given. But that's it. If the fact pattern is different, the precedent likely will not apply. And even if it does, the rule of the previous case will not tell us what the verdict in the new case will be.

Appellate Court Lawmaking: Powers and Limits

The main work of appellate courts is to *interpret* the criminal statutes of the jurisdiction. With few exceptions, courts lack the authority to overturn policy decisions of the legislature. And yet one does not have to read many judicial opinions on criminal law issues to see that considerations of criminal justice policy play an important role in many appellate court decisions. How can this be? This constitutes one of the central questions of jurisprudence, which we certainly will not resolve here. But we can clear away some of the mystery. Simply stated, legislatures delegate a certain amount of rule making authority to appellate courts, authority which implies both the ability and need to consider policy in statutory interpretation.

In enacting criminal statutes, legislatures make the big decisions about offense definition and punishment through the wording of statutes. But because criminal statutes must apply to a wide variety of fact patterns, they must be phrased in fairly general terms. This often leaves a number of lesser issues to be resolved by the courts. In this way the legislature implicitly grants courts what might be called interstitial lawmaking authority. Courts may fill in the details of the legal picture that was sketched in broad strokes by the statute. Courts cannot simply paint over the legislature's legal scheme, however.

Students often ask why legislatures do not do a better job of writing criminal statutes. Sometimes the problem lies in unusual fact patterns, new technologies or new social practices that legislators could not have foreseen. More often, legislatures just prefer courts to resolve the details. Courts are often better suited to this kind of legal work by virtue of training and experience. It's even true that sometimes legislators prefer broadly worded statutes on controversial topics, both because this makes passage more likely and it allows courts to be blamed for any unpopular applications.

Whenever an appellate court issues a nonconstitutional decision on the criminal law, that decision is subject to legislative override. The legislature may alter the appellate court ruling by modifying the old statute or creating a new one. What is remarkable is how rarely legislatures do this.[11]

Reality Check: Case Book Criminal Law

The essential text, indeed, virtually the scripture for most law school courses on American criminal law is the case book, comprised primarily of appellate decisions on whether trial verdicts should be affirmed or reversed. Such decisions provide a rich resource for learning, but they can also perpetuate common misconceptions about criminal law in the United States. They suggest that most cases go to trial and that on appeal convictions are often overturned, leading to the release of probably guilty and dangerous individuals. This is not the reality of contemporary criminal justice. Time for a quick reality check.

Cases in the casebook are almost always appeals based on trial verdicts, but in most U.S. jurisdictions roughly 90% of criminal cases are resolved by guilty plea. Cases that go to trial and are appealed do have a potentially disproportionate impact on the system as a whole, however, both because they may set legal precedent, and because their outcomes may influence the plea bargains offered and accepted in similar cases.

In terms of success on appeal, recall that because of the prevalence of guilty pleas, appeals are taken in only a small percentage of criminal

---

11. For an example of legislative overturn of appellate court decisions in California relating to mens rea, particularly in homicide, See Stephen J. Morse, Undiminished Confusion in Diminished Capacity, 75 J. Crim. L. & Criminology 1, 25–26 (1984).

cases. *Still most appeals fail; the great majority of convictions obtained at trial are affirmed on appeal. Because affirmances are less likely to produce opinions worthy of classroom study than are reversals, however, the former predominate in case books.*

Finally, reversals obtained on appeal are not worth as much as you might think. Generally the successful appellant does not go free. Under the American law of double jeopardy, a case reversed on appeal usually returns to the trial court where the prosecution may try the defendant again, this time in a proceeding which avoids the mistakes of the preceding one. Only if the reversal is for insufficient evidence (a relatively uncommon ground for a successful appeal) or if the prosecution has lost evidence critical to a retrial, as where witnesses have died or disappeared, does a successful appeal result in complete exoneration. Successful appeals may improve the defendant's negotiating position with respect to plea bargaining, however.

There is one way in which the appellate cases studied in law school reflect the reality of criminal adjudication: they are more whydunits than whodunits. The appellate cases generally turn on legal responsibility for proven conduct, not on who did what. The same is true for criminal trials. (Though we must immediately note that there are a significant number of cases, especially those involving stranger violence, that do turn on issues of identity.) For example, in a white-collar fraud case where the defendant allegedly exaggerated the financial worth of his company, the defense will more likely prevail by asserting that the defendant sincerely, though perhaps mistakenly, believed the truth of his financial assertions rather than by denying that he ever made the representations, or that they were true. The whydunit nature of most contested cases means that principles of criminal law often play central roles in determining the outcome of criminal trials.

Constitutional Limits on Criminal Legislation and Interpretation

The legislative power to create and punish crimes is subject to constitutional limits. Unfortunately, this topic is too big and complex—and depends too much on law yet to be covered—for a detailed discussion here. A quick overview of the way in which our nation's most important constitutional court, the United States Supreme Court has handled issues involving criminal law must suffice.

To oversimplify—but not by that much—the Court has over the last 30 plus years occasionally threatened to deploy various constitutional provisions to oversee legislative enactment of criminal statutes, but in the end has largely deferred to legislators. When the Court has used the Constitution to invalidate criminal enactments, it has been primarily to enforce the state's obligation to provide clear notice of its own criminal prohibitions.

The most basic aspect of the notice requirement is that the state may not retrospectively criminalize conduct. Under the ex post facto clause of the Constitution, any new criminal statute may apply only to conduct that occurs following passage of the law. Nor may the legislature retroactively increase penalties for an offense. Again, any increase in punishment may only be applied prospectively. Finally, in a recent decision, the Court held that the ex post facto prohibition invalidates efforts to prosecute crimes for which the previously enacted statute of limitations had already expired.[12]

Notice limitations may also limit the judiciary. At least in theory, a change in the judiciary's view of the criminal law, at least if it negatively affects the accused, may be so significant and unexpected as to violate the notice principle—that citizens should have fair warning of what is and is not criminally prohibited.[13]

In support of the notice requirement, the Court has read the due process clause of the Constitution to prohibit excessively vague criminal prohibitions. A jurisdiction's law defining a criminal offense (the statute and any clarifying interpretation offered by the judiciary) must: (1) provide notice to individuals in society of what conduct is criminal; and (2) provide guidance to police, prosecutors and courts so as to avoid arbitrary or discriminatory law enforcement. Recently, the United States Supreme Court struck down a Chicago loitering ordinance that permitted police to arrest any person who the officer "reasonably believed" to be a gang member and was engaged in loitering, meaning that he or she remained "in any one place with no apparent purpose."[14] The Court held this law provided neither clear notice to citizens, nor guidelines for law enforcement of what was criminal conduct. An important consideration for the Court was the difficulty of distinguishing between innocent and criminal conduct under the statute.

---

12. Stogner v. California, 539 U.S. 607 (2003).

13. See Rogers v. Tennessee, 532 U.S. 451 (2001) (rejecting constitutional challenge to appellate court's change in common law "year and a day" rule in Tennessee homicide prosecutions); Keeler v. Sup. Ct., 470 P.2d 617 (Cal. 1970) (rejecting judicial interpretation of murder statute to include a fetus as a human being).

14. City of Chicago v. Morales, 527 U.S. 41 (1999).

For the most part the Court has refused to employ the Constitution to regulate the content of criminal statutes. The Court, for example, has generally refused to make the presence or absence of mens rea a matter of constitutional concern. Whether a crime imposes strict liability is purely a question of legislative intent.[15] As discussed further in Chapter 4, the Court has held that the due process clause requires the government to prove the essential elements of any crime beyond a reasonable doubt, but the Court has left the definition of essential elements largely to legislatures. The Court has taken a similar view of the double jeopardy clause, permitting legislators to create multiple offenses and multiple punishments for similar conduct if they wish.[16]

Finally, the Court has generally refused to overturn legislative decisions about the length of prison sentences. Outside of the death penalty and criminal fines, the Supreme Court has found little application for the eighth amendment's prohibition on cruel and unusual punishment to legislatively authorized punishments. While punishments must not be "grossly disproportionate" to the wrong punished, the Court has only once struck down a sentence of incarceration under the eighth amendment. Life imprisonment without chance of parole was found cruel and unusual punishment for a habitual offender convicted of passing a bad check worth less than $100, who had a long record of nonviolent felonies.[17] More recently, the Court approved a 25 years to life sentence for a repeat offender convicted of the theft of three golf clubs, the Court holding that the defendant's extensive criminal history, though nonviolent, justified the state's imposition of a long prison sentence.[18]

Constitutionally speaking, the United States Supreme Court is concerned only with the federal constitution. The highest court of each state also has authority to set limits on criminal law according to the applicable state constitution.

---

15. See, e.g., Montana v. Egelhoff, 518 U.S. 37 (1996) (upholding Montana law that prohibits defendants from introducing intoxication evidence to negate mens rea in any form). Like many appellate courts, however, the Supreme Court often uses its interpretive powers to find mens rea requirements in statutes where they do not expressly appear. See, e.g., X-Citement Video, Inc., 513 U.S. 64 (1994); Staples v. United States, 511 U.S. 60 (1994); Morisette v. United States, 342 U.S. 246 (1952). For an example of another approach, the Canadian Supreme Court has held that proof of mens rea is required under that nation's charter of rights for any offense involving a deprivation of liberty. See Reference Re Section 94(2) of the Motor Vehicle, 23 C.C.C.3d. 289 (1985)

16. See Missouri v. Hunter, 459 U.S. 359 (1983); United States v. Dixon, 509 U.S. 688 (1993). See generally, George Thomas, *Double Jeopardy* (1998).

17. Solem v. Helm, 463 U.S. 277 (1983).

18. Ewing v. California, 538 U.S. 11 (2003). See also Lockyer v. Andrade, 538 U.S. 63 (2003).

Trial Level Decision Makers: Judges and Juries

Just as criminal lawmaking authority is divided between legislatures and appellate courts, so decision-making authority over criminal trials is divided between juries and judges. Again the broad outlines of the division of power seem clear enough: judges decide issues of law; juries decide issues of fact. Yet the actual division of power between juries and judges is highly complex, reflecting the way that factual and legal issues are often closely intertwined.

In American criminal trials, pride of place is given the jury. The authority of lay persons to decide criminal trials is historically one of the most celebrated features of American criminal procedure. Thomas Jefferson once famously declared that if forced to choose between the right to jury trial and right to vote, he would select the jury because he considered it more important to democracy.[19]

But we should not become so intoxicated with the rhetoric of the jury trial right that we mistake the reality of contemporary practice. Modern penal laws and practice strongly encourage guilty pleas, meaning that few cases ever reach a jury. And even in jury trials, the judge oversees the legal action in the courtroom. For this reason, we start our review of trial level decision makers with the lone figure in black who presides over the criminal courtroom from the bench.

Judges

Judges rule on all pretrial motions,[20] from requests for bail to motions to exclude evidence based on illegal searches or interrogations, to questions about the legal validity of the criminal charge. Judges also preside over the guilty plea process, should a defendant desire to plead guilty (which most eventually do).

At a jury trial, the judge serves as referee, setting the terms for the factual and legal contest waged by the prosecutor and defense attorney. The judge functions as evidentiary gatekeeper, deciding what evidence is admitted and for what purpose. With a few limited exceptions, the evaluation of that evidence

---

19. "Were I called upon to decide whether the people had best be omitted in the Legislative or Judiciary department, I would say it is better to leave them out of the Legislative. The execution of the laws is more important than the making of them." Letter to the Abbe Arnoux, 1789, 15 *The Papers of Thomas Jefferson* 283 (1958).

20. A motion is a formal request for court decision.

is left to the jury.[21] American trial judges generally may not comment on the evidence or otherwise attempt to influence how the jury evaluates the facts presented. This contrasts with the English adjudication system, where the judge performs a "summing up" at the close of the case in which she or he summa-rizes the evidence and frames the legal issues. Summing up gives the English judge considerably more influence over the jury's factual and legal decisions than the American jurist has.[22]

The judge is the final arbiter of all purely legal questions at the trial, whether procedural, evidentiary, or substantive. At the close of the case, the judge gives the jury an elaborate set of oral instructions on the law, covering everything from basic principles of evidence law to essential distinctions in substantive criminal law.

Instructing the Jury

Legally speaking, jury instructions are critical. Appellate courts view accurate instructions as essential to the legal validity of any jury verdict. This is why mistakes in jury instructions represent one of the most com-mon grounds for appeal in criminal cases. Good trial lawyers often begin their strategizing about an upcoming trial by considering the jury in-structions likely to be used; most are standardized and can be readily found in practice books. Yet when we look closely at the matter, there's some-thing very odd about U.S. law's approach to jury instructions. Although the whole point of such instructions is to inform jurors of the law, courts take a curiously diffident view of whether jurors actually understand them. What seems to matter most is how they are understood by lawyers. It is as if we assessed the quality of education entirely by what teachers say in class and not at all by what students comprehend.

As traditionally administered, jury instructions represent remark-ably poor instruments for conveying practical legal knowledge. The in-structions are usually given orally, the judge reciting them in a monotone to the jury, frequently when jurors are already tired from listening to the

---

21. Following the presentation of the state's evidence at trial (known as the case in chief), the defense may make a motion for a directed verdict of acquittal, which the court must grant if it finds that, considering the evidence in the light most favorable to the prosecution, no reasonable jury could convict. See Fed. R. Crim. Proc. 29; United States v. Holloway, 731 F.2d 378 (6th Cir. 1984). A directed verdict means that the case will not go to the jury. Di-rected verdicts can only be granted on behalf of the defense.

22. This power is a frequent source of distress for that quintessential (albeit fictional) English defense counsel, the barrister Horace Rumpole. See John Mortimer, "Rumpole a la Carte" in *The Best of Rumpole* 157, 190–91 (1993). See also William Pizzi, *Trials Without Truth* 143–44 (1999).

lawyers' final arguments and are anxious to begin deliberations (and hopefully, go home). Sometimes judges also provide a written copy of instructions for jurors to study at their leisure, but this is by no means standard practice. Most jury instructions are written in a highly abstract manner. They offer generalizations about the law designed for use in a wide variety of cases, with only minimal variation. As a result, jurors often struggle with how the instructions apply to the case before them.

Jury instructions frequently take their language directly from past appellate decisions. This may establish their legal accuracy in the eyes of appellate courts, but at the considerable cost of using often archaic or specialized legal expressions that confuse jurors. Nor are jurors encouraged to ask questions about the instructions. If they do, trial judges generally repeat the previously given instruction, word for word, without further explanation. This is because appellate courts have, with some frequency, reversed convictions where trial courts tried to explain key legal concepts in their own words, but failed to do so in a way that is perfectly accurate, complete and balanced. Finally, jurors are never asked or tested in any way to determine if they understand their instructions.

The hard truth about jury instructions is that courts refrain from inquiring too closely about jury comprehension for fear of what this might reveal. The legally trained do not necessarily hold a high personal opinion of jury comprehension of the law and many presume that the current "black box" system of instruction and decision-making (no inquiry into the substance of jury deliberation) is necessary to the preservation of jury trials.

In recent years there have been greater efforts in a number of jurisdictions to take the needs of jurors more seriously. In some jurisdictions, courts have made serious efforts to simplify the language of jury instructions. Such instructions even employ examples from everyday life to illustrate legal concepts. But the conservatism of the legal profession with respect to time-honored methods such as formalistic jury instructions cannot be underestimated. For many lawyers and judges, the risks of altering traditional legal language always loom larger than the problem of juror (non)comprehension.

Court Trials

Occasionally defendants choose trial by judge rather than by jury. So-called court trials occur when a defendant waives his right to a jury trial; in a number of jurisdictions, a waiver must also be obtained from the prosecution. In such trials, the judge performs all decision maker functions. Defendants may choose a court trial because of respect for a particular judge or in the belief that a particular defense will play better to a judge than to a jury.[23]

Sentencing

Last, but certainly not least, in any case where a conviction is obtained, the judge serves as sentencer. Over the last quarter century, the judge's sentencing authority in many jurisdictions has become more restricted due to determinate sentencing schemes and especially minimum mandatory sentences. Nevertheless, in many cases judges retain significant discretion concerning whether a convicted defendant will serve time, and if so, how much.

Selection of Trial Judges

In the federal system, trial judges (known as U.S. district judges), are selected by the President, with the consent of the Senate. Nominations are often suggested by the Senator or Senators from the jurisdiction of the President's political party. Like federal appellate judges, federal trial judges are appointed for life.

State trial judges are initially selected in a number of different ways. They may win the position in an election, or be appointed by the governor or some other governmental authority. In most state jurisdictions, trial judges must at least be reelected, and while judicial elections involving an incumbent are not usually contested, a single controversial decision can change that.[24] In general, state judges are far less insulated from the bite of popular censure than are federal judges.

Juries

Although modern criminal justice places heavy practical limitations on its exercise, the right to jury trial remains an extraordinary and important feature of American criminal adjudication. In a heavily professionalized legal system, where all other major participants, from police to judges to lawyers, have

---

23. A court trial may also be seen as improving the prospects for a successful appeal from a conviction because a judge normally provides more explicit grounds for his or her verdict than a jury would.

24. In some jurisdictions, persons may be appointed to perform judicial functions without being granted the full office of judge. In California, for example, judicial functions may be carried out by a duly appointed commissioner or referee.

extensive specialized training, jurors have none. Indeed, cynics often quip that the main qualification for jury service is ignorance about the issues to be adjudicated. Although unfair (there is a difference between lack of exposure to particular controversies and incapacity for resolving them), this comment has bite for the small truth it contains.

In a legal system where critical decisions are usually reached in a public forum and must be supported by a statement of reasons on which an appeal to a higher authority may be based, jurors deliberate in secret and offer no reasons for their verdict of guilty or not guilty. No record is made of jury discussions and normally neither courts nor lawyers may formally inquire into the content of these discussions.[25]

But the most remarkable feature of jury trials concerns acquittals. If a jury finds the defendant not guilty, that decision is absolutely final. For reasons discussed further below, acquittals cannot be appealed by the prosecution in the U.S., even if the acquittal is legally erroneous. (By contrast convictions may be appealed. Even here, though, the jury findings presumed to support the conviction are granted considerable deference by appellate courts.)

What explains the extraordinary powers of the jury? As a full answer would require reviewing large chunks of English and American history and culture, we must be satisfied here with a brief inspection of the two historic roles of the American criminal jury: (1) to resolve cases according to common sense views of the facts and legal responsibility and (2) to serve as a democratic check on overzealous prosecutors and judges.

Explaining the first of these roles is fairly easy. Jurors bring a wealth of human experience to the courtroom which arguably provides them with greater insight into human behavior than any single judge. In terms of making responsibility judgments—determining, for example, whether a criminal killing should be labeled first-degree murder, second-degree murder or manslaughter—jurors may better represent the standards of the community than a judge. Finally, even if jurors lack certain skills and experience that judges have in evaluating evidence and deciding responsibility, we might prefer jury decision making for the same reason that we prefer electoral democracy to its alternatives: it protects us against the excesses and corruptions of power common to elitist decision making.

---

25. Verdicts may be overturned because a juror was improperly selected, as when he or she lied during the selection process, or when jurors improperly considered matters not before them, as in a non-court supervised trip to the crime scene or other independent investigation of the facts. Courts will refuse to hear evidence about how jurors actually conducted their deliberations, however.

The political role of the jury represents the complicated part of the jury story. In both English and American history, the jury has served as a popular check against overreaching governments, especially in attempts to quelch political dissent through criminal prosecutions. But the days of kings jailing citizens for political dissent are long gone, raising the question: what is the political role of the jury in a modern democracy? Again we encounter a question bigger than the space we can afford its answer. Thus I offer only a partial response.

Criminal juries keep the legal system responsive to popular values that may not be reflected in the electoral process. To give a particular example, the death penalty has often proven more popular at the ballot box than in the jury box. Even jurors who support the death penalty often prove reluctant to impose it in a particular case. This suggests that juries represent an important real-world check on penal excess.

The Right to Jury Trial

Defendants charged with felonies or with misdemeanors whose maximum sentence exceeds six months have a constitutional right to a jury trial. Traditionally the jury is comprised of 12 persons who must vote unanimously to return a verdict of either guilty or not guilty. In recent years both the numbers of persons on the jury and the requirement of unanimity have changed in some states, however. The Court has approved state use of unanimous juries as small as six persons (Florida) and nonunanimous juries in which a supermajority vote produces a verdict (9–3 vote permitted in Louisiana).[26]

The selection of jurors from the local population depends on a mix of constitutional and statutory rules, local practices and decisions by the attorneys in the case. The United States Supreme Court has held that jurors must be selected from a group of local citizens of the trial venue (the geographic region from which the particular courthouse draws) that represents a rough cross-section of the local population. This means that the jury pool—the citizens summoned to the courthouse as potential jurors—must be selected in a way that does not significantly discriminate against any racial, ethnic or gender group. For example, if the local population is 20% Latino, the jury pool cannot be only 5% Latino.[27]

---

26. Williams v. Florida, 399 U.S. 78 (1970). Interestingly, the Sixth Amendment right to jury trial still requires a 12 person unanimous jury for federal criminal trials. See id. at 86. On the constitutionality of nonunanimous jury verdicts, see Apodaca v. Oregon, 406 U.S. 404 (1972); Johnson v. Louisiana, 406 U.S. 356 (1972).

27. See Taylor v. Louisiana, 419 U.S. 522 (1975); Duren v. Missouri, 439 U.S. 357 (1979).

Jury pools have also become more representative as a result of new juror recruitment schemes. In order to implement reforms for jury service such as "one day, one trial," state authorities have eliminated exemptions for certain groups or professions; in combination with constitutional rules concerning jury selection, the result is that American jury pools are probably more representative of the local population than they have ever been before.

Selection of an actual trial jury (also called a *petit jury*) from the pool of prospective jurors depends on challenges exercised by the trial attorneys. Attorneys may make an unlimited number of challenges *for cause*. By law, a judge must excuse any prospective juror for cause who is ineligible to serve because of legal grounds such as a blood relationship with the defendant or clear bias for or against the prosecution or defense.

In contrast to challenges for cause, which must have a specific legal basis, attorneys also may make a limited number of *peremptory challenges*, based entirely on the attorney's assessment of the prospective juror. Statutory law in the jurisdiction will determine how many peremptory challenges attorneys may make in a case. Peremptory challenges normally can be made for any reason. An attorney may use a peremptory challenge to excuse a juror because of her tattoos, her hairstyle or the way she sits. But—there is a limitation on peremptories, relatively new to the criminal process. The United States Supreme Court has held in a series of decisions beginning with Batson v. Kentucky, that neither the prosecution nor the defense may employ peremptory challenges to exclude persons from the jury based on their race, ethnicity or gender.[28] Although this rule has proven difficult to enforce, because virtually all other reasons for exclusion are legally permitted, it has changed the dynamic of jury selection. Attorneys cannot systematically exclude persons from a jury because of assumptions about their loyalty to certain racial or gender groups, as was common in the past.

The Mystery of Jury Nullification: Rule of Law v. Democratic Check

No aspect of the American criminal jury trial is as controversial, or as misunderstood, as the phenomenon known as jury nullification. Jury nullification refers to the jury's power to acquit a defendant *for any reason*. As noted earlier, a jury's verdict of acquittal is nonreviewable. This means that even if the jury blatantly disregards the judge's instructions on the law in reaching a

---

28. See Batson v. Kentucky, 476 U.S. 79 (1986), J.E.B. v. Alabama, 511 U.S. 127 (1994) (gender discrimination); Georgia v. McCollum, 502 U.S. 1056 (1992) (defense challenges).

not guilty verdict, that verdict will stand. The reverse is not true, however. If a jury's verdict of conviction cannot be reconciled with the facts or the law, the verdict will be overturned.

Jury nullification contradicts a central premise of criminal justice, that verdicts should follow the law. It also violates the express obligations of jurors to the court. An individual becomes a juror in a case when she takes an oath promising to obey the law as given by the trial judge. No wonder that judges and many legal commentators find jury nullification an embarrassment and seek to restrict its occurrence. Yet jury nullification remains legally protected. Why? The answer lies in the history of Anglo-American democracy.[29]

The most celebrated jury acquittals in Anglo-American jurisprudence occurred when jurors refused to do what the law of the day required. The only way this power can be maintained is if jurors retain the ability to acquit *against the law*, that is, contrary to legal instruction. The problem is that we cannot both review acquittals for legal accuracy and permit juries to defy the law by acquitting. The result is that acquittals cannot be reviewed on appeal.

Current law on jury nullification constitutes a rough compromise between the values of legal accuracy and raw democracy. Courts maintain that while juries retain the *power* to acquit against the law, they do not have the *right* to do so. In practice, this means that trial courts instruct the jurors as if jury nullification did not exist. Jurors are told, via the juror's oath and other means, that they are obliged to follow the law given by the trial judge. In most jurisdictions, jurors are never informed of their power to acquit against the law. Nor may trial lawyers explicitly argue for jury nullification.[30] Yet acquittals are sacred; if jurors *do* acquit against the law, that verdict will stand.

The rationale for this state of affairs (to the extent there is a rationale as opposed to a crude compromise of tradition and legal uniformity) is that if jurors *really* disagree with the law in the case they will follow their own beliefs, regardless of instructions. Judges (and others) worry that if jurors are told about nullification, they would employ its powers more frequently. Jurors would often disregard the law, seriously undermining its deterrent force.

---

29. Jury nullification also has roots in early American legal practice. In the early 19th-century, juries often determined the law as well as facts. At this time judges often had no formal legal training, which meant that they were not necessarily better able to ascertain the law than jurors. As the legal system became more professionalized, judges gradually took control of questions of law. By the end of the nineteenth century the current division of courtroom labor was generally accepted: judges decided what the law was, juries applied that law to the facts of the case.

30. See United States v. Dougherty, 473 F.2d 1113 (D.C. Cir. 1972).

While the power of juries to nullify represents a direct threat to core legal values, its threat to actual justice should not be exaggerated. In fact, modern juries rarely make a conscious decision to disregard the law in a criminal case. Most cases of purported jury nullification—where outside observers believe the verdict to be at odds with the facts and applicable law—represent instances where juror views of the criminal law or law enforcement practices influence the jury's fact-finding. A jury offended by the conduct of police undercover officers in a drug case probably will not acquit the defendant to send a political message to law enforcement, but may be more open to defense arguments that the police testimony in the case should not be believed. Similarly, jurors who have reservations about the legal definition of rape in an acquaintance rape case may view the complainant's account more suspiciously than they otherwise would. In this fashion, jurors reconcile (for themselves) the competing claims of law and justice.[31]

Juries and Sentencing

The last major piece in the rather anomalous puzzle of judge-jury relations is sentencing. We might expect that given their other powers, juries would have some say about punishment as well as guilt. At a minimum, we might expect that jurors would take punishment considerations into account in rendering verdicts. It is common human experience that knowing the consequence of a decision can affect the decision itself. Nevertheless, outside of a handful of states, except in capital cases juries, have no say in sentencing, nor may they consider punishment in reaching a verdict. Even as their guilty verdicts may set the outer boundaries and sometimes the precise terms of punishment, in many jurisdictions, jurors are told nothing about the penal consequences of their decisions.

Lawyers: Prosecutors and Defense Attorneys

Now we turn from decision makers to advocates. Criminal trials in the United States form a critical part of our adversarial system of justice. The adversarial system is built on the notion that a public contest between attorneys

---

31. This decision process illustrates how legal training influences one's approach to legal problems. The lawyer normally tries to separate normative and factual analysis; lay persons tend to treat them as intertwined.

representing opposing parties over evidence and law will best reveal the facts and the moral and legal considerations critical to individual responsibility. In criminal cases, the key adversaries are the prosecutor and the defense attorney.

Prosecutors

The prosecutor represents the executive branch of government in seeking the conviction and punishment of those who have committed criminal wrongs. Most prosecuting attorneys are full-time government employees who work under an elected or appointed chief prosecutor. Among the common titles for the chief prosecutor in state courts is the District Attorney, State's Attorney, or Commonwealth Attorney. The chief prosecutor for most federal cases is the United States Attorney, who represents a federal district, usually comprised of a significant portion of a state.

Unlike most lawyers, prosecutors do not have individual clients. Although the prosecutor may work closely with police and victims, may solicit their views and forcefully advocate on their behalf, the prosecutor does not legally represent either. Thus a prosecutor may refuse to pursue a case that victims and the police wish prosecuted; conversely, a prosecutor may proceed on a case over the objections of police or the citizens involved.[32] The prosecutor is a public official who must independently assess the needs of all members of the public, even including the defendant. As is frequently stated, though not always heeded, the prosecutor's job is to do justice, not just convict.

The prosecutor's greatest power comes from the authority to initiate criminal charges, an authority which usually includes the power to dismiss charges once filed. In the United States the prosecutor must agree to bring criminal charges; unlike many other nations, citizens may not force a prosecution by presenting evidence directly to a judge. Under American law, a prosecutorial decision *not* to charge is final. The most important recourse for persons disappointed by refusals to charge is in the court of public opinion. The heads of prosecutorial agencies are either elected officials or appointed by elected of-

---

32. Not that either is common. Generally prosecutors pay close attention to police and victim desires in making case decisions. Pursuing a case against police or victim desires often presents significant evidentiary obstacles. The best example of cases that may be pursued over the objections of the victim comes in domestic violence. Victims of domestic abuse sometimes reconcile with their assaulter following the incident and want criminal charges dropped. Here prosecutors may proceed regardless, relying primarily on evidence gathered by police and medical personnel at the time of the incident.

ficials and so they are sensitive—to varying degrees—to public sentiment in the locality.[33]

The multiplicity of jurisdictions in the United States provides another potential avenue for relief for persons disappointed by a prosecutorial refusal to charge. Depending on the nature of the case, dissatisfied police or victims may ask a different prosecutorial authority, either state or federal, to consider the case.

When the prosecutor does file criminal charges, the case will be subject to some form of pretrial screening, normally by presentation to a grand jury or a preliminary hearing before a judge. In most cases, neither represents a significant hurdle for the prosecution, as prosecutors need only show probable cause to believe that the defendant committed the charged offense, rather than the proof beyond a reasonable doubt required for conviction at trial. The rules of evidence for such proceedings are also usually favorable to the prosecution.[34]

Prosecutorial charging decisions are usually made based on the strength of the case assembled by the police, the severity of the wrong and the resources available for prosecution and punishment. In most urban jurisdictions, police encounter more instances of criminal violations than can be fully prosecuted and punished. As a result, prosecutors often develop general guidelines for less significant criminal cases that will either be declined or diverted pretrial for some alternative resolution. Variations in local crime rates, as well as varying attitudes towards crime and its punishment, frequently contribute to large disparities in charging between urban and more rural localities. Similar disparities often appear in plea-bargaining, conviction rates and sentencing.

In recent years, changes in sentencing laws have given prosecutors new powers over punishment. Minimum mandatory sentences and determinate sentencing schemes increasingly tie the sentence in a case to the charge. This means

---

33. One criticism of the Independent Counsel law under which the so-called Whitewater investigation of President Clinton was conducted (the investigation which later became concerned with his relations with Monica Lewinsky) was that this prosecutor was not answerable to the electorate or any elected official and had most unlimited resources for investigation and prosecution.

34. There is one constitutional check on the prosecutor's decision to file criminal charges: the doctrine of selective prosecution. Here the defendant must show that the prosecutor charged the defendant with a crime because of the defendant's race, sex, religion or exercise of a fundamental right like free speech. See United States v. Armstrong, 517 U.S. 456 (1996); United States v. Wade, 388 U.S. 218 (1967). Intentional discrimination is the key. It will not be enough to show that the prosecutorial agency prosecutes many more persons of one race than another for a particular offense; the defendant must also show that the *reason* for this disparity is racial hostility and not other causes, including a disparity in arrest rates. As a result, successful claims for selective prosecution are rare.

that prosecutors may exercise unilateral power over sentencing by deciding what to charge originally, and what charges, if any, to later dismiss. If an offense involving the use of a gun carries a mandatory five-year prison sentence under state law, the prosecution may insist on that sentence following conviction even if the judge believes a lesser punishment is warranted. This also gives the prosecutor additional leverage in plea negotiations.

For those cases that do go to trial, the prosecutor functions as the primary producer of evidence. Because the state bears the burden of proof (discussed further in Chapter 4), the prosecutor must present the witnesses and exhibits that establish the criminal wrongs of the defendant. It is not unusual for the prosecutor to be the only one to call witnesses at trial.

Many prosecutor's offices are staffed predominantly by younger attorneys who come to the office to gain courtroom litigation experience and then go on to other legal work, often in criminal defense or civil litigation. Almost all offices have some long-term or career prosecutors, however.

Defense Attorneys

The defense attorney represents the accused. Consistent with a defendant's wishes, defense counsel works to prevent conviction if possible, and in the event of a conviction, to minimize any penalty imposed. Regardless of how the defense attorney is selected (i.e. no matter who pays for his or her services), the attorney represents only the accused. The only larger cause that defense counsel serves is to advocate for the rights of all citizens by enforcing those rights of the accused that may have been infringed by the government.

The role of defense counsel in contemporary criminal justice system has been heavily shaped by constitutional decisions. In the 1960s, the Warren Court (the United States Supreme Court under the leadership of Chief Justice Earl Warren) revolutionized American criminal procedure in the nation with a series of decisions establishing a fundamental right to appointed counsel in most criminal cases.[35] Previously the sixth amendment right to counsel had been read to mean a right to a lawyer if the defendant could afford one. As a result, outside of capital cases, many defendants in criminal cases had no lawyer. The Court's new-found *right to appointed counsel* changed the nature of criminal adjudication by requiring the establishment of public defender's offices and similar agencies and helped raise the standard of practice for both defense counsel and prosecutors in criminal cases.

---

35. E.g., Gideon v. Wainwright, 372 U.S. 335 (1963) (right in felony cases).

A criminal defendant has a right to counsel in all felony cases, in any misdemeanor case in which a sentence of imprisonment is imposed, or in any case where the defendant is given a suspended sentence (where incarceration may be imposed if probation is violated).[36] Defendants also have a right to self-representation—to give up the right to counsel—if they so desire and have been adequately warned about the consequences of the decision.[37]

The most frequently litigated aspect of the right to counsel is the requirement that any defense attorney, whether privately retained or court-appointed, must competently represent the defendant. The defendant is entitled to *effective* representation of counsel. A conviction must be reversed if the defendant shows that his attorney failed to meet the basic standard of lawyer competence—in practice a low standard that gives great leeway to a lawyer's strategic decision making—and that the lawyer's incompetence was reasonably likely to have adversely affected the outcome of the case.[38]

Defense attorneys may be either hired (retained) by the accused or appointed by the court. The best-known criminal defense attorneys are members of a relatively small group of the bar who can charge significant fees for their services. Personally selected by the defendant, family or friends, such attorneys tend to have the trust of their clients. Although there are important exceptions to this rule, attorneys with successful private practices in criminal defense are among the most experienced and skilled practitioners of criminal law and are generally the best paid.[39]

Unfortunately, many of those accused of crimes, and their families, assume that any attorney they can hire is better than any attorney appointed by the court to represent them. As a result, lawyers with little or no expertise in criminal practice may be retained because they are known to someone close to the defendant and their services are (barely) affordable. Charging only a modest fee for the case may discourage the lawyer from vigorous use of pretrial motions or going to trial; a guilty plea becomes the most cost-effective outcome.

---

36. Argersinger v. Hamlin, 407 U.S. 25 (1972) (right to counsel in misdemeanor cases); Alabama v. Shelton, 534 U.S. 654 (2002) (right in misdemeanor cases with suspended sentence). As a practical matter, a court must appoint counsel in any misdemeanor case if the court wishes to preserve jail as a sentencing option.

37. Faretta v. California, 422 U.S. 806 (1975).

38. Strickland v. Washington, 466 U.S. 668 (1984).

39. Just a few of the reasons that public reputation may not match suitability for a case: (1) a lawyer's fame may owe more to promotional abilities than courtroom skills; (2) determination and ability demonstrated in past cases does not necessarily translate into capability or aptitude for a present case; different cases require different skills; (3) successful lawyers sometimes take on too many cases; and (4) even the best trial attorneys can suffer burnout.

Meanwhile an attorney's lack of experience in criminal litigation may translate into less effective negotiations with prosecutors over the terms of a guilty plea.

The great majority of defendants accused of crimes are represented by court-appointed attorneys. In many urban areas, indigent defendants are appointed an attorney who works in the public defender's office. These attorneys do nothing but criminal defense. While public defenders are often overworked and operate with minimal resources, training opportunities are often better than elsewhere (though this definitely depends on the office) and their familiarity with local prosecutors, judges and juries often gives them a good sense of the legal marketplace in negotiating pleas. Unfortunately, the pressures of contemporary caseloads often mean that public defenders can spend little time with clients except in the most serious cases.

Defense attorneys may also be appointed by the court from a preapproved list of qualified counsel. In some jurisdictions, these lists are used only when the public defender's office is unable to represent an indigent defendant, as when the office already represents a codefendant. In other jurisdictions, all appointments come from a judicially approved list. How the appointment list system works varies greatly depending on jurisdiction, as does the quality of resulting representation. The fundamental disadvantage of a list appointment system is that the appointed attorneys depend upon trial judges for future appointments, creating a disincentive to litigate as hard as the attorney might otherwise. The attorney who displays adversarial enthusiasm beyond what the court deems appropriate, may not win reappointment.

A big problem for all appointed counsel is earning the trust of clients, who often perceive appointed counsel as adjuncts to the prosecutor's office because they also are paid by the government.

So You Want to Practice Criminal Law

You've seen them pontificating on TV, you've read their quotes in the paper and now you want to be a famous criminal lawyer too. Or perhaps you feel called to the criminal courthouse by a strong sense of justice, or injustice. Maybe you just find something enormously compelling about the human and moral drama of criminal cases. Whatever your motivation, you think maybe you would like to practice criminal law. Where do you sign up?

During law school, clinics and externships can offer invaluable introductions to criminal litigation. Prosecution and defense agencies may also offer summer internships, either paid or unpaid. The value of these opportunities depends on the quality of supervision and amount of responsibility given. The highest quality clinics offer excellent supervision and give students significant responsibility for the defense or prosecution of criminal cases.

When you're ready to look for a job in the field, do your research. Ask lots of questions of criminal lawyers in the area where you would like to practice. Don't be shy. Most lawyers enjoy giving advice and love to talk about their work and their colleagues. Ask about the different prosecution and public defender offices and what they look for in new lawyers. Ask how the offices are run, what morale is like, and about the offices' reputations in the local bar.

While there also may be good opportunities in private practice, for a new lawyer it is hard to beat working in either the local prosecutor's or public defender's office. Although training and supervision can vary enormously, the work usually provides a wide range of cases and significant professional challenges.

With relatively few exceptions, criminal law tends to be local. While there are opportunities for geographic mobility on both the defense and prosecution sides, most criminal lawyers spend their careers in a single geographic area. Many concentrate on either state or federal court.

What about the difference between federal and state criminal practice? Federal practice is the more prestigious and, not coincidentally, federal prosecution and defense offices often require fancier academic credentials and more practice experience from new hires than do their state counterparts. On the other hand, most crimes, especially crimes of violence, are prosecuted in state court. State criminal practice generally involves more of the human drama that draws many to the field. By contrast federal criminal cases tend to be heavy on legal paperwork with many written motions and trials dominated by documents. This makes federal criminal practice closer to civil practice, an advantage for those who may wish to do civil litigation later on.

What about choosing between prosecution and defense work? Often this question is answered by which office wants you. It's also true that some lawyers have ideological objections to either prosecution or defense work. Just remember, both sides have critical roles to play in doing justice. Prosecutors have more direct power over the system, but opportunities for creative justice work can be limited by office policy. Meanwhile, although defense attorneys "win" fewer cases than prosecutors, they help ensure that individual justice is done, that persons accused of crime are not reduced to mere case numbers with criminal records attached.

CHAPTER 2

BASIC PRINCIPLES OF PUNISHMENT AND RESPONSIBILITY

You don't need to understand punishment theory to understand basic criminal law. It just helps. A lot. Just as one can drive a car without knowing how the internal combustion engine works, or use a computer without comprehending programming or microprocessors, so one may practice criminal law without being able to hold forth on the deterrent, retributive, or any other theory of punishment. But as with cars and computers, not understanding the basic principles behind the mechanism can leave one at the mercy of others who claim expertise in the area. At the least, you want to know the language, and at best you'd like to understand essential working principles.[1] With this in mind, this chapter introduces basic terms and concepts in punishment theory.

Logically speaking, punishment theory comes before criminal doctrine, because logically the justifications for rules come before the rules themselves. We need to know why the state has the power to punish in order to know what rules of criminal liability and sentencing it should follow. This is not to say that law actually develops from theory, however. In practice, lawyers, courts and legislatures come up with particular solutions to particular problems without much theoretical introspection. Only later does the larger pattern emerge,

---

1. Another way of explaining the importance of punishment theory is by the example of the frequently incomprehensible instructions that come with various "easy to assemble" manufactured items. These instructions invariably provide a step-by-step method for assembly with accompanying pictures, but they remain difficult to comprehend because the author rarely indicates the purpose behind the steps. Why is it important to do step 1 before step 3? Why must the item be turned on its side as in figure 7B? And exactly what is shown in that figure? An explanation of the theory behind each step or procedure would assist enormously. The same is true of criminal law.

assuming it does. As a result, it would make almost as much sense for this to be the book's final chapter. Still, logically, the basics of punishment theory come before legal doctrine.

Most of this chapter concerns the two most important theories of punishment in criminal law today: deterrence and retribution. These will be considered both in general terms and with specific examples of their applications. The chapter closes with a brief consideration of some other important theories, including the expressive theory of punishment and restorative justice.

Two Styles of Moral Reasoning: Consequentialist and Nonconsequentialist

Punishment theory is a subset of philosophy and shares with that discipline several initially off-putting traits. Not only is the terminology strange, but critical moves depend on small distinctions ignored in everyday life. A certain amount of linguistic and logical nitpicking is critical to success in both punishment theory and philosophy.

We begin by distinguishing fundamentally different (at least from the philosophic perspective) ways of thinking and talking about right and wrong. We need to distinguish *consequentialist* and *nonconsequentialist* arguments.

To call an argument consequentialist is simply to give a fancy name to the most familiar kind of normative[2] proposition, one that depends on the consequences of a decision or action. For a consequentialist, right or wrong depends on the rightness or wrongness of the consequences of the decision. You should vote for candidate X because she will lower your taxes (personal finance consequences). Or, you should go to college, because then you will be able to get a better-paying and more fulfilling job (personal finance and fulfillment consequences). Or, you should tell the truth, because otherwise no one will want to be friends with you (social consequences). In each instance the key to what you should do is what will happen as the result of your action.

The most familiar kind of consequentialist argument and the most important in criminal law is *utilitarian*. A utilitarian judges what is best to do by what will produce the greatest amount of good for the greatest number of peo-

---

2. Normative simply refers to a judgment about better or worse. A judgment about whether a painting is good is normative, as is an assessment of a basketball player's ability to hit the winning shot, or whether the Federal Reserve made the right decision last week on interest rates.

ple. The good to be maximized can be defined in different ways, but for our purposes can be called happiness. Whatever promotes happiness or pleasure counts as a good, also called utility. Whatever causes pain counts as a negative, or disutility. A good social policy is one that maximizes the total amount of happiness (utility) and minimizes the total amount of unhappiness (disutility). For example: democracy provides the best form of government because in the long run it produces the greatest degree of collective happiness—economic, social and individual—for its citizens.

Group Consequentialism, or, What's Good for Us

Most consequentialist arguments are utilitarian, but not everything that sounds utilitarian actually is. Often consequentialist arguments seek to maximize the good of a particular group—usually a group with whom the proponent identifies—without seriously considering the good of others. For example, one might say that a decision or action is good if it produces good consequences for business. Conversely, one might argue that an action will be good if it benefits wage earners, or the poor. In either case, one might support a tax cut—or tax hike—because it would help a particular group even if, considered on a society-wide basis, the social and economic costs would outweigh the benefits.

Here we see the difference between philosophic theory and application. While few will argue for a public policy on a nakedly selfish basis, many will effectively do so using what appears to be a utilitarian argument. Whether they acknowledge it or not, many say that they wish to produce the greatest good for the greatest number, when in fact their overriding priority is to maximize goods for a particular group. The point is that we must listen carefully to consequentialist arguments to see if they are truly utilitarian in seeking the greatest good for the greatest number, or if utilitarian language is used to promote a particular group's interests. The challenge is to take benefits and harms for all persons into account.

The second major form of normative argument is nonconsequentialist. Nonconsequentialist arguments are somewhat less common in the modern discussion of public policy, for they require initial agreement on essential moral principles, something difficult to achieve in a heterogeneous society. A nonconsequentialist judges an action or decision according to a predetermined principle, *regardless* of the consequences. For example, one might contend that telling the truth is always right and lying is always wrong, regardless of the consequences. No matter how minor the deception or how devastating the immediate consequence, lying is always immoral.

Consequentialist and nonconsequentialist arguments often produce the same results. Indeed, in ordinary conversation we tend to use them interchangeably. For example, most parents teach their children not to lie. The parent may emphasize social or economic consequences: no one will want to be your friend or do business with you. Or a parent may use a non-consequentialist argument: "A good person always tells the truth, even if hurts. No matter what, you should tell the truth because that's the right thing to do."

At this point readers may wonder: What's the big deal? If consequentialist and nonconsequentialist arguments lead to the same result, why bother to distinguish them? Yet the distinction matters not just in philosophy, but in all manner of human affairs. We just do not normally recognize how often both personal and public disagreements turn on the difference between consequentialist and nonconsequentialist reasoning.

As a simple, perhaps simplistic example, consider the political and legal controversy which surrounded the investigation by Independent Counsel Kenneth Starr of wrongdoing by President Bill Clinton in the late nineties. Putting aside the many legal issues involved, this was a conflict between two men who took a fundamentally different approach to decision-making. Bill Clinton, the career politician, took a largely consequentialist approach. Clinton's handling of the Monica Lewinsky scandal was marked by consideration of political consequences. He considered the effect on his own approval ratings of various strategies, and ripple effects on the economy and foreign policy, just as he did in making other important presidential decisions.

By contrast, Kenneth Starr, the career lawyer and conservative·thinker, made critical decisions in the case without much consideration for political, economic, diplomatic or other consequences. In the conduct of his investigation, Independent Counsel Starr appears to have been driven by a deep conviction of the wrongness of the president's conduct and the moral and legal need for him to be held responsible through the impeachment process. How much the investigation cost the nation in terms of money and political divisiveness was irrelevant to Starr's effort to fulfill what he saw as his mandate as a prosecutor to bring a law-breaker's wrongdoing to the attention of the appropriate legal decision maker.

The point here is not to say that consequentialism or nonconsequentialism was uniquely appropriate to resolve the impeachment controversy, or that Starr and Clinton necessarily represent the best—or worst—of each approach, but to demonstrate that we cannot understand the dispute entirely until we recognize the fundamentally different ways that each man framed the critical issues.

As another example, consider the long-running debate about the death penalty in the United States. The consequentialist worries about whether the death penalty deters others from killing. This means that empirical[3] data on comparative homicide rates and punishments, among other information, will be critical to assessing capital punishment. By contrast, the nonconsequentialist asks whether executing an offender is ever justified according to essential moral principles, regardless of the execution's effects. Again we see that failing to grasp the difference between consequentialist and nonconsequentialist arguments will preclude constructive debate because each side frames the issue in a fundamentally different way.

Deterrent Theories of Punishment

The main consequentialist considerations in punishment can be grouped under the general heading of *deterrence*. Deterrence holds that perpetrators should suffer punishment in order to—and to the extent needed to—discourage the commission of further criminal harms and thus produce the greatest good for the greatest number. English philosopher and utilitarian Jeremy Bentham put the basic case for a deterrent approach to punishment as follows:

> The general object which all laws have, or ought to have, in common, is to augment the total happiness of the community; and therefore, in the first place, to exclude, as far as may be, everything that tends to subtract from that happiness: in other words, to exclude mischief.
>
> But all punishment is mischief: all punishment in itself is evil. Upon the principle of utility, if it ought at all to be admitted, it ought only to be admitted in as far as it promises to exclude some greater evil...."

To put this in more modern language, Bentham argues that the purpose of law is to maximize happiness and minimize pain, and because punishment involves the infliction of pain, punishment should be used only to the extent that it prevents persons from suffering other, greater pains. In this respect an important criterion for the utilitarian approach is *efficiency*. The best punishment is that which most efficiently, meaning with the least amount of punishment, addresses criminal harms. Bentham continued:

> The immediate end of punishment is to control action. This action is either that of the offender, or others: that of the offender it

---

3. Meaning based on data that can be verified by independent observers.

controls by its influence, either on his will, in which case it is said to operate in the way of *reformation*; or on his physical power, in which case it is said to operate by *disablement*; that of others it can influence no otherwise than by its influence over their wills; in which case it is said to operate by way of *example*.[4]

An assumption of deterrent theory is that human beings are rational calculators who prefer pleasure to pain and that individuals will refrain from otherwise pleasurable activities if they know that they will suffer greater pain as a consequence.

Deterrence can be broken into a number of subcategories, the most important of which are specific and general deterrence. *Specific deterrence* means punishment designed to prevent the particular offender from reoffending. Thus for a young offender, one night in jail might be an appropriate sentence if it would scare him enough to prevent him from committing any future crimes. *Incapacitation* is a form of special deterrence. It refers to punishment, usually incarceration, which physically prevents the defendant from committing crimes against society for the duration of the punishment. The recent trend to extremely long sentences for repeat offenders attests to the popularity of this punishment rationale.

General deterrence means punishment aimed at dissuading persons other than the offender from committing similar crimes in the future. The idea here is that the example of one person's punishment will scare others into obeying the law.

Finally we come to *rehabilitation*. Clearly the least popular of penal considerations in the modern U.S., rehabilitation represents the use of the state's coercive powers to change the offender's outlook and behavior so that he or she will be a constructive member of society and not commit crimes. Rehabilitation involves internal change in the offender's character so that he or she no longer wishes to commit crimes rather than simply being coerced by the threat of punishment into obeying the law. To the extent that rehabilitation aims at preventing future wrongdoing, it may be seen as a form of specific deterrence. It can also be conceived as independent of deterrence, though. We might believe, for example, that the government should seek to rehabilitate offenders not just to prevent future crime but because they need or have a right to such treatment. The most recent trend in punishment thought, called restorative jus-

---

4. *An Introduction to the Principles of Morals and Legislation* (1789) (emphasis in original).

tice, is also the most sympathetic to rehabilitative concerns. It is discussed at the end of the chapter.

Problems in Deterrence

To understand deterrence we need to see how it works in particular cases. Here we consider, in turn, problems in sentencing, in responsibility, in degree of offense, and in offense definition.

Deterrence and Sentencing

Carla is a young woman with a drug problem. Addicted to methamphetamine, she sells all her possessions to support her habit, and when that money runs out, turns to armed robbery. She is arrested and convicted of the armed robbery of two tourists at a local park. It is her first criminal offense. The presentence report in her case indicates that a brief jail sentence combined with probation and a drug rehabilitation program promises the best means of keeping Carla off drugs and out of crime.

At sentencing, the prosecutor notes that the local community has a significant problem with armed robberies. These offenses are extremely dangerous, sometimes leading to serious and even fatal violence. Many robberies are committed by young people with serious substance abuse problems. In addition, the local economy depends heavily on tourism, which will be severely damaged unless the legal system acts forcefully to deter future criminality against visitors.

Under a deterrent approach, how should the court sentence Carla?

Specific deterrence and rehabilitation coincide here to support a sentence of a modest jail term plus drug rehabilitation program. When the court considers that a lengthy prison term might increase Carla's alienation from society, worsen her chances of lawful employment, further indoctrinate her into criminal culture, and do little or nothing for her drug problem, the option of more severe punishment seems even less attractive.

But what about general deterrence? What happens to the deterrent force of criminal law if robbers such as Carla receive modest punishment and expensive drug treatment at taxpayer expense? Perhaps rational individuals with drug problems will decide that they will be better off, or at least not much worse off, if they commit robberies, because the worst that can happen to them is not very bad and might even prove beneficial in the long run. Compounding the problem with a lesser sentence is its consequences for the tourist economy.

Perceptions that the community is soft on tourist crimes will have serious economic effects that a utilitarian calculus must consider.[5]

In Carla's case, considerations of general and special deterrence conflict. General deterrence argues for a significant prison term; specific deterrence argues for jail plus rehab. The judge must decide which aspect of deterrence should weigh more heavily in this case. In this respect, punishment theory—at least at this level of generality—identifies the questions to be asked, but does not necessarily provide concrete answers about particular cases.

Deterrence and Excuses from Responsibility

Police arrest a disheveled looking man for attacking with a baseball bat three teenagers on their way to high school. The arrestee, who identifies himself as the "X-man" admits the attacks but says they were necessary because each of the teens was wearing Space Invader shoes, a new brand of sneaker. Huge billboards around the city declare: Light Years Ahead—Space Invaders. The X-man believes that young people who wear the shoes are being slowly indoctrinated by aliens from Alpha Centauri who are bent on destroying human civilization. The X-man has a long history of serious mental disease for which he has been hospitalized many times. According to the deterrence theory of punishment, should the X-man be held criminally responsible for his attacks?

Given the severity of the X-man's delusions concerning aliens and sneakers, deterrence theory may support an excuse from criminal responsibility. The X-man simply does not seem to be a rational calculator, capable of assessing the costs and benefits of his conduct in the way that the deterrent theory of criminal law presumes. Conviction and punishment will not likely affect his future behavior and arguably will have little effect on others, who do not share the delusions that motivated his conduct. The only clear deterrent justification is incapacitation. While locked up, the defendant cannot attack any other sneaker-wearers in free society.

Developing these arguments further, the defense would contend that the X-man's mental illness removes the case from the usual deterrent concerns. Putting the X-man in prison makes no more sense under deterrence than putting a dog in jail for biting a mail carrier. As with the dog, society's proper re-

---

5. Note that here there is a potential disjunction between perception and reality. Harsh punishment of Carla may or may not deter other potential robbers. But it will have done economic good if it persuades potential tourists that the city is safe enough to visit.

sponse is to defend itself using civil law protections rather than the condemnatory and punitive powers of the criminal law. Under civil commitment laws, if found to be crazy and a danger to others, the X-Man may be involuntarily held in a secure institution for mental treatment.

Law-enforcement officials may not want to give up so easily on general deterrence here, however. They may argue that excusing the X-man from criminal responsibility would undercut the force of criminal law by permitting deliberate, unjustified and dangerous acts of violence to go unpunished. They will argue that other persons inclined to violence, whether suffering from mental problems or not, will be encouraged to act on their antisocial inclinations because, based on the X-man's case, they may think they can escape punishment.

Deterrence and Degree of Offense

Tom is a hot-tempered man who, because of his upbringing, is especially sensitive about his mother's reputation. When a drunken stranger at a bar makes explicit reference to the extraordinary sexual generosity of his mom, Tom pulls out the knife he always carries for protection and stabs the stranger once, killing him.

Under these facts, Tom is clearly guilty of criminal homicide; the only issue will be the level of offense. According to a deterrent theory of punishment, should Tom's be classified as criminal homicide of highest severity, of moderate severity or relatively low severity (for homicide)?

Under deterrence we ask: how much disutility does a homicide of this sort cause as compared with other kinds of homicides? Another way of putting this might be to ask, how threatening was Tom's conduct to the basic social order? Is it less threatening to the basic social order than most intentional killings because it was a spontaneous reaction to the victim's ugly words? Certainly we generally *feel* less threatened by crimes of passion than by carefully planned attacks. Tom's offense seems more understandable, more traceable to ordinary human faults than if it was premeditated. We might also say that the kind of choice that Tom made indicates that the threat he poses to society is highly situational. Don't insult his mother and he will not bother you.

On the other hand, this pattern of behavior, in which two men engage in a heated argument leading to fatal violence, is among the most common patterns of criminal homicide. Statistically, many more people die in this fashion than from the kinds of homicides portrayed on television or in the movies, which tend to feature calculation. Perhaps we need to expend considerably more penal resources to deter persons like Tom from resorting to fatal violence, which would argue for treating this as one of the more serious forms of homicide.

Tom's case illustrates a potentially important distinction between our experience of fear and statistical evidence of threat. Generally speaking, we fear the calculated killer much more than the hot-tempered one. Witness the proliferation of serial killers on television and in the movies. Our lesser fear of spontaneous killings helps explain why such homicides are usually categorized by the criminal law as of medium or lesser severity. But should we be ruled so much by our emotions here? What if statistical evidence of threat points in another direction? Again, deterrence sets the questions, but does not provide the answers.

Deterrence and Offense Definition

The Governor has on his desk for consideration two bills passed by the legislature in its most recent session. He wants to sign one of them, but must decide which. Each bears the popular title: One Drink and You're Slammed. Each of the proposed laws is designed to combat the problem of fatal accidents caused by intoxicated drivers. Each of the bills imposes a mandatory jail term for any driver involved in an accident causing a fatality in which the driver had a blood alcohol level above .03. This is a lower blood alcohol level than the legal limit of .08 set for the crime of driving under the influence (DUI); it is a level that would be met by almost any person who had a single alcoholic drink within four hours of the accident.

Bill No. 1 is the tougher of the two bills because it does not require that the driver have been at fault in the accident or that intoxication have contributed to the accident. By contrast, Bill No. 2 requires that the driver be at fault in the accident and that the accident occur in a way "consistent with impairment by alcohol ingestion." If the governor follows a deterrent approach to punishment, which of these two bills should he sign?

The deterrent arguments for Bill No. 1 seem clear. Because the requirements for conviction are few—low blood alcohol plus involvement in a fatal accident—the law would cover more cases of harmful conduct by persons who had been drinking and driving than Bill No. 2. Thus, Bill No. 1 promises more in terms of both specific deterrence of drivers who drink and are involved in serious accidents, and general deterrence of those who might consider driving after drinking.

But remember that under the deterrent approach to punishment, our use of criminal law must produce the greatest good (happiness) for the greatest number. Because by design punishment creates unhappiness, not just for the defendant but also for the defendant's relatives and friends, and imposes larger economic costs to society, we should use it to the *minimum* extent needed to gain the countervailing benefits of reduced future crime. We should punish efficiently. Punishment that produces high costs with relatively little benefit fails the utilitarian calculus. The problem with Bill No. 1 is that it may punish the wrong people in some cases.

Some of those convicted and sent to prison under Bill No. 1 will have done very little, if anything, wrong. In this respect the legislation appears *overinclusive*, criminalizing too much conduct. The driver need not have been at fault in the accident, meaning that the cause of the fatality may be attributable to road conditions or the conduct of someone else, perhaps another driver or a pedestrian. Nor does the driver's blood alcohol amount of .03 necessarily make the driver a wrongdoer. Driving with this small amount of alcohol in the bloodstream does not constitute DUI and would not be criminal except for the—perhaps entirely fortuitous—occurrence of a fatal accident.[6]

Following the logic of Bill No. 1, we would obtain even more deterrence if we reduced the blood alcohol level to an even lower level or included within its purview all accidents, regardless of whether they involved injury to a person. Each of these changes would extend the coverage of the law and thus increase its power to deter drinking and driving. The only limitation on this process—if we do not consider efficiency—is that at some point prosecutors, judges, juries and others may perceive the law as so unfair that they will refuse to apply it.

The deterrent argument for Bill No. 2 is that it is better tailored to the problem that needs to be addressed, and thus represents a more efficient use of penal resources. The requirements of fault in the accident and linkage to alcohol intoxication mean that those who are convicted under Bill No. 2 will have engaged in some wrongdoing. Thus the second bill does a better job of punishing *only* those who we both wish to deter and believe can be deterred because they made significantly culpable choices. Not that Bill No. 2 has no downside. Placing additional proof requirements on the prosecution means that some persons who truly were at fault in causing the fatal accident will escape criminal liability, because the prosecution will not be able to prove beyond a reasonable doubt either the fault element or the connection to intoxication element of the law.

---

6. Here we confront an issue about how fault is proven, something that will be important in future discussions about doctrine, particularly mens rea. Many will consider the fact that the accident was fatal as strong evidence of significant fault on the part of the driver. Common experience says that fatal accidents are usually associated with bad driving. Similarly, there is a statistical connection between alcohol intake and injury accidents. As a result, we might decide that proof of alcohol intake and a fatality establishes individual fault. But what is generally true about alcohol and fatal accidents is not always true, meaning that some persons who have satisfied the elements of this offense will not have demonstrated actual culpability.

The Pros and Cons of Deterrence

Is deterrence a good theory of punishment? While this question goes far beyond the scope of this work, a quick review of frequently made arguments for and against may be useful.

Supporters of deterrence argue that it provides the only reliable justification for, and limitation on, punishment in a modern democratic society. By requiring that punishment produce good consequences, deterrence makes the law subject to empirical testing. It seems to promise that well-designed studies will give us the necessary information to create optimal rules for liability and sentence. For the same reason, deterrence places a rational limit on punishment, a practice which can be readily abused due to the often extreme and highly personal passions aroused by crime. Finally, deterrence rests on measures of pain and pleasure—utility and disutility—which have broad acceptance. It works despite our many disagreements about moral principles in a diverse society.

Critics of deterrence frequently argue that its exclusive focus on consequences permits punishment of the innocent. In theory, deterrence could justify punishment of a person who did nothing wrong, as long as the person's punishment would significantly deter others. More realistically (for in the great majority of instances, punishment of the innocent would undercut the general deterrent force of law) deterrence may support the over-punishment of the guilty. An offender may receive greater punishment than his individual culpability would merit in order to set an example for other would-be offenders. For example, a getaway driver in a bank robbery is given a life sentence for murder for a shooting committed by a co-felon inside the bank, even though the driver was personally opposed to any violence and did not know the co-felon carried a gun. Though not fully deserved, the conviction and sentence may efficiently deter others from involvement in bank robbery.

Critics also argue that the empirical basis for using deterrence to shape rules of liability and determine extent of sentence is more promise than reality. Studies indicate that the most critical factor in deterring bad conduct is likelihood of discovery.[7] This means that arrest rates make more difference to crime fighting then do rules of liability. By the same token, increasing or diminishing criminal penalties for a particular offense, has even less impact on criminal behavior, for these depend on the contingencies of arrest *and* conviction. As

---

7. See Guyora Binder, The Culpability of Felony Murder, 83 Notre Dame L. Rev. 965, 983 & n.74 (2008). See generally, Daniel S. Nagin & Greg Pogarsky, Integrating Celerity, Impulsivity, and Extralegal Sanction Threats into a General Model of Deterrence: Theory and Evidence, 39 Criminology 865 (2001).

a practical matter, few who commit crimes seriously consider their chances of conviction at trial if caught, or what sentence they might receive if convicted. Most don't think much about the chance of being caught. Criminologists in recent years have emphasized the impulsivity of many criminal offenders. In this sense many offenders do not engage in the long-term rational calculation that utilitarian theory presumes. They seek short-term benefits regardless of long-term costs either to themselves or others. At least as to such offenders, manipulating the rules of criminal liability or sentence seems unlikely to have much deterrent effect.

Finally, critics say that deterrence does not constitute the check on penal passions that proponents maintain, because deterrence appeals to our fear of future criminality, a fear which is commonly exaggerated in certain kinds of cases. That we fear child kidnapping more than fatal highway accidents demonstrates the pattern of our emotions, but not necessarily their rationality. We are much more likely to suffer the latter than the former. Thus arguments phrased in terms of a rational calculus of deterrence may in fact express nonrational fears about certain persons or conduct, including exaggerated fears tied to race and economic class.

Retributive Theories of Punishment

Retribution is a nonconsequentialist theory of punishment that says punishment is just when it is deserved according to the wrong done by an offender. A wrongdoer should be punished to the extent of his wrong action, with wrongness measured according to the nature of the harm done and the nature of wrongdoer's choice. The underlying principle that guides punishment for most contemporary retributivists is respect for basic human rights. A thief should be punished for his choice to steal another's property and thus disrespect the owner's property rights. A rapist should be punished for his choice to violate another's sexual integrity and thus disrespect the victim's right to sexual autonomy. The rape should be punished more than the theft because culpable violation of sexual autonomy is a more serious form of disrespect than is stealing: a worse harm and a worse choice to harm.

In contrast to deterrence, which emphasizes future considerations, retribution looks to the past for its judgments. Under a classical view of retribution, punishment depends entirely on what the person did, and not at all on the consequences that may flow from the person's punishment.

Although in everyday usage, retribution connotes harsh punishment, the theory of retribution does not necessarily lead to harsher results than does deterrence. In fact, there are cases where retribution may support less or no punishment where deterrence argues for major penalties. The reverse may be true as well. By calling a punishment retributive we mean only that the punishment is deserved according to the wrong done.

One of the most influential proponents of a retributive approach to punishment was the German philosopher Immanuel Kant. Kant built his concept of punishment on the principle that all persons should be valued for their ability to choose for themselves. This requires that we take their choices seriously: we should reward good choices and punish bad. When persons commit wrongs against others, punishment must follow, he contended. He argued that deserved punishment values persons for their choosing abilities, and so is a good in itself.

According to Kant, just punishment depends on the nature of the crime and not on the consequences, good or bad, that follow from punishment. As the following oft-quoted passage indicates, he was very much an opponent of the utilitarian view of criminal law.

> "The penal law is a Categorical Imperative; and woe to him who creeps through the serpent-windings of Utilitarianism to discover some advantage that may discharge him from the Justice of punishment, or even from the due measure of it.... for if Justice and Righteousness perish, human life would no longer have any value in the world."[8]

Kant illustrated his commitment to the idea of deserved punishment with a hypothetical concerning the last murderer on earth. He wrote that if human society was about to be disbanded, with the last survivors of the race to scatter across the globe, each to live alone, and it was discovered that one of their number had committed murder, still the murderer must be punished. Although obviously such punishment would do no good in terms of future society, since there would be no future society, Kant believed that punishment was morally required to expiate the wrong already done.

Not all who follow a retributive approach believe that deserved punishment must be imposed in every case, however. Some see retribution as setting an upper limit on punishment: a person should never be punished *more* than he or she deserves, but in some cases, lesser punishment may be merited due to nonretributive considerations. Further discussion of such approaches will come under the heading of mixed theories of punishment below.

Some modern proponents of retribution justify it as a way to restore the essential balance of burdens and benefits in society. Working from a social con-

---

8. *The Philosophy of Law* 194–95 (W. Hastie trans. 1887).

tract theory of government, the notion here is that the offender has refused to bear the burden of an essential obligation—obeying the criminal law—and has thereby obtained unmerited benefits (as in stolen property or unconsented sex) which must be taken back by means of punishment. This approach does not change how retribution is applied, but proponents contend it gives a better account of the justification for retribution than do more traditional versions such as Kant's.

Problems in Retribution

As with deterrence, we need to look at a number of particular punishment problems in order to understand how retribution informs criminal law decision-making. Again we will look at problems in sentencing, excuses from responsibility, degree of culpability and offense definition.

Retribution in Sentencing

When he was a teenager, Mike wanted to be the meanest, scariest guy in the neighborhood. He succeeded. Mike always carried a gun and liked to use it, especially for robberies. During a robbery of a jewelry store, the owner talked back to him, so Mike shot him in the heart. Watching the man die, Mike realized the terrible nature of his deed. He threw away his gun and vowed to change his life.

The police investigation of the crime goes nowhere. Meanwhile Mike changes his life. Ten years later, now a college graduate, a married father of two, and a well-respected high school teacher, Mike confesses his crime to the police. He is charged with robbery and murder, convicted and now must be sentenced. If we take a retributive approach to punishment, what should his sentence be?

Under retribution, because Mike committed severe offenses, he deserves a severe sentence. Regardless of the consequences to Mike, his family and supporters, or even to society generally, punishment depends on the nature of his choice to do wrong and the nature of the harm he did. Given that Mike's worst crime—murder—was among the worst imaginable, retribution argues that his sentence should be proportionately severe.

(Note that if deterrence were the primary consideration, Mike's attorney could argue that because Mike has already become law-abiding, punishment is not required for specific deterrence and certainly not for rehabilitation. The only deterrent argument in favor of significant punishment would be general deterrence: the need to avoid the impression that one may avoid punishment for serious crimes as long as one says sorry and doesn't do it again. The question is whether Mike's situation is so exceptional that a lenient punishment would not undercut the force of the law's promise to punish robbery and murder.)

Victims, Punishment and Punishment Theory

Mike's case gives us the chance to consider how punishment theories deal with an important contemporary controversy in sentencing: the role of victims. Under a retributive theory of punishment what is the relevance of the desires of the surviving relatives of a murder victim? In real life there is no question that the strongly expressed views of victims or their family can affect both how a case is prosecuted and the sentence imposed following a conviction. Fitting these views into a retributive theory of punishment can be difficult, however.

Under a deterrent theory, the concerns of victims go to both the harm done by the crime and the potential positive consequences of punishment. Indeed there is a variant of deterrent theory, called revenge utilitarianism, which holds that a primary purpose of punishment is to satisfy the emotional needs of victims and others for payback in order to prevent them from taking private revenge, thus jeopardizing the rule of law.

Under a retributive approach, punishment depends on the nature of the offense rather than the reactions of victims or others to the offense. Thus, it should make no difference under retribution whether the victim of Mike's murder was a homeless person whose death would otherwise go unnoticed or that of a leading citizen whose killing inspired widespread grief and anger. A court concerned with imposing deserved punishment may properly listen to victims and victims' families for their views on the seriousness of offense, but the quantity or intensity of such views is, by itself, irrelevant to the court's ultimate determination of the severity of offense under retribution.

Retribution and Excuses from Liability

Recall the earlier example of the X-man and his attacks on young people because of his delusion that persons wearing Space Invader shoes are being indoctrinated by dangerous aliens. What does retribution say about the X-man's criminal liability?

The question here is whether the X-man has rationally chosen to harm others so that he deserves punishment for his harm-doing. In this respect, retribution focuses on the same issue as deterrence—the defendant's rationality.

Arguing in favor of an excuse, one might say that because of his delusions, the X-man never rationally chose to disrespect or harm other persons. He might be analogized to a toddler with a gun or a wild animal: beings who may be dangerous, but who lack the qualities of rationality needed for criminal responsibility. Thus because of his madness, his irrationality, the X-man does not *deserve* criminal punishment.

Against this conclusion, a prosecutor may argue that even if the X-man was mentally ill, he was rational enough to understand the basics of what he was doing. He still knew that his victims were human beings and not extraterrestrials and he made a deliberate choice to attack and kill them, thus satisfying the basic requirements of personal responsibility under retribution.

Again, the point is not to identify the winning argument, but to illustrate how the debate proceeds under retribution.

Retribution and Degrees of Culpability

Recall the case of Tom, the hot-tempered man especially sensitive about his mother's reputation, who killed a man in a bar in retaliation for a maternal slur. Tom is clearly guilty of criminal homicide here; the only issue will be the level of offense. According to a retributive theory of punishment, should Tom's be classified a criminal homicide of highest severity, of moderate severity or relatively low severity?

Tom's killing of the stranger was intentional; Tom purposely killed the man. Normally we see purposeful wrongs as more serious forms of disrespect than we do knowing or reckless or negligent actions. We might therefore place all intentional homicides in a single offense category. As we will see in subsequent chapters, however, current law makes a number of category distinctions between different kinds of intentional homicides.

Tom's was a spontaneous killing without much prior thought. Some believe that as a spontaneous choice to kill represents a less serious form of disrespect for human welfare than does homicide committed in cold-blood, following careful deliberation. It is a more emotional and less deliberate choice, and therefore somewhat less culpable. If true, Tom should be convicted of, he deserves punishment for, a homicide offense of middle or lower severity. Similarly, some will argue that Tom had good reason for anger at the stranger, based on the stranger's insult to Tom's mother, and for this reason Tom's responsive killing does not represent as serious a form of disrespect to human value as do other intentional homicides. While his choice to kill was bad, it was not as bad as that of an intentional killer who had no good reason for hostility toward his victim; therefore Tom deserves conviction for a lesser homicide offense.

Retribution and Defining Criminal Offenses

Recall our earlier discussion of two proposed bills that seek to impose mandatory jail terms on drivers with a low level of blood alcohol who have been involved in fatal accidents. Bill No. 1 required proof only of .03 blood alcohol and involvement in a fatal accident. Bill No. 2 also required that the accident have occurred in a fashion "consistent" with alcohol impairment and the driver must have been at fault in the accident. What should the governor do with respect to these bills if he takes a retributive approach to the criminal law?

With respect to both proposed laws, the governor must decide whether persons convicted under each proposal would deserve the conviction and sentence the law would impose. The answer with respect to Bill No. 1 is clearly negative. For the same reasons that the law appeared overinclusive under deterrence, it cannot be justified under retribution. Some persons convicted of a crime and sentenced to incarceration under Bill No. 1 would in fact be innocent of any significant wrongdoing and thus would not deserve any punishment. As we saw previously, a person could be convicted for involvement in an accident that was not his fault, an accident not linked to alcohol impairment, when the driver had an otherwise lawful amount of alcohol in his system.

Under retribution, there are also serious questions about Bill No. 2. In order to sign this piece of legislation, the governor would have to believe that all drivers at fault in causing a fatal accident, who had a low level of blood alcohol, and whose accident occurred in a manner "consistent" with alcohol impairment, had done a sufficient wrong to deserve incarceration. The governor must believe that any person who chose to have at least one drink, then drove, and was involved in a fatal accident committed such a serious wrong that he or she should go to jail. A retributive argument against Bill No. 2 would be that, at least in some cases, the offender was not truly culpable and that what is being punished here is simply the fatal result, which may have been beyond the defendant's control.

The Pros and Cons of Retribution

Proponents of retribution contend that it is the only theory that does justice because only retribution measures conviction and sentence by what the offender chose to do rather than by the consequences of punishment. Under retribution, punishment must be deserved according to the crime; larger social needs can never alter or override an assessment of individual responsibility.

Proponents also argue that retribution gives a better account than deterrence of what most people do in deciding criminal responsibility. For all the talk of preventing crime that we hear in connection with criminal legislation, conviction and sentencing, most persons assess justice by what they believe the wrongdoer deserves according to the nature of his wrongdoing. In other words, most people intuitively judge crime according to retributive principles.

Critics respond that while retribution sounds good in principle, in practice it is empty. Where do these first principles on which retribution is supposedly based come from? For example, who says that respect for autonomy is the principle on which we should build our whole legal structure? Perhaps more important, exactly what does this principle say about deserved punishment? Does it really tell us what a person deserves for burglarizing a house, for stealing a car, or even for committing a serious assault? Critics say that judgments of deserved punishment are just statements of personal preference based on subjective, not objective, criteria. Retribution just rationalizes emotional reactions. Worse, it may encourage penal excess. By asking what a wrongdoer deserves, retribution appeals to the rage of the law-abiding, an emotion not easily distinguished from the desire for revenge, which many believe law should check.

Other Theories

Outside of academia, few in criminal justice take either a purely deterrent or retributive approach to crime. Instead, given a particular responsibility question to decide, we draw on whatever principles seem most appropriate to the situation. Some complain that such eclecticism is incoherent. It's sloppy thinking. But it may be that the complexities of real-world justice will always lie beyond the reach of any one punishment theory.

There are also theories of punishment that do not fall in either the retributive or deterrence camp. We will briefly consider three: mixed theories which seek to combine retribution and deterrence, an expressive theory which marries a retributive method to a consequentialist end, and restorative justice, which reconceptualizes the aims of criminal justice.

Mixed Theories

Most lawyers, legislators and judges subscribe to a mix of punishment theories, using both deterrent and retributive arguments according to context. The normative question is whether this mixing of approaches is principled: Is it a worthy effort to achieve universal principles of justice through an eclectic use of punishment theories, or is it just a way of rationalizing whatever outcome the individual prefers in a given situation?

An example of an effort at a principled mix is where in sentencing, some have argued that retribution should set the maximum amount of punishment, but that deterrent concerns should determine whether any lesser penalty should be imposed. Thus an offender like the reformed killer Mike in our earlier example who would receive a severe penalty under a purely retributive approach, would receive a moderate sentence under a mixed theory based on considerations of specific deterrence, rehabilitation and general deterrence.

Unfortunately, mixed theories of punishment often owe more to expediency than to principle. A lawyer or legislator may shift from retribution to deterrence and back again depending on what works best to achieve a particular desired end. In other words, there is no theory, only disparate arguments cobbled together to support a preexisting preference for a particular outcome.

The Expressive Theory

The expressive theory, also called the educative or communicative theory of punishment joins a consequentialist justification of punishment with a nonconsequentialist application of punishment principles. The central idea is that society punishes to express society's condemnation of the offender's conduct. By publicly convicting an offender and then imposing punishment on him, the state publicly condemns the offender's conduct and forcefully—through punishment—communicates that condemnation to the offender and all other citizens. The expressive theory differs from retribution primarily in its justification. Under the expressive approach, punishment is justified in whole or in part by its potential effect on offender and society.

In application, the expressive theory is normally identical to retribution: to achieve its educative ends, punishment must be and appear to be just, meaning that it must be deserved. In its justification, however, the expressive theory varies from retribution in valuing a consequence of punishment, that punishment should communicate a moral message to the offender and the society at large.

Restorative Justice

The newest idea in Anglo-American punishment theory draws on some of the oldest of punishment practices. This is the concept of restorative justice, that the criminal justice process should seek to repair the social damage done by crime by a process of reconciling offender, victim and community. Although the subject of much writing and experimentation throughout the Anglo-American criminal justice world (meaning those nations that trace their legal heritage to England) it harks back to values and procedures used by many indigenous peoples and small communities in times past.[9]

Restorative justice has important implications for how criminal cases are adjudicated, but it has been promoted primarily as an alternative punishment method.[10] The basic idea of restorative justice is that crime represents an assault on community relations and therefore requires a community-based, relational response. Following determination of guilt, restorative justice envisions a meeting of offender, any identified victim, and other community representatives to discuss the harm done by the offender, and to permit the offender to take personal responsibility, including offering apologies for his or her conduct. The assembled group then devises a plan for the offender to make the victim whole and restore community trust. When the offender has fulfilled this plan, the offender can be received back into the community as a fully restored member. When it works, restorative processes can be transformative for those involved, especially for victim and offender.

Restorative justice represents a serious conceptual challenge to current law and methods of punishment because it sees justice as about relations and not just rules. In practice it is highly dependent on the individuals involved in the restorative process and public trust in that process.

Restorative justice is not likely to supplant other punishment theories or conventional legal processes, especially in larger urban areas where transparency can be critical. Its relational—meaning highly personal—processes may be too hidden from public view to satisfy the citizens of large urban community. Nevertheless it has the potential to inspire important change in criminal policy. In particular, its ideas may subvert the contemporary tendency to seek the permanent exclusion of wrongdoers from society, regardless of its fiscal, social, or moral cost.

---

9. For an introduction, see Howard Zehr, *The Little Book of Restorative Justice* (2002). For the importance of offender reconciliation in an early Puritan community, see *Colonial Justice in Western Massachusetts (1639–1702): The Pynchon Court Record* (Joseph H. Smith ed. 1961).

10. For consideration of restorative justice values in adjudication, see Stephanos Bibas, Forgiveness in Criminal Procedure, 4 Oh. St. J. Crim. L. 329 (2007); Stephanos Bibas & Richard A. Bierschbach, Integrating Remorse and Apology into Criminal Procedure, 114 Yale L. J. 85 (2004). I should also note that some proponents see restorative justice as a complete substitute for incarceration. See Jordan J. Ballor, To Reform or Abolish? Perspectives on Punishment, Prison and Restorative Justice, 6 Ave Maria L. Rev. 481, 491–93 (2008) (reviewing various abolitionist perspectives).

CHAPTER 3

THE LIABILITY FORMULA: ESSENTIAL ELEMENTS AND AFFIRMATIVE DEFENSES

A critical part of criminal law analysis is identifying the type of legal rule that applies to a particular situation. We need to name the doctrine or set of doctrines that address the problems that the facts and law present. This chapter provides the first step in the naming process by identifying the major categories of rules in substantive criminal law. It sets out an analytic device called a liability formula that groups criminal law doctrines into basic categories. The formula distinguishes between so-called essential elements of an offense and affirmative defenses. It breaks down essential elements into four major subcategories: the act requirement, mens rea, causation, and additional circumstances.

The categorization of legal arguments matters because it differentiates arguments that may otherwise be confused and also because it may affect the burden of proof, a topic covered in the next chapter. Finally, introducing the formula here serves to introduce the most important topics covered in the rest of the book.

The Liability Formula

Because of the variety of criminal offenses, doctrines and fact patterns, it can be hard to know where to start in analyzing criminal responsibility in any given case. There are so many trees to examine that we can lose our way in the forest. In order to assist my students in this regard I have long used a basic formula for criminal liability, a shorthand list of legal requirements in the form of a mathematical formula.

The liability formula places all substantive criminal law issues into five basic categories: the act requirement, mens rea, additional circumstances, causation and affirmative defenses. This formula structures much of the discussion of the rest of the book and should prove useful in structuring criminal law analysis generally. It provides a general grouping of legal rules, directing us to the particular rules and analytic methods of a variety of criminal law doctrines. In its full form the formula is written as follows:

Act + Mens Rea + Additional Circumstances → Result w/o Affirmative Defense = Guilt.

This formula provides that if (1) defendant voluntarily committed an act or acts prohibited by statute (or in some instances omitted to act in a legally critical respect) (2) with the mens rea required by statute, (3) under any additional circumstances required by statute, (4) and thereby caused any required result, (5) without evidence supporting an affirmative defense, then defendant should be found guilty.

The first four of these doctrinal categories—the act, mens rea, additional circumstances, and result requirements together constitute what are called the essential elements of an offense. The prosecution has the burden of proving all of the essential elements of an offense beyond a reasonable doubt. By contrast, the burden of proof for affirmative defenses may sometimes be placed on the defense.

While useful, the formula set out above has some major limitations. Most importantly, not every category appears in every offense. The act requirement and affirmative defense requirements are universal, but some criminal statutes do not include any mens rea requirements. Such offenses are termed strict liability. Meanwhile other offenses contain multiple mens rea requirements. There may or may not be an element or elements that constitute additional circumstances. Finally, the result requirement, while critical to the offense of homicide, appears in relatively few other crimes. The great majority of offenses do not require proof of a result.

Given so many exceptions to the formula's rule, the reader may well ask: How does the formula help? The answer is that the formula provides a general, though necessarily provisional, guide to the different kinds of criminal rules that may apply to a given offense. It gives us a starting point and an order in which to consider liability issues. While such guidance may appear of minimal value, even modest help in organization proves welcome in criminal law.

The best way to explain the formula is to illustrate how it applies to a particular case. The following set of facts will be used to introduce each category of doctrines under the formula. Subsequent chapters provide further discussion of each.

On a Thursday afternoon, a sports car enters an intersection near an elementary school while traveling at high speed. The car suddenly veers to the right, then left and strikes a school crossing guard. The guard is taken by paramedics to a local hospital, where she receives medical treatment for serious injuries. That night her condition dramatically worsens after she is given the wrong medication. She dies two hours later.

The Voluntary Act Requirement

Under the liability formula our first issue involves what is called the voluntary act requirement. We ask: Did the defendant voluntarily act in a way prohibited by the criminal statute under which he is charged? In this instance, whether charged with a simple speeding offense, a more serious vehicular offense such as dangerous driving, or a homicide offense such as murder or manslaughter, the critical act will be the defendant's driving of the sports car.

In most cases involving injury by vehicle, the only issue concerning the act requirement is identity: can the prosecution prove that the defendant was the person behind the wheel at the time the injury occurred? If the defendant is proven to be the driver, we will generally presume that the defendant voluntarily drove the car. Under some unusual circumstances, issues about the voluntariness of the defendant's conduct might arise, however.

If it turns out that just before entering the intersection the accelerator of the car malfunctioned, resulting in sudden acceleration, we would have to decide if this rendered the driver's conduct involuntary. Likewise, if a child in the passenger seat of the car grabbed the steering wheel at the critical moment, and this movement led directly to the accident, then the defendant might argue that he was not voluntarily "driving" the car at the critical time. Neither argument is necessarily a winner for the defense, for in both instances the prosecution might argue that defendant should be held responsible for the events that purportedly interfered with his control. Thus the prosecution might argue that the defendant made voluntary choices concerning car maintenance or child control, respectively, that make him responsible for subsequent failures in these respects at the time of the accident. For more extensive discussion of the voluntary act requirement, see Chapter 5.

Mens Rea

The next issue to arise under the formula—and the most hotly contested criminal law issue in most cases—is that of mens rea, what is sometimes called criminal intent. Assuming that the defendant voluntarily drove the car, we need to determine whether: (1) the driver purposely hit the crossing guard, or

(2), if not, whether he was aware of the dangers his driving posed to the guard and others, or (3) if not aware, he should have known of those dangers. These are some of the critical mens rea distinctions that might be presented in a criminal prosecution. Such distinctions might make the difference between criminal and civil liability or between conviction for murder, or for a lesser offense, such as dangerous driving. For certain offenses, like speeding, no mens rea is required, however. Mens rea is the subject of Chapters 6, 7 and 8.

Additional Circumstances

The criminal law formula next requires us to analyze what I call "additional circumstances." This necessarily opaque phrase designates statutory circumstances that must be proven but do not require mens rea. They represent circumstances as to which the prosecution need not show any awareness or negligence on the part of the defendant.

Consider the prosecution of the driver in the crossing guard case under a statute which creates a separate crime of reckless driving within 1000 ft. of an elementary school. For reasons discussed in Chapter 7, a court will likely hold here that recklessness applies only to the dangerousness of the driving and not the location of the school. Thus, the location element represents an additional circumstance. As long as the prosecution can show that the accident occurred within the 1000 ft. vicinity of the school, no proof need be presented that the driver was aware that the school was nearby.

Causation

Some offenses, most notably homicide, contain a result element, a requirement that the defendant's conduct cause a certain kind of harm. If the driver is charged with either the murder or manslaughter of the crossing guard, then the prosecution must not only show that the defendant voluntarily drove the car, with the required mens rea, but that this wrongful conduct caused the victim's death. Causation involves analyzing the connection between the driver's wrongful conduct and the death of the victim. The defendant may wish to argue that although he was responsible for the accident, the guard's death was attributable primarily to the conduct of others and therefore no *homicide* conviction is warranted.

The driver might try to place primary blame on the crossing guard herself, saying that her own careless conduct in the intersection was the primary cause of the accident. Given that drivers must generally watch out for pedestrians and should proceed with special care in the vicinity of schools, this causation argument is not likely to succeed without facts—not given here—indicating that the guard's conduct was exceedingly dangerous.

More plausibly, the defendant might also argue that the primary cause of the victim's death was incompetent medical treatment, that the "real" cause of death was the administration of the wrong medication. Causation is the topic of Chapter 13.

Affirmative Defenses

Affirmative defenses constitute the final category of doctrines under the liability formula. These are special excuses or justifications for the defendant's conduct which preclude conviction despite proof that the defendant satisfied all of the other elements of the offense. Affirmative defenses include doctrines such as self-defense, insanity, or duress. Affirmative defenses usually—though not always—involve issues not explicitly mentioned in the statute that defines the criminal offense.

In our crossing guard accident case we need additional facts to raise a potentially viable affirmative defense. Assume, for example, that following his arrest the driver tells police that:

> "You're right, I did hit her. Ran her right over. But she's not who you think she is. She's not a crossing guard really. She's an criminal agent. They're kidnapping all of the children and taking them away for medical experiments. I had to do it to save them." Does this statement support any defense to liability?

This statement raises the basis for an affirmative defense of insanity.

Note that here the driver has confessed to voluntarily driving the car that struck the guard and has admitted a high level of mens rea with respect to injuring or even killing the guard. Insanity involves different considerations than mens rea or the act requirement. If the defendant was legally insane at the time of the accident, then even if he intentionally struck the guard with his car, he should be acquitted. While he may be civilly committed for mental treatment, an insanity verdict precludes criminal punishment. Affirmative defenses are discussed in depth in Chapters 18 (self-defense) and 20 (insanity).

Element Analysis and Criminal Statutes

Having provided a quick overview of the basic families of criminal law doctrines that we will be studying, we now turn to analysis of the basic building block of all criminal law: the criminal statute. As was discussed in Chapter 1, every criminal charge brought in an American court is based on a particular criminal statute enacted by the legislature of the jurisdiction. The statute defines the basic requirements for conviction, and it, or associated statutes, will determine the range of punishment for the offense. Therefore, legal analysis of a criminal offense should always begin with the statutory definition of the relevant offense.

Criminal law analysis would be considerably simpler if criminal statutes came with their parts clearly labeled. If the legislature specifically labeled one part of an offense definition as the act requirement, another as the mens rea requirement, and so on, much confusion could be avoided. But legislatures never do this. Instead, criminal statutes take the form of basic English sentences, albeit with often strange words and difficult grammatical constructions. For every criminal offense, the reader must determine the function of every part of the statutory definition. She must ascertain how statutory phrases should be categorized under the liability formula. The first step in this process is to break the criminal statute down into its constituent elements. Once we've done this we can decide into which category each element falls.

An element of a statute is simply a phrase in the statute which describes a particular requirement for conviction that may be conveniently separated from other requirements in the statute. As noted previously, statutes generally take the form of fairly complicated sentences; breaking a statute into component parts usually makes analysis easier by providing smaller parts to work with, at least initially.

There are no particular rules for how to divide the statute into elements. We simply look to see what makes logical and grammatical sense as a particular unit. Different people may divide the same statute into somewhat different elements. This should not matter. This initial division into elements is largely a matter of convenience, a preliminary to the real work of determining what each part of the statute means.

The following criminal statute should serve to illustrate basic element analysis.

> Whoever threatens a peace officer with a deadly weapon, with the purpose of inflicting great bodily injury or immediate apprehension of such injury, is guilty of a felony.

We might break the statute down into the following elements:

> Whoever
> (1) threatens a peace officer with a deadly weapon,
> (2) with the purpose of inflicting great bodily injury
> (3) or immediate apprehension of such injury,
> is guilty of a felony.

Next we categorize these elements according to our criminal law formula. The easiest way to do this is to try to match the formula categories with words or phrases within the statute.

What part of the statute correlates with the voluntary act requirement? Here we look for verbs—descriptions of prohibited conduct. The first element's requirement that the defendant *threaten* the victim with a deadly weapon describes the prohibited act. The conduct must be of a sort that meets the definition of threatening and it must have been committed voluntarily.

What about mens rea? As we will see in succeeding chapters, the adverbial phrase "with the purpose of" represents a common form of mens rea requirement. The defendant must have committed the act of threatening with the goal of either inflicting great bodily injury on the victim or inducing apprehension of such injury in the victim.[1]

We have now covered the main elements of the statute *except* that the victim be a peace officer and that the threat be committed with a deadly weapon. The important question is whether these requirements are strict liability or not. Must the defendant be proven to have had a particular level of awareness with respect to the victim being a peace officer? Such a requirement would generally limit prosecutions to cases involving uniformed officers; attacks on undercover or off-duty officers would be made difficult because of the need to prove the defendant knew of the victim's law-enforcement status. Similarly, did the legislature intend to require proof that the defendant knew or perhaps should have known of the dangerousness of the weapon used?

Questions such as this will be pursued in greater depth in Chapter 7. For our purposes here it is sufficient to note that the word sequence of the statute suggests that the mens rea requirement is limited to the infliction of injury or creation of apprehension of injury. Therefore the peace officer and deadly weapon elements may be termed additional circumstances. The prosecution must prove that the victim was a peace officer and that the item used was a deadly weapon but not that the defendant had any culpable state of mind with respect to these facts.

---

1. Note that to make sense of the apprehension element, we have to use words and combinations that do not expressly appear in the statute. Since this is a criminal offense targeting the conduct of an individual, and apprehension is a central wrong to be punished here, apprehension must be something caused by the defendant, hence the use of the word "inducing" in the text. Similarly, the mens rea of "with the purpose of" is applied to the apprehension element as well as they bodily injury element, since these two seem to be alternative forms of harm doing in the statute.

What about causation here? Initial appearances notwithstanding, the statute contains no result requirement. As discussed further in Chapter 13, causation becomes an issue only when the statute requires that defendant's conduct cause a particular *physical* harm. With respect to this assault offense, defendants must have either attempted to inflict physical injury or acted so as to create the apprehension of such injury; no physical harm is required. (It is true that a defendant might be convicted of this assault offense if he actually did inflict a great bodily injury on the victim, assuming he acted with the required mens rea. This demonstrates the potential range of conduct that the statute covers; it does not change the statutory requirements.)

Nor does the assault statute make any mention of affirmative defenses. This is not unusual. Affirmative defenses tend to be set out in general statutes independent of particular criminal offenses. Sometimes the dimensions of affirmative defenses are set by judicial decisions.

A Language Note: Distinguishing Arguments about Essential Elements and Affirmative Defenses

As we have seen, the first four categories of the liability formula—voluntary act, mens rea, additional circumstances, and causation—constitute the essential elements of an offense. As we will soon see, an important reason to distinguish the essential elements of an offense from affirmative defenses involves issues of burden of proof. But in addition to the challenge of distinguishing essential elements and affirmative defenses, we encounter a terminological problem in discussing these matters. We need a language that separates arguments about essential elements of the offense from arguments about affirmative defenses. For example, in the traffic guard case, we considered a number of defense arguments about essential elements, specifically the act requirement, mens rea and causation. In the legal literature, such defense arguments are commonly termed "defenses," as in a "defense" of no voluntary act or a mens rea "defense." The problem with using the term defense this way is that it sounds like it is an affirmative defense about which the defendant must produce evidence and persuade. Yet because the controversy concerns an essential element of the offense, the burden of proof remains on the prosecution.

In order to distinguish between defendant arguments about essential elements and those that concern affirmative defenses, in this book the term defense when used alone will be reserved for affirmative defenses. A defendant's efforts to rebut prosecution presentations on essential elements of the offense will be referred to as defense presentations or defense arguments.

CHAPTER 4

Proof and Persuasion

So, what happened?

This is almost always the first question in any criminal case. In the practice of law it is often the most important question. But in criminal law, determining the facts is usually just preliminary to the main event. As appellate courts do in their decisions, we commonly summarize the facts in order to concentrate on the real controversy, which is how the law applies to those facts. When factual disputes are mentioned, they are usually presented in binary form: the prosecution's version versus the defendant's version. In the analysis that follows, the truth of first one and then the other version is assumed in order to decide the legal question: how the rules of criminal law should resolve liability.

But this oversimplifies adjudicative reality. Factual disputes in criminal cases are many and complex. There are usually not just two versions, but multiple versions or possibilities, according to the number of witnesses and pieces of physical evidence. Nor is it easy to distinguish between matters of fact and law. In short, factual disputes are often at the center of the controversy in criminal cases, and although they will not be the focus of our study of criminal law, we need a basic grasp of the challenges of factual proof to understand the significance of the requirements of offense definitions and defenses considered in the rest of the book.

In this chapter we look—briefly—at how principles of criminal law interact with questions of proof and persuasion. When a matter of fact remains in dispute after all the evidence has been presented, we need a method for dealing with the remaining uncertainty: this is the work of rules on burden of proof. Here we will also examine some of the practical problems of proving criminal culpability, especially proof of mens rea.

Burden of Proof

To understand why rules about burden of proof matter and how such rules work, it will be help to start with a concrete example.

It all happened on the subway on a hot summer afternoon.

The Prosecution's Evidence

Elinor, 54, an office manager at a downtown law firm, was riding the subway home from work. She had had to stay later than usual and was very tired. There were no seats available; she barely made it into the crowded car.

About halfway between stations, the subway car jolted and she felt a hand on her right breast. The hand squeezed her. She screamed and grabbed the hand. She yelled at the young man to whom it belonged, accusing him of molesting her. He was arrested by police at the next station. Elinor told police that she felt "totally violated" and that there was no question at all that it was deliberate, and he was "a filthy dirty, perverted man" who had been staring at her before the incident occurred.

The Defense's Evidence

Ahmed, 22, was on the subway car after a long day of looking for a job. He had recently come to this country at the behest of his uncle who had helped obtain the necessary immigration papers. Ahmed had only ridden the subway five or six times before. In his native country, it is extremely rude to stand close to unrelated women, let alone touch them and he was trying to avoid any contact. He had taken his hand off the pole which he had been holding when the subway car jolted and he was thrown forward. Off balance, instinctively he reached out and accidentally touched someone, and then realized to his horror that he was touching a woman's breast. "I am a good man. I would never do such a thing. It is unthinkable," he told the police. He also says that Elinor called him a "dirty filthy Arab" and had looked at him with disgust before the incident occurred.

The Criminal Law Question

The criminal law question in this case involves why Ahmed touched Elinor. Assume that the charge requires that Ahmed have committed an intentional sexual touching, that he touched her breast for sexual purposes. Elinor claims that Ahmed acted with this intent but he contends that the touching was entirely accidental.

The Proof Problem

There is no scientific test to resolve this dispute. There is no DNA match or fingerprint or other scientific technique to determine which version—if either—is accurate. Other witnesses may testify to the character of the parties and the context of the event, but even a security camera may not record enough visual information to be determinative. As in many criminal cases, the determination of mens rea will depend on the testimony of one or two key witnesses—here certainly the testimony of the victim and likely also the accused.

The case also illustrates how important a legal resolution is. The stakes for both Elinor and Ahmed are personally very high, even if the actual penalty for this offense proves modest compared to other crimes. Society also needs a definitive resolution to the controversy. How can our system of law resolve cases like this where there is a critical factual dispute?

Initially we hope that any factual uncertainty will be resolved by the trial process. We hope that the jury, in listening closely to the witnesses and observing their demeanor, comparing the details and consistency and coherence of their accounts, will be able to decide what occurred. If so, we need not worry about burden of proof. But if after considering all of the evidence the jury still has doubts, is uncertain—to some extent—about what occurred or why, then rules about burden of proof may be critical. It is to these rules that we now turn.

In a criminal case in the United States, *the prosecution bears the burden of proving all essential elements of an offense beyond a reasonable doubt.* With respect to affirmative defenses, some or all of the burden of proof *may* be placed on the defense, though in many instances the most important burden, that of persuasion, will remain on the prosecution.

To understand what this means, we must begin with the values that inform this basic rule structure. It is the familiar notion that an accused should not be convicted of a crime and be subjected to the serious social and penal consequences of a conviction unless the fact finder is certain—beyond a reasonable doubt—that he is actually guilty.

Convicting the Innocent, Acquitting the Guilty: Risks of Error and Burden of Proof

Most are familiar with the old adage that it is better that 10 guilty men go free than that one innocent be convicted.[1] This expresses the precept of Anglo-Amer-

---

1. William Blackstone, 4 *Commentaries on the Criminal Laws of England* 352 (1979) (1769) ("for the law holds, that it is better that ten guilty persons escape, than that one innocent suffer.")

ican criminal justice that because we value personal liberty and reputation so highly, we believe that convicting the innocent is far worse than acquitting the guilty. Obviously, we would prefer totally accurate verdicts: convicting the guilty and acquitting the innocent. But given the fallibility of human judgments, especially in a setting where emotions run high and information is imperfect, we need an adjudicative system that minimizes the worst kinds of errors.

Generally we believe that mistakes are most likely where factual uncertainty appears greatest.[2] Thus we assume that the greatest risk of an erroneous conviction in Ahmed's case is where there remains significant doubt in jurors's minds about the prosecution's proof once all the evidence has been heard. As a result, Ahmed should be acquitted—found not guilty—unless the jury is convinced beyond a reasonable doubt that his touching of Elinor's breast was an intentional sexual act.

Essential Elements, Affirmative Defenses and the Burden of Proof

We have already seen that the prosecution bears the burden of proof on all essential elements of an offense, *in potential distinction* to affirmative defenses. We will see that constitutionally, the burden of proof on affirmative defenses *may* be shifted to the defense. Why this constitutional distinction?

Some argue that affirmative defenses do not present the same risks of error as do essential elements. A mistake about mens rea represents a fundamental error about whether the defendant committed a crime. If Ahmed is found guilty of a sex offense when his touching was truly innocent, this represents a fundamental error about both culpability and dangerousness. By contrast, consider if Ahmed's attorney argued that he should be acquitted, even if he committed an intentional sexual act, because he was insane. Such a defense would not raise the same concerns about convicting a person entirely innocent of wrongdoing.

Another explanation for the constitutional distinction between essential elements and affirmative defenses involves the relative availability of evidence to the prosecution and defense. The prosecution generally will have evidence about the defendant's actions and intentions relevant to the essential elements

---

2. Unfortunately, this assumption may not always be warranted. Recent cases of miscarriages of justice revealed by DNA testing show that several kinds of evidence, especially eyewitness testimony and to a lesser extent, confessions, may be seen by fact finders as considerably more trustworthy than they actually are. See Barry Scheck, et al., *Actual Innocence* (2000); Samuel Gross, Loss of Innocence: Eyewitness Identification and Proof of Guilt, 16 J. Leg. Stud. 395 (1987).

of an offense from witness accounts and physical evidence. With respect to at least some affirmative defenses—insanity being an example—the defense may have a major evidentiary advantage. That is, when it comes to insanity, the defendant personally has access to evidence that the prosecution may not. As a result, fairness may dictate that at least some of the burden of proof on insanity shift to the defendant.

Setting Burden of Proof Rules

The initial decision about burden of proof in criminal cases is up to the jurisdiction's legislature. The legislature can direct the allocation of burden of proof explicitly through criminal statutes, or may do so implicitly by the manner in which it defines offenses and affirmative defenses. Courts must then apply these rules to the case at hand. Where the legislature has not spoken on the issue, courts must make their own decision about burden of proof according to principles and traditions of criminal justice in the jurisdiction.

But there is one other important potential consideration here, and that is the requirement of due process under the federal constitution. The United States Supreme Court has held that in all criminal cases, the prosecution must prove all essential facts or elements beyond a reasonable doubt. What *exactly* does this mean? Unfortunately, a satisfactory answer to this question would take us well beyond the bounds of our present task. A summary of the Court's approach here is found in the accompanying sidebar, Constitutional Decisions on Burden of Proof. But overall, the Court's treatment of this issue is similar to its constitutional treatment of other matters of substantive criminal law: deference to legislative decision-making is the overriding theme of the Court's burden of proof jurisprudence.

Constitutional Decisions on Burden of Proof

The United States Supreme Court has relied on three sets of considerations to determine what is an essential part of the prosecution case: (1) the statutory definition of the offense; (2) historical treatments of the particular issue; and (3) policy considerations relating to both substantive criminal law and evidence.

The Court first looks to the language defining the offense because this provides important information about the legislature's view of what is essential to the offense. When the contested issue is an explicit part of the statutory offense definition, this strongly suggests its status as an essential element both for purposes of substantive criminal law and for constitutional burden of proof. By contrast, when the issue is left out of the defining statute but is denominated an affirmative defense in separate statutory language, that status will probably hold for constitutional purposes as well. Similarly, express statutory language shifting the burden of proof on a matter onto the defense indicates legislative intent to treat the matter as an affirmative defense and may carry significant constitutional weight.

Statutory language is often be ambiguous, however. If so, the Court may look to criminal justice traditions. For example, consider a statutory definition of murder that requires that the killing be "unlawful." Because killings committed in self-defense are lawful, this language could be read to make the lack of self-defense an essential element of murder. The prosecution would have to disprove indications of self-defense beyond a reasonable doubt to convict for murder. But the fact that self-defense has traditionally been termed an affirmative defense, with at least the burden of production placed on the defense, has persuaded the Court that this statutory language does not require the prosecution to bear the burden of proof as a matter of constitutional law.[3]

Historical treatment of similar criminal offenses is also influential. The closer the affinity between the contested issue and a traditional mens rea requirement of the offense, the more likely it will be held an essential feature of the prosecution's case. For example, the Supreme Court has held that where a jurisdiction employed a traditional common law definition of murder, provocation constitutes a negative element of murder because it negates the requirement of malice aforethought.[4] By contrast, where the jurisdiction defines murder in a way that makes no explicit or implicit mention of provocation, the Court affirmed the legislature's choice to treat an expanded version of provocation taken from the MPC as an affirmative defense as to which the defense bears the burden of proof.[5]

Finally, the Court has also looked to policy considerations in setting constitutional requirements for the burden of proof. Where the legislature has sought to expand the scope of defense arguments beyond those traditionally permitted, the Court is most likely to approve a shift of the burden of proof onto the defense. The Court may also be influenced by considerations of which party has the best access to evidence with respect to the particular issue.[6]

---

3. See Martin v. Ohio, 480 U.S. 228 (1987).
4. Mullaney v. Wilbur, 421 U.S. 684 (1975).
5. Patterson v. New York, 432 U.S. 197 (1977).
6. See Patterson, 432 U.S. at 206–10.

The Two Kinds of Burdens of Proof: Distinguishing the Burden of Production from the Burden of Persuasion

There are actually two different kinds of burdens of proof: the burden of production and the burden of persuasion. Unfortunately, in talking about the burden of proof, courts and others often do not distinguish between these, and simply refer to burden of proof without further distinction. Mostly, such references are to the burden of persuasion. As we will see, the most serious issues with respect to burden of proof usually involve the burden of persuasion. Nevertheless, a basic understanding of the topic does require distinguishing between these two kinds of burdens. So, what is the difference between burden of production and burden of persuasion?

The burden of production refers to the obligation of producing credible evidence concerning an issue in order for that issue to be considered by the fact finder. The burden of production represents a kind of gateway into legal evaluation of an issue. In legal terms, the burden of production involves the obligation of the moving party (the one seeking to change the legal status quo) to produce enough facts on the issue to have it considered by the decision maker.

Meanwhile the burden of persuasion is the burden of convincing the fact finder to a certain level of certainty once all of the evidence has been admitted. The burden of persuasion is what resolves any lingering uncertainty that remains at the end of the case.

Burden of Production

Imagine that the phone rings at your home. It's after dinner time, and no election is approaching, so feeling safe from telemarketers and political campaigners, you pick up. You say hello. And then you wait for the person on the other end to identify herself and give the purpose of the call. According to the etiquette of phone calling, the caller has the burden of production. You would think it quite odd and possibly threatening to receive a phone call from someone who fell silent after stating hello. You did not make the call, so why should you have to establish who is calling and why? Of course, if it is your four-year-old niece calling, then the usual rules may not apply and you will have to carry the conversation.

In a criminal case, the prosecution bears the burden of production *and* the burden of persuasion on all the essential elements of an offense. This is what it means to say that the prosecution has the burden of proof on all essential elements.

Usually when there is a serious issue about burden of proof, it has to do with the burden of persuasion rather than production. But not always. Consider the following.

> Buster is taken into custody at a rock concert after being involved in a fight. Found in his pocket in a glassine container are what appear to be three rocks of crack cocaine. The evidence is weighed and booked into the police evidence room. The material is later is incinerated pursuant to a police department policy of destroying all illegal drugs after six months. Normally by this time the drugs have been tested in a lab and the laboratory technician's testimony can be used at trial to prove chemical composition and amount. In this case, this step is either neglected or the paperwork on the testing has been lost.
>
> Buster is charged with possession of crack cocaine, but the trial is delayed for almost a year. At trial the arresting officer testifies that the material found in Buster's pocket had the characteristic appearance and was packaged in the characteristic manner of crack cocaine sold on the street. The prosecution introduces no evidence about chemical testing of the substance, however.
>
> The defense moves for a verdict of acquittal on the grounds that the prosecution's evidence that the defendant possessed crack cocaine was insufficient. The result?

Here it appears the defense will prevail because the prosecution has not met its burden of production concerning an essential element: that the material in Buster's pocket actually was crack cocaine. Without evidence of a chemical test of the material, the prosecution simply has not produced enough evidence about the nature of the substance. Note that the same decision might be rendered according to the burden of persuasion. If, for example, the arresting officer had conducted a field test that showed positive for cocaine, but a defense expert questioned the efficacy of such a test, the court might hold that the prosecution had not met its burden of persuasion on this element. A failure on either burden of proof will bar further proceedings in the case.

With respect to affirmative defenses, the obligation to come forward with evidence—the burden of production—is normally placed on the defense. Indeed, this is usually seen as one of the defining features of affirmative defenses.

The trial judge has the initial responsibility of determining whether a burden of production with respect to an affirmative defense has been met.[7] Often

---

7. Generally speaking, the trial court need not make a specific ruling concerning the prosecution's burden of production, because as to the essential elements of the offense, the

courts speak of the requirement to present *credible evidence sufficient to raise a reasonable doubt.* The judge's role in determining whether this burden is met is a sensitive one, for in jury trials it goes to the heart of the distinction between the judge's role as a legal gatekeeper and the jury's role as the ultimate judge of the credibility of witnesses and significance of physical evidence.

If the defense does not satisfy its burden of production with respect to an affirmative defense, then the jury will not be instructed on the defense.

Officer O'Reilly of the Highway Patrol is driving in a marked patrol car in the middle lane of the interstate at midmorning when he notices a car flash by in the fast lane going at least 100 miles an hour. Officer O'Reilly starts a pursuit in which he observes the Driver execute a number of extremely dangerous maneuvers, going in and out of lanes and then, on surface streets, driving on the wrong side of the street. The chase ends at the Emergency Room of the hospital. In the hospital lobby, Driver hits and kicks the Officer before he is finally subdued. Driver is charged with reckless driving and assault on a peace officer.

At trial, using the testimony of Officer O'Reilly and two civilian witnesses, the prosecution establishes all of the essential elements of both offenses. Cross-examination by defense attorney establishes that while he struggled with the Officer, the Driver was yelling that he needed to be with his wife who was in labor with their first child.

Outside the presence of the jury, the defense attorney argues to the court that based on the evidence presented thus far, the jury should be instructed on the doctrine of necessity. Necessity is an affirmative defense which will excuse Driver if he honestly and reasonably believed that his otherwise criminal conduct represented the lesser evil in the circumstances—that the consequences would have been worse had he obeyed the law. Defense attorney states that Driver believed his wife and/or new child would die if he were not present during labor.

Should the jury hear an instruction on necessity if the burden of production for this affirmative defense is on the defendant?

Most judges will probably say no based on this evidence. Without further testimony, there is insufficient evidence that a reasonable person might believe that Driver's presence with his wife was so important to make such risky driv-

---

prosecution will also have the burden of persuasion and that is usually the main focus of attention.

ing and fighting with a peace officer the lesser evil. There is no indication of any medical necessity for Driver's immediate presence. As a result, the court is likely to rule that the defense has not met the burden of production on this affirmative defense and the issue will not go to the jury unless more evidence is presented.

Shifting Burdens: The Interaction of Burden of Production and Burden of Persuasion with Affirmative Defenses

As we have seen, the burden of production for an affirmative defense usually rests on the defense. What happens once it is satisfied? There are two different possibilities.

We have already seen that, constitutionally, jurisdictions *may* place the burden of persuasion for an affirmative defense on the defendant. There has been a trend in this direction with certain affirmative defenses, especially the insanity defense, as we will see in Chapter 20.

With respect to many affirmative defenses, however, once the defense's burden of production is met, the burden of persuasion falls back on the prosecution. The prosecution then must disprove the elements of the affirmative defense to secure a conviction. A return to our previous case will illustrate how this works.

> Driver takes the stand in his own defense. He says that it all began when he received a hysterical call on his cell phone from his wife saying she had prematurely gone into labor and she was frantic because she was at the hospital and couldn't reach him. (He had been in a meeting.) He stated that given her medical condition (high blood pressure, diabetes, and other ailments) and her psychological state, that he believed if he was not present in the labor room to calm her down, that there was a good chance either she or their baby, or maybe even both, would die. He believed that there were no sedative drugs that she could safely take under the circumstances.
>
> If in this jurisdiction the burden of persuasion for the affirmative defense of necessity is on the prosecution, how should the jury be instructed in this case on the burden of proof?

Assuming that the Driver's testimony is sufficient to meet the burden of production and therefore get the issue presented to the jury, the ultimate burden of persuasion here falls on the prosecution. This means that the jury will be instructed on the requirements of necessity, and told that unless the prosecution can *disprove* the elements of necessity beyond a reasonable doubt, then Driver should be acquitted. In other words, unless the prosecution can prove beyond a reasonable doubt either that Driver *did not* believe that he had to be present in the labor room to save a life, or (more likely in this case) prove that his belief *was unreasonable*, then Driver should be acquitted.

Anticipating such an instruction, the prosecution might want to consider calling a rebuttal witness to provide medical testimony on the unreasonableness of Driver's account. Otherwise any lingering uncertainty on the question of necessity will, because of the burden of proof, produce an acquittal.

Proof Beyond a Reasonable Doubt? Instructions and Practice

As a matter of constitutional due process, the prosecution must prove each essential element of a criminal offense beyond a reasonable doubt. This is the highest standard of proof used anywhere in Anglo-American law. It has also been a hallmark of U.S. criminal law since the late 18th century. Exactly what amounts to proof beyond a reasonable doubt remains a remarkably difficult question given the pedigree of this concept, however.[8]

Legal instructions on beyond a reasonable doubt rarely go beyond general truisms. For example, jurors often hear that reasonable doubt does not require the exclusion of all doubt, because that would be impossible (something that prosecutors emphasize). They are also frequently told that it signifies a degree of confidence similar to that required for making an important decision in one's life (generally emphasized by defense counsel). Further guidance in the form of examples or statistical measures is virtually never provided. Courts assume that jurors will be able to resolve for themselves what beyond a reasonable doubt means in the case before them.

This brings us to one of the more sensitive questions in criminal adjudication. How do jurors really understand the requirement of proof beyond a reasonable doubt? In particular, do they apply the same standard in all cases? As a matter of law, the requirement of proof beyond a reasonable doubt is invariant. It does not change from case to case, or jurisdiction to jurisdiction. But veterans of criminal litigation know that juries in some cases convict on far less proof than do other juries. The disturbing truth is that the standard of proof required for conviction varies considerably from case to case and courthouse to courthouse.

Perhaps the most important real life variable is the emotion the case inspires in jurors. A horrific crime creates emotional pressure to find

---

8. For a revealing historical account of reasonable doubt, see James Q. Whitman, *The Origins of Reasonable Doubt* (2009).

someone guilty. The result is that, as a practical matter, the prosecution needs relatively less evidence in such a case to persuade the fact finder of the accused's guilt. The attractiveness of the defendant, or preconceptions concerning his or her character may also influence fact finders. This helps explain why criminal prosecutions of defendants with significant accomplishments in business or entertainment, or against members of respected professions such as police officers, often prove far more difficult for the prosecution than other kinds of cases. The extent to which the victim in the case (if any) or the prosecution witnesses are sympathetic to the fact finder can make a difference, even independent of the facts adduced. Most troubling of all, fact finders may unconsciously alter the burden of proof under the influence of their own (often unconscious) preconceptions about persons based on race or ethnic background.[9]

Obviously this is not the way criminal adjudication should work. If the fact finder can be shown to have been biased against the defendant, or have decided based on emotions not connected to facts or law, this may form the basis of a successful appeal of a conviction. But it would be naive to suppose that legal rules can entirely eliminate these kinds of influences. They are a fundamental part of human nature and while the law may minimize their effects, they cannot be entirely eliminated, which means they must always be a matter of serious concern to lawyers.

The Practical Challenges of Proof

The discussion so far of factual uncertainty and the prosecution's burden of proof may strike some readers as unsatisfactory. How can crimes be proven to this level of certainty? If the prosecution must prove mens rea and other aspects of culpability beyond a reasonable doubt and the prosecution cannot require the defendant to testify because of constitutional limitations, then how can any criminal prosecution succeed except where the defendant has already confessed? Who besides the defendant can provide insight into what the defendant knew or sought, information critical to ascertaining defendant's purpose, knowledge or reck-

---

9. The point can be exaggerated, but many defense attorneys take racial bias in fact finders very seriously. For example, consider this exchange involving a young black man facing criminal charges in the Los Angeles area. The defendant's "lawyer told him, completely apart from the evidence ... [that] a conservative jury he was likely to face in the ... suburb in which the crime took place, in all probability, would not believe him no matter what he said...."You are the jury's worst nightmare. Young black male with a gun." Edward Humes, *No Matter How I Shout* 196–97 (1996).

lessness? And even if all witnesses testify to their own understandings of events, as with our initial case involving Elinor and Ahmed, how can we possibly *prove* one account true beyond a reasonable doubt, when it conflicts with another and we have no scientific evidence on the point?

These questions point to the practical difficulty of proof in criminal cases, a problem largely for the prosecution. In the remainder of this chapter we will consider how culpability may be shown in the criminal courtroom. Initially we take up a common concern, that such proof requires the ability to read minds, which proves exaggerated. Then we consider the use of presumptions, which assist the prosecution in its proof, though not without legal controversy.

The Reading Minds Problem

Sometimes lawyers and others assert that proving mens rea and other subjective aspects of culpability is nearly impossible because it requires us to read the defendant's mind. As one nineteenth century judge wrote concerning a claim of self-defense: "The prisoner says he believed his life was in danger. Who can look into his heart? If the *law* allows *him* to judge, who can contradict him? The [physical] circumstances are nothing; it is his *belief* that justifies him."[10]

The notion that we need to read minds—or hearts—to establish culpability is a misconception. Neither telepathy nor extraordinary psychological insight is required, just an ability to assess the reasons for which a person acted. Usually we can ascertain these reasons from information about the person's conduct from third parties.

In analyzing culpability, we compare the actions of the accused with generally recognized patterns of human conduct. We assess the defendant's conduct according to: (1) what we know about human nature generally and (2) what we learn about the defendant in this situation. Consider two different incidents of alleged theft at the airport.

> In the first case, a man is seen closely examining the luggage tags of a number of bags on a baggage carousel before removing from the carousel a suitcase that belongs to someone else. He is then arrested.
> In the second case, a man is observed in a stall in the men's room rifling through a red woman's purse—a purse belonging to a stranger.
> In neither case do we have any statements from the accused. How can we establish whether either of these individuals acted with an intent to steal?

---

10. State v. Harris, 46 N.C. (1 Jones) 190, 195 (1853).

Whether these men were engaged in theft or innocent activity depends on their beliefs concerning the ownership of the suitcase and the purse respectively. But without any direct information from them about what they thought about ownership, how can we tell? We can tell a considerable amount by comparing their conduct to general patterns of human behavior.

The man seen examining luggage tags is probably in less danger of conviction than the one with the purse in the men's room. Why? Because common experience teaches that many persons have difficulty identifying their luggage and that a careful examination of luggage tags may be necessary to get the right bag. As a result, there is nothing inherently suspicious in his conduct up to the point that he took the suitcase from the carousel. That he took another's suitcase, *after* checking baggage tags provides some indication of an intent to steal, but without more evidence, including leaving the area with the suitcase, we do not have enough information to come to any firm conclusion about his understanding of the ownership of the suitcase or his plans for depriving the rightful owner of it permanently.

By contrast a man looking through a woman's purse—a purse that in fact belongs to a complete stranger—in a men's restroom is much more suspicious. Such conduct is more consistent with intent to steal and less consistent with any generally recognized pattern of innocent behavior. The selection of a private place and the unlikelihood that any man would be mistaken about his right to look in an unrelated woman's purse strongly suggest an effort to steal money and valuables that the man knows are not his. Would this definitively prove the man's intent to steal? No. It's possible that the man has an innocent explanation. But without such an explanation, his conduct looks very consistent with intent to steal.

From these examples we may draw two related conclusions, one reassuring and the other not so much. The first is that proof of mens rea and other aspects of culpability does not require the insights of a mind reader, a skilled psychologist or a great novelist. It involves determining the reasons for which a particular person acted based on all that is known about the particular situation and human nature generally.

The second is that proving culpability beyond a reasonable doubt is difficult. This brings us to one last matter important to proof in criminal cases: the use of so-called presumptions.

The Dangerous Magic of Presumptions

Presumptions invite fact finders to make legal inferences from what are called predicate facts. They permit the fact finder to use common sense observations, general truths, in their assessment of the particular facts of the case. Such presumptions are enormously attractive to the prosecution, because they permit a fact finder to move from an undisputed predicate fact to a disputed legal conclusion, usually about mens rea. Such presumptions are for the same reason strongly resisted by the defense, especially if they relate, as they often do, to an essential element of the offense. The following illustrates.

Pulled over for running a red light, Loretta is found to be driving a car stolen just two hours earlier. She is charged with possession of a stolen vehicle, an offense that requires proof beyond a reasonable doubt that the Loretta knew that the vehicle was stolen.

In deciding whether Loretta knew that the vehicle was stolen it is relevant that the car was stolen only two hours before. This fact, known in law as a predicate fact, makes it more likely that Loretta was herself involved in its theft or had knowledge of its theft from whoever gave her access to the car. From the predicate fact of the car being recently stolen, we might infer her knowledge about it being stolen. But how do we do this legally? We use a presumption.

Presumptions are statements of general truths that factfinders may use to assist them in making legal determinations, especially about mens rea. For example, a judge may tell jurors in Loretta's case that they may infer from the possession of recently stolen goods (the predicate fact), knowledge that goods are stolen (the legal conclusion). Another common instruction holds that the deliberate use of a deadly weapon on a vital organ (predicate facts) may indicate a purpose to kill (legal conclusion).

You can see why prosecutors like presumptions. They potentially make proof of mens rea much easier. For the same reason, defense counsel view them as dangerous, especially with respect to essential elements of the offense that must be proven by the prosecution beyond a reasonable doubt.

Presumptions raise potentially important and difficult constitutional issues because they may violate the prosecution's constitutionally required burden of proof. Assuming that the presumption applies to an essential element of the offense, such as mens rea, the key legal issue is whether the presumption is mandatory or permissive.

A presumption is *mandatory* if it requires, or might be read to require the fact finder to believe that the prosecution's proof of an essential element is sufficient based on the predicate fact alone. This is problematic because it undercuts the prosecution's requirement of proving the element beyond a reasonable doubt. Instead, the prosecution need only prove the predicate fact beyond a reasonable doubt and then it's up to the defense to rebut this, effectively shifting the burden of proof onto the defense.

If the presumption as to the essential element is only *permissive*, the same constitutional concerns do not arise. A permissive presumption gives the fact finder the option of making a legal inference from the predicate fact but still requires the prosecution to prove the element beyond a reasonable doubt.

An example will illustrate the basic distinction. But a warning: the distinctions can be quite subtle.

> Alan is part of a group of second semester high school seniors who think it is hilarious to make fun of senior citizens at a movie matinee. Alan sits in an aisle seat in the middle of the theater. An elderly man who walks with a cane comes down the aisle. Just before he gets to Alan, Alan sticks his leg out. The man trips over Alan's foot and falls. The man suffers a broken leg. Allan is later charged with a crime that requires proof that he acted with "purpose to cause injury."
>
> The prosecution would like to have the jury instructed as follows: "*The law presumes that persons intend the natural and probable consequences of their actions.*" Assuming that the purpose to cause injury element is an essential element of the offense, is this presumption constitutional?

The question is whether this is a mandatory or permissive presumption. This is clearly a mandatory presumption. It states that "the law presumes" so that the fact finder may believe that he or she *must* follow its direction, though perhaps subject to rebuttal by the defense. In effect this seems to shift to the defense the burden of proof on mens rea (purpose to injure) once the prosecution has proven the predicate fact, that the victim is likely to be hurt by defendant's act. As a result, it violates the prosecution's constitutional requirement of proving all essential elements beyond a reasonable doubt.

> Assume the same facts as previously, but the prosecution suggests the following instruction: "*The natural and probable consequences of an action may indicate the actor's purpose in acting.*" Any problem now?

This would appear to be a permissive presumption, because while it permits the fact finder to make the inference of intent from the predicate fact, it does not require it. As a result, it should pass constitutional muster.

Introduction to Part Two

Act and Mens Rea

To learn how to play a musical instrument, a sport, or learn a craft, there are certain essential skills and concepts one must master. They are the building blocks of the entire enterprise. Learning them can be tedious and frustrating, however, because although they seem simple, they prove surprisingly difficult to grasp. Worse, they are not what you came to learn; they are not what you had in mind when you signed up.

Enough with the scales, I want to sing a song. Okay, I can dribble, basically, let's play a game of one-on-one. Or better yet, let's scrimmage. Anybody can simmer, I'm here to learn gourmet cooking! And yet neglect of such building block skills and concepts will stunt the development of the future musician, athlete, or chef. He or she will always have certain weaknesses, bad habits to work around or somehow compensate for.

So it is with the material presented in Part Two. After the preliminaries of Part One, the reader will be particularly anxious to start in on particular crimes, especially the crimes of violence which are the subject of Part Three. Let's get to the real action, the fun stuff. The good news is that the act and mens rea material covered in Part Two is part of the fun stuff. It is just presented in a different manner and on a smaller scale than the reader might expect. We focus here not on the definition of particular offenses, but on two of the main building blocks of criminal offenses, the act requirement, and especially, mens rea.

Mastery of these concepts is essential for all of criminal law. Learning the analytic methods presented here will be invaluable. In other words, it's worth the time.

CHAPTER 5

THE VOLUNTARY ACT REQUIREMENT

When my eldest daughter was a toddler, like most children her age she frequently spilled drinks and upset plates when eating. Dinner time was often punctuated by emergency efforts to stem a tidal wave of food-stuffs that threatened anyone nearby, and even some who weren't so near. This made meals at home interesting and eating out an activity fraught with social hazards. Yet when my wife and I urged our daughter to be more careful, she often denied responsibility.

"I didn't do it. My arm did it," she would say.

No doubt this is how she experienced the event. She did not direct her arm to knock over the milk; she did not will her leg to trip on the chair, causing her to spill the plate and its contents on the floor. These were the independent acts of her limbs. In essence she argued that her bodily movements were involuntary.

Of course things that make sense to a three-year-old don't always make sense to adults. So it is that in law and elsewhere we generally hold persons accountable for the movements of their bodies. Despite the many occasions in which we feel as if our bodies control us, the criminal law recognizes only very limited exemptions from responsibility for bodily control. The voluntary act requirement recognizes three kinds of problems with bodily control: (1) physical coercion; (2) unconsciousness; and (3) reflex or convulsion.

The act requirement ensures that every person convicted of a crime is the author of, the conscious uncoerced chooser, of conduct that is legally prohibited. It may be satisfied in two different ways: by an affirmative act or by an omission to act where there was a legal duty to act. In the great majority of cases the defendant satisfies the requirement by affirmatively moving his or her body in a way covered by statute. He hits, fires, takes, speaks or otherwise directs his body such that he may be convicted of an offense based on that action. In most cases a failure to act, what is termed an omission to act, will *not* suffice for criminal liability in Anglo-American criminal law. Only if the person had some special duty to act, and failed to do so, will an omission satisfy the act requirement.

Although the act requirement is an issue in relatively few cases, it is a central building block of criminal law. Learning its workings is important not only for where act issues arise but also as an introduction to some basic concepts of responsibility in criminal law. It also introduces us to the interaction of different parts of the criminal law formula, especially between the act requirement and mens rea.

Punishing for Acts, Not Thoughts

A central purpose of the act requirement is to ensure that the state punishes for harmful actions, not mere wrongful thoughts. In contrast to earlier ages, when legal authorities sought to ferret out and punish dangerous thinking or talk about king or church, modern U.S. criminal law is generally limited to physical deeds—and occasionally omissions—which involve significant harms or hazards to other individuals in the society. Thus criminal liability generally depends on proof of a physical act prohibited by statute.

Act analysis begins with the criminal statute and the statutory verb or verbs which define the act or acts prohibited. We look for words like kills, takes, destroys, threatens, obstructs, transports, possesses and so on, which indicate the actions prohibited. Then we look to the facts of the case for particular examples of such conduct. Sometimes the criminal act will be obvious; thus the violent pummeling of another person will be the basis for a criminal assault, the firing of a gun for an attempted murder, or the setting of a fire for arson. Depending on context, though, much less dramatic bodily movements may suffice to satisfy the conduct requirement of the statute: in some instances even a few words spoken, or a physical gesture might be enough. It all depends on what the statute seeks to prohibit and the facts presented.

> In a burglary of her house, Amelia's diary is stolen from a locked desk drawer. It is later recovered by the police. In an effort to identify the diary's owner, a police officer reads the diary. Shocked by its contents, the officer turns it over to a federal prosecutor. Amelia, who detests the current occupant of the White House, wrote in her diary: "I'd like to nuke the White House and watch him die."
>
> Assume that it is a crime to "threaten the life" of the President.[1] Has Amelia done a sufficient act to be charged with this offense?

---

1. For current federal law on threats to the President, see 18 U.S.C. sec. 871(a).

The prohibited act here is to "threaten the life" of the President. Therefore we ask, did Amelia voluntarily act to threaten the nation's highest elected official? Amelia will likely argue that to threaten the President she must do more than just think nasty thoughts about the executive, but must threaten, which means that she must *communicate* the threat to another person. Here she just wrote down her own private thoughts in a private place. It was a police officer, without consent or direction from Amelia, who communicated her words beyond the pages of her private diary. This was not Amelia's voluntary act and therefore she committed no offense.

The issue will turn on statutory interpretation: what did the legislature mean by the word "threaten"? Given the traditional distinction between thoughts and actions, it is likely that a court would agree with Amelia that writing threatening words in a private diary does not violate the statute; the offender must voluntarily communicate the threat to another person (though not necessarily to the President personally).

Note that if Amelia wrote the same words in a letter that she sent to the President, or perhaps even to a friend, she might be subject to prosecution because she communicated her threat to another. The voluntary act requirement, at least, would be satisfied. Mens rea is another question.[2]

Why does the criminal law limit its reach to wrongful acts instead of wrongful thoughts? The answer involves concerns with both proof and the proper role of government in a liberal democracy.

The obvious reason we do not punish for bad thoughts is that they are nearly impossible to prove. Generally our thoughts are private and cannot be reliably ascertained by others.[3] As Amelia's case shows, however, there may be cases where mere thoughts can be proven. Even here a proof concern remains, however. Even if we know what the person thought, we do not know the seriousness of their thoughts. Perhaps Amelia uses her diary to blow off steam, writing outrageous things that she would never speak aloud, let alone do. Such private musings do not present a significant public concern.

The need to distinguish idle thoughts from plans for action brings us to the second major justification for the act requirement: that to protect individual freedom, the government should limit its penal powers to punishing socially

---

2. For the mens rea requirements of current federal law, see United States v. Miller, 115 F.3d 361 (6th Cir. 1997).

3. "[A]s no temporal tribunal can search the heart, or fathom the intentions of the mind, otherwise than as they are demonstrated by outward actions, it therefore cannot punish for what it cannot know." William Blackstone, 4 *Commentaries on the Laws of England* 21 (1979) [1769].

harmful *conduct*. In a society that values individual freedom, the government should only infringe a citizen's liberty if the individual has acted in an anti-social way. We need to remember that the criminal law gives the state the right to use violence: to forcibly imprison and even, in some cases, to kill. It should be used sparingly.

Affirmative Bodily Movements: Involuntary Acts Due to Coercion, Unconsciousness, Reflex or Convulsion

Courts often speak of the voluntary act requirement, thus referring to the requirement that the affirmative bodily movement or omission be the product of the actor's will. But what does it mean, exactly, for an act to be "voluntary?" Issues concerning what is voluntary arise in a wide range of legal contexts. For example, voluntariness can be critical to the validity of a release from civil liability in tort law or to the constitutionality of a consent to a police search under the fourth amendment. But in each legal context the term voluntary means something different. As applied to the act requirement in criminal law, voluntariness presents a narrower set of concerns than some dictionary definitions of the word might suggest.

As a practical matter, the law presumes that human conduct is voluntary unless there is evidence of direct coercion, unconsciousness, or reflex/convulsion. As a result, voluntariness is best understood by reference to those exceptional situations where there is some dramatic interference with the conscious mind's direction of the body. More than for most criminal doctrines, the exceptions (instances of involuntariness) define the rule (of voluntariness).

We all sometimes feel out of control. Because of fatigue, stress, intoxication, or simple inexperience with a particular activity we may feel as if we do not control our own bodies. Yet for the most part these experiences do not represent instances of involuntary conduct. The person remains the author of his or her own conduct and that is the key to voluntariness here.

Coerced Action

An action is coerced if it results from the direct application of physical or legal force on the actor. In such cases the action should be attributed to the person exerting force and not the person forced. As with all act analysis, identifying the particular act or acts on which liability rests is a critical first step.

By Force

Joe tells his lawyer. "There I was, sitting at home, minding my own business, having a couple beers, watching the football game (Go Gators!) with some of the guys when the cops show up. The cops want to ask me some questions, but it's the fourth quarter, score's tied, one minute left, and my team's on the fifty yard line, third down and 5, so I tell them to get lost. That's when they drag me out into the street. And yeah, I kind of lost it then and swore at them pretty good."

Joe has been charged with violation of a statute that states: "Any person who appears in public and manifests a drunken condition by loud and profane language is guilty of a misdemeanor." What should Joe's lawyer argue on his behalf?

As this case presents a problem with the act requirement, we start with the statutory verbs: "appears" and "manifests." The most appealing argument for the defendant involves the first of these. Joe's lawyer may argue that Joe never voluntarily appeared in public as the statute requires. His appearance outside his house was coerced by the police. In effect, the police are to blame for Joe's appearance in public while drunk. This should be a winning argument.[4]

The importance of statutory wording here becomes clear when we make a small change in the offense definition.

Same facts as above but the statute now reads: "Any person who manifests a drunken condition by loud and profane language in public is guilty of a misdemeanor." What voluntary act argument, if any, should Joe's lawyer make on his behalf now?

Under the new statute the only voluntary act required seems to be that one manifest a drunken condition by loud and profane language. Now Joe's case looks much less promising because his manifestation—his verbally abusive response to police—appears the product of his own will. It may have been provoked by the police conduct but it was nevertheless the product of Joe's choice. Joe was clearly the author of his own cursing at the police. Thus the prosecution will argue—successfully—that his manifestation was voluntary.

On occasion we may have to go beyond the verbs in the statute to identify the needed voluntary acts. Consider, for example, a further variation which concerns neither appearance in public nor manifesting a drunken condition, but how the accused became drunk.

---

4. See Martin v. State, 17 So. 2d 427 (Ala. App. 1944).

Because of his religious beliefs, Bob does not drink. Nevertheless, in order to be sociable, Bob accompanies some colleagues from work to the local tavern one night. These colleagues think it would be fun to see Bob drunk. Two of them hold Bob down while a third pours a double strength kamikaze (a stiff alcoholic drink) down his throat. Bob becomes very intoxicated, and on leaving the restaurant shouts and curses at a variety of people walking along the street. Assuming a statute which criminalizes only "manifesting a drunken condition in public," can Bob be convicted?

Here the prosecution might argue that the only voluntary act required is manifestation and that Bob voluntarily manifested: no one forced him to use loud and profane language when in public. Some people act this way when drunk, but most do not, indicating that there is a voluntary choice involved.

In response, the defense should argue that implied in the statutory prohibition is the requirement that one voluntarily become intoxicated. The legislature meant to criminalize loud and profane language in public by persons responsible for their own intoxication. Thus the voluntary act requirement is not met unless the accused voluntarily manifested after having *voluntarily consumed* intoxicants. Normally this second condition is not an issue because in the vast majority of cases, persons who become intoxicated do so voluntarily. Under the expanded reading of the statute suggested here, because Bob's intoxication was coerced and therefore involuntary, Bob should be acquitted.

Supporting the argument that intoxication as well as manifestation be voluntary are our theories of punishment. Public bad conduct due to intoxication is hard to deter unless the consumption of intoxicants is also deterrable. Clearly individual consumption is not deterrable when it is coerced. Similarly, under retribution, given that Bob did not choose to become drunk and drunkenness is the immediate cause of his bad conduct, Bob does not merit significant, i.e. criminal, blame for his actions.

By Legal Command

An anonymous caller reports to the police that a short, heavy set man wearing a long coat is exposing himself (displaying his genitalia) to women who come out of the Park Street subway station. While driving around the block near the station the police spot a short, heavy set man wearing a winter coat, though the weather is warm. The pair of officers stop the man. One of the officers tells the man: "Okay. Open the coat." The man opens his coat, revealing that he is wearing no clothes underneath. The police arrest the man for indecent exposure, an offense consisting of the "public display of a person's private parts to another." In subsequent investigation, police are unable to find those who originally complained about the man's flashing. The prosecutor decides to charge the man with public exposure in revealing himself to the police officers. Is there any problem here with the voluntary act requirement?

Even though the man clearly did engage in the conduct prohibited by the statute—he publicly displayed his private parts to the officers—he did not do so voluntarily. This case is essentially a rerun of Joe's original public drunkenness case except that the coercion here comes in the form of a police command rather than the direct application of physical force. The defendant can argue that the statement: "Okay, open the coat," was an order that the defendant felt legally compelled to obey, such that his subsequent display was effectively the act of the police officer and not the defendant. Obviously none of this would be a problem with respect to the man's exposure to those who had originally complained to the police—but as noted in the facts, that evidence is not available to the prosecution.

The Problem of Psychological Compulsion

Sara Hubble is a well-off suburban housewife in her fifties who loves to shop. Now that her children are grown and her doctor husband is doing well in his cosmetic surgery practice, Mrs. Hubble has both the time and resources to devote to the acquisition of material objects. Unfortunately for local merchants, Mrs. Hubble also likes to steal. She is a practiced shoplifter who regularly takes expensive items of cosmetics, jewelry and lingerie from stores without paying for them. She has been caught on several occasions, but has been able to talk her way out of an arrest. Then she is stopped outside a store with a "zero tolerance" policy on shoplifting and found to have $100 worth of cosmetics from the store in her purse which she did not purchase.

Mrs. Hubble admits that she took the cosmetics without paying for them. She says: "I don't know what it is, but sometimes I just get desperate and I have to do it. I get all tense and then I steal something and I feel much much better." She is examined by a psychiatrist who declares that Mrs. Hubble suffers from kleptomania, which he describes as a compulsion to steal. The psychiatrist states that without treatment, persons such as Mrs. Hubble cannot refrain from stealing. *Assuming that we believe* the psychiatrist's account, is there a voluntary act problem with prosecuting Mrs. Hubble for theft of the cosmetics?

The psychiatrist, by finding that Mrs. Hubble was compelled to steal, seems to suggest that her act of stealing was involuntary, that she had as little choice in the matter as if someone else were directing the actions of her hands. But is this what the law means by involuntariness? The answer is no.

We need to distinguish here the psychological concept of compulsion from the concept of voluntariness in criminal law. The criminal law is built on a strong presumption of free will, that persons are responsible for what they physically do. Only if there is evidence of dramatic interference with the conscious mind's direction of the body will the law consider the person's physical action to be involuntary.

The medical and behavioral sciences suggest that many persons suffer from conditions that involve powerful internal compulsions to conduct that may be both personally and socially harmful. Drug addicts, alcoholics, and some sex offenders are among those who act in destructive ways due to drives they—apparently—cannot control by themselves.[5] As a result they may commit crimes. But generally we do not believe that these compulsions make the person legally nonresponsible. We blame the alcoholic and the social drinker alike for drunk driving because both are seen as the authors of their own conduct. No one else coerced their conduct and their conscious minds directed their bodies.

It may be true that Mrs. Hubble suffers from a significant mental problem that made it difficult or even impossible for her to refrain from stealing in some situations, but without any evidence that another person coerced her action, her "compulsion" to steal will not count as involuntariness in criminal law. She remained in charge of her own conduct such that she is responsible for taking the cosmetics. Her kleptomania argument may be important for sentencing, but should not prevent conviction.

Unconsciousness

Some of the most difficult issues involving the voluntary act requirement concern claims of unconsciousness. Sleepwalking, convulsive fits due to disease, hypnosis and extreme trauma, especially to the head, are among the conditions that may produce unconscious "action." In each of these cases the accused's conduct occurs when we have reason to believe that the conscious mind does not control the body.

---

5. It is always difficult to distinguish between impulses one cannot resist and those one chooses not to resist, but at least in some instances of compulsive behavior there is evidence of the former and not just the latter.

Saul has very occasionally suffered from sleepwalking. Especially when he was younger he would sometimes wake up in a different room than where he went to sleep, not knowing how he got there. He has never done anything dangerous when sleepwalking, however. On this particular night Saul leaves his bed at around 2:00 in the morning, goes outside and starts up the backhoe[6] which he has rented to excavate for a room addition to his house. He drives the machine down the street and turns into a neighborhood gas station where the shovel of the backhoe sheers off a gasoline pump, setting off an explosion and fire. Despite the noise, a police officer finds Saul behind the wheel of the backhoe, snoring. Upon being woken, Saul says he has no idea what just happened, and no idea how he got to be where he was. "I really should be in bed," Saul observes.

Assuming that Saul drove the backhoe while "sleepwalking," can he be held criminally liable for his conduct?

The answer is that although Saul "acted" in a very dangerous fashion, he did not commit a voluntary act for purposes of criminal liability. Assuming he was sleepwalking, his conscious mind did not direct the movements of his body.

An important issue in a case like this will be whether Saul had prior notice of any tendency to dangerous sleepwalking. On the facts given this does not seem to be the case, but in the section on timing issues at the end of the chapter we will see how such an argument might be made in some cases.

A Question of Proof: Memory Loss and Unconsciousness

One hallmark of unconsciousness is no memory of an otherwise memorable event. But does such a loss of memory necessarily prove unconsciousness? The answer is no, though it may be an important part of proof.

All of us perform conscious acts that we cannot later recall: a person due to extreme fatigue, stress, or intoxication may undertake activities without any later memory of having done so, even shortly thereafter. In such cases, the part of the brain in charge of making memories does not function even as the conscious mind directs the body. Thus we pull into the driveway without any awareness of how we managed the drive home. But this does not mean that we were legally unconscious while driving home. We were still "driving," still using our mind (albeit some small part of it) to direct the operation of the car.

---

6. A kind of tractor with digging apparatus used in construction.

It also remains true, however, that one who is unconscious during an event will have no memory of it. Thus a complete lack of memory of an important recent event provides some indication of prior unconsciousness.

A trier of fact presented with evidence of a defendant's loss of memory must address two related questions: (1) whether the defendant in fact has no present memory of the incident (i.e., determine whether the defendant is telling the truth about lack of memory); and (2) if there is a lack of memory, whether that lack is due to unconsciousness at the time of the critical event.

Habit

The treatment of habitual action by the criminal law provides a further refinement on the kind of choice-making needed for a voluntary act. The key again is whether we can say the person was the author of her own actions. The basic rule is that a habitual act is also a voluntary act

> Jennifer works the graveyard shift, which means that she leaves for work at 11 p.m. when the roads are nearly deserted. Because traffic is so light she develops a habit of ignoring the stop sign at the bottom of the hill near her house. One day she is told to start work in the late afternoon. Driving from her house she does not stop at the stop sign and hits an elderly man crossing the street, causing severe injuries. Jennifer tells police: "I was totally unconscious of the stop sign. I never saw the man. I'm so used to driving at night, it just never registered at all."
>
> Jennifer is charged with dangerous driving. Assuming she is telling the truth about what happened, did her conduct satisfy the voluntary act requirement for this offense?

Jennifer may assert that she was acting out of habit and so was totally unconscious of both the sign and the pedestrian. Since we know that an unconscious act is not a voluntary one, it *sounds* as if Jennifer has a good argument that she committed no voluntary act of dangerous driving. But this is a classic language trap, confusing the ordinary language meaning of voluntary with its legal definition. Jennifer drove her car without being coerced by another or suffering a dramatic mind-body interference such as an epileptic fit or sleepwalking. Instead, her failure to see or heed the stop sign was the result of a bad habit, which was itself the result of previous voluntary choices. For purposes of act analysis, she voluntarily drove the car. [7]

---

7. The MPC specifically distinguishes habitual and conscious acts, but categorizes both as voluntary. Sec. 2.01(2)(d). In nonMPC jurisdictions, habitual acts are generally not dis-

Again punishment theory may help us understand doctrine. Jennifer's conduct was sufficiently under her own control for us to see that she might have been deterred by the prospect of punishment and that punishment will likely deter her from future carelessness of this sort. Likewise, persons in her situation in future may well behave better—that is, work on their own bad habits—spurred by the example of her punishment. Finally, we can say that she deserves punishment both for the wrongful choices involved in developing a bad habit and for having failed to correct it.

Convulsion and Reflex

Instances of convulsion or reflex are similar to unconsciousness in that they involve such substantial interference with the conscious direction of the body that they render the person's actions involuntary. Such episodes may or may not involve loss of mental understanding; for purposes of the voluntary act requirement what counts is that the actor's conscious mind loses control of the body at the time of the otherwise criminal deed. A clear example is an epileptic fit. If a driver suffers a sudden and unexpected epileptic seizure while behind the wheel of his car, causing a serious accident, he will not be criminally liable because at the time of the accident he was no longer voluntarily driving the car.

As we saw with respect to coercion, we need to distinguish involuntariness claims based on convulsion or reflex from arguments about psychological compulsion. Mental health experts may state that, given the individual's background and psychological makeup, his otherwise criminal conduct represented an "automatic" or "reflex" reaction compelled by his personality and the situation.[8] Such language suggests that the individual lost conscious control of his body, but not in the sense needed to establish involuntariness. Instead, the expert's testimony should be understood as describing the psychological dynamics of decision-making which will be relevant, if at all, to mens rea or perhaps to an affirmative defense such as insanity.

Omissions to Act

So far we have considered only affirmative bodily movements, where the individual's body causes some effect on the human or natural world. Now we

---

tinguished from other forms of voluntary acts. Regardless, Jennifer has no valid argument concerning the act requirement.

8. E.g., Commonwealth v. Carroll, 194 A.2d 911, 916 (Pa. 1963).

take up the problem of omissions to act. When may criminal liability be based on the individual's failure to act?

The Requirement of a Duty

The general rule is that an omission to act will not support criminal liability unless the law provides that the individual has a special duty to act on behalf of a particular person.

> While walking to the store, Darryl notices a small child playing near a high voltage electric generator. The generator is surrounded by a chain link fence that is covered with warning signs. Darryl sees that the gate to the enclosure has been left open. Darryl could easily close the gate, which would prevent the toddler from approaching the generator. He does not. Nor does Darryl say anything to the child's mother who he sees running down the sidewalk, frantically calling for her missing child. As Darryl watches, the child goes through the open gate, touches the wires coming out of the generator and is electrocuted.
>
> Can Darryl be convicted of a homicide offense for the death of the child?

Morally we should condemn Darryl's conduct. His callousness is appalling. Nevertheless the criminal law absolves him of guilt. Unless he had some special relationship to the child or personal responsibility for the generator—neither of which is apparent on the facts given—under Anglo-American law he had no duty to safeguard the child. His omission to act therefore will not satisfy the voluntary act requirement.

Justifications for the Rule

Why does the criminal law take this seemingly extreme position? What would be wrong with basing criminal liability on an omission to act when the omitted act is so simple and the consequences of inaction so grave? The justifications for the current rule fall under two general headings: practical problems with proof and a political commitment to maximum individual liberty.

In order to understand the proof concerns, we need to look beyond the act requirement to another part of the criminal formula: mens rea. We often depend on the proof of a prohibited physical act for information about mens rea. For example, when a person takes an item from a store shelf, secretes it in a bag and walks out of the store, these physical actions not only constitute the taking needed to satisfy the act requirement of theft, they also give us important information about the taker's understanding of the wrongfulness of the taking and his intentions with respect to future ownership of the item. Taken as a whole, the actions strongly suggest an intent to steal. By contrast, a failure to act generally gives us much less information about the nature of a defendant's choice.

In Darryl's case, to prove mens rea the prosecution might have to prove his awareness of the hazard to the child posed by the open gate and the generator. If the case is based on affirmative acts that Darryl did with respect to the gate or generator, that will provide much more information about recklessness than if, as here, Darryl simply stood by and did nothing.

There is also a personal liberty argument for the limitation on omission liability. Some argue that the state should have the power to interfere with individual autonomy *only* when an individual affirmatively acts to harm others. In the absence of affirmative harm-doing, the state should not force persons to act better. Basing criminal liability on a wide range of omissions to act would create obligations to others that would impermissibly interfere with individual freedom.

In the end, the controversy about omissions concerns where we draw the liability line. All agree that *some* omissions to act should suffice for liability. All also agree that we must restrict liability here, for permitting *all* omissions to suffice would present too many risks of wrongful convictions and infringe too much on individual freedom. The serious question therefore is what *kinds* of omissions should support liability. The answer given by Anglo-American criminal law is that an omission to act supports criminal punishment when the accused owed a special legal duty to the person in need of assistance.

Legal Duties to Others

Anglo-American criminal law recognizes five major categories of legal duties, each of which may make an omission to act criminal: (1) relationship; (2) statutory; (3) contractual; (4) undertaking care or rescue; and (5) creation of the peril.

One person may have an obligation to assist another based on a family relationship such as husband-wife or parent-child. Modern courts have also sometimes found obligations based on nonfamilial relationships, as between fellow workers and between roommates.

A duty may be statutorily created. For example, current law imposes duties to report traffic accidents, to file income tax returns, to register for the draft, or to register as a sex offender. In many jurisdictions, a wide range of individuals from teachers to nurses to clergy have a statutory duty to report evidence of suspected child abuse to police or other authorities.

A duty to act may be based on contract. Child care providers, grade school teachers and life guards are among those whose employment agreements create a duty to safeguard those in their charge.

Persons who undertake to assist another in a time of peril assume a duty to either complete the rescue or to ensure that someone else undertakes it. The rationale behind this duty is the concern that a would-be rescuer who desists before completing the rescue may have placed the person in peril in a worse position by having dissuaded other potential rescuers. This may also extend to caretakers who have voluntarily taken on the care of another.

Finally, one who creates an individual's peril has an obligation to come to her assistance. Thus a person who pushes another down a flight of stairs has a legal obligation to obtain medical assistance for the person's injuries. This obligation may even arise if the defendant was not at fault in creating the peril. A person who accidentally and nonnegligently knocks another down a flight of stairs might still be required to obtain medical help.

The Voluntariness of Omissions—Capacity to Act

Though rarely an issue, an omission to act must be voluntary to be legally sufficient. This is usually described as the requirement that the person be capable of the omitted act. This language covers the same set of voluntariness problems discussed with respect to affirmative acts. Thus if the omission was coerced (the accused was physically restrained from action) or the result of unconsciousness (sleepwalking, epileptic fit and the like), then the failure to act will be deemed involuntary.

Liability for an omission to act also requires the person be physically able to do the omitted act. Thus to have a duty to save a drowning person the accused must have been physically strong enough to accomplish the rescue given the materials at hand. Similarly, if the omission involves failure to summon medical help, the means of summoning that help must have been readily available.

A Final Wrinkle: Timing Issues

In every criminal case we need to decide *when* the defendant committed the act for which he may be criminally liable. Generally the act occurs at the moment of actual harm-doing or of discovery of the offense. We focus on when the shot was fired, the accident occurred or the drugs were found in one's possession. In some cases, however, there are possibilities for liability based on acts taken before this, and in other cases liability may be based on omissions to act which occur later.

Moving the Act Back in Time

David has recently developed a medical condition which causes temporary seizures. These seizures never last long—usually ten to thirty seconds—but during a seizure David cannot see or hear and he experiences uncontrolled convulsions in his arm and leg muscles. While driving on the interstate one morning, David suffers a seizure. His car veers into oncoming traffic and strikes a motorcyclist, killing him instantly.

David is charged with vehicular manslaughter. Did he commit a voluntary act which would support criminal liability?

David's lawyer will argue that at the time of the accident David's mind did not and could not direct his body, thus he did not commit a voluntary act of driving. Once the seizure occurred, David ceased to function as the driver of his car. If the prosecution cannot disprove this, it may try to shift the time frame for act analysis. The prosecutor may say that liability should rest on David's *pre-seizure* driving. David's driving of the car before the seizure was voluntary—uncoerced and conscious—and was performed with notice of the risk of a seizure that might endanger others. The prosecutor must then make a related mens rea argument, that in his pre-seizure driving David was either actually aware of the dangers of having a seizure while driving (needed for a reckless offense) or should have known of the dangers (for a negligence offense) and therefore there is a union of act and mens rea prior to his suffering the fit.

The same reasoning applies when a person knowingly consumes intoxicants that render him unconscious. In almost all U.S. jurisdictions, anyone who, with notice of its intoxicating qualities, consumes a substance that leads to loss of consciousness may not claim involuntariness with respect to actions he takes thereafter. Courts reason that any loss of consciousness due to intoxication was voluntarily risked by the defendant and so should not excuse from responsibility. As a result, arguments about intoxication normally involve other parts of the criminal formula, usually mens rea (see Chapter 19). Note also that many claims of unconsciousness due to drinking really describe loss of memory rather than loss of basic mind-body control at the time of the incident. Most persons rendered truly unconscious by alcohol, our most popular intoxicant, are also rendered physically inert and so are incapable of doing anything that would constitute an affirmative criminal act.

Moving the Time Frame Forward: Omissions to Act after Causing Harm

There are other cases where the prosecution may seek to shift the time frame forward to establish liability based on an omission to act that occurs *after* the defendant's affirmative conduct. Consider the following case.

It is the spring of 2000. Harold E. is late for a meeting with investors concerning his latest dot com start-up. Trying to avoid a freeway tie-up, he speeds through a residential neighborhood, somewhat above the posted speed limit. Jessie, a teenager, comes out from behind a parked car riding his scooter. Harold slams on the brakes but still strikes Jessie with his SUV. Harold gets out and sees that Jessie is bleeding from the head and having trouble breathing. Harold sticks his business card in Jessie's shirt pocket. "Call me. I gotta run. And next time, look both ways before you cross." Harold drives off.

If the teenager Jessie dies because of lack of prompt medical attention, which Harold could have obtained by using his cell phone, could the prosecution prove a voluntary act in a homicide case?

Here we have an affirmative act that should be fully sufficient for criminal liability: Harold's driving leading to the collision. There are no voluntariness problems with Harold's driving: no coercion, reflex/convulsion or unconsciousness problems. Therefore criminal liability may follow as long as other parts of the criminal formula, notably mens rea and causation, are satisfied. But what happens if they are not?

Let us assume for the moment that the prosecution cannot prove that Harold drove his car with the recklessness or negligence needed for a criminal offense. Instead, Jessie's recklessness on his scooter was the primary cause of the accident. But what about criminal liability for Harold based on an omission to act *after* the accident?

Because Harold's driving led to Jessie's injury, he had a duty to assist Jessie, to make sure the injured teen received medical treatment. [9] Harold did not do this, even though with ready access to a phone he certainly could have. Thus the requirements for a sufficient omission to act are met. Again liability will depend on mens rea—but here the prosecution has more facts to work with. It

---

9. This responsibility is clear if Harold was at fault in the accident. Even if Harold was not at fault, however, his involvement in the collision may trigger a duty to aid. See Sandford Kadish, Stephen Schulhofer & Carol Steiker, *Criminal Law and Its Processes: Cases and Materials* 206 (8th ed. 2007)

may be easier for the prosecution to show Harold's recklessness or negligence with respect to a failure to aid—given Harold's awareness of the accident and Jessie's obvious injuries—than with respect to the original accident, where Jessie appeared in the road without warning.

CHAPTER 6

INTRODUCING MENS REA

"[E]ven a dog distinguishes between being stumbled over and being kicked."

Oliver Wendell Holmes, Jr.[1]

At the heart of criminal law is *mens rea*, a Latin term variously translated as "evil mind," "evil will" or "guilty mind." Mens rea refers to the requirement that to be convicted of a crime, a person must have chosen to act badly, not just act in a way that produced bad results. To use Holmes's analogy, mens rea tracks the difference between kicking and stumbling.

We will speak of *mens rea* here rather than mental state or intent, because the very foreignness of mens rea emphasizes that we deal with a legal concept distinct from ordinary language. A large part of the challenge of mens rea analysis is to distinguish legal from ordinary language concepts of blame.

Mens Rea's Challenge

Problems with mens rea tend to hide in the ambiguities of language and common assumptions about wrongdoing. It is the question not asked, the issue not pursued that causes the most confusion. As a result, we have to be careful about how we frame mens rea questions.

The standard mens rea problem comes in the form of a fact pattern detailing what the accused did and said, to be analyzed according to an offense defined in a criminal statute. We must determine if the accused's conduct meets the statute's requirements for conviction. Four basic issues must be addressed: (1) what mens rea term or terms the offense includes; (2) the standard definition of each mens rea term; (3) what element or elements of the offense each

---

1. *The Common Law* 3 (1881)

mens rea term modifies and how; and (4) whether the accused can be shown to have acted with the required mens rea on the facts given. This chapter concerns primarily steps one and two and four. Step three involving statutory interpretation will be the main preoccupation of Chapter 7.

Sound mens rea analysis requires patience. Often issues concerning basic wrongdoing seem so obvious that we jump to a legal conclusion without the necessary analysis of statutory terms. In the process, vital legal distinctions may be missed. Consider in this regard the opening quote by the legendary jurist, Oliver Wendell Holmes. Holmes introduces us to an important distinction in criminal wrongdoing in characteristically acerbic fashion: even dogs recognize the difference between intentional and accidental harm-doing. The person who deliberately kicks a dog deserves blame because she intends to hurt the animal. The person who stumbles over a dog should not be blamed because the pain she caused was neither intended nor foreseen.

But Holmes's analogy takes us only so far. As applied to criminal law, his observation suggests that we should punish only the kickers of the world and not its stumblers. And it is true that criminal law generally follows this pattern. But what is usually true, is not always so. Consider driving while intoxicated— a significant criminal offense, carrying increasingly serious penalties—but one that does not require any purpose to harm or even awareness of harm. The intoxicated driver is more of a stumbler than a kicker, yet we believe punishment is warranted because the intoxicated driver should be aware of the significant, unjustified hazards of his conduct. This demonstrates that at least for some kinds of wrongdoing, the intentional versus accidental distinction that we rely on in ordinary responsibility discourse is inadequate. In the criminal law we need a further set of distinctions to separate careless conduct that merits punishment from conduct that does not.

This brings us to the real difficulty of mens rea analysis. While most persons (and perhaps dogs) have an intuitive grasp of responsibility principles, most lack the intellectual and linguistic tools to make careful arguments about moral and legal culpability. The lay person normally sloughs over distinctions that can make the difference between freedom and imprisonment in a criminal case. Thus we must replace old habits of quick intuitive judgment with careful, deliberate and self-conscious analysis.[2]

---

2. An analogy may be drawn to relearning any ingrained custom: learning to speak without "like" or "uh" or "you know," improving one's posture or breaking bad driving habits. It can be done, but it requires a will to change and the realization that the effort will often prove frustrating.

Basic Mens Rea Terms: The Model Penal Code Quartet

We begin with the Model Penal Code's basic quartet of mens rea terms: *purposely, knowingly, recklessly* and *negligently*. We start here *not* because the MPC terms are universally employed in U.S. law, but because they have generally accepted definitions. Once we grasp the meaning of each MPC term we will have a basic conceptual vocabulary that will permit clearer understanding of the many common law mens rea terms used in Anglo-American law. We can translate common law terms into MPC terminology, thus establishing the meaning of any mens rea term in context.

As an introduction to mens rea under the MPC, we will apply each of the basic mens rea forms to the offense of homicide, that is, the killing of another human being. The aim of the exercise is not to establish the definitions of different homicide offenses, however. That will be the work of Part Three of the book.

One other important note on mens rea before we take up definitions. Mens rea terms *never* work in isolation but *always* in partnership with other words in a statute. Mens rea terms are commonly adverbs which modify both verbs and other phrases in the offense definition. As a result, simply identifying the mens rea term and its standard meaning is never sufficient; the mens rea term must always be joined with the element or elements that it modifies.

Purposely

The MPC provides that a person purposely causes a result when it was her "conscious object" to achieve that result.[3] Consider the following facts as the basis for a charge of attempted murder. To be guilty of such a charge the individual must have acted with purpose to kill the victim.

> Although brothers, Richard and Mike have long despised each other. Upon reaching adulthood, their mutual animosity has only increased. A reunion at a holiday celebration at their parents' house triggers a lengthy and bitter argument about the family business, in which Mike accuses Richard of stealing. Richard pulls a loaded handgun from his waistband, points it at Mike's head, says, "Die, creep!" and pulls the trigger. The shot barely misses Mike, grazing his scalp. Richard is

---

3. Sec. 2.02(2)(a)(i).

about to shoot again when he is knocked down from behind by his
father. Richard is charged with attempted murder based on the one shot
fired. Did Richard act with purpose to kill? What are the arguments
for and against?

We might start the analysis by asking about Richard's conduct: Why would
anyone act in this way? Why would anyone take a loaded gun and fire it at the
head of a disliked person during a bitter argument? The circumstances of the
altercation and our background knowledge of human nature suggest that
Richard acted with purpose to kill. Feeling hatred for his brother, Richard took
a lethal weapon, directed it at a vital organ, and pulled the trigger, seeking to
cause a fatal injury. Richard's efforts to get off a second shot also tends to show
a homicidal goal.

Note that the failure to kill, or even seriously injure Mike does open the
door to rebuttal arguments. Richard might argue that he shot only to scare
his brother, meaning that he did not desire to kill him. Mike is, after all,
his brother. Not that the brother-slaying-brother scenario is exactly unprecedented.

In considering analysis of purpose here, remember the point made previously that mens rea terms always have partners; they don't work in the abstract. In this situation, the mens rea of purpose partners with the element of
death. Without that partnership, mens rea analysis can easily go astray. For
example, some might argue that since Richard purposely pulled the trigger of
the gun, Richard should be convicted of a purposeful attempt. But attempted
murder requires not a purposeful act of violence but an act done with *purpose
to cause death*. If he only meant to scare, Richard did not act with purpose to
kill.

In the criminal law, the most common synonym for purpose is intent. Thus
courts commonly distinguish intent-to-kill homicides from other varieties.
But we need to be very careful with "intent." In some contexts courts use intent or intentional to mean purposeful; in other situations it may extend to
knowing or reckless conduct as well.

Knowingly

The MPC provides that a person knowingly causes a result when she is
"practically certain" that the result will occur.[4] The accused acts knowingly toward a result when the accused realizes that her action will cause the result.

---

4. Sec. 2.02(b)(ii).

The difference between knowingly and purposely here is that with knowingly there is no requirement that the individual desire the result.

Marina has had enough. Edgar, her husband of ten years has filed for divorce. Relying on a prenuptial agreement he has deprived her of her home and money. Edgar has even given her (prior to the divorce) a sexually transmitted disease courtesy of his own philandering ways. She decides she cannot beat him legally (he has all the money) so she will employ violence. Using her internet skills she learns how to build a bomb, builds it and places it on the small business jet which her husband uses, under the seat he normally takes. She realizes that the plane is flown by a professional crew and usually carries a number of passengers besides Edgar. She is too mad to care. The bomb explodes at the plane's next take off, as Marina planned. The bomb kills all ten persons aboard, but not Edgar, because, unknow to Marina, he missed the flight due to a hangover. Police arrest Marina when she is spotted at the airport, dancing and shouting: "He's dead, he's dead, he's dead. The wickedest man in the world is dead." Marina tells police that "Edgar just had to die. I'm real sorry about the others though. They were just in the wrong place at the wrong time."

What mens rea did Marina have with respect to the possible death of Edgar and the actual deaths of the 10 people aboard?

Here the facts show that Marina acted with clear purpose to kill Edgar, the mens rea needed for an attempted murder charge. Her previous relationship with Edgar, her construction of the bomb, its detonation and her celebration speak powerfully to her homicidal object; it was her conscious aim to end Edgar's (in her view) sorry life.

Marina's attitude towards those actually killed by her bomb is somewhat different, however. Assuming she told the police the truth about her intentions, (that in her statements to police she was sincere and not lying) Marina did not consciously seek the death of the 10 on board. Consequently, as to the 10 killed she may not be convicted of an offense requiring purpose to kill. There are other forms of mens rea that her conduct may satisfy, however.

What about an offense requiring that one knowingly kill another? Was Marina practically certain that her bomb would cause their deaths? The answer must be yes, based both on general knowledge of bombs, planes and human anatomy and Marina's statements which indicate personalized knowledge. To articulate the obvious (a frequently important task in the law, if only to show where the true controversy lies), virtually any adult knows that setting off a powerful bomb in a plane that has left the ground is very likely to kill those aboard, either through the force of the explosion or the resulting plane crash. Confirming that Marina knows these facts of life and death, she tells the police that she is sorry about the "others," indicating on the one hand a lack of purpose to kill but also that she was aware of the deadly consequences to others. The only remaining issue will be just how certain she was of death to others. The defense might argue that she was only aware of a significant risk of death to others and therefore was only reckless. Which brings us to our next mens rea: recklessness

Recklessly

The MPC provides that a person recklessly causes a result when she acts with awareness of a high and unjustifiable risk that the result will occur. The Code states that the actor is reckless when she "consciously disregards a substantial and unjustifiable risk" of a particular result.[5] Recklessness thus is comprised of three elements: (1) proof of awareness of risk; (2) proof of a substantial risk; (3) proof that the risk under the circumstances was unjustifiable. We will call these the awareness, risk and justification elements.

Issues about recklessness usually involve awareness—whether the accused was actually cognizant of the risks involved in his conduct. The fact finder must examine the accused's statements, actions and other circumstances to determine whether the accused realized the risks involved, meaning whether he was aware of the facts that demonstrated the dangerousness of his or her conduct.

Recklessness requires that the risk involved in the defendant's conduct be substantial. How much risk is substantial will depend to some extent on what is placed at risk. When, as in homicide, the risk is of loss of life, we may find a risk substantial even when statistically it presents a low chance of occurrence. The MPC explains: "The risk must be of such a nature and degree that, considering the nature and purpose of the actor's conduct and the circumstances known to him, its disregard involves a gross deviation from the standard of conduct that a law-abiding person would observe in the actor's situation." Simply stated, the greater the potential harm, the more careful we expect people to be.

The risk must also be unjustified. Again this requires a normative judgment. But unlike risk assessment, only a small percentage of cases raise any real issue concerning this element. Excused here are those who have some specially good reason for engaging in risky conduct: the police officer who engages in a high-

---

5. Sec. 2.02(c).

speed chase to capture a dangerous suspect or a surgeon who performs a dangerous operation in an effort to save a critically ill patient. Even if the police chase causes the death of a pedestrian or the surgery kills the patient, we would not hold either the police officer or surgeon for reckless killing, because although each may have been aware of the hazards of their conduct, and nevertheless engaged in highly risky action, each had an overriding justification (law enforcement and medical necessity respectively) for their conduct.

Bud Walters is a veteran high school football coach in a small town in east Texas, where high school football is revered. Coach Walters believes in rigorous physical conditioning, not just to prepare his players for the game, but to prepare them for life. He sees himself as a molder of men, not just a sports coach. In the heat and humidity of late August the coach works his players hard, in full equipment, both morning and afternoon. Seeing that his biggest players need conditioning the most, he works them the hardest. In his twenty years of coaching, none of his players has suffered serious injury due to heat.

The medical truth is that overweight, out of condition football players are at significant risk of heat stroke in summer practices. Symptoms include disorientation and dizziness. Heat stroke is a serious condition that can cause death or permanent brain damage. Like all Texas football coaches, Coach Walters has received a recent letter from a doctor associated with high school athletics, providing detailed information and warnings about heat stroke.

During the first summer practice, Ed, a bulky lineman appears in physical distress during wind sprints. Ed's face is pale; he staggers and looks lost. Coach Walters orders him keep going. Ed runs for another five minutes, then collapses. Within the hour he is declared dead due to heat stroke.

Coach Walters tells the police he had no idea that Ed was in any danger. Coach Walters is clearly devastated by the afternoon's events.

Can Walters be convicted of recklessly causing the death of the player?

The critical question here is whether Walters was *actually aware* that his actions posed a substantial risk of death to Ed. As in most cases, there is no issue concerning justification. Though high school football takes on religious importance to people in some parts of this country, it does not constitute an activity that justifies training practices that seriously endanger the lives of players. There are hazards to football that may be nearly unavoidable, such as injuries from physical collisions, but heat stroke is not one of them. It also appears that the coach's conduct was, in fact, quite dangerous. The medical background given suggests that the coach's order to Ed to continue to run after the signs of his physical problems were apparent, created a significant risk of danger to Ed's life.

The awareness of risk issue turns on Coach Walters' credibility. If Walters told the truth when he said that he did not realize the risks involved, he should be acquitted, because he did not consciously disregard a substantial and unjustifiable risk of causing Ed's death. If we disbelieve his account, we may find that, based on the warning letter and perhaps other information, he consciously disregarded the health risks of pushing players like Ed so hard.

In cases such as this, warnings of risk, both direct and indirect, often play a critical role. For example, if the year before the incident a player suffered a serious heat stroke while under his direction, this would provide strong evidence that Walters realized the risks involved in his training methods at the time of the latest incident. The letter mentioned in the facts will assist the prosecution in this regard, but only if it can be shown that Walters actually read it or was aware of it.

Under a strict reading of recklessness, it will not be enough to prove that the coach was presented with warnings, he must also have understood their import, thus making him aware of a significant risk to players like Ed. If Coach Williams states that he had heard medical warnings about heat stroke but considered them "a bunch of nonsense from fools in white coats that don't know nothing about kids and football," he still can claim that he did not act recklessly. *Assuming we believe he is telling us the truth about his own state of mind,* he should not be convicted because the coach never consciously disregarded a substantial risk of death to his player—he thought the medical warnings were nonsense.

There can be an important difference between law in theory and in practice here, however. In practice, fact finders often equate notice of risk with the awareness needed for recklessness. Many jurors will decide that proof that the coach was warned about heat stroke means that he *must have* realized the risks involved. The defense can certainly argue that awareness cannot be proven from warning alone, but the decision about this inference belongs to the decision maker.

It is also worth noting that the case provides a good example of the difference between the ordinary meaning of a word and its legal definition. Coach Walters acted recklessly *in the ordinary sense of the word.* He exercised poor judgment in ordering Ed to continue running after he displayed clear signs of heat stroke. But assuming we believe his account, Coach Walters did not act recklessly under the MPC definition of that term. He was not aware of a significant risk of death or serious harm to Ed.

Negligently

The last of the MPC's mens rea terms is negligence. In contrast to purpose, knowledge and recklessness which focus on what the accused *actually* aimed for or realized, negligence judges what the accused *should have* realized. Thus negligence sets an objective, universal standard rather than a subjective, individualized standard. A person acts negligently with regard to causing a risk when a reasonable person would have realized and heeded the risk in the same situation.

The MPC states that a person acts negligently with regard to causing a result when she "should be aware of a substantial and unjustifiable risk" that her conduct will cause the result.[6] As with recklessness, this mens rea has three components. These are: (1) notice of risk; (2) degree of risk; and (3) lack of justification for risk. The risks of the person's conduct must be so readily apparent, and so unjustified in context, that the person may be criminally punished for failing to heed them.

Unlike the other three mens rea states we have examined, criminal negligence does not depend on the accused's actual state of mind. As a result, courts and commentators sometimes call negligence an objective standard based on general expectations of attention and care in the situation, in contrast to subjective standards which assess defendant's actual purpose or awareness.

A person acts negligently when she fails to meet a basic minimum standard of care that we expect of all persons in society. Our general notion is that a reasonable person — the ordinary, law-abiding individual — would have acted more carefully in the same situation than did the defendant. Exactly what counts as reasonable — and who counts as the reasonable person — will be a matter for argument in many cases.

The MPC assesses negligence according to what the reasonable person would do "in the actor's situation," leaving room for argument about what individual attributes of the accused or the circumstances might be included to effectively individualize the standard. Most jurisdictions permit some consideration of the defendant's physical characteristics, such as age or physical abilities in setting the standard of care for the situation. Otherwise questions of individualization are generally left to the arguments of counsel and decisions of juries.

The MPC defines negligent risk-taking in explicitly normative terms: "The risk must be of such a nature and degree that the actor's failure to perceive it,

---

6. Sec. 2.02(2)(d).

considering the nature and purpose of his conduct and the circumstances known to him, involves a gross deviation from the standard of care that a reasonable person would observe in the actor's situation." This language is designed to require a more extreme form of carelessness than that required for a civil judgment in tort law, and thus is usually termed gross negligence as opposed to ordinary negligence.

> Return again to the case of Coach Walters. Under the facts given above, could the coach be found guilty of negligently causing Ed's death?

The answer depends on the amount of warning information concerning heat stroke available to one in Coach Walters' position. We would want to know what sort of medical information was distributed to coaches generally. With that in hand we would be able to judge whether Coach's failure to perceive this risk represented a gross deviation from the perceptions of a reasonable person in the coach's situation.

In this situation, the criminal negligence standard requires the decision maker to judge the reasonableness of Walters' conduct with reference to that of other coaches. We expect a person who has taken on the responsibility of directing high school athletes to take more care for their physical safety, including undertake more investigation of heat stroke, than we would others.

In contrast to recklessness analysis, Coach Walters' statement that he did not realize the risk is not determinative under negligence. It is a factor to consider in the reasonableness equation, but the ultimate question is whether he should have been aware, not whether he was.[7]

Reasonableness Talk: Distinguishing Mens Rea and Credibility Arguments

When a court mentions reasonableness or should-have-been-aware as part of its mens rea analysis, this usually indicates that the crime is satisfied by negligence as to that element. Similarly, when courts speak of the requirement that the defendant have actual awareness of certain facts, we can infer that a

---

7. Again we should note a possible distinction between theory and practice. While in theory recklessness and negligence represent different *kinds* of mental states—actual awareness v. should-have-been aware—in practice, the difference may be more of *degree*. In deciding between a reckless and a negligent offense, decision makers may be swayed more by the degree of risk, the extent of warning and lack of justification for risk-taking than by the often subtle distinctions between actual awareness and should-have-been-aware that dominate the formal analysis of legal culpability.

minimum mens rea of recklessness or knowledge as to the particular element is required for conviction.[8]

There is one important, though potentially confusing way in which talk about reasonableness may be relevant to proof of an actual awareness mens rea (knowledge or recklessness), however. In some cases the reasonableness or unreasonableness of the defendant's account goes to the defendant's *credibility* concerning his or her claim of no awareness. Generally speaking, the more unreasonable the defendant's story, the harder it will be for a fact finder to believe. For example, a fact finder might consider Coach Walters' claim that he heard but entirely discounted medical warnings about heat stroke to be highly unreasonable. The fact finder might further decide that since the coach otherwise appears to be a reasonable person, he is probably lying about being ignorant of the risks involved. The fact finder might conclude that the coach *was* aware of significant risks because of the medical warnings, and is just denying awareness now in order to avoid criminal or other liability.

Reasonableness might also be used to bolster a defendant's credibility. The more that a reasonable person would perceive the situation in the same way as the defendant did, the easier it will be for us to believe the defendant's subjective account. Thus if it appears that most coaches in Walters' position would not have seen Ed's condition as serious prior to his collapse, this will make Walters' subjective claim—that he was not aware of a significant risk—more plausible.

The bottom line is that we must always pay attention to how reasonableness is used. Reasonableness in reference to the requirements for conviction indicates a negligence mens rea. Reasonableness with respect to the credibility of the defendant or witness concerns fact-finding.

Proof of Lesser Mens Rea by Proof of Greater Mens Rea

Under the MPC proof of a higher mens rea will suffice to satisfy the proof required for a lesser mens rea. For example, if the charged offense requires killing knowingly, proof that the defendant killed purposely will suffice to prove knowingly. Similarly proof of knowledge will satisfy both recklessness and negligence, and recklessness will also cover negligence.[9] The key question there-

---

8. Often courts do not carefully distinguish between these two mens reas, because many offenses that require awareness permit conviction based on proof of either knowledge or recklessness. Thus for this discussion I will assume that the minimum mens rea under consideration is recklessness.

9. Sec. 2.02(5).

fore is what is the *minimum* mens rea that will support a conviction. Any mens rea greater than that, i.e., one involving more awareness or goal-orientation, will also suffice for conviction.

One last important caution with respect to mens rea language. In our analysis of liability, we must always distinguish between the mens rea required for conviction and the actual mens rea of the defendant. In the end, these must match up for a conviction—the defendant must be proven to have acted with a mens rea sufficient to match the statutory requirements—but if we are not careful in distinguishing these two, confusion about statutory requirements could result. We might believe that a defendant should be found guilty because he has a particular mens rea without regard to what the statute actually requires. We will consider the challenges of statutory analysis in much greater depth in the next chapter.

What about Common Law Mens Rea Terms?

Traditionally, the common law expressed mens rea in highly moralistic terms: criminal conduct was described as "malicious," "depraved," "intentional," "wilful" or "wanton." Such phrases gave judges and jurors a general idea of the moral character of the conduct but did not specify the particular aims or awareness of the accused. The advantage of this approach is that it permits consideration of a wide range of morally relevant factors in assessing guilt. It allows the decision maker to consider the kind of harm done, the actor's aims or awareness, his passions and motivations, among other factors. But this flexibility carries a high price in clarity and certainty. Suggestive moral phrases provide little guidance in the hard cases where we need law most. Worse, they increase the risk of nonmoral decision making, of judging the accused based on factors such as race or class which should be irrelevant to conviction and punishment. Without ever realizing it, decision makers may make intuitive character judgments based on feelings concerning the defendant's group status rather than his proven conduct.

Using the MPC mens rea quartet as a reference, we can hazard a rough approximation of a few common law terms. Many jurisdictions define "intentional" to mean either purposeful or knowing. "Malicious" usually encompasses the MPC mens rea terms of purposeful, knowing and reckless.[10] "Wanton" may be knowing or reckless; in some cases it may extend to negligence.

---

10. To put this another way, moral blame may be a necessary condition of criminal liability, but it is not a sufficient condition. Many morally blameworthy acts are not, and

The problem with these generalizations is that while they may be generally true, *none is always correct*. We cannot predict with certainty how a court will translate a traditional mens rea term, *especially* without considering statutory context. When we take up statutory interpretation we will see that a great deal depends on what parts of a statute the mens rea term modifies and how it modifies that term.

Finally, we should note at this point that there are some mens rea forms that cannot be translated directly into MPC terms. In homicide, we will find assessments of premeditation, indifference and provocation all involve qualities of decision making, attitudes, motives or emotional states that go beyond any of our four standard mens reas. We will leave their exploration to Part Three of the book.

Crimes Without Mens Rea: An Introduction to Strict Liability

Although offenses are generally built around the mens rea requirement, there is an important category of crimes known as strict liability offenses for which no mens rea need be proven. A person may be found guilty of such an offense if he or she committed the prohibited conduct without regard to intention, awareness or even culpable carelessness. Guilt is complete with proof that the person voluntarily committed the prohibited act, assuming all other requirements of the offense are also met.

A brief consideration of the rationale for, and the working of strict liability offenses is worthwhile here because it illuminates some of the important pluses and minuses of mens rea. In the following chapter we will look at strict liability in more depth in connection with statutory interpretation.

The most familiar example of strict liability offenses is traffic violations. An individual may be guilty of speeding even if she had no idea how fast she was going. In the exercise of their discretion, traffic judges may listen to mens rea type arguments in ruling on a case and often do in setting a fine, but the law does not require such solicitude. (Police officers have the same or even greater discretion in deciding whether to issue a ticket.) Guilt under *law* depends solely on whether the vehicle, driven by the accused, exceeded the legal speed limit.

Strict liability offenses frequently share three basic attributes: (1) penalties for the offense are relatively minor; (2) the prohibited activity provides inher-

---

should not be criminal. For example, while many crimes center on telling lies, such as fraud or perjury, lies are also a common feature of everyday life; most have no criminal consequences.

ent notice of potential wrongdoing to the actor; and (3) requiring proof of mens rea would be costly both in terms of litigation and deterrence. Again the offense of speeding provides a ready illustration. Most people who speed are either aware of it or should be aware, so that we can say that if they truly were going above the speed limit, they deserve punishment for their violation of the rules of the road. In those few cases where the driver was not at fault, for example, because of a speedometer that malfunctions without warning, the fiscal and social/moral costs of the resulting conviction are modest. Conviction may be unfair but the consequences are not so severe as to require the proof of mens rea in all cases. We also hope that at some stage of the proceedings in such cases, legal authorities—police, prosecutor, judge—will exercise discretion to recognize exceptional circumstances that the law does not.[11]

Consider also the litigation costs of requiring proof of mens rea for speeding offenses. Police officers would have to conduct and record their interviews with drivers more carefully in order to preserve evidence about awareness of wrongdoing that could be critical to proving mens rea. In general, we would expect that more persons cited would insist on a trial because there would be more to litigate at such a proceeding.

Proof problems may also undercut deterrence. Knowing that one could make a mens rea argument to prevent conviction would encourage many drivers to go faster on the assumption that they would still have an excuse if pulled over for speeding. 'Oh I never saw the sign,' or, 'My speedometer said that I was going under the speed limit,' and so on. In response, authorities might lower speed limits below their optimal level to minimize successful mens rea arguments. In sum, at least as to speeding offenses, the costs of mens rea easily exceed its benefits.

Strict Liability and the Voluntary Act Requirement

The only issue to be litigated when a person is charged with a strict liability offense is whether he or she acted in a way prohibited by the statute. For example, was the accused the driver of the car? Was the car in fact going over the speed limit? In a few cases, there may be an issue concerning the voluntary act requirement. The next problem illustrates.

> Louisa wants your legal advice. She has been charged with a curfew violation. The relevant part of the law reads: "No driver under

---

11. Note that the discussion here concerns traffic offenses which generally neither carry a penalty of incarceration, nor result in significant personal or social stigma. Our willingness to tolerate the conviction of a nonculpable defendant may change when the consequences include loss of liberty or a criminal label that does real damage to one's reputation.

the age of 17 may drive on the public highway between the hours of midnight and 5 a.m." Louisa, who is 16 years old, was cited by a police officer who found her asleep at the wheel of car that was partially pulled over to the side of the road at 12:15 a.m. The car's engine and lights were still on. Awakened by the police officer's loudspeaker, Louisa followed his instructions to pull the car off the road. She then told the officer that she had no idea it was after midnight and noted that she wasn't driving dangerously.

Louisa wants to know if she has any defense to the charge, because "the whole thing is like totally unfair. Don't the police have anything better to do?"

Assuming this is a strict liability offense, Louisa's claims of ignorance and safe driving do not present promising arguments. As written, the law does not require any awareness of the time of day or night, just that a person under the age of 17 drive on the highway during the prohibited time period. Nor does the violation require proof of dangerous driving. There is an interesting possibility concerning the act requirement, however. Louisa might argue that there was no evidence of her voluntarily driving the car on the road after midnight because the officer never saw her driving prior to issuing his loudspeaker instruction. She can argue that her driving following the officer's instruction was a response to a police command and therefore was coerced and not voluntary. (See Chapter 5).[12]

---

12. There is an interesting set of driving violation cases which involve the voluntary act requirement and mechanical failures. The legal question these cases present is whether the person behind the wheel was voluntarily driving at the time of the offense when the "driving" may be attributed to a mechanical failure of the vehicle's equipment. Generally, if the mechanical failure involves a basic part of the car's equipment such as throttle or brakes and the driver has no prior notice of the problem, the defendant will not be held to have voluntarily driven the vehicle following the failure. In some cases though, courts have held that the driver remains responsible for the failure of a nonessential feature of the car such as a cruise control device, on the theory that the driver voluntarily delegated control to the device and therefore remains responsible for its functioning. See State v. Baker, 571 P.2d 65 (Kan. Ct. App. 1977).

CHAPTER 7

MENS REA IN STATUTORY CONTEXT: THE ART OF READING CRIMINAL STATUTES

There is a magic to written language that lawyers especially should appreciate. We should recall Charles Sequoya, a member of the Cherokee nation who in the early 19th-century was so impressed by white men's ability to "talk at a distance" by marks on paper that he devoted himself to inventing an alphabet for the Cherokee tongue. Sequoya's creation led to the development of a Cherokee literature that included a written constitution.[1]

There is a special magic to legal writing because of its ability to not only communicate but to govern at a distance. Consider how extraordinary it is that people in one place and time can set down words that will decide major issues of property and liberty involving unknown persons in distant times and places. It's worth taking a moment to appreciate the successes of written legal language, for the main task of this chapter is to consider its difficulties in the context of criminal law.

In studying mens rea we have so far concentrated on the definitions of individual mens rea terms. We have not paid much attention to statutory context. In practice, however, statutory context often proves critical to the meaning of a mens rea term or terms.

---

1. See John Ehle, *The Trail of Tears: The Rise and Fall of the Cherokee Nation* 159–61, 152–53 (1988). Despite the Cherokees' adoption of many Western ways, including a well-developed legal system, the federal government forcibly removed tribal members from their lands and sent them to western territories, an action accompanied by great loss of life, property, and culture.

Sequoya likened the struggle to develop a written language as akin to "catching and taming a wild animal," which might also describe the effort to capture the essence of a crime in statutory language. James Wilson, *The Earth Shall Weep: A History of Native America* 158 (2000).

We all know that context can make a big difference. Depending on context, the statement: "He should be taken out and shot" might be a lighthearted joke or an execution order. We interpret such statements according to what we know of the persons involved, the topic discussed, facial expressions, physical gestures, and many other indicators of the speaker's intent. Note how much of this interpretive information depends upon physical presence. When speaker and audience communicate only by writing, interpretation becomes much more difficult.

In drafting criminal statutes, legislators face an additional challenge in that they must devise rules to govern cases whose particulars are unknown—after all, the crimes have not yet been committed. To perform their function, criminal statutes must capture the essential idea of a crime in relatively general terms that will guide decision makers (judges and jurors) in the assessment of a wide range of fact patterns. But such general language can also be ambiguous.

In addition to problems with the definitions of mens rea terms, in this chapter we confront problems with statutory grammar. By grammar I mean the set of principles that govern the interaction of words within a sentence, that tell us, for example, what is the subject of the sentence, the verb and the object; what terms adjectives or adverbs modify. As we will see, ordinary English grammar often does not answer the most important interpretive questions with respect to criminal statutes and their mens rea requirements.

To fill in the gap left by ordinary grammar we must exercise our legal imaginations. We have to imagine how the law would work under each possible interpretation. We have to imagine the kinds of convictions that would be included and excluded.

This chapter aims to provide an introduction to basic principles and methods of statutory interpretation in criminal law. It presents a methodology for reading criminal statutes and their mens rea requirements in the form of a sequence of questions to be asked and answered by the statute's reader. We also consider methods for applying statutory mens rea requirements to particular facts.

What the chapter cannot promise, indeed what no one can promise, is clear, universal rules for determining the mens rea requirements of many different criminal offenses. We can identify some basic techniques and guidelines for statutory interpretation, but in the end, each criminal offense must be considered in its own right.

Interpreting Statutes: The Role of Appellate Courts

As we saw in Chapter 1, in theory the shape of criminal law depends almost entirely upon the legislature. Elected representatives of the public draft and enact statutes which criminalize particular offenses, subject only to the approval or veto of an elected executive. In practice, though, appellate courts have a vital role to play in shaping criminal law through the interpretation of criminal statutes—especially with respect to mens rea.

In interpreting statutes, courts seek readings consistent with the general aims of the criminal law. Thus courts may find a mens rea requirement where a legislature has not clearly enunciated one in order to bring the statute into conformity with long-standing principles of just punishment. Or to the same end the court may give a mens rea term a more limited reading than we might expect.

To understand the judicial role here it helps to consider the different perspectives of courts and legislatures with respect to criminal law. The legislature is a body comprised of politicians concerned most with the public's current hopes and fears. When it comes to crime, public fears about being victimized by crime tend to outweigh concerns with unjust convictions. As a result, in drafting criminal legislation politicians tend to worry more that the law might permit the guilty to go unpunished than that it may condemn the innocent. Legislators often figure that if they do write a statute too broadly, the law's overbreadth will be cured by prosecutorial discretion, judicial interpretation or the judgment of juries.

Meanwhile courts must resolve the fates of particular defendants according to statutory language, precedents and general principles of criminal law. Courts are generally more sensitive to the ways that even well-motivated prosecutors may go astray, and as a result courts are more likely to insist that convictions be based on proof of mens rea.

Interpretive Sources: Language, Legislative History, Tradition, and Policy

How do courts go about interpreting criminal statutes? The court's most basic guide to statutory meaning is statutory language. The court begins by reading the statute according to standard language rules: definitions, grammar and punctuation. This reading may be supplemented by legislative history, relevant criminal law traditions and policy considerations.

When available, legislative history can be important to statutory interpretation. Knowing what problems the legislature sought to address in the statute may help determine its proof requirements. Sources of legislative history range from reports of code revision commissions and legislative committees, to more informal sources such as newspaper accounts of floor debates.[2] Regardless of documentation, however, legislative history is often ambiguous, because it tends to record the views of the strongest proponents (and sometimes opponents) of the legislation rather than the consensus of all members. As a result, judges vary considerably in the weight they assign to legislative history, some considering it direct evidence of legislative intent, others treating it with caution, knowing that it can be manipulated by skilled partisans to suggest a position not shared by the legislature as a whole; some judges ignore it entirely, believing that only the text of the statute matters.

Criminal law traditions represent another important influence on statutory interpretation. Judges often look to how earlier tribunals have interpreted similar offenses and assume that, absent a clear legislative indication to the contrary, the new offense should be interpreted in the same fashion as its predecessors. For example, in interpreting a statute criminalizing the distribution of cigarettes to minors, a court may look to other underage offenses to decide whether the legislature meant to require proof of mens rea as to the age of the minor. Because crimes involving underage sex or the provision of alcohol are usually strict liability as to age (that is, have no mens rea requirement as to age), the cigarette offense may well be read similarly.

Finally courts read statutes in light of basic criminal justice policy, a policy that generally links significant penalties to the proof of subjective mens rea — an intent to do wrong or awareness of wrong. As Justice Robert Jackson so memorably put it: "The contention that an injury can amount to a crime only when inflicted by intention is no provincial or transient notion.... A relation between some mental element and punishment for a harmful act is almost as instinctive as the child's familiar exculpatory 'But I didn't mean to'...."[3]

---

2. The clearest example may be the commentary provided by the drafters of the Model Penal Code. Where legislatures adopt a particular provision of the MPC, courts often look to the MPC commentary for guidance on its meaning. See American Law Institute, *Model Penal Code and Commentaries* (Official Draft and Revised Comments 1985). Similar sources of legislative history in committee reports are also usually available for federal statutes. Formal legislative history in the form of debates or committee reports is not available for many state statutes, however, leaving courts with less reliable sources of information about the legislative process.

3. Morisette v. United States, 342 U.S. 237, 251 (1952).

Mens Rea Analysis: A Four Step Approach

The process of ascertaining mens rea requirements in a criminal case can be broken down into four stages:

1. Identify all possible mens rea terms in the criminal statute under which defendant is charged.[4]
2. Identify the usual meaning of each mens rea term.
3. Through analysis of the statute determine:
   (a) what element or elements of the statute each mens rea term applies to; and
   (b) how the mens rea term applies to each element (assuming it does apply).
4. Analyze the facts of the case to determine whether the prosecution can prove that the defendant acted with the required mens rea.

Each of these stages may require its own complex analysis. Much of what is needed in the first two steps we covered in Chapter 6. In this chapter we focus on steps three and four.

Example 1: Obstruction of a Criminal Investigation

To illustrate the complexity of statutory interpretation, consider the following statute:

> Whoever obstructs the progress of a criminal investigation by providing false or misleading information to the police or other legally authorized investigators and does so willfully is guilty of a crime.

Simply by reading through the statute once, we gain a general sense of the sort of wrongful conduct—willful obstruction of a criminal investigation—that legislators meant to prohibit here. We can all probably come up with a particular example of the sort of conduct that the statute was meant to address: bribing a judge or juror, threatening a witness, destroying evidence. We would expect that the statute would cover such conduct. But perhaps it goes further. In any event, we must determine the statute's coverage from its language.

We begin with the vocabulary of mens rea: what does "willfully" mean? Although willfully is a common mens rea term, especially in federal law, there is no standard definition. In fact, its meaning can vary according to context. Its

---

4. In the case of a statute which does not contain a mens rea term, we must also ask if a court will imply a mens rea requirement. If so, we would then have to determine how that requirement would apply to the facts presented.

connotation of intentionality suggests that it might be limited to purposely, but courts standardly interpret it to cover knowingly and recklessly as well.

Mens rea turns not just on definitions but on grammar. Linguistically, mens rea terms are adverbs or adverbial phrases; they work by modifying verbs. Recall the basic principle that mens rea terms always act in partnership with other words and phrases. Here we must decide what terms in the statute that willfully modifies—and how. We will see that the same mens rea term can have different meanings as applied to different terms within the same stature.

For purposes of discussion let us assume that a court decides that willfully has a general meaning of purposely, knowingly, or recklessly. (This means that the prosecution can gain a conviction by proof of defendant's purposeful or knowing or reckless mens rea.) We must now decide whether this mens rea requirement applies to:

(a) the obstruction of the investigation;
(b) that the information provided is false or misleading;
(c) that the recipient of the information was a police officer or other authorized investigator.

What are the possibilities? Willfully might apply to all three elements (a–c), two of the three (probably a & b), or even just one of the three (probably a or b). Grammatical rules may assist here, but they cannot provide the whole story. Too much turns on this decision to let it rest on grammar alone. We must also exercise our legal imagination, imagining how different mens rea rules would produce different results in a variety of cases.

What does the concept of obstructing an investigation suggest about mens rea? Would we expect a person to be convicted if that person was entirely unaware that the information provided was false or misleading? This seems unlikely because such falsity lies at the heart of the criminal wrong. This means that willfully should modify the false or misleading element.

Would we expect a person to be convicted of this offense if she was aware that she was providing false or misleading information, but not that it would obstruct an investigation? This seems unlikely, because although there is moral fault in conscious deceit, deceit without any understanding that the deceit was legally significant does not seem to describe the offense of obstruction of justice. People lie all the time with no criminal consequences. It's lying about a matter of legal significance that constitutes the essential wrong of this offense. This tends to indicate that willfully should partner with—should modify—both the obstruction *and* the falsity elements (a & b).

Whether willfully should also apply to the final element, that the recipient of the information be a law enforcement officer is less clear. Once mens rea is established as to obstruction and falsity, the essence of the wrong seems established.

From analysis of this particular statute we may form a general guideline concerning statutory interpretation and mens rea. In general, *where a statute includes a mens rea term, that term should apply to the element that defines the essential wrong of the defendant's conduct.* In other words, the mens rea term should apply to whatever it is in the defendant's conduct that makes that conduct criminal as opposed to noncriminal.

Example 2: Destruction of Property

In this jurisdiction it is a misdemeanor to "maliciously destroy the property of another." Translating this into the mens rea language of the MPC (purposely, knowingly, recklessly, or negligently), what mens rea might be required for conviction of this offense as to: (1) destruction of property, and (2) property of another?

The legislature here has included a traditional mens rea term: "maliciously." What does this usually mean? We know from the brief discussion of common law mens rea terms in Chapter 6, that maliciously generally does not bear the same meaning in criminal law as in ordinary usage; it does not require that the defendant act in a wicked or mean-spirited fashion. Instead, modern courts usually interpret maliciously to mean purposely, knowingly, or recklessly. Its meaning here will depend on factors particular to this offense, however. Context matters.

The first and probably most important issue in interpreting this statute is deciding whether "maliciously" modifies only "destroy the property" or whether the mens rea term also extends to the phrase "of another" which deals with ownership. We begin by breaking up the statute into its smallest elements:

Whoever
maliciously
destroys the property
of another ...

Clearly, maliciously modifies destroy. We know this because English grammar dictates that adverbs appear next to the verbs they modify. Unfortunately, ordinary grammar does not tell us whether maliciously modifies *only* destroy or whether it also modifies "of another." To put this in legal terms, the issue is whether the mens rea requirement involves only destroying property, or destruction *and* ownership.

Note that we now have two different sets of mens rea issues going simultaneously. We have the issue of (1) how to translate maliciously into MPC terminology and we have the issue of (2) whether maliciously modifies one or both of the elements of the statute.

If we adopt the limited reading of maliciously, that it modifies only destroy, and translate the term maliciously into the MPC mens reas of purposely, knowingly, or recklessly, then the defendant will be convicted if he destroyed another's property with the aim of destroying the property's value (purposely); or while aware of a substantial certainty that such destruction would result (knowingly); or while aware of a significant and unjustified risk that his acts would destroy the property (recklessly). The state would have to prove that the property belonged to another but *not* that the defendant was aware that it belonged to another. We would chart the statutory elements under this reading as follows.

(1) defendant must maliciously (purposely, knowingly, or recklessly) destroy property,

(2) which property belongs to another (strict liability element)

The question is: is this is the best way to read the statute? Is this likely what the legislature intended?

Again we exercise our legal imaginations to consider legislative reactions to different outcomes produced by different statutory readings. Do we think the legislature meant to convict someone of a criminal offense for deliberately destroying property she honestly—but mistakenly—believed to be hers? Would anyone expect to be *criminally* punished, as opposed to being held civilly liable, for purposely smashing a china vase that one sincerely believed was one's own, if it turned out to belong to another? It appears more likely that the legislature envisioned criminalizing the act of deliberately smashing another's valuable vase when the individual knew it belonged to another or perhaps when she knew of a high risk that it belonged to another.

If maliciously modifies the ownership element as well as the destruction element, then in addition to proving purpose, knowledge or recklessness as to the property's destruction, the prosecution would also have to prove purpose, knowledge, or recklessness as to the property being owned by another. This reading is consistent with ordinary grammar, traditional legal interpretations of maliciously and comports with our basic policy of attaching mens rea to the aspect of conduct that makes it morally wrongful.[5]

---

5. This discussion does not cover all of the possibilities for statutory interpretation here but is limited to some of the most likely possibilities.

The Mystery of Changing Meaning Within a Statute

Sometimes the same mens rea term may have different meanings within the same statute according to the terms that it modifies. This seems strange as a matter of ordinary language, but it makes sense in terms of the work that mens rea does in criminal statutes. Consider the following statute.

"A person is guilty of a felony who purposely receives stolen property." Assume that purposely here is defined in accord with the MPC definition of purposely. Exactly what mens rea must be proven for conviction?

Because we have a definition of the mens rea term of purposely, the only challenge here is deciding how it works in the statute. Again we must decide what statutory element or elements the mens rea term modifies.

Because of its placement in the statute, purposely must modify receiving; that is, the defendant must have had the conscious object to take possession of (to receive) the property. If that is all the work that purposely does, i.e., it does not modify any other part of the statute, we would chart the statute this way:

(1) defendant must purposely receive property &

(2) the property received must have been stolen (strict liability element)

The problem with this interpretation is that here the mens rea term does almost no work. It does not help us distinguish between criminal and non-criminal conduct. Receiving property—essentially agreeing to a transfer of property from one person to another—is generally a purposeful act anyway. Even more worrisome is that receipt of property is generally an innocent act. What could be more common (and lawful) in our modern capitalist society than the purposeful transfer of property between persons? If purposely is to fulfill its usual task of distinguishing criminal from noncriminal conduct, it must modify stolen; the fact that the item is stolen is key to the criminality here. This suggests the following reading of the statute:

(1) defendant must purposely receive property

(2) with the purpose that the property have been stolen

But this may go too far. Consider what this interpretation would include and what it would exclude. Only persons who received stolen property with the conscious object, with the desire, that it be stolen would be guilty. Yet most of those who merit punishment for receiving stolen property do not take the property *with the purpose that* it have been stolen. Even the professional fence (one who is in the business of purchasing and reselling stolen goods) does not act with the conscious object that the item be stolen; his object in receiving the property is to make money. The fact that the items are stolen means he takes special risks in the transaction for which he may be compensated by heightened profits. He can buy especially cheaply and thereby make a significant profit even if he sells at a below-market price. This means that the typical fence of stolen property acts with knowledge, or perhaps recklessness that the item was stolen. And, in fact, receiving stolen property is normally interpreted in this fashion:

(1) defendant must purposely receive property,
(2) being reckless as to the risk that the property was stolen.[6]

Linguistically this interpretation may seem odd in that the word purposely here takes on two different meanings in the same statute. One must act with the purpose to receive property, but need only be reckless with respect to that property being stolen — two different forms of mens rea that come from the same original mens rea term of purposely. Can we do this? The answer is that we can.

This interpretive method holds for many so-called conduct offenses, those offenses that punish wrongful acts without a requirement that the acts produce particular physical harms.[7] In such offenses, purposely carries its ordinary meaning with respect to the conduct prohibited, and then effectively converts to a mens rea of knowledge or recklessness with respect to the circumstances that make the conduct wrongful (as in, awareness of a high risk that the property received is stolen). This same interpretive method may apply when the mens rea is a common law terms such as maliciously or intentionally or willfully. In essence the legislature has required mens rea for the offense, and the court must interpret that requirement to best accomplish the legislature's practical intention.

Reading Mens Rea In — and Out: Is This Strict Liability?

One might expect that recognizing a strict liability offense would be relatively simple: any offense that lacks a mens rea term in its statutory definition must

---

6. See MPC sec. 223.6 on receiving stolen property: "A person is guilty ... if he purposely receives ... movable property of another knowing that it has been stolen, or believing that it probably has been stolen." This makes clear that the mens rea for stolen status is satisfied either by knowledge or an awareness of a likelihood that it was stolen, the latter mens rea being akin to recklessness.

7. See MPC sec. 2.02 (2) (a) (ii).

be strict liability. But this is not true. Some offenses without an explicit mens rea term will be read to include a mens rea requirement. And, some offense definitions that contain explicit mens rea terms will be so narrowly read that they effectively become strict liability. While the presence or absence of mens rea terms plays an important role in determining whether an offense is strict liability, at least three other factors may affect the analysis: (1) traditional interpretations of similar crimes in the past; (2) the severity of penalty; and (3) inherent notice of risk provided by the prohibited conduct.

Reading Mens Rea into a Statute

The willingness of courts to read in a mens rea term when one is not included in the statute is a less radical move than it may at first appear. Many of the old common law offenses of English law—especially so-called general intent crimes—often did not include an explicit mens rea term in their definitions, yet these have traditionally been interpreted as requiring some form of mens rea. Thus modern courts follow a long tradition in holding that mens rea may be required even when it is not explicit in the offense definition.

In general, the more that a statutory offense looks like a traditional crime that requires mens rea, the more likely it is that a court will interpret the offense as requiring mens rea. For example, assume the legislature creates a new offense of theft by electronic means, but does not include any explicit mens rea term in the definition. A court may well decide that this offense is essentially an updating of traditional theft offenses to accommodate new technologies—and since all forms of theft traditionally required mens rea, a court may well conclude that the legislature intended the same with respect to the new offense.

Severity of penalty also tends to argue for mens rea. The more severe the penalty, the more likely that a reviewing court will presume that the legislature intended to require mens rea. The same will be true of the amount of social stigma that attaches (or does not) to conviction of the particular offense. In general, the worse the consequences of conviction, the more likely that mens rea will be implied.

Finally, the extent to which the conduct prohibited contains inherent notice of wrongdoing or special risks to the public often carries significant weight with interpreting courts. For example, a court may find that an offense that criminalizes the unauthorized possession of explosives does not require proof of awareness of lack of authorization on the ground that the prohibited conduct is so inherently dangerous and unusual that anyone engaged in it must realize that special rules must apply.[8] Given the nature of the prohibited conduct, the chances are great that anyone who does engage in it without authorization will be aware that they are engaging in illegal activity. The same reasoning obtains if the prohibited activity poses special hazards to the public as a whole, such as transportation of hazardous materials or harms to the community's food supply. In these instances, a court may deem notice of the hazard to be inherent in the activity, making proof of mens rea morally and legally unnecessary. By contrast, an offense which criminalizes certain kinds of financial transactions, might require mens rea concerning the illegality of the transaction on the ground that otherwise truly innocent persons might be convicted of significant offenses.[9] (For more on the problem of mens rea with respect to statutory elements of authorization and legality, see the next chapter's discussion of mistake of law.)

Reading Mens Rea Out—By Reading It Narrowly

As noted above, even the presence of a mens rea term in a statute does not necessarily signal that the offense requires proof of a particular culpable mental state or attitude. Courts sometimes read the mens rea term so narrowly—limiting its application to such a small part of the statute—that the crime in effect becomes one of strict liability. The same three factors discussed above apply here.

> Consider an offense that prohibits purposeful sexual contact with a person under the age of 14. Defendant admits that he had sexual contact with the victim but states that it was consensual and he reasonably believed that she was sixteen years of age. He argues that as a result he lacked the required mens rea with respect to age. The prosecution maintains, however, that the statute is strict liability as to age. Who is correct?

The word "purposeful" in the statute clearly modifies the sexual contact element, meaning that the prosecution must prove that the accused had a sexual purpose in touching the victim. But notice that the very concept of a *sexual* touching implies a sexual purpose, which means that this part of the statute would be much the same without the word purposeful. This suggests that, pur-

---

8. See, e.g., United States v. Freed, 401 U.S. 601 (1971) (no mens rea required as to registration requirement for possession of hand grenades). Compare United States v. Staples, 511 U.S. 600 (1994) (knowledge that weapon was fully automatic required for conviction on unregistered firearm offense).

9. See, e.g., Ratzlaf v. United States, 510 U.S. 135 (1994) (mens rea required with respect to the criminality of structuring a financial transaction to avoid currency reporting requirements in federal law).

poseful probably should modify another element as well. Also arguing against a restrictive reading is our general guideline that mens rea should apply to that aspect of conduct essential to wrongdoing. Sexual touching between adults is perfectly lawful, if consensual. Here the touching is criminal only because of the age of the person touched. From this we would expect that the mens rea of purposeful would extend to the age element of the offense, perhaps being converted into a requirement of knowledge or recklessness in the process.

Despite all this, a court will likely deem the age element to be strict liability. This means that the prosecution must prove that the victim was under 14, but not that the defendant was aware of this, or even had reasonable notice of it. We can predict this with some confidence because of a long-standing criminal law tradition that age elements in underage offenses—especially sex offenses—are strict liability. This tradition is supported by an equally long-standing policy of using the criminal law to provide special moral and legal protections for the young.[10] A court is likely to presume that the legislature would not vary from the strict liability tradition without a more definitive expression of a mens rea requirement as to age.[11] The result is that, in effect if not in wording (the statute does still contain a mens rea term), this crime is a strict liability offense.

Proving Mens Rea: Application of Mens Rea Requirements to the Facts

We move finally to the last phase of mens rea analysis: the application of statutory requirements to the facts of a particular case. Once we have determined what the statute requires, then we see if those requirements match up with the evidence adduced at trial. The key here is to separate the different stages of analysis, which usually means determining the statute's meaning—or at least the different possibilities for its meaning—before going to the facts. Otherwise, we are likely to succumb to the temptation, all too frequently indulged by lawyers and courts, of reading statutes to conform to our view of the particular defendant.

---

10. See People v. Olsen, 685 P.2d 52 (Cal.1984) (holding that statutory language: "Any person who shall willfully and lewdly commit any lewd or lascivious act … upon or with the body, or any part or member thereof, of a child under the age of 14 years, with the intent of arousing, appealing to, or gratifying the lust or passions or sexual desires of such person or of such child, shall be guilty of a felony …" does not require mens rea as to age.)

11. Courts might also believe that the obvious youthfulness of the victim—that he or she appeared to be an adolescent, even if not as young as 13—provides inherent notice of the moral and legal riskiness of the sexual touching.

State health and welfare officials are appalled to discover that someone has created a web site called "Lowlifes.com" which provides access to confidential state welfare files of some particularly nasty or
colorful cases. Investigation reveals that the web site is the creation of
18-year-old high school student, Darryl, a dedicated computer hacker.
Welfare officials come to you, a state prosecutor, to see if Darryl can
be charged with a crime. Research reveals a new state statute that
makes it a misdemeanor to knowingly and without authorization read,
distribute, download or otherwise gain access to confidential government information. What kind of evidence would you need to prove a
criminal case under this statute against Darryl?

Before we can look at—or look for—evidence of Darryl's guilt, we must
determine the mens rea requirements of the statute. Read most broadly, the statute
requires proof that Darryl: (1) knew that he gained access to confidential government information; and (2) knew that he lacked authorization to do this.[12]

As a prosecutor, you would first seek evidence tending to show Darryl's
awareness of the confidentiality of the information taken. This could be shown
by warnings posted on the original government sites and welfare files. Also
useful would be any admissions that Darryl may have made to friends or others about what he did to gain access. The contents of the files themselves may
also provide notice of confidentiality, in that they may contain such personal
information that all readers would understand it was meant to be confidential.

The same evidence would probably also show Darryl's awareness of lack of
authorization. The more explicit restrictions on access are placed on the state
welfare website, the more that Darryl's efforts to defeat those restrictions
demonstrate an understanding (and disregard for) the rules concerning authorized access.

The prosecution presents evidence at trial that the web site was
Darryl's creation and that the listed data—which includes details of
child sexual abuse, domestic violence, and drug abuse—was taken
from state welfare files, all of which are clearly marked confidential.
The state also introduces a number of e-mails from Darryl, in which
he proudly announces his ability to hack into any government site,

---

12. There is a possibility that the mens rea of knowingly would apply only to the confidentiality of the document and not to "without authorization," but because Darryl as a
high school student had no grounds to believe that he had authorization for access to confidential government documents, this possibility need not be explored here.

and that he will soon be providing "worldwide proof" that he is a "totally awesome hacker." Is Darryl likely to be convicted at trial?

The simple answer is yes. The challenge is articulating why.

First, what is the evidence to show that Darryl knew that the files represented confidential government information? The warnings on the files provide clear notice of government confidentiality. The private nature of the information provides a degree of inherent notice of their confidentiality as well. Finally, the e-mails from Darryl indicate his active interest in violating the electronic security of others, revealing general awareness that his conduct violates norms of privacy and confidentiality that security measures are designed to protect.

Second, what is the evidence that Darryl knew that his access to the government site was unauthorized? Again we will employ much of the same evidence that we did with respect to the confidentiality element.[13] Nevertheless, we should keep the analysis of the elements separate in order to preserve any distinction there may be between them. The warnings posted on the government site, the nature of the information accessed and electronically published by Darryl, and Darryl's electronic crowing about his hacking abilities all strongly suggest his awareness that his conduct was unauthorized. The e-mail evidence directly indicates Darryl's knowledge of his lack of authorization to gain access, indeed indicates that lack of authorization motivated his conduct, because he wanted to demonstrate that he can defeat any government electronic security. In addition, a prosecutor might note that as an 18-year-old high school student, Darryl had no reason to believe that he had any special authorization for access to such records.

Putting It All Together: Determining Statutory Mens Rea Requirements and Analyzing Facts

Assume that Darryl was convicted of the misdemeanor offense described above, was fined, given a term of community service and placed on probation. Unfortunately, he does not seem to have learned his lesson.

Two years later, the primary computer system for the United States Department of Defense (DOD) crashes and is down for three hours

---

13. The same facts often may be used for multiple purposes in criminal law analysis. For example, the same facts with respect to the display and firing of a gun by the defendant may be relevant to voluntary act analysis (did the defendant act unconsciously?), mens rea (did he seek to kill?), and even an affirmative defense (did he act in self-defense?). We must always distinguish the different uses of the same facts according to legal context, however.

as the result of an unauthorized electronic intrusion. The intrusion automatically triggers software that brings the system down before there can be a serious security breach. It leaves certain core defense functions running, but creates massive disruption of all other functions. The intrusion is traced to Darryl. Darryl has devised a sophisticated hacking program specifically designed to defeat the DOD security protections. When questioned by the FBI, Darryl admits everything. (He is a slow learner in this regard as well.)

Darryl is charged with the following federal offense: "Whoever willfully acts in any way to endanger the national security by damaging, destroying, or in any way interfering with the proper functioning of a defense installation of the United States, including by electronic means, is guilty of a felony." The statutory language "including by electronic means" was added several years ago to include all computer and related electronic facilities. The original statute was passed during World War I at a time when acts of physical sabotage against military installations were feared.

Darryl's attorney contacts the federal prosecutor in this case, stating that Darryl is willing to plead guilty to a misdemeanor charge of unauthorized access. Darryl simply wanted to demonstrate his hacker prowess and had no intention to, or awareness that he would, endanger national security. In fact, Darryl desperately wants to become a federal law enforcement agent when he grows up (assuming he ever does). FBI investigation tends to corroborate this account. The shutdown of the system was triggered by a new software program, whose existence was secret outside the DOD.

The DOD would like Darryl prosecuted to the "full extent of the law, at a minimum." But everyone agrees that the most important thing is that Darryl be convicted.

Should the federal prosecutor accept the defense offer of a guilty plea to the misdemeanor? What are the government's chances of prevailing at trial on the felony charge?

The great temptation for prosecutors here is to judge the defendant culpable and then read the statute accordingly. Certainly Darryl appears a worthy subject of prosecutorial attention, given his history of hacking and the seriousness of the intrusion and its consequences. Turning now to the felony statute, a prosecutor might argue that all of Darryl's conduct was intentional, and therefore meets the statutory requirement of willful. He intentionally acted to gain access to confidential government documents related to the national defense. The nature of the intrusion plus Darryl's past hacking offense strongly indicate his understanding of the wrongfulness of his conduct. As far as the endanger the national security element goes, Darryl must either have known that such an intrusion would harm national security, or should have known, the prosecutor will argue. He appears guilty as charged.

There is a problem with this analysis, however. This reading of the statute owes more to the government's dark view of Darryl as a culpable, dangerous hacker, than it does to the specific requirements of the felony statute. If we start our analysis with the statutory language, we may reach a different conclusion.

The statute contains the mens rea term of "willfully." This term usually translates into the MPC terms of either purposely and knowingly or purposely, knowingly and recklessly. The term almost certainly excludes negligence. The critical question for statutory interpretation is what element or elements willfully modifies.

Willfully may attach to any combination of: (1) acts; (2) endangering national security; and (3) gaining access to confidential electronic files relating to national defense. The government might argue that willfully applies only to the first-mentioned element, the defendant's acts, but this seems unlikely. Such a reading would make persons guilty of a felony who accidentally gain access to confidential defense records and accidentally harm national security in the process. Such a reading would violate the principle that mens rea terms should attach to the element or elements of the offense essential to wrongdoing. Wrongdoing here involves unauthorized access and risks to national security.

Assuming that willfully does modify more than "acts," the hard question is whether it applies to one or both of the remaining elements: (1) endangering the national security and (2) interfering with a defense installation. The latter requirement would pose fewer problems for the prosecution in this case. Everyone knows that access to DOD files is highly restricted and this plus the sophisticated nature of the program required to gain unauthorized access demonstrate that Darryl had a high degree of awareness that his unauthorized intrusion would represent an interference with the proper functioning of this defense "installation."

The big question is whether willfully applies to the endangering national security element. If it does, the government is in trouble. It lacks evidence that Darryl sought to endanger (was purposeful as to endangering) the national security. Nor did he know that the national security would be endangered. Recklessness seems more promising, but there is no direct evidence that Darryl was actually aware of a substantial and unjustifiable risk that national security would be endangered. The only mens rea that the government could readily prove with respect to endangering national security is negligence. The government would like to argue that anyone who purposely attempts an unauthorized intrusion into a DOD computer system should be aware of a range of potential negative consequences for the nation's security. But as we noted previously, willfully as a mens rea term does not normally include negligence.

The bottom line is that prosecution would *like* to read the statute as requiring purposeful, knowing, or perhaps reckless interference with the proper operation of the Defense Department's computer network (its facility) but either no mens rea or a negligence mens rea as to endangering the national security. The government certainly can make a policy argument that persons who engage in this kind of activity pose a significant danger to DOD computer security and demonstrate significant disregard for security measures. But is this the best way to read the statute?

The first aspect of wrongfulness mentioned in the statute after willfully—and the most serious form of wrongdoing mentioned in the statute—is danger to the national security. Both factors suggest that willfully should apply to endangering the national security. The legislative history of the statute bolsters this reading. The original harms that legislators sought to address were acts of physical sabotage, acts characterized by a purpose to interfere with defense operations.

The point of this extended analysis is not that the defense reading of the statute will necessarily be accepted by a court and the prosecution's necessarily will be rejected. The point has been to show how if we focus primarily on the culpability of the defendant we may (consciously or unconsciously) distort our reading of the legislative intent behind the statute. Darryl may have committed acts worthy of criminal punishment. But the critical question is whether the Congress intended to cover Darryl's conduct under this particular federal offense, a question that will turn on whether willfully modifies the endangerment element—and if so, how.

CHAPTER 8

MISTAKES OF FACT AND LAW

"OK, it's true I did that, but not like you said. I had no idea I was doing anything wrong because I made an honest mistake about the situation. You can't commit a crime by mistake."

Or can you? This chapter concerns claims that a defendant's mistake about facts or law should preclude criminal responsibility. Primarily these involve the mens rea requirement of the particular offense. As a result, general rules are hard to come by; we can though construct useful *methods* of analysis and identify some general trends.

We will consider two basic types of mistakes, those involving facts and those involving law. Courts are generally more receptive to mistake of fact arguments than mistake of law, but again there are no reliable, universal rules. Much depends on the particulars of the offense and the mistake claim.

An important caveat before we proceed any farther and that is to admit a particular bias in approach to mistake questions here. The chapter will largely track the approach of the MPC, which holds that mistake claims constitute a particular form of mens rea arguments.[1] Determine what the mens rea requirements for an offense are and you'll know what mistake claims may be made. This contrasts with the tendency of some courts and legislatures to set out general mistake rules that seem to create affirmative defenses, independent of mens rea. Such rule statements can create great confusion in interpretation and conflict with particular offense definitions.[2] They will not be covered here.

Before beginning the analysis, a brief note on the distinction between factual and legal mistakes. Factual mistakes involve a wide array of errors that a

---

1. Section 2.04(1)(a) provides that a claim of mistake of fact will be a valid defense to a charge if "the ignorance or mistake negatives the purpose, knowledge, belief, recklessness or negligence required to establish a material element of the offense."
2. We will also encounter a few mistake of law claims that should be categorized as affirmative defenses.

defendant may make in the assessment of a particular situation. Mistakes about whether a gun is loaded in a homicide case, or about who owned the laptop computer taken by the defendant in a theft case are typical kinds of mistakes of fact. Mistakes of law concern mistakes about *specialized* legal knowledge, matters that lie beyond the knowledge of most laypersons. So, for example, a legal mistake might involve the legal status of a divorce decree in a bigamy case, or tax obligations in a criminal tax prosecution.

Mistake of Fact

What is a mistake of fact claim?

A mistake of fact claim usually involves the defendant taking the witness stand and admitting that he or she did the conduct charged by the prosecution, but did so subject to some mistaken belief about the situation which rendered the conduct noncriminal or of lesser criminality. For example, if the defendant is charged with unlawful sexual intercourse with a person under the age of 18, the defendant may testify that she did have intercourse with the alleged victim, a 15-year-old boy, but she reasonably believed he was 18. Or, a defendant charged with theft of a laptop computer from another student's dorm room might testify that he took the computer, but he thought it was his own.

In mistake of fact cases defendants normally admit that they voluntarily committed the acts prohibited the statute, but seek acquittal because of a critical mistake about their understanding of the situation, mirroring in some ways the typical "yes, but" structure of an affirmative defense. In substance, however, mistake claims involve mens rea.

The only difference between a mistake of fact claim and the sort of mens rea arguments we have already considered is the kind of evidence involved. With prior mens rea arguments, defendants simply argued that the prosecution evidence was inadequate. With mistake of fact, the defendant adds his or her own affirmative evidence concerning an innocent state of mind. But either way, the issue is mens rea.

The following examples illustrate the essential similarity between standard mens rea arguments and most mistake of fact claims.

> Defendant is charged with reckless endangerment of human life. The prosecution at trial presents evidence that Defendant, following a storm which took down power lines, cuts a length of downed power line and sells it to a scrap metal dealer. The defendant leaves one end

of the electric line dangling from a utility pole, bare wires exposed. When the power company restores power to the line several days later, the severed ends of the line touch a metal pipe, delivering a severe electric shock to a plumber working in a nearby building. The defense does not present any witnesses.

The offense requires that the defendant have acted recklessly—with awareness that his conduct created a substantial and unjustified risk to human life.

How might defense counsel construct a mens rea argument on behalf of defendant in this case?

Here we have a standard mens rea problem of the sort explored in the previous chapter. Defense counsel may argue that the prosecution did not prove that defendant was aware that cutting a downed power line could endanger to a plumber working nearby. The prosecution would argue that the obvious dangerousness of cutting electrical lines without permission means that defendant was almost certainly aware of a grave risk of electrocution to a wide range of persons nearby—and it was certainly an unjustified risk. The issue concerns defendant's state of awareness.

Now let us consider the same case, slightly reworked to present a mistake of fact claim.

Assume the same criminal charge and the same evidence presented by the prosecution. This time, however, defendant testifies in his own defense, claiming that he checked to make sure the power was off before he cut the line and that he deliberately severed the wires high on the power pole so that no children or bystanders could be injured. He stated from his past experience as a utility lineman, he believed that the power company would never restore power without assuring the integrity and safety of all lines first.

In what ways, if any, does the defendant's testimony change the analysis of this case?

The first thing to note is what remains the same. The defendant's physical actions are the same and produce the same result. The charge is the same. Again the only issue is proof of the defendant's recklessness towards endangering human life. The difference is that now we have affirmative evidence from the defendant on the mens rea question.

Defendant's testimony suggests that because of his prior experience he believed that the power company would take precautions before restoring power and that therefore cutting the line would not pose any danger of electrocution.

In other words, he believed that his conduct would not endanger life; hence he did not act recklessly with respect to the plumber. The prosecution must establish that the Defendant is lying about his understanding of risk in order to convict.

Matching Mens Rea Requirements with Mistake Claims

Mistake of fact claims generally involve two questions: (1) does the defendant's alleged mistake relate to an element of the offense as to which mens rea is required, and, if so, (2) does the evidence of the defendant's mistake contradict that mens rea? This analytic method simply restates that set out in the previous chapter: first determine what the statute requires for mens rea, then analyze the facts in light of those requirements.

Mistakes and the Difference between Awareness and Negligence Mens Reas

The most common problem in mistake of fact doctrine involves the question of whether the mistake must be honest, or honest *and reasonable*. Using the MPC approach introduced at the outset, the question is whether the statute requires a form of mens rea that requires some degree of actual awareness as to the critical element, or merely negligence. The awareness forms of mens rea—purpose, knowledge, or recklessness—all match up with honest mistakes.[3] That is, if conviction requires proof of a mens rea of purpose, knowledge or recklessness toward element X, then if defendant is honestly mistaken about element X, he cannot be convicted because proof of awareness of X fails.

By contrast, if the defendant can be convicted based on negligence toward X, then an honest mistake about X will not be sufficient. The mistake must also be reasonable.

If element X is strict liability, no mistake of fact is possible with respect to X. The following three examples illustrate.

---

3. Strictly speaking, we do not need to make separate mention of honesty, for honesty is included in the idea of mistake. A person is mistaken when she (honestly) believes that certain facts about a situation are true. If the person is dishonest and lies to us about what she believed, then she was not in fact mistaken. Nevertheless, because there are times when the issue of the reasonableness of a mistake is important, it helps to distinguish between an honest mistake that may be unreasonable and a mistake that is honest *and* reasonable.

Example 1: Dealing in Stolen Property

Amelia sells a $10,000 diamond bracelet to a Brie for $500 cash. When asked by Brie why the price is so low, Amelia responds: "You wouldn't believe me. But believe this: it's worth a whole lot more than $500." When pressed by Brie, Amelia says, "It's better if you don't ask any more questions."

Brie turns out to be an undercover police officer investigating a series of burglaries of expensive homes. The bracelet had been stolen from a house in the city less than three days before the transaction.

Amelia is charged with dealing in stolen property. The relevant statute provides: "Whoever sells or otherwise engages in a transaction for material benefit involving stolen property, knowing it to be stolen, is guilty of a felony."

Amelia tells her defense attorney that she was given the bracelet by an elderly homeless woman who Amelia had helped cross a busy street.

On these facts, will Amelia be convicted?

We begin with the statute's mens rea requirement. The prosecution must prove that Amelia knew that the bracelet was stolen at the time of the transaction. The prosecution will argue that, considered in their entirety, the facts show Amelia's awareness that the bracelet was recently stolen. Amelia clearly knew she was selling it for far less than its market value, and she refused to discuss its provenance. The strength of this proof may persuade Amelia that she will be convicted unless she takes the witness stand to tell her own side of the story.

But will her story, *if believed*, prevent conviction? The answer is yes. According to Amelia she (mistakenly) believed that the rightful owner of the bracelet had given it to her (Amelia) as a reward for a good deed. She believed that she became the rightful owner of the bracelet because of the gift; she did not believe and therefore did not know that the bracelet was stolen. (Of course there is no guarantee in real life that the fact finder will believe Amelia.)

Now we will change the case in order to reveal some important distinctions concerning the reasonableness of mistake.

Assume that Amelia works cleaning an office building. She says that she found the bracelet in trash emptied from the trash containers in the building. She says that she believed someone had just thrown the bracelet away, that the owner did not want it any more. Therefore, she believed she could do with it what she wanted, just as other workers commonly take soda cans out of the trash to sell for recycling.

Does Amelia have a mistake of fact claim under these circumstances?

Again the issue is Amelia's mens rea with respect to the item taken. Again Amelia states she believed she obtained the bracelet lawfully, by recovering abandoned property, and had thereby become its lawful owner and could dispose of it as she wished. Her belief in lawful ownership contradicts the mens rea required for conviction of the charged offense. If she believed that she lawfully obtained the bracelet then obviously she did not believe that her possession was unlawful. But a problem remains. Amelia's belief that such an expensive bracelet was simply thrown away is unreasonable. We would not expect an item so valuable to be disposed of in this way. This may cause many to balk at an acquittal. It doesn't seem right that she should escape responsibility based on such a weak excuse. But as we have seen before, it all depends on what the statute requires for conviction.

Amelia cannot be convicted of this offense unless the prosecution proves that she knew the bracelet was stolen. *If* Amelia sincerely believed that the bracelet was abandoned (just thrown away), then she did not have the requisite awareness that it was stolen. It would not matter that her belief concerning the lawfulness of her possession and ownership was unreasonable. She is not being charged with being negligent as to its stolen status; the mens rea required is knowledge. An honest mistake about lawful possession will suffice for acquittal, even if unreasonable.[4]

So far we have assumed that Amelia is telling the truth about her belief in lawful ownership. In the real world, however, her credibility will be very much at issue. In assessing her credibility we will look to a number of different factors, including the unreasonableness of her story. In general, the more unlikely—the more unreasonable—a version is, the less believable it is. Since a reasonable person would not believe that anyone would simply throw away an item as valuable as this bracelet, we may doubt whether Amelia truly believed that the bracelet was abandoned. The unreasonableness of her story may persuade the fact finder that Amelia is lying about her mistake and conclude that she did know the item was stolen. Of course we could also decide that Amelia is just the sort of person who believes lots of crazy things and therefore even though her account of finding the bracelet in the garbage and believing it was hers seems ridiculous, it might be just the sort of thing that she would believe, meaning she did lack the knowledge required for conviction.

---

4. This isn't to say that there couldn't be an offense of interference with property rights based on a negligence mens rea. It's just that this statute appears aimed at punishing persons who knowingly deal in stolen property.

Finally we consider mistake of fact claims when the critical mens rea is negligence.

Example 2: Sexual Assault

Jennifer, a college freshmen, attends a wild spring break party at Brad's fraternity house. Brad is a sophomore. Both have consumed a considerable amount of alcohol prior to meeting, though Brad, being a large football player, is much less affected than Jennifer. They dance together in a style known as "freak dancing" in which the partners rub sensually up against each other. Several times Jennifer stumbles and Brad has to hold her up. Brad invites Jennifer to his room upstairs to lie down. They go to his room and Jennifer collapses on his bed. When Brad tries to remove Jennifer's blouse, she makes a groaning sound and shakes her head, as if to say no. Nevertheless he undoes his pants and engages in a sexual act by rubbing his genitals against her body. Shortly thereafter Jennifer screams at Brad, apparently disgusted by the results of his sexual act.

Jennifer tells investigators later that she tried everything she could to keep Brad off her in the bedroom, but she was dizzy from alcohol and Brad took advantage of that to "get himself off." Brad tells investigators that by virtue of her whole course of conduct that evening, he believed that Jennifer wanted to have sex with him. He admits that because of intoxication and his own arousal, he may have been mistaken about her degree of sexual interest. He says that she seemed "totally okay" until after it was over.

Brad is charged with sexual assault, an offense which requires: (1) a sexual act (2) committed upon or with a nonconsenting victim and (3) with knowledge, recklessness or negligence as to the victim's nonconsent.

Assume that the facts show that the sexual event occurred without Jennifer's consent. Assume also that Brad is telling the truth that he believed Jennifer did consent. Should Brad be convicted or acquitted of sexual assault?

The issue again is mens rea, here as to the victim's nonconsent. We need to decide whether the facts show that Brad acted with the required mens rea as to Jennifer's nonconsent.

The problem tells us to assume that Brad is telling us the truth about his state of mind: he believed Jennifer consented to the sexual act. As a result, Brad should be acquitted of any offense that requires an awareness mens rea (purpose, knowledge, or recklessness) as to nonconsent. But the *minimum* mens rea for conviction (the lowest level of mens rea that will still suffice for conviction) with respect to nonconsent is negligence. Defendant is guilty if he or she did not know of the victim's nonconsent, but should have. This means that Brad may be convicted even if he was unaware of Jennifer's nonconsent, *if* a reasonable person in his situation would have been aware. To put this in mistake of fact terms, Brad may not claim a mistake of fact as to Jennifer's consent unless his mistake was honest *and* reasonable.

Brad's problem is that his lack of awareness of Jennifer's nonconsent might be deemed unreasonable. The prosecution would contend that a reasonable person—which means a sober individual—would likely have realized that Jennifer was not interested in engaging in sexual interaction with him in the bedroom.

Example 3: Speeding

Ruth is a 75-year-old widow and a careful driver. She tries to obey all the rules of the road. In preparation for a long drive to visit her grandchildren, Ruth takes her one-year-old car into the dealer for service. She asks the nice man at the service counter to check the car's speedometer because she recently received a warning from a police officer for driving too slowly on the highway, even though it seemed to her that all the other cars were going too fast. Two days later when she picks up the car, the service representative tells her that the speedometer has been "brought up to factory specs," meaning it is now working perfectly.

On her subsequent drive to see her grandchildren, Ruth pays close attention to the speedometer and tries to drive just below the speed limit. To her great surprise she is pulled over and given a speeding ticket by a police officer who says she was going five miles above the speed limit. He explains that the jurisdiction has imposed a "zero tolerance" policy on speeding, and assures her that it has nothing to do with budget problems experienced by local government. Ruth is charged under a law which states: "It is an infraction punishable by up to $150 to drive faster than the posted speed limit."

Ruth later discovers that the dealer had calibrated her speedometer incorrectly so that it underestimated her speed. She now comes to you for advice. Surely a broken speedometer—which was not at all her fault—gives her a defense to the speeding charge, doesn't it? A nice old lady like her shouldn't be convicted of anything. Right?

Ruth has a problem here. The infraction has no mens rea term and defines an offense—speeding—that is normally strict liability. The prosecution must prove that Ruth actually was speeding, but not that she was aware of such speeding or even that she should have been aware. Ruth would like to argue that she was honestly and reasonably mistaken about her speed, based on her broken speedometer and the flow of traffic, but she cannot because the offense is strict liability. The bottom line here is simple. With respect to any element that is strict liability, defendants cannot claim excuse based on mistake, however reasonable.

Summing Up—So Far

What we have done so far is to reconcile mistake of fact claims with standard mens rea analysis. In effect we have translated mistake of fact arguments into mens rea arguments. The following chart provides a schematic view of the relationship between mistake of fact and mens rea. On the left side of the chart are the different forms of mens rea that the prosecution may be required to prove for conviction. On the right hand side of the chart are the equivalent mistake of fact claims that will excuse a person from conviction. The point of the chart is to demonstrate how arguments about mens rea may be translated into arguments about mistake of fact and vice versa.

The first level of the chart describes the rules covered in Amelia's stolen property cases. The second level of the chart describes the rules covered in our discussion of Brad's sexual assault case. The third level of the chart describes the rules covered in Ruth's speeding case.

Mens Rea Required for Conviction	Mistake of Fact That Excuses
Purpose, Knowledge, or Recklessness re X	= *any* honest mistake re X excuses
Negligence re X	= honest *and reasonable* mistake re X excuses
Strict liability re X	= *no excuse* for any mistake re X

Mistake of Law

Among the most familiar adages of Anglo-American criminal law is its rule on mistake of law: "Ignorance of the law is no excuse," or in the original legal

Latin: "Ignorantia legis neminem excusat." For all the apparent clarity of this rule, however, the actual doctrine of mistake of law is complex and its operation is often unpredictable. While ignorance of the law is usually no excuse, there are a number of important exceptions. The more accurate statement of law might be: *ignorance or mistake concerning the existence or meaning of the law generally will not excuse, except that ignorance or mistake about law may excuse if it negates a mens rea requirement for the particular offense.* This doesn't exactly roll off the tongue like "ignorance of the law is no excuse," which may help explain why the latter is the rule constantly cited, despite its inaccuracy.

We begin our exploration of mistake of law with a look at why mistake of law issues are difficult for courts. Understanding how mistake of law claims threaten values important to the law and the judiciary helps us understand why outcomes can be unpredictable. We then consider several distinct affirmative defenses relating to mistake of law. Finally we address the heart of mistake of law doctrine, those instances where a defendant's mistake about a matter of specialized legal knowledge may negate a mens rea required for the offense.

Value Clash: Fairness versus Certainty

The law concerning mistake of law is difficult. Here we will find cases involving statutes with very similar wording where courts reach opposite conclusions about whether a defendant's mistake of law matters. The reason for the outcome variation is that mistake of law claims often ask courts to reconcile the irreconcilable. The cases involve two critical but competing legal values: being fair to individual defendants and maintaining the certainty of criminal law generally. The importance of both fairness and certainty mean that no universal rule on mistake of law is possible and that mistake of law issues will be determined according to the relative significance of each policy in the context of a particular offense and defendant's claimed mistake.

Considerations of individual culpability (fairness) generally argue in favor of recognizing a mistake of law claim. If the defendant truly did not understand the wrongfulness of his conduct because of a mistake concerning the law then how does that defendant deserve punishment? Even deterrence may raise questions about liability, for a defendant who tried to do right may still be convicted, which hardly sends a clear deterrent message to either the defendant or the public generally.

On the other hand, recognizing even the most limited mistake of law claim— one based on an honest and reasonable mistake—will diminish the certainty of the criminal law. As we have seen, interpreting the criminal law can be a difficult business under the best of circumstances. If we excuse individuals based on their own mistaken interpretations of criminal law, then we necessarily make the criminal law less certain and its deterrent force weaker. We may also have a hard time catching bad faith claims of mistake of law, those instances where persons lie about their supposed ignorance or mistake.

By comparison, mistake of fact claims tend to be easier to assess. Here jurors and judges, drawing on their own life experience, may be able to assess the credibility of defendants with some degree of reliability. Jurors will use their common sense to determine whether someone like Amelia in the stolen property case discussed earlier, is telling the truth. By contrast, mistake of law claims involve relatively obscure legal rules with which most people have no experience. Remember, such claims involve mistakes about *specialized* legal knowledge. They are not matters of ordinary common sense. And probably no one knows *everything* that the criminal law prohibits.[5] The bottom line is that mistake of law claims seem to present greater risks of erroneous acquittals than do mistake of fact claims.

Last, but not necessarily least, recognizing mistake of law claims requires courts to give up some of their control over legal interpretation. Allowing a defendant an excuse for a mistake about lawfulness seems to give that defendant some authority over the effective reach of the criminal law. No wonder that courts hesitate to recognize such mistakes.

Understanding why mistake of law claims can appear threatening to courts helps us identify some important features of the doctrine. As we will see in our next section, it will initially help us distinguish a mistake of fact from a mistake of law. It will also give us some indicators for when a mistake of law claim is likely to be recognized.

Distinguishing Factual and Legal Mistakes

We have special concerns about mistakes of law because of the way in which such claims threaten the certainty of the criminal law. But this threat only arises when the mistake concerns something about the law that most lay people do not know. This provides the key to distinguishing between mistake of law and fact.

---

5. For example, did you know that it is a federal offense to impersonate a 4-H member or representative for purposes of defrauding? 18 U.S.C. sec. 916. Would you be surprised to learn that anyone who "stamps, prints, places, or inserts any writing in or on any product or box, package, or other container containing a consumer product offered for sale" in California is guilty of a misdemeanor? Calif. Penal Code sec. 640.2 (a). (This California statute was enacted in response to a series of incidents in which race hate literature was placed in items sold at supermarkets.)

Assume we have a statute that prohibits unlawful entry into a motor vehicle: *whoever knowingly and unlawfully breaks and enters the motor vehicle of another is guilty of a criminal offense.* We might think that any mistake claim about the lawfulness of the breaking and entering would constitute a mistake of law claim. But this would be wrong. The following illustrates.

> You attend a concert and return to the parking lot where you parked your car. To your great dismay, you cannot find your car keys. You believe that you have locked them in your car. Because it is late at night, and the neighborhood seems shady, you do not want to wait around for a tow truck or locksmith. You take a rock from the street and use it to smash in one of the side windows and unlock the door. Unfortunately, you then discover that the keys are not inside. Worse, you discover that the car that you have just broken into does not belong to you, though it is the same color, make and model as your own. Worst of all, a police car has just pulled up behind you.
>
> If charged with unlawful entry into a motor vehicle (see definition above), you will seek to avoid conviction with a mistake argument. You made a mistake about whose car it was. But is this mistake about car ownership better categorized as a mistake of law or mistake of fact?

Note that the mistake claim here turns on ordinary facts about identifying the car and therefore its lawful owner. Yes, the question involves ownership, which is ultimately a legal question, but it turns on ordinary facts about ownership. You need no legal training, no legal research to distinguish your car from someone else's. As a result, even though your claimed mistake involves the element of lawfulness (ownership), it should be categorized as a mistake of fact and analyzed according to the principles set out in the first part of this chapter.

With a change in facts, however, we will see that the same statutory element may give rise to a mistake of law claim.

> Again you break into the car by smashing in a window, but in this instance you do so knowing that the car is not yours. Instead you know the car belonged to your business partner who recently fled to another country with assets stolen from your joint business. You have done legal research which suggests that because the car was bought with business assets, you have the right to seize it. It later turns out, unfortunately, that this conclusion is erroneous because of a little-known provision in the jurisdiction's vehicle code which states that, unlike other forms of movable property, vehicles can be seized only with

a court order. This was enacted in the jurisdiction to address certain abuses by repossessors of motor vehicles.[6]

If charged with unlawful entry into the vehicle under the same statute as above, you will want to defend by claiming you made a mistake about the lawfulness of your action. In this case, should your mistake be classified as a mistake of law?

Now the mistake involves legal expertise. Only a person particularly knowledgeable about the law of seizure would know about the need to obtain a court order. Thus the mistake should be categorized as a mistake of law. This does *not* mean that the mistake claim will fail. It just means that the policy concerns raised by mistake of law claims are present here, with the result that courts will be more reluctant to recognize defendant's argument than in the previous case.

Notice that in terms of culpability, the two cases are quite similar. In neither instance have you demonstrated any propensity or inclination toward serious wrongdoing. Nor is there any difference in the statute, or statutory element, involved. The critical difference between the two cases is the extent to which the mistake about lawfulness involves a matter of common or specialized legal knowledge.

Affirmative Defenses Relating to Legal Mistakes: Erroneous Official Statements of Law and Inadequate Publication

Like mistake of fact claims, most mistake of law claims are arguments about mens rea. But before we explore mistake of law mens rea arguments, we need to distinguish a small subset of mistake of law claims that constitute affirmative defenses. These can be grouped under two headings: (1) reasonable reliance on an official statement of law later changed or deemed invalid and (2) inadequate publication of law. Neither is raised very often.

Both of these doctrines are affirmative defenses because they operate independent of the essential elements of any criminal offense. As a result, the defendant will bear at least the initial burden of producing credible evidence on the defense in order for it to be considered in the case.

---

6. This should not be taken to describe current law. The example is a hypothetical to illustrate the kind of legal knowledge we might describe as specialized.

Reasonable Reliance on Erroneous Official Statements of Law

A number of jurisdictions permit mistake of law claims, regardless of the nature of the criminal charge, when the defendant's ignorance of the criminal law is based on a previous, erroneous statement of law by a legally authoritative institution or official. This may occur when a court interprets a statute in a way later reversed by another court. It may occur when the defendant relies on a statute later declared unconstitutional. Or it can occur when a public official with special authority to give opinions about the law, such as the jurisdiction's Attorney General, gives a formal legal opinion that is later changed or overruled. This defense is based on the principle that citizens should be able to rely on statements of the law by an authoritative source, delivered in an authoritative manner. When such statements prove erroneous, the practical effect is that the law has changed, and it would be fundamentally unfair to expect a defendant to predict that change.

This form of affirmative defense is quite narrow and does not include many forms of otherwise reasonable efforts to figure out what criminal law prohibits and does not. Most importantly, an individual may *not* rely on the advice of a private attorney to bar a criminal prosecution. The law's concern here is pragmatic, that attorneys by virtue of ignorance, lack of expertise in the area, or self-interest (telling clients what they wish to hear makes clients more willing to pay fees) may provide erroneous advice. Lawmakers also worry that such a defense would encourage persons to fabricate mistake claims, claims which would be difficult for fact finders to evaluate. Who knows what the attorney actually told her client? Perhaps the client heard only what he wanted to hear.

For related reasons, citizens cannot cite the advice of a police officer as the basis for this affirmative defense. Nor may the defendant claim that she reasonably read the criminal statute or other law in a particular way that a subsequent court found erroneous.

The affirmative defense of reasonable reliance on an official statement of law must not be confused with the mens rea-mistake of law doctrine discussed below. As we will see, *if* lawfulness is an element of the offense to which mens rea applies and *if* the court holds that this mens rea element extends to matters involving legal expertise, then arguments that would be rejected under an affirmative defense may be accepted as a negation of mens rea. For example, the previous example of legal mistake about seizure of a car clearly would not fit the affirmative defense discussed here, but it might support a mens rea argument of the sort discussed further below. (In short, you might argue that you did not "knowingly and unlawfully" break and enter the vehicle.)

Inadequate Publication

Some jurisdictions also provide an affirmative defense for the jurisdiction's failure to adequately publish the criminal prohibition. Thus, if a legislature or other proper body enacts a criminal ordinance but does not promulgate it in the authorized fashion, so that it is not available to citizens in the ordinary way, then later prosecutions may be barred by this defense. No one should be convicted for a secret crime.

Mens Rea and Mistake of Law

A defendant's best chance at a mistake of law excuse usually depends on mens rea. Such claims may be recognized when the statute includes mens rea as to lawfulness. We can separate these claims according to types of mens rea, whether the mens rea concerning lawfulness involves actual awareness (purpose, knowledge, recklessness) or negligence. If the lawfulness element is strict liability—or the offense as a whole is strict liability—then there will be no excuse for mistakes about lawfulness.

Mens rea as to some aspect of lawfulness is usually a prerequisite to a successful mistake of law claim. But it is not sufficient. Courts may interpret the lawfulness mens rea requirement broadly, to include mistakes about specialized legal knowledge, i.e. mistake of law, but in other instances they may construe the mens rea requirement narrowly, to encompass only certain underlying facts or wrongfulness generally, but not including the specialized legal knowledge that defendant claims to lack.

As with mistake of fact, everything turns on statutory interpretation, and thus focuses on the details of particular offense definitions.

Example 1: Theft and Claim of Right

Jake rents a house for a year. During the course of the year, at his own expense and with the approval of the landlord, he removes the old carpet in the dining room and installs a hardwood floor over the original plywood sub-floor. At the end of the year's lease, the landlord decides to sell the house. Upset at losing the rental, Jake decides to take his flooring with him to use at his next residence. He pulls it up. When the landlord discovers what Jake has done, she goes to the police, saying that Jake deliberately and criminally stole the flooring from the house. Based on this report, Jake is arrested.

When Jake speaks with his court appointed attorney, Jake says he is not guilty because he had permission to put the flooring in and he paid for it, so it was his to remove if he wished. His attorney informs Jake that under well-established but not especially well known principles of property law, once the hardwood floor was installed, it became a fixture of the house. Legally the flooring became part of the structure and therefore the property of the landlord.

Jake is charged with theft of property, that he "knowingly and unlawfully took property belonging to another, with intent to deprive the owner thereof permanently." Can Jake win an acquittal based on his mistake of law?

First, notice that this is a mistake of law claim because Jake's mistake concerns a rule of property law unknown to most people.

Jake has in fact taken property belonging to another: by virtue of the law relating to fixtures, the flooring that he took was the property of the landlord. Jake had no lawful reason for the taking, making it unlawful. Jake plans to use the flooring himself so he might be said to have acted with the purpose to permanently deprive the landlord of the flooring. The real question concerns whether there is any mens rea with respect to the element of "belonging to another?"

The first step to recognizing Jake's mistake of law claim turns on whether the "knowingly" mens rea that appears early in the statute modifies the "property of another" element that appears later. (We could also try to see if knowingly modifies unlawfully, but for purposes of simplicity we will focus on the "property of another" element.) Knowing probably should apply to property of another, because a taking only starts to look like stealing when the taker *knows* that the property belongs to another. Accidentally taking the property of another does not sound like stealing.

But it won't be enough for Jake to establish that "knowing" modifies "property of another." Jake's mistake involves *specialized* legal knowledge about property law. It is a mistake of law claim. Courts are often reluctant to recognize such claims for reasons set out earlier, and one way of doing so is to limit the reach of mens rea as to any lawfulness requirement. Here, for example, a court might say that to be convicted a defendant must know the basic facts relevant to ownership but not all the relevant details of property law. This reading would make Jake guilty of stealing, which doesn't seem right, because given his mistake he had no idea that his taking was wrongful, which is normally a prerequisite to theft.

Also in Jake's favor here, is that his mistake involves property law. This makes his argument less threatening to the certainty of the criminal law. Permitting Jake to make this claim will hardly open the floodgates to theft defendants conjuring up all sorts of excuses concerning the law of fixtures or other obscure parts of property law.

The bottom line is that Jake's mistake of law should be recognized. If he sincerely believed, due to ignorance of the law of fixtures, that he was the rightful owner of the flooring, then he should not be convicted of this offense.

Note that although Jake's mistake may in this instance be reasonable, reasonableness is not legally required. Under this statute, the prosecution must prove that Jake *knew* that the flooring belonged to the landlord when he took out. Even if we judge that Jake's belief that he owned the flooring was unreasonable, if his belief was sincere, the prosecution's proof of mens rea will fail.

Example 2: Tax Offenses

Courts and commentators sometimes divide criminal offenses into two general categories: malum prohibitum and malum in se. Malum in se offenses are those that are wrong in themselves, that is, those whose wrongdoing is morally obvious. Such offenses range from murder to burglary to rape. No one in our society needs to peruse the criminal code to understand that such conduct is a crime because the violation of social norms is so basic. By contrast, malum prohibitum (literally, prohibited wrong) offenses are entirely legislative creations. Their wrongs may not otherwise be obvious. A wide range of modern regulatory offenses fall under this category, involving everything from tax to environmental offenses.

By their nature, prosecutions for malum prohibitum offenses are particularly likely to inspire mistake of law claims. Defendants in malum prohibitum cases can claim, more plausibly than with most crimes, that they were not aware of the unlawfulness of their conduct. On the one hand, because the prohibited conduct does not provide the same notice of serious wrongdoing as in malum in se offenses, recognizing mistake of law here may be important to proving actual culpability. On the other hand, recognizing such claims for malum prohibitum offenses also presents greater threats to the certainty of the criminal law than for other crimes.

An interesting example of how courts have resolved this conflict comes in the area of federal tax crimes.

> Shirley has been a truck driver for ten years. For seven of those years she filed federal income tax returns. For the last three years she has not filed returns, even though neither her employment status nor her income has significantly changed. She has attended a number of tax protest meetings where she heard that if she declares herself a "free and independent citizen," she will no longer owe any obligations to the federal government. Shirley is convinced and stops filing annual income tax forms.

Shirley is charged with willful failure to file federal income tax returns. During pretrial proceedings the court rules that Shirley has a legal obligation to file returns; the court deems "specious at best" Shirley's legal arguments to the contrary.

Can Shirley claim a mistake of law based on her own sincere but erroneous interpretation of her legal obligation to file an income tax return?

At first glance, Shirley's case seems most unpromising. She is claiming a mistake about the meaning of the criminal statute under which she is charged, an argument that not only threatens the interpretive role of the criminal court but directly threatens the certainty of criminal law in this area. Given that the tax code is complex and widely misunderstood, this kind of mistake claim would seem especially threatening to the system. Many tax defendants might make similar claims, and these would be hard for a fact finder to evaluate. Finally, Shirley's purported mistake seems highly unreasonable. After all, the only certain things in life are death and taxes, right?

On the other hand, the statute does contain a mens rea element which may apply to an aspect of lawfulness: the legal obligation to file a return. The statute requires that the defendant "willfully" fail to file. The prosecution would likely argue that to satisfy this mens rea requirement, it is sufficient to show that Shirley knew that wage earning citizens, based on their annual income, are required to file income tax forms and that Shirley knew her own annual income. The prosecution would argue that it need not prove that Shirley understood the specifics of federal income tax law as applied to her. Shirley will respond that the statutory language requires that she specifically understand her obligation to file, otherwise her decision not to do so could not be deemed a "willful" one.

Federal courts have generally sided with defendants like Shirley in interpreting such statutes. The prosecution must prove beyond a reasonable doubt that Shirley knew that she was legally obliged to file a federal income tax return.[7] Therefore, like Jake in the earlier case, Shirley may claim an honest, though unreasonable mistake of law as a defense to the criminal charge. If she truly believed what she heard at the tax protester meetings, she could not be convicted of the criminal offense because under these facts she was not actually aware that she violated any tax obligation. Federal courts have read criminal statutes in this way because of indications that Congress did not in-

---

7. Cheek v. United States, 498 U.S. 192 (1991).

tend to criminally punish citizens for tax violations unless they demonstrate clear awareness of their own wrongdoing, an awareness that in the tax field (because malum prohibitum) extends to all critical aspects of unlawfulness including specialized knowledge of tax obligations.

Example 3: Other Regulatory Offenses

While courts often recognize mistake of law claims in tax offenses and other financial crimes, they have been less sympathetic to legal mistake claims involving other kinds of regulatory crimes. Even where the wording of the criminal statute suggests mens rea as to unlawfulness, the mens rea requirement may be narrowly interpreted to exclude claims of mistake of law.

> Congress has enacted a statute which makes it a crime to know-ingly violate any regulation of the Interstate Commerce Commission. Among the regulations of the Interstate Commerce Commission is a rule that requires that shippers of hazardous materials to specifically describe the material in shipping papers. Defendant is the shipping agent for a company involved in the shipping of hazardous materials—various dangerous acids—which are not specifically mentioned on the company's shipping papers. The shipping agent is charged with a criminal violation. As part of his defense, the shipping agent argues that the prosecution must prove defendant's knowledge of the regulation violated. The defendant testifies that because he was inadequately trained by his company, he was unaware of the relevant regulation.
>
> Should the Defendant's claimed mistake of law be recognized as a valid defense to this prosecution?

Supporting Defendant's claim here is the mens rea language of the statute. We have a mens rea term—knowingly—that both by virtue of linguistics and the essential wrong principle seems to apply to the "regulation of the Interstate Commerce Commission" element. Because the offense is based on what are probably fairly technical regulations, it appears to be a malum prohibitum offense and as such we may need proof of knowledge of illegality to be assured that the defendant is culpable of wrongdoing. Otherwise we might end up convicting of a federal offense someone who honestly believed that his conduct was lawful.

On the other hand, accepting an expansive interpretation of knowingly in this statute, one that would encompass a full mistake of law argument, would require the prosecution to prove beyond a reasonable doubt that every defendant prosecuted was personally aware of the existence, meaning and application of the particular regulation the defendant is charged with violating. This could be difficult, and significantly undercut the criminal law as a deterrent force in interstate transportation.

Another important consideration here is the extent to which even a limited reading of knowingly in the statute provides proof of defendant's culpability. In this case, the prosecution would have to prove knowledge of the transportation of particular acids, widely known to be dangerous. Any person who is engaged in the transportation of such materials should know that they are dangerous and that they are subject to significant state and federal regulation. Therefore, we might judge that any person engaged in this trade has a special duty to learn about and follow applicable regulations. If true, this tends to undercut one of the more powerful arguments for recognizing mistake of law, that it is necessary to prevent the conviction of the morally innocent.

The bottom line is that in a similar case (though one brought against a company rather than a single employee) the Supreme Court held that the prosecution was required to prove that defendant knew that it was transporting certain acids and that they were not listed on the shipping papers as particular hazardous materials, but not that the defendant knew that such transportation violated an ICC regulation.[8] Thus the Court rejected defendant's mistake of law claim.

Example 4: Offenses without Mens Rea

John is a corrections officer—a guard—at a federal prison. He likes law enforcement work and wants to carry a handgun with him when off-duty, as many police officers do. He goes to the trouble of looking up the state law on carrying a concealed weapon. The law makes it a crime for anyone to carry a concealed weapon without a license; peace officers are exempt from this requirement, however.

Under state law a peace officer includes any officer in a "state correctional facility or of any penal correctional institution." John figures that because he is a corrections officer in a federal penal institution, he falls under the "or of any penal correctional institution" provision.

---

8. United States v. International Minerals & Chemical Corp., 402 U.S. 558 (1971). There was a dissent in the case by Justice Stewart, joined in by two other justices. Id. at 565–69.

The weapons charge is a strict liability offense; as long as the individual knows about the weapon, no knowledge or other mens rea is required as to the licensing provision.

John gets in a fight at a nightclub which leads to the discovery of his weapon and being charged in state court with carrying a concealed weapon without a license. The state court determines, after considerable debate, that the catch-all provision in the statute does *not* apply to federal prison guards. Now John argues that he made a good faith and reasonable effort to determine the legality of his conduct by reading the relevant criminal statute. Will John's mistake of law claim be recognized?

This example, based loosely on a New York case, presents a troubling mistake of law claim. In defendant's favor, his reading of the statute was facially reasonable and his particular mistake is not likely to be repeated. But the essence of his claim—that he misunderstood the meaning of the criminal law under which he is charged—directly threatens the certainty of the criminal law and the court's powers of legal interpretation. Worst of all for the defendant, the offense is strict liability. There is no mens rea that can be attached to a lawfulness element. Therefore there can be no mens rea-mistake of law claim.

The bottom line here is the same as it was with respect to mistake of fact claims. If the defendant is mistaken about an element of the offense which is strict liability, the mistake is irrelevant. The law does not excuse for any mistakes with respect to strict liability elements.

For a defendant like this correctional officer, the only possibility is to argue an affirmative defense of mistake of law under the official statement rule, but as we have seen this will generally only apply if there was a previously issued official statement of law that was subsequently changed.[9]

---

9. The facts of this case are roughly similar—but should not be taken to be identical to those of People v. Marrero, 507 N.E. 2d 1068 (NY 1987).

INTRODUCTION TO PART THREE

CRIMES OF VIOLENCE: HOMICIDE AND RAPE

Now we turn to the definitions of basic crimes of violence, specifically: murder, manslaughter, and rape. By in-depth exploration of these offenses we gain a deeper understanding of essential element analysis. These particular offenses have been selected both because of their importance to our general conception of criminal law and their doctrinal richness. One who masters these crimes should have the analytic tools to understand most others.

Murder ranks as the most serious crime in American criminal law and convictions normally lead to severe sentences. These qualities alone call for special attention. The law of murder and manslaughter is also of interest because of its legal and moral ambition. Here we find an elaborate hierarchy of offenses according to mens rea. In homicide we find more different forms of mens rea than in any other criminal offense. Several are unique to homicide.

Rape merits attention both because recognizing its wrong is central to civilized society and because its reconceptualization over the last 30 years presents some important questions about culpability. Modern rape law challenges the assumption that actual awareness is critical to criminal culpability. It also presents problems in interpretation, as traditional doctrinal terms and concepts must be applied in light of modern understandings of sexual violence.

Criteria for Crimes

Before we take up the definitions of particular crimes of violence, we might ask a more general question: What does a good criminal statute look like? What are the criteria for judging offense definitions as a matter of both policy and practice?

In essence, we want rules of criminal law that guide decision-makers to make just decisions in all cases. No small task. I suggest four basic criteria: (1) that rules be consistent with principles of justice; (2) that they be susceptible of universal and reliable application; (3) that they be

---

sensitive to important factual variations; and (4) that they produce publicly acceptable results. Unfortunately, these values are often in tension with each other, and sometimes in outright conflict.

First, the rules of criminal law should be consistent with principles of justice, meaning that they should be drawn from and be informed by basic theories of criminal responsibility. Academics usually take this to mean that criminal law should be the product of a particular theory of punishment. But because in a democracy criminal law must reflect the values of many, reaching consensus on a single theory will likely prove impossible. Indeed the effort to impose a single concept may be counterproductive, for criminal justice is famous for converting high ideals into unanticipated, unintended results. Nevertheless, principles matter here. The worst of criminal law is driven by a desire for a particular result, without concern for larger principle.

Second, the rules of criminal law should be consistent across all cases. This has two aspects: equality and reliability. As to equality, criminal law rules in one area should follow the same principles of responsibility that guide other areas. An excuse recognized for white-collar offenders should also be recognized for shoplifters and car thieves, for example. In addition, criminal rules should provide sufficient criteria for decisions to ensure that individual case decisions are not biased. Purely discretionary judgments are susceptible to the human tendency to sympathize—or not—according to personal similarities between decision maker and defendants or victims. This generally argues in favor of clear, specific rules, because such rules give us criteria for comparing outcomes of legally similar cases. Simply stated rules are also needed for reliable application. We want decision makers to decide based on legally approved factors. Given that in the American criminal system, lay persons are critical decision makers, the rules must be stated in terms comprehensible to nonlawyers.

Third, criminal law must be fact-sensitive. The complexity of human behavior is such that it is impossible to create rules that anticipate every variation in criminal cases. Thus we must grant decision makers discretion, allowing them to take into account the particulars of the case. Of course too much discretion will violate our second norm. No one said this would be easy.

Fourth, criminal law must produce results that meet public approval. In the United States, criminal law must not only have democratic origins, but must maintain public respect over time. A rule of law that comports with a particular theory of punishment will not survive if it produces results that consistently violate the electorate's sense of justice. The rule will lose its power to guide decisions—decision makers will ignore the rule, at least sometimes—or the rule will be changed.

CHAPTER 9

PURPOSE TO KILL MURDER

Murder is the most basic crime of all, and probably the most ancient. It would also seem to be one of the easiest to define. Yet murder and its lesser partner in crime, manslaughter, are among the most complex offenses in Anglo American law.

American jurisdictions generally distinguish between at least two kinds of criminal homicide: murder and manslaughter. Within each of these categories lie a number of subcategories distinguished by different forms of mens rea. Many rest on doctrines that date back centuries, with the richness and ambiguity that such a long legal history usually brings. Adding to analytic interest, the legal stakes for proper categorization of homicide are very high. Whether the defendant is guilty of murder or manslaughter, and what kind of murder or manslaughter, can make the difference between life and death, or more commonly, between a life sentence and a shorter one.

The law of murder and manslaughter raises questions of both moral responsibility and legal process. What criteria should we use to grade the severity of criminal homicides? How much of this grading should be done by rule and how much should be left to the discretion of decision makers, according to the facts of each case?

Criminal homicides divide into three large groups according to the core mens rea involved: (1) intentional killings, i.e. those involving purpose to kill; (2) unintentional killings, those involving a reckless or negligent mens rea; and (3) felony murder and associated doctrines, in which the commission of certain other crimes cause death. This chapter focuses on a subset of intentional killings: murder based on proof of purpose to kill. The following chapter will cover another form of intentional killing: voluntary manslaughter based on provocation. Chapter 11 covers unintentional killings and Chapter 12 covers felony murder and associated doctrines.

Before proceeding, I should explain why the discussion of murder here organizes according to mens rea and not degree of murder. Within the category of murder, jurisdictions commonly distinguish between first and second and sometimes third degrees. These degrees set different levels of punishment, making them very important in practice. But to understand how murder law works, we need to understand differences in mens rea forms. To illustrate, in many states, first-degree murder may be based on either premeditated murder or felony murder. Premeditated murder involves premeditation and purpose to kill; felony murder requires proof of a death caused in the commission of a designated felony such as rape or robbery; the only mens rea required is for the underlying felony. The proof required for each form of first-degree murder is therefore quite different.

The first step to determining the degree of murder is determining what kind of murder might be charged, according to mens rea.

A Brief History of Purpose to Kill Murder

We need a little history to understand the modern law of murder. At English common law, murder was a killing committed with malice aforethought and was always a capital offense. Defendants convicted of murder were hung unless pardoned by the king. The origins and exact meaning of malice aforethought, or malice prepense as it was also called, are today somewhat murky. Legal historians suggest that its original meaning probably included a notion that the killing was intentional and deliberate, involving some degree of calculation. This contrasted with voluntary manslaughter, in which the defendant's homicide was more spontaneous and impassioned.[1]

One of the first tasks of the new American states after the founding of the United States was to enact new criminal codes. The new American crimes were largely based on English law, but many legislators wanted to reform the "sanguinary" (bloody) nature of English crimes and punishments. In the field of murder, the most influential changes were undertaken by the Pennsylvania legislature in 1794, which created two degrees of murder. First-degree murders were punishable by death; second-degree murders were not. The Pennsylvania legislation designated premeditated murder as one form of first-degree murder. Many states followed Pennsylvania's lead and by the middle of the 19th-century most states had placed premeditated murder at the top of their hierarchy of criminal offenses.

The next stage of premeditation's history concerns its judicial interpretation. From early in the 19th-century until the present day, courts have strug-

---

1. Malice aforethought gained a broader meaning over time, however, to encompass other killings, including death caused in the course of certain felonies (felony murder) and a killing caused by extreme recklessness (depraved toward murder). For more on malice, see Resisting the Siren Call of Malice below.

gled with the relationship between premeditation and purpose to kill. Some courts have interpreted premeditation strictly, as a requirement clearly *independent* of purpose to kill. In such jurisdictions, premeditation requires proof that the defendant considered the moral consequences of homicide prior to its commission. In other jurisdictions, appellate courts interpret premeditation broadly, meaning that they grant juries significant discretion in deciding premeditation as long as purpose to kill is clear.

Over the last generation, premeditation has become a somewhat less important part of murder doctrine. Some jurisdictions have eliminated it entirely. In most states, premeditation survives as one form of first-degree murder, but it no longer plays the critical role in distinguishing between capital and noncapital offenses. In reaction to a series of United States Supreme Court constitutional decisions in the 1970s, many American states enacted capital punishment schemes for murder in which specific aggravating facts must be proven in addition to other requirements of murder to qualify an offense for the death penalty. Such aggravating facts may include particular motives, the number or identity of victims, or other special harms. Even with these changes, however, premeditation can still make a major difference in penalty by distinguishing between first and second degree murder.

Resisting the Siren Call of Malice

In many U.S. jurisdictions, murder is still formally defined as a "killing with malice aforethought." As a result, courts in many jurisdictions consider the presence or absence of malice as critical to distinguishing murder and manslaughter (manslaughter being a killing without malice aforethought.) Malice itself is subdivided into express and implied forms. Express malice usually refers to those forms of murder mens rea based on purpose to kill, while implied malice refers to the recklessness and indifference required for depraved heart murder; it may also encompass felony murder.

There are few more venerable phrases in Anglo-American jurisprudence than malice aforethought. But longevity, as Oliver Wendell Holmes noted long ago, is an insufficient justification for any rule of law. In the contemporary context, talk of malice aforethought is mostly unhelpful, either just introducing the main issue of mens rea, or suggesting something not actually at issue.

In contemporary law, malice aforethought is synonymous with murder: it represents a name for all the forms of mens rea sufficient for murder. But since these different forms of murder mens rea do all the real work of distinguishing murder and manslaughter, and different types of murder, it makes more sense to focus on these forms rather than worrying about malice aforethought.

The phrase itself can be misleading. It does not require malevolence or evil intent toward the victim; it includes unintentional killings, as in depraved heart murder covered in Chapter 11. Nor does it require "aforethought" in the sense of premeditation. Premeditated murders are included within its capacious reach, but so are forms of murder that involve no pre-calculation, no afore-thought.

There has been at least one occasion in recent years where malice of forethought mattered though. It seems to have influenced a pair of U.S. Supreme Court decisions on the burden of proof in murder and manslaughter.[2]

The bottom line is that while malice aforethought persists as a part of murder law in many jurisdictions, the careful student will use the phrase sparingly—or not at all. Most of the time, we will do better without it.

Premeditated Murder: Purpose to Kill and Premeditation

The original language of the Pennsylvania murder statute is found in many American statutes to this day: "all murder, which shall be perpetrated by means of poison, or by lying in wait, or by any other kind of willful, deliberate, and premeditated killing ... shall be murder in the first-degree."[3] Most legal attention focuses on the requirement that the killing be "willful, deliberate, and premeditated." Cases of administration of poison or murder by lying in wait are not that common, although they do provide good examples of what early legislators viewed as premeditated killings.

The statutory premeditation language appears to set out three distinct mens rea elements: willful, deliberate, and premeditated, but in practice there are but two: purpose to kill and premeditation.

"Willful" is a common law mens rea term that in this context probably stands for purpose to kill. I say probably because courts rarely address the word specifically in their considerations of premeditated murder mens rea. Instead judges often speak of the "specific intent" required, by which they mean purpose to kill here.

---

2. See Mullaney v. Wilbur, 421 U.S. 684 (1975); Patterson v. New York, 432 U.S. 197 (1977). For more on burden of proof see Chapter 4.

3. E.g., Cal. Pen. Code sec 189.

The word "deliberate" can have several different meanings. It may be a synonym for purposeful, as in purpose to kill, in which case we would do better to simply speak of purpose to kill. Or it may refer to deliberation, referring to defendant's contemplation of homicide, in which case it is a synonym for premeditation. As a result, I think it simpler and clearer to speak of just two forms of mens rea: (1) purpose to kill and (2) premeditation.

Purpose to Kill

In jurisdictions that recognize premeditated murder, a prerequisite for conviction is that the offender have acted with purpose to kill, that is, with the conscious object to end the life of the victim. This is in addition to any requirement concerning premeditation.

It makes sense to begin the analysis of premeditated murder with purpose to kill for a number of reasons. Of the two mens rea forms, purpose to kill is usually easier to resolve. If purpose to kill is lacking, we can skip premeditation analysis entirely and move to unintentional forms of homicide. Finally, by taking up purpose to kill first, we will see more clearly the relationship between premeditation and purpose to kill.

As a legal concept, purpose to kill is straightforward. Did the defendant aim to end the life of the victim? Was the death intentional or did the offender mean only to hurt or scare the victim? Or perhaps the defendant intended no harm at all, and the injury was entirely accidental. In determining purpose to kill, the main challenges involve evidence and articulation. What facts demonstrate that the defendant did—or did not—act with purpose to kill? Often we can infer a purpose to kill from the nature of the fatal assault and the dispute which preceded it.

> Stephen is an angry young man with reputation for settling disputes violently. He is especially touchy when behind the wheel of his large SUV. When another vehicle cuts him off in traffic, Stephen gives the other Driver the finger and forces the Driver's car off the road. Stephen jumps out of his SUV and screams profanities at the Driver. The Driver responds with his own insults.
>
> Stephen pulls out a gun from his waistband and fires six shots at the Driver, striking him twice in the head and four times in the torso. The Driver dies before medical assistance can arrive. Did Stephen act with purpose to kill?

This is not a hard case with respect to this mens rea. The circumstances indicate that Stephen was very angry with the Driver because of the incident on the road and after expressing his feelings in gestures and words, and being further infuriated by the Driver's responsive insults, Stephen expressed his rage in ultimate violence, using a deadly weapon in a deadly fashion. He shot at vital areas of the Driver's body—head and torso—in order to accomplish maximum damage and therefore to kill. Once Stephen began shooting, all of the evidence suggests that it was his conscious object to end the life of the (in his view) offending Driver.

Tobias is a brooding, even sullen 17-year-old who rarely responds directly to the harsh criticisms and taunts of his Father, but feels them deeply nevertheless. When on a family trip the car suffers a flat tire, the Father orders Tobias to change it, even though Tobias is the least mechanically adept member of the family. As Tobias tries to figure out how to use the tire iron to loosen the wheel nuts, Father calls him hopeless idiot, a wimp and a druggie. (Tobias occasionally smokes marijuana.)

Father turns away, laughing. Tobias stands up with the tire iron in his hand. With a baseball swing, Tobias strikes Father with the tire iron once in the back of the head. Father drops to the ground, unconscious. Within a day Father is dead of his head injury. Did Tobias act with purpose to kill?

This is a harder case. Arguing that Tobias acted with purpose to kill, we might note that he intentionally used a heavy club, the tire iron, against a vital organ, the head. Given the history between Tobias and Father, and Father's taunts, it may be that Tobias was so angry that he wished to kill Father, and chose an efficient method to do so. But the defense can raise many questions here. Did Tobias understand the dangerousness of his action? The defense might argue that he meant only to scare or hurt his father, but that with a single, unlucky blow—remember Tobias's apparent lack of physical skills—there is no proof beyond a reasonable doubt of a conscious object to kill.

Assuming we have established purpose to kill, the next stage in the analysis of premeditated murder is: premeditation itself.

The Weight of Homicide Cases

All practice of law has its moral hazards, ways in which the work may make the practitioner less morally aware or concerned. The same is true of the study of law.

A moral hazard of studying criminal law is becoming casual about the pain of criminal cases, especially homicides.

Homicide cases are an apparently endless source of entertainment in our society. Where would the Law and Orders, the CSI's, the murder mystery novel or even the local news be without homicides? Homicide may even be featured in first year law school classes partly because of its entertainment value. Homicides are inherently dramatic. They catch and keep our interest, becoming colorful stories that we discuss and debate. But every homicide has its own moral weight that should be respected.

The effects of a homicide are hard to overestimate. It's not just the life suddenly ended. A tear is made in the social fabric that will have effects on others that last not just for weeks or months, but years and even generations. The burden that sudden violence imposes can crush the spirit of survivors. On some level we all know that. It's why observers try to tame homicide through story, why we hear so much professional talk of "closure," though almost never from those who are most affected.

So this is just a reminder. Most of the examples used in this book are fictional, but the decided cases on which homicide law is based are quite real. They're not just stories.

Premeditation

While the statutory language setting out the definition of premeditated murder is essentially the same from jurisdiction to jurisdiction, the meaning of these words can vary significantly according to judicial interpretation. Why? Why do appellate courts in different states read the same language in such different ways? The answer has to do with, among other things, disagreements about what makes one homicide more severe than another, and the relative value of jury discretion in this context.

Premeditation is supposed to distinguish the very worst murders from other murders. The idea is that well considered, cold-blooded killings represent a more heinous moral choice and signify a more dangerous offender, than do other killings. The hired hit man and serial killer present classic examples. Appellate courts are well aware though, that heinousness may not always track reflection. Some heinous killings are committed almost spontaneously. Courts desiring to include such killings within the worst form of murder may want to read premeditation broadly. (For more on this see the sidebar on The Worst of the Worst.)

Also implicated in premeditation's definition is the question of jury guidance. Courts that believe that juries generally can be trusted to decide offense severity based on the particular facts presented are more likely to leave the nuances of premeditation to jury discretion. Such judges may believe juries better situated to make the severity assessment on a case-by-case basis rather than try to capture its complexities in a single rule. Other courts worry that without clear legal direction, juries may fall victim to bias, especially unconscious bias. Jurors may judge certain defendants more harshly than others based on improper considerations such as the race or gender of the defendant or victim. Such courts are likely to prefer strict rules for premeditation, whose application appellate courts can then review.

The overall statutory scheme of murder must be considered as well. In many jurisdictions, in cases where purpose to kill is evident, the difference between a first and second-degree murder conviction will depend on proof of premeditation. This indicates that the legislature meant premeditation to be the deciding factor, which indicates that it must mean something different than purpose to kill. This favors what we will call a *strict* interpretation of premeditation because of the insistence that premeditation represent a rule independent of purpose to kill.

The Strict Approach: Proof of Reflection

Courts that take a strict view of premeditation understand it as the defendant's *pre*-meditation or thinking about killing prior to the actual commission of the deed.[4] Just as the most important decisions in life are generally the product of careful thought over time, involving the deliberate weighing of advantages and disadvantages, so premeditation suggests that the very worst decisions (most culpable, most dangerous) are those that result from calculation or reflection. Where the person has taken the time and care to weigh the consequences of killing but nevertheless proceeds with the deed, the person demonstrates the highest degree of moral culpability and threat. As a shorthand, we may think of this kind of premeditation as assessing the defendant's degree of internal calculation or *reflection* on the act of homicide.

A significant problem with the strict approach to premeditation is that it seeks to assess an internal mental process. The law distinguishes killings ac-

---

4. E.g., State v. Guthrie, 461 S.E.2d 163 (W.Va. 1995); People v. Bingham, 699 P.2d 262 (Wash. App. 1985); People v Anderson, 447 P.2d 942 (Cal. 1968).

cording to what the defendant considered prior to acting. Unlike most forms of mens rea, this test does suggest the need for mind reading. To avoid demanding the impossible of prosecutors and decision makers, courts have suggested particular markers of premeditation. These fall into three general categories: timing/planning, relationship/motive and the manner of killing/coolness of defendant's action.

Timing/Planning

One indicator of premeditation is a significant gap in time between an initial decision to kill and the actual killing. This lapse in time tends to indicate a period of reflection or calculation about killing. A number of ambiguities lurk here, however. Initially, we have the problem of determining when an individual might first have contemplated killing. Sometimes there is a particular precipitating event which may start the reflection "clock," but in many cases a decision to kill, like other decisions, is impossible to time precisely. Even if we know the exact chronology of events, a gap in time between initial thought and action does not necessarily show that the intervening time was used for homicidal reflection. About the most that we can say with respect to timing is that the more time that elapsed between a decision to kill and the killing, the more that premeditation is indicated. The reverse will also be true.

A much stronger indication of premeditation, indeed, an activity virtually synonymous with premeditation, is homicidal planning. Recall the two specific examples of premeditated murder included in the original Pennsylvania statute: administration of poison and lying in wait. Both methods of homicide require planning. Planning is a form of calculation and reflection on the homicide and provides strong evidence that the defendant weighed the consequences of the deed.[5]

Relationship/Motive

The most misunderstood premeditation factor is the assessment of motive according to the prior relationship between killer and victim. Again keep in mind our object: determining whether the defendant reflected on homicide prior to killing. Analyzing the prior relationship between killer and victim pro-

---

5. Planning also involves observable activity such as the purchase of a weapon, scouting of a location for attack, or preparations for cover-up and escape. Concrete evidence of planning thus obviates the need for decision makers to make difficult inferences about internal mental processes.

vides potential insight into motive which in turn may tell us about homicidal reflection.

Here is the key point: some motives to kill support reflection, but other motives to kill do not. Establishing that the defendant had a motive to kill is *never enough by itself*; all purposeful homicides have a motive, however senseless or trivial it may seem to others. We need to see what the defendant's particular motive says about reflectiveness.

Killing for money is a motive that supports reflection about homicide because it suggests a cold-blooded, well considered homicidal decision. By contrast, killing to avenge an immediate insult to honor is a motive generally inconsistent with prior reflection on homicide; it suggests a hot blooded, impulsive, poorly considered action, one that is not premeditated.

Manner of Killing/Coolness of Defendant

How the offender kills may also speak to reflectiveness. The sniper's single fatal shot to the head or heart indicates planning and therefore premeditation. It is also indicative of coolness in execution, earning the description "cold-blooded." By contrast, a fatal beating in which the assailant uses whatever weapons are available at the scene—a chair, shoes, fists—and attacks in a frenzy, suggests an impassioned, impulsive homicide, not one that has been previously reflected upon.

An important caution: manner of killing often provides important evidence on *both* premeditation and purpose to kill, but the two mens reas should be separately analyzed. For example, the cool efficiency of the sniper indicates that he acted with a clear aim to end the victim's life—a purpose to kill. The same evidence, as noted above, indicates calculation and reflection—premeditation. However, in the case of the fatal assailant, the same evidence may point in different directions on these two elements. The fury of the assault may support purpose to kill, but would not generally point toward premeditation.

Now to illustrate the strict approach to premeditation with a particular example.

> Sleepy has been working low level jobs in the drug trade for years. Then he gets his break: acting as agent for a drug wholesaler in the sale of two kilos of cocaine to a major street dealer, Roscoe. Sleepy arrives with the two kilos and Roscoe gives him cash in exchange. The transaction occurs in an apartment building owned by Roscoe. On leaving the building, Sleepy is robbed at gunpoint of the cash by Roscoe's men, who tell him they are acting on Roscoe's orders who doesn't like Sleepy's "attitude."

Two weeks later, Sleepy happens to see Roscoe through the window of a downtown restaurant, sitting with his girlfriend. Sleepy enters the restaurant, pulls out the gun he has been carrying with him since the robbery, and shoots Roscoe three times in the head, killing him. Sleepy is then arrested. On these facts, what are the chances of Sleepy being convicted of premeditated murder in a jurisdiction that follows the strict view of premeditation?

Purpose to kill is clear. The prior robbery and Sleepy's manner of killing (three gunshots at close range to the head) strongly indicate that it was his conscious object to kill Roscoe. What about premeditation?

The prosecution is likely to argue that Sleepy must have been contemplating homicidal retaliation for the robbery since the moment that he learned that Roscoe was behind it. He is carrying a gun, which may indicate prior preparation for the killing.

The defense will protest that this is all speculation. All that is actually known is that after being robbed at gunpoint, Sleepy decided to arm himself and, when he happened to see Roscoe, decided to confront him. From the defense perspective, the time gap to be assessed is that between pulling out the gun and shooting, or at most, spotting Roscoe in the restaurant and shooting; under neither scenario is there substantial opportunity for planning or weighing of consequences.

The relationship between these men—rivals in the drug trade—would generally support a cold-blooded killing. The prosecution would argue that this is murder for business purposes, suggesting a well considered, self-interested deed. The defense might emphasize the personal aspect of the dispute between defendant and victim to make the homicide appear more emotional and spontaneous.

In terms of manner of killing, the prosecution would contend this was virtually execution style, highly efficient and again, cold-blooded. The defense would say that when the opportunity appeared, Sleepy took advantage. The method says nothing particular about prior reflection.

Bottom line: should the jury be so inclined, it may find reasonable doubt as to premeditation, but a more likely result would be a finding of premeditation, based on the cold-blooded nature of this drug trade homicide.

Recall the previous case in which Stephen, the prickly driver of a SUV, after being cut off, forces another Driver off the road, gets out of his own vehicle and shoots the Driver dead. Purpose to kill was clear in this case, but what about premeditation under the strict approach?

Here the defense should have the advantage in a premeditation argument. The events leading to death occurred rapidly, and without any prior notice. The homicide was not planned—unless additional facts can be adduced that Stephen carried a gun in anticipation of such an incident. The relationship between Shooter and Victim was nonexistent prior to the incident, and the motive for the shooting—road rage—indicates a hot tempered, impulsive homicide rather than one that was carefully reflected upon before commission. The manner of killing is efficient, and arguably cold-blooded, but it is also perfectly consistent with a hot blooded and unreflective homicide. Overall, this killing does not look premeditated *if* we take the notion of prior reflection seriously.

The Broad Approach: Jury Discretion

As previously noted, many appellate courts eschew strict interpretations of premeditation, preferring to give fact finders wide discretion in its determination.[6] In these jurisdictions, premeditation is broadly defined, or more accurately, left broadly undefined. Appellate courts typically say more about what is not required, than what is. As long as purpose to kill is evident, such courts are not inclined to second-guess juries on premeditation.

In these jurisdictions, premeditation does not require a substantial time between decision and action. We hear the prosecutorial cliché taken from Commonwealth v. Drum that "no time is too short for a wicked man to frame in his mind the scheme of murder."[7] Indeed, jury instructions may indicate that "no appreciable time" is required to premeditate. Appellate courts here hold that premeditation does not require a cool emotional state, nor evidence of planning or any other specific indicator of reflectiveness. In fact, in such jurisdictions there is virtually no judicial review of premeditation distinct from purpose to kill.

Under the broad approach, it is a legitimate question whether premeditation actually represents a requirement distinct from purpose to kill. Perhaps

---

6. E.g., Commonwealth v. Carroll, 194 A.2d 911 (Pa. 1963); Young v. State, 428 So.2d 155, 158–59 (Ala. Crim. App. 1982).

7. See, for example the use of this phrase in Carroll, 194 A.2d at 916. A more complete quotation from the Drum case provides a more complex view of premeditation, however. "It is true that such is the swiftness of human thought, that no time is so short in which a wicked man may not form a design to kill, and frame the means of executing his purpose; yet this suddenness is opposed to premeditation, and a jury must be well convinced upon the evidence that there was time to deliberate and premeditate. The law regards, and the jury must find, the actual intent; that is to say, the fully formed purpose to kill, with so much time for deliberation and premeditation, as to convince them that this purpose is not the immediate offspring of rashness and impetuous temper, and that the mind has become fully conscious of its own design." Commonwealth v. Drum, 58 Pa. 9, 16 (1868).

the most accurate description of the law in such jurisdictions distinguishes between the law at trial and on appeal. Assuming clear proof of purpose to kill at trial, courts will not overturn jury determinations of premeditation on appeal. Similarly, jury instructions may give fact finders broad discretion in determining premeditation. But the issue still must be decided.

In all jurisdictions, defense counsel at trial can argue to the jury that the defendant did not premeditate, even if purpose to kill is shown. Skilled defense counsel may still persuade a jury—even in a broad approach jurisdiction—that factors such as timing/planning, motive and manner of killing may be considered in determining whether the defendant did reflect on homicide. Remember, even in those jurisdictions where appellate courts opine that premeditation *may* occur quickly, there is no requirement that the fact finder decide that it *did* occur rapidly in the case at hand.

Return once more to the case of Stephen, road rage killer. How would this case be analyzed under the broad approach to premeditation? If convicted of premeditated murder at trial, in a jurisdiction following the broad interpretation approach, Stephen would have no hope of overturning the premeditation finding on appeal. With purpose to kill clear, the appellate court can surmise that the jury may have found that Stephen reflected on killing at any time from the moment of being cut off up to the instant of shooting. Perhaps he began reflection when he forced the other car off the road, or when he got out of his own vehicle, or in the moments between removing his gun from his waistband and shooting.

What about the same case at trial? At trial the prosecution can make the same arguments about rapid premeditation, which may prove convincing. Certainly Stephen is not a very sympathetic defendant. It's also true though, that the defense at trial may still argue that the swiftness of events and hot blooded nature of the killing suggest that Stephen did not *in fact* reflect upon the consequences of killing prior to his shooting the driver. While the broad approach holds that premeditation may occur under these facts, it does not mandate that result. In practice, the jury has essentially unreviewable discretion on premeditation here.

The Worst of the Worst

What makes one killing worse than another? What makes the assassin's homicide more culpable or dangerous than a killing committed out of sudden, jealous passion? Making distinctions in relative severity is one of the basic tasks of homicide law. It also presents one of the more difficult questions of criminal law policy. With this in mind, consider the work of premeditation in identifying the worst of homicides.

The worst killers — the hit man, the political assassin, the serial killer — represent classic examples of premeditated murder. We imagine each making a cold-blooded, calculating, careful decision to take another's life. Based on these examples, premeditation appears a reliable guide to homicide severity. But there are counterexamples.

Imagine a wife who has cared for a terminally ill spouse for months or years, and after long agonizing, decides to end his life to alleviate his terrible suffering. Such a homicide is certainly premeditated, but by virtue of premeditation should it merit treatment as the worst kind of homicide, receiving the most severe punishment? Surely this crime does not belong with those mentioned above. Meanwhile some relatively unconsidered killings, especially if associated with other criminal activity, would seem to merit treatment in the worst category, despite a lack of premeditation.

If premeditation does not always work, what are the alternatives? Some possibilities may be found in contemporary law of capital punishment. Many jurisdictions have designated particular aggravating factors which will determine whether an offense is eligible for the death penalty. These fall into four general categories: (1) victim status; (2) degree of dangerousness; (3) cruelty in method and (4) motive.

Victim factors may track especially vulnerable victims, such as children, or public servants killed in the exercise of their public duties, such as police officers, firefighters, prosecutors or judges. This category overlaps significantly with motive, because victim factors either implicitly or explicitly require a particularly bad motive related to victim status.

Dangerousness factors track the number of persons killed or endangered by the accused.

Cruelty in method factors include the use of torture as part of the crime. The essence of the aggravation here is in the infliction of particular pain on the victim prior to the homicide. Again this could be seen as an implicit motive factor, indicating the sadism behind the defendant's actions.

Explicit motive factors include killing for material gain, and killing out of race or other group bias.

For myself, I believe that motive represents the best candidate for premeditation's replacement, and that the examples of the worst premeditated killers mentioned above are also examples of homicides committed for the worst motives.[8]

8. See Samuel H. Pillsbury, *Judging Evil: Rethinking the Law of Murder and Manslaughter* 98–124 (1998).

Purpose to Kill Murder (Without Premeditation or Provocation)

In most American jurisdictions that recognize premeditation, if a killing is committed with purpose to kill but without premeditation—and without provocation—it will generally be classified as a second-degree murder. Purpose to kill has already been discussed; provocation will be the subject of the next chapter.[9]

There is one additional form of intentional murder that deserves mention here: murder based on purpose to do great bodily harm. Great bodily harm is harm involving significant physical injury, the sort of injury that requires immediate medical treatment to avoid death or permanent injury.

In most jurisdictions, an act taken with purpose to do great bodily harm that produces death will also result in a second-degree murder conviction. This can occur in three different ways.

First, some jurisdictions explicitly list purpose to do great bodily harm as an alternative mens rea sufficient for second-degree murder.

Second, juries may be instructed that they may infer purpose to kill from acts demonstrating purpose to do great bodily harm. This does not change the requirement of proof of purpose to kill beyond a reasonable doubt, but the presumption makes such proof easier as a practical matter.

Third, we will see in Chapter 11 that all jurisdictions recognize a form of murder based on extreme recklessness known as depraved heart murder, which effectively includes homicides committed with purpose to do great bodily harm. That is, it will virtually always be true that if a person acts with purpose to do great bodily harm and ends up causing death, that person will also demonstrate the recklessness necessary for depraved heart murder, assuming no affirmative defense, such as self-defense, applies.

---

9. A purpose to kill homicide may also be reduced from murder to manslaughter in some jurisdictions by virtue of imperfect self-defense, covered in Chapter 19.

CHAPTER 10

PROVOCATION

Provocation is the great politician of Anglo-American criminal law, winning broad support by stating general truths on which all may agree (but understand in different ways) and by promising something to each opposing faction (but not everything desired). One of the oldest doctrines in our law, it has prevailed, as successful politicians are wont to do, by compromise and adaptation. No wonder it can be hard to pin down.

Also known as heat of passion, a killing upon a sudden quarrel, or in a few jurisdictions extreme emotional disturbance, the rule of provocation always seems to operate in the in-between, forging a compromise between opposing forces. It reduces certain murders to manslaughter, lowering punishment for defendants but not eliminating liability. A legally provoked defendant will still be convicted of voluntary manslaughter, a serious felony that often carries a lengthy sentence.

The rule contains internal tensions that verge on outright contradictions. All versions of provocation grant mitigation because of the reason-obscuring effects of strong emotion, yet the rule requires that this emotion must be in some sense reasonable. The doctrine normally looks to the standard of an ordinary reasonable person for guidance, yet no ordinary reasonable person would commit this felony. These tensions have inspired a long-running debate in academia about whether provocation is better understood as a partial excuse or partial justification.[1]

For such a venerable and widely accepted doctrine, coming up with a clear, concise and accurate rule statement proves surprisingly difficult. Indeed, some standard rule statements are positively misleading. Often a better guide to the rule are particular case examples. Yet even here we find considerable controversy, as previously classic cases may no longer serve as trustworthy guides. In short, there is much to discuss here.

---

1. A debate I find unhelpful. The rule has elements of both: justification in its requirement of reasonable passion and excuse in its mitigation for violence inspired by this passion.

The rule of provocation varies significantly according to jurisdiction. Three approaches are covered in this chapter: (1) the categorical approach under the common law; (2) the discretionary approach under the common law; and (3) the Model Penal Code's Extreme Emotional Disturbance (EED) rule.

A Brief History

In early English criminal law, the doctrine of provocation took its shape from principles of manly honor. It reduced murder to manslaughter when the individual killed in quick retaliation for a grave insult or injury to person or family. Paradigm cases involved killings in response to a serious physical attack, a serious challenge to bodily honor and integrity (in the 17th-century this included tweaking another's nose, and a form of road rage known as taking the wall), or discovery of a wife in the act of adultery. In all instances, the man—and this was clearly a man's doctrine—reasonably believed that he had been seriously assaulted or otherwise wronged, and was therefore justifiably outraged. The killing was nevertheless criminal because there was no legal excuse or justification for homicide.

The doctrine's coverage has always been limited. "Slight" provocation would not suffice. Most incidents which inspired rage and violence would not constitute legal provocation.

The provoked killing also needed to occur relatively swiftly after the provoking act, "before a reasonable time has elapsed for the blood to cool and reason to resume its habitual control."[2] This was a killing upon a *sudden* quarrel. The man who was truly overwhelmed by passion resorted to violence sooner, not later. A delay in retaliation suggested both a lack of courage and underlying malevolence.

As the law of provocation developed, both in England and in the United States, it saw a gradual, though not smooth or consistent development from a male oriented rule of mitigated punishment for homicide inspired by honorable passion, to one that emphasized the debilitating effects of strong emotion on the reasoning process, measured by the general norms of a reasonable person. Modern courts frequently speak of a passion that might prompt one to "to act on impulse and without reflection," thus emphasizing the negative effects of strong emotion on individual judgment. Courts explain that it is a doctrine that mitigates "out of indulgence to the frailty of human nature."[3]

---

2. Maher v. People, 10 Michigan 212, 219 (1862).
3. Id.

The furthest development of this more psychological understanding of provocation is the Model Penal Code's Extreme Emotional Disturbance rule.[4]

Provocation in the Liability Formula

Where does provocation fit in the liability formula: is it a form of mens rea or an affirmative defense? The answer depends primarily on statutory wording. In some jurisdictions it counts as a negative element of murder; in other jurisdictions, provocation is denominated an affirmative defense. The important practical issue is which party bears the burden of persuasion on provocation.[5]

Normally the defense must produce some significant evidence of provocation to raise the issue before the jury. Once the issue is raised, the question becomes who has the burden of persuasion. Must the prosecution must persuade the fact finder beyond a reasonable doubt that there was *no* legal provocation, or must the defense affirmatively persuade that there *was* provocation? In most jurisdictions, it is the former: the prosecution will have to persuade concerning a lack of provocation, once the issue is properly raised. Although the question of burden of proof can be critical in some cases, for the sake of simplicity, the discussion that follows will address provocation requirements without reference to the allocation of proof.

We also need to distinguish provocation from the affirmative defense of self-defense. As we will see in a subsequent chapter, self-defense operates as a full defense to homicide when the defendant actually and reasonably believed in the immediate necessity of deadly force to repel an unlawful, deadly threat to self or others. It is based on reasonable fear. By contrast, provoked killings are more retaliatory than defensive, and generally involve not reasonable fear but reasonable anger. Although the provoking incident may have involved physical violence or threat of violence, and therefore fear may be part of the defendant's passion, the provocation rule is only needed when there is no reasonable threat to life at the time of the fatal attack. Otherwise, self-defense will apply.

---

4. One word on contemporary practice versus legal concept. In practice, prosecutors often agree to guilty pleas to voluntary manslaughter in cases that do not strictly meet its description according to the law of the jurisdiction. This may be because of evidentiary problems or a judgment about appropriate sentence, regardless of whether the facts support a provocation claim.

5. If provocation is a negative element of murder, then constitutionally the burden of persuasion must rest with the prosecution. For more on this, see Chapter 4.

Provocation and self-defense significantly overlap when it appears the defendant killed because of an honest but unreasonable belief in the need for self-defense. Some jurisdictions recognize a separate doctrine to cover this situation called imperfect self-defense. Such a defense is partial and will result in a voluntary manslaughter conviction. In those jurisdictions that do not recognize imperfect self-defense, the defendant may try for the same result through the rule of provocation. The defendant can argue that the victim's threats or violence were sufficient to inspire anger and fear to constitute a reasonable passion.

Basic Elements

At a minimum, provocation involves three elements: that the defendant acted with (1) murder mens rea, while (2) actually and (3) reasonably impassioned by the provoking incident.

The first item on our list is to determine whether the defendant acted with sufficient mens rea for a murder charge. If not, the doctrine of provocation, which serves to lower murder to manslaughter, simply does not apply. The murder mens reas of purpose to kill, purpose to do great bodily harm, or depraved heart recklessness all may apply to provocation, but most cases involve purpose to kill. Most cases of provocation involve instances of the defendant acting out of extreme anger toward the victim, a state of emotion consistent with desiring the victim's death.

There are two forms of murder that cannot be mitigated by provocation. First, provocation has no impact on felony murder. We will see in Chapter 12 that felony murder requires only mens rea for the underlying felony and not the death of the victim; thus it lacks a murder mens rea to be mitigated. Second, there can be no provocation if there is proof of premeditation. A legally provoked killing is one where the defendant's passion caused him to act rashly, meaning he did not reflect on killing as premeditation requires. In this respect, provocation is premeditation's opposite number. One excludes the other.

Assuming murder mens rea is present, under the common law we next look to see whether the defendant acted while impassioned as a result of the provoking incident. The central concept of provocation or "heat of passion" is that the defendant acted in a moment of such strong emotion that it affected his ability to think clearly about his actions and their consequences. We know that when feelings run strong, clear thinking is hard; we tend to speak or act without considering the consequences.

Establishing that the defendant acted while impassioned by the provoking incident is usually fairly straightforward. We look to see if the provoking incident was the kind that would normally arouse strong emotion, and to the defendant's words and actions to see if they show an individual under the influence of strong feeling. Finally, the act of homicide itself, depending on its manner and timing, may provide an indication of strong feeling. Throughout there must be evidence that it was the provoking incident that aroused the defendant's passion rather than something else.

Doing almost all the work in provocation doctrine—meaning that it decides most cases—is the requirement that the defendant's emotional reaction, his or her passion, be reasonable. Before we delve into the mysteries of reasonableness, we must be clear about *what* must be reasonable. *It is the defendant's passion that must be reasonable, not the killing itself.*

Although courts, statutes and commentators often speak of the reasonableness of the defendant's action, this cannot be correct. In law, reasonable refers to the perceptions or conduct of the average *law abiding* person. Yet a legally provoked killing is a serious felony. The ordinary reasonable person does not go around committing felonies. The only way out of this definitional conundrum is to recognize that reasonableness applies to the *emotions* inspired by the provoking situation, and not the defendant's subsequent killing. Where the defendant's passion is reasonable, we sympathize with the defendant's situation. We believe that what the defendant experienced in the provoking incident would "sorely tempt" a reasonable person to kill, but nevertheless blame the individual for succumbing to that temptation.

In most jurisdictions, the focus for reasonableness analysis is the provoking incident or incidents which inspired the defendant's passion. As we will see, jurisdictions vary considerably concerning what sorts of provoking incidents might constitute "legally adequate" provocation, however. Those jurisdictions that follow the MPC do not explicitly require any provoking incident, making assessment of reasonableness there especially challenging.

In some jurisdictions, provocation rules include a third element: the lack of a cooling-off period. The provocation may not be too "remote" from the fatal attack. Courts hold that the killing must occur before a reasonable cooling off period following the original provoking incident has elapsed. In other jurisdictions, timing has been eliminated as a formal requirement, although it may still affect decision maker assessments of reasonableness. Conceptually, I think it is simplest to consider timing issues under the general heading of reasonableness. We ask whether the defendant's emotional state *at the time of* the homicide was reasonable based on the nature of the original provoking incident and the amount of time that passed between incident and homicide.

Finally, a word about jurisdictional variation. The discussion here, which sets out three different rules, represents an oversimplification of legal reality.

There are actually many more variations on provocation than the three presented here, but for our purposes these will suffice to introduce the most important variations in the American law of provocation.

The Categorical Approach to Common Law Provocation

Jurisdictions that take the most restrictive approach to provocation employ what may be called a categorical approach. In these jurisdictions a jury may not consider provocation unless there is evidence of certain types of provoking incidents, usually incidents that involve violence or serious sexual wrong done to the defendant or a loved one. In these jurisdictions, judges play an important gatekeeping role, permitting jury consideration of provocation only if certain prerequisites are met. In these jurisdictions, legal provocation is implicitly restricted to instances where the defendant experienced great anger, or a combination of anger and fear.

The legal motto of the categorical approach is that "words are never enough." Courts here believe that a clear line must be drawn between verbal hurts, taunts and insults, and provocations involving violence, sexual violation or marital infidelity. While words may be considered a part of legal provocation in combination with physical wrongs, they will not suffice on their own, no matter how egregious.

Legally Adequate Provocation—The List of Approved Provoking Events

Modern courts following the categorical approach often set out the following list of legally approved provoking incidents taken from centuries-old English cases: mutual combat, extreme assault and battery on a defendant, injury or serious abuse of a close relative of defendant, illegal arrest of defendant, or sudden discovery of a spouse's adultery.[6] I wonder about the usefulness of this list as a guide to current law, however. For example, it is very difficult to find a modern case of legal provocation based on illegal arrest. Two centuries ago in England, when there were no professional police and arrests were often made by ordinary citizens, we can understand how an illegal arrest might rep-

---

6. E.g., Girouard v. State, 583 A.2d 718, 721 (Md. Ct. App. 1991).

resent a major wrong inspiring great and violent passion. Given the professional status of police today, it's hard to imagine a situation—outside of self-defense—where a reasonable person would be "sorely tempted" to kill an arresting officer.

Questions may also be raised about the discovery of adultery ground. Classically, the defendant needed to discover his wife in the physical act of infidelity. Such a discovery provided the moral and visceral equivalent of the violence inherent in other approved categories of provocation. In contemporary American society where divorce is relatively easy to obtain and an individual's social standing does not depend on a spouse's chastity, we may ask whether there will be many cases where discovery of adultery would make a reasonable person feel "sorely tempted" to kill. To preview a distinction detailed later, facts showing discovery of adultery may be enough to get a provocation claim before a jury in a categorical jurisdiction, but that does not mean the jury will necessarily find provocation. The jury must still make its own judgment about whether the defendant experienced the actual and reasonable passion necessary for mitigation.

The mutual combat ground of provocation is one of the most venerable forms of provoking incident, going back to medieval times when the doctrine was called "chance-medley." The common law's identification of killings "upon a sudden quarrel" or upon a "sudden falling out" between victim and killer probably referred to just such situations. Today this remains a part of provocation law in many jurisdictions, but is subject to important limitations. It refers to situations in which armed combatants mutually choose to engage in a deadly contest on essentially equal terms. Many potential cases of mutual combat will turn out to fall either under self-defense (because the defendant reasonably believed the use of deadly force necessary for self-preservation), or murder (because the defendant either took unfair advantage of his opponent or there was no mutual combat, just a one-sided attack.).

Summing up, the most important instances of legal provocation under the categorical approach involve either serious physical assault on or sexual wrong done to defendant or a loved one, what I will call serious violence or violation.

Timing: The Cooling Off Period

In categorical jurisdictions, the timing of the homicide with respect to the provoking incident is an important feature of the rule. Courts may bar consideration of provocation evidence if the killing clearly occurred after a cooling off period elapsed. In all cases that reach the jury, courts will instruct fact finders concerning the cooling-off requirement. The notion here is that any reasonable person would have regained emotional balance by the time that the homicide occurred. If the defendant nevertheless remained in a high state of passion, then even if originally reasonable, the passion would become unreasonable by the time the killing occurred. Unfortunately for the law student, there is no clear rule as to the length of a cooling off period. The best we can do is to note that the worse the original provocation, the longer the cooling off period will be, and vice versa.

Judge and Jury Roles: Law and Facts

In a categorical jurisdiction, analysis of provocation is a two stage process, the first involving the judge and the second the jury. Courts have the responsibility of defining the outer limits of provocation as a matter of law; juries determine the facts and render a final verdict on provocation. At trial, the judge determines if testimony presented or proffered might constitute legal provocation, if believed by the jury. If there is sufficient evidence to pass this preliminary test, the jury will make its own independent assessment of the evidence, guided by the court's instructions. As always, the jury must decide any credibility issues. For example, one witness might describe the provoking incident as involving serious violence, while another witness might describe it as a trivial shove. In most instances the trial court would not seek to resolve this factual dispute but would leave it to the trier of fact, the jury. The jury would then make its own assessment of the provoking event and, based on this, decide whether the defendant was actually and reasonably provoked.

Having set out the basic rule of provocation in categorical jurisdictions, it's time to see how the rule works with facts.

Bill and his new girlfriend LeeAnn are drinking at a tough neighborhood bar on a Friday night. LeeAnn complains that the "biker guy" at the table across from them keeps "undressing me with his eyes" and making crude gestures at her. Bill confronts the man, Pete, and tells him to keep his "dirty eyes" off of LeeAnn. Pete laughs and insults Bill's manhood. Bill shouts insults back. Pete then takes a bottle of whiskey from the bar and smashes it over Bill's head. Bill falls to the floor, stunned. Bill's friends pull him away to a distant booth, where he gradually recovers his senses. He is bleeding but not profusely.

Some minutes later—as little as 10 minutes, or as much as 30— Bill gets up and approaches Pete again, a hunting knife in his hand. Bill often carries a knife with him for protection. Pete sees Bill coming and, playing to the others in the bar, imitates the way that Bill fell to the floor after being hit with the bottle. The other men laugh. Bill screams epithets while rushing up and stabbing Pete five times in the chest, killing him. Is this murder or manslaughter?

Murder mens rea is evident here. Multiple stabs to the chest by a hunting knife (a large knife) accompanied by epithets, following a previous assault and insults, all indicate that Bill was very angry at Pete and did everything he could to end the man's life. The question is whether, in addition to acting with purpose to kill, Bill was legally provoked.

Actual provocation is also pretty clear. The circumstances of the evening gave Bill many reasons to be angry with Pete, and his words and furious assault indicate that he was in a state of great anger at the time of the fatal assault. There could be an argument here that Bill was not actually aroused to a great state of passion after being stunned, but the facts suggest otherwise. The question of whether a reasonable person would have cooled off by the time of the stabbing will be dealt with shortly. It doesn't look like Bill did.

The major question, as it nearly always is with provocation, is whether a reasonable person in Bill's situation also would have been so impassioned as to be "sorely tempted" to kill. In a categorical jurisdiction, this requires a preliminary judgment that the incident falls into one of the approved categories. Chances are good that there is enough here to get the issue to the jury. The defense will argue that Pete's assault with the whiskey bottle, smashing it over Bill's head, constitutes a serious physical attack. I would be inclined to agree. This is the kind of assault that could cause serious head injuries, permanent facial scars and extensive blood loss. Bill is lucky to get off with perhaps a minor concussion. The prosecution can argue that, just like in the movies, that this sort of bottle-breaking-over-the-head is a minor physical blow, unworthy of legal provocation. Most likely this argument would not be sufficient to keep the issue from the jury, though it might ultimately prove persuasive with the jury.

A related issue in a categorical jurisdiction is whether a cooling off period had passed such that the homicide occurred too late for provocation. Here the provoking incident was significant and the retaliation occurred within the hour, without any break in sequence — neither party ever left the location — suggesting that a reasonable person probably would not have cooled off during this interval. Again the prosecution might argue to the contrary, reviving earlier stated arguments about the minor nature of the assault.

The bottom line is that the defense has a decent chance at a manslaughter verdict in this case in a categorical jurisdiction.

Carol is a 28 year old single mother of three who never graduated from high school. She is barely making ends meet for herself and her family. Her oldest son, Tai, is 12 years old and a very talented basketball player. Everyone tells her that he has the makings of a college star, and maybe even a professional player, with the right coaching. Tai currently plays on an all-star club team for Coach Harold, who is a famous former college basketball coach. After several weeks, Tai starts acting strangely. When Carol questions Tai, the boy reports that Coach has molested him on two occasions. Carol confronts Coach Harold. Coach Harold denies doing anything wrong and calls Tai a liar. The Coach threatens Carol that if she tells anyone about these allegations, he will make sure that Tai never plays again for a good team. He says that no one will believe the allegations anyway. He offers Carol $5,000 if "things stay quiet." Carol goes away devastated, convinced that the molestation occurred, but that she has no chance of bringing charges against the Coach. Carol herself was sexually abused as a child.

Three days later, Carol confronts Coach in the parking lot outside the gym. She draws a gun from her purse and says, "you'll never touch another kid." She fires all five rounds in the revolver into his torso, killing him. Murder or manslaughter?

Again murder mens rea will not be a serious issue. Five shots to the torso following Carol's promise that Coach will "never touch another kid," given the suspected prior molestation and Carol's personal background all indicate that Carol acted with the conscious object to end the Coach's life.

We next consider whether Carol was in an actual state of great passion, whether she was actually provoked. Considering her son's complaint against the Coach, Carol's personal history and the shooting itself, it's likely that Carol was extremely upset at the time of the shooting. The prosecution may argue, however, that given the three-day time lapse between the initial confrontation in the shooting, that Carol must have thought long and hard about her action, clearly reflected on it, and decided to inflict cold-blooded revenge. If Carol was not experiencing strong passion at the moment of killing, she would not meet this threshold requirement for provocation. Under the circumstances of this case, however, this is a hard argument for the prosecution.

Assuming that Carol was actually provoked, was she reasonably so? This case should fall under the category of a serious wrong to a loved one. We do not know if the allegation against the Coach was true, but the defense will argue that Carol had a reasonable basis for believing it so. A mistaken belief concerning what happened to Tai will not be fatal to a provocation claim as long as the mistake is reasonable. Along these lines, the prosecution might contend that there was not sufficient evidence for a reasonable person to believe that the Coach was guilty of molestation. The prosecution might argue that Carol's emotional reaction was due more to her own personal history than to a reasonable assessment of the facts.

Finally there are concerns about timing. Would a reasonable person have remained as upset as Carol apparently did for three days? Given the severity of the initial wrong and the callousness of the Coach's response, the defense would have a good argument that three days would not be enough for a reasonable parent to cool off from learning of a child's molestation.

The bottom line is that in a categorical jurisdiction, there is a good chance that this claim will reach the jury—which must then make its own decisions about reasonable passion and timing.

A variation on this case will illustrate the difference between the categorical approach and the discretionary approach that we will next consider.

> Assume the same background facts as before, but in this case Tai told his mother that he was upset because the Coach used ugly racial epithets toward him and discriminated against him on the team on the basis of race. When Carol confronts Coach, he uses racially offensive language to her. Carol has been the victim of serious racial discrimination in her life, as have other members of her family.
>
> The homicide occurs three days later, in the same fashion as described originally, with Carol condemning Coach's bigotry prior to shooting. Murder or manslaughter?

Words of racial insult can be enormously hurtful, and race discrimination, especially toward the young, can be deeply destructive. Carol may well have been actually provoked—enormously enraged— by Coach's words and actions, but would her passion be reasonable according to the norms of provocation doctrine? In a categorical jurisdiction, unless accompanied by serious violence or violation, the Coach's conduct would not be sufficient to qualify for legal provocation. His "mere words" and acts of discrimination would not constitute serious violence or violation and therefore would not support mitigation of Carol's homicide from murder.

The Discretionary Approach to Common Law Provocation

Rejecting the categorical approach, a number of jurisdictions give juries primary authority to decide provocation claims. The same basic structure of common law analysis holds here—murder mens rea plus actual and reasonable passion due to a provoking incident—but in these jurisdictions, the provoking incident need not involve serious violence, violation or discovery of adultery. Here words *may* be sufficient as legal provocation. In such jurisdictions there is often no requirement that the homicide take place within a particular span of time following the provoking incident, though timing may still influence decisions about the reasonableness of passion. Many discretionary jurisdictions also permit defendants to argue that words or actions that occurred well after the initial provocation may "rekindle" the defendant's reasonable passions. Finally, such jurisdictions often take a broader view of the passion involved, allowing juries to find that any strong emotion may constitute reasonable provocation.

As a result of its potentially broad view of the provoking incident, the discretionary approach places more decisional weight on the reasonable person. This person provides the standard of emotionality against which to assess the passion of the defendant. But who is this person? Especially, how much is the reasonable person is imbued with the particular characteristics of the defendant? This is a critical question, yet courts give juries only the most general guidance on the issue.[7]

The previous case involving Bill's barroom stabbing of Pete illustrates the potential overlap between categorical and discretionary approaches. This case would be analyzed in substantially the same way under a discretionary approach; the only potential distinction is that in a discretionary jurisdiction, it would be a purely jury question whether Pete's breaking of a bottle over Bill's head would support reasonable provocation.

The case involving Carol's shooting of Coach would also follow similar lines except with respect to timing. In a discretionary jurisdiction, the jury would have considerable leeway in deciding how the timing of previous events and the homicide affected—or did not—the reasonableness of Carol's passion at the time of the killing.

---

7. For example in California, jurors are told that reasonableness includes the defendant's "circumstances." Juries are instructed: "The heat of passion which will reduce a homicide to manslaughter must be such a passion as naturally would be aroused in the mind of an ordinarily reasonable person in the same circumstances." The instruction then warns, however, that a "defendant is not permitted to set up [his] [her] own standard of conduct and to justify or excuse [himself] [herself] because [his] [her] passions were aroused unless the circumstances in which the defendant was placed and the facts that confronted [him] [her] were such as also would have aroused the passion of the ordinarily reasonable person faced with the same situation." California Jury Instructions: Criminal (CALJIC) Sec. 8.42.

The most dramatic differences between the two common law approaches appear in cases in which the provoking incident did not involve serious violence, violation or discovery of adultery.

Celeste is a 38 year-old mother of two who suffers from depression and has a drinking problem. A former model, she gave up her career at her husband Antonio's insistence and is now very concerned about her economic future. She is also very sensitive about losing her looks to age. Celeste's situation worsens dramatically when Antonio announces that he has filed for divorce in order to marry a 22 year-old summer intern in his office. This decision leads to acrimonious arguments between husband and wife about child custody and property. At the conclusion of this argument, Antonio calls Celeste an "aging cow with a drinking problem" and vows that he will "litigate to eternity" to make sure that she gets nothing from his law practice. Antonio moves out of the house and rents an apartment.

Two days later, Celeste learns that Antonio has taken all of the family money, leaving her and the children nothing. She drives to Antonio's apartment building in her super size SUV and when he walks out, she runs him over, three times. He dies of his injuries. Murder or manslaughter?

Looks like purpose to kill: running over someone in a large SUV, *three times.* The situation certainly suggests that Celeste was upset at Antonio, quite likely upset enough to want him dead. As for provocation, this is a nonstarter in a categorical jurisdiction, because for all his apparently brutish behavior, Antonio did nothing that would fit an approved category. Things are different in a discretionary jurisdiction, however. First we would have to determine if Celeste was actually provoked, if she was in a state of high passion. Although there is no direct proof, there are enough indications of actual passion in the provoking situation and Celeste's conduct that we should move on to the question of whether that passion was reasonable. Here we discover just how much leeway a decision maker may have in a discretionary jurisdiction.

The prosecution will argue that the case involves a garden-variety separation/divorce dispute in which emotions run high but which would not make a reasonable person "sorely tempted to kill." The prosecution would argue that the worst verbal provocation occurred two days before the fatal assault, making it more likely that Celeste had calmed down, and if not, that a reasonable person would have calmed down by the time of the attack.

The defense will emphasize the particular vulnerabilities of Celeste, of which Antonio was presumably aware, and argue that once these are taken into account, Antonio's verbal taunts and threats, combined with actions that threaten the economic well-being of herself and her children, were such as to inspire in a reasonable person in her situation a high state of anger and fear, making her susceptible to aggressive impulses. My guess is that the prosecution has better of the argument here, but that is just a guess, by a former prosecutor. The analytic point is that the jury will have the first and also likely the final word on provocation in a discretionary jurisdiction.

Is Provocation Sexist?

Provocation has gotten some pretty tough press in the academic literature in recent years. It has been accused of permitting or promoting gender discrimination, homophobia, violence generally, and even race and class discrimination. Some have called for its abolition; a number of commentators have urged its conceptual or structural reform. Central to these criticisms is the way that the doctrine may reflect questionable social attitudes or expectations.[8]

The most sustained critique of provocation has centered on gender: that it is built on patriarchal norms and a male model of aggression. Traditionally one of its central examples, discovery of adultery, involves a situation much more likely to provoke violence from males than females, and may be linked to traditional concepts of male control of female partners. In at least one jurisdiction, this ground for provocation has been eliminated, and it is no longer emphasized in most accounts of the doctrine.[9]

Another gender-problematic feature of provocation may be its timing element. A brief cooling off period, critics claim, reflects a typically male use of aggression. Boys and men are socialized to use aggression instrumentally, to respond to insult or threat with a nearly immediate aggressive response. Girls and women by contrast are socialized to be peacemakers and diplomats, to avoid aggression at almost all costs, which means that when females do resort to violence it tends to be after a significant lapse

---

8. For a sampling of these criticisms, see Donna Coker, Heat of Passion and Wife Killing: Men Who Batter/Men who Kill, 2 So. Cal. Rev. L. & Women's Stud. 71 (1992); Victoria Nourse, Passion's Progress: Modern Law Reform in the Provocation Defense, 106 Yale L. J. 1331 (1997); Robert B. Mison, Comment, Homophobia in Manslaughter: The Homosexual Advance as Insufficient Provocation, 80 Cal. L. Rev. 133 (1992); Jeremy Horder, *Provocation and Responsibility* 186–97 (1992); Samuel H. Pillsbury, *Judging Evil: Rethinking the Law of Murder and Manslaughter*, 146–59 (1998). For a defense of the doctrine against at least some of these criticisms, see Joshua Dressler, Why Keep the Provocation Defense?: Reflections on a Difficult Subject, 86 Minn. L. Rev. 959 (2002).

9. Md. Code, Criminal Law sec. 2-207.

> of time from the original provoking incident. But this slower, more typically female resort to violence is not necessarily more culpable or dangerous than the quicker, more typically male response.[10]
>
> I have argued for three changes in provocation, in part to remedy its patriarchal tendencies: (1) development of gender-neutral paradigmatic examples; (2) a recasting of the doctrine in terms of reasons for violence (motive) rather than reasonableness of passion and (3) more flexibility with respect to timing.[11]

Extreme Emotional Disturbance

Finally we turn to the most distinctive American rule on provocation, a rule so distinctive that it goes under a different name: the Model Penal Code's rule on mitigation for Extreme Emotional Disturbance (EED).

I will not mince words here. I believe the EED rule is incoherent. Its rule combines psychological explanation with moral judgment without giving fact finders clear guidance on reconciling these fundamentally different perspectives on human behavior. The terms of the rule are also obscure, so that even sophisticated legal decision makers often articulate their decisions in moral or emotional terms not found in the rule.[12] The practical bottom line is that decision makers have considerable discretion concerning mitigation and may decide the issue largely on a case-by-case basis.

The conceptual problems of EED are the result of a deliberate compromise. (At least in this regard the doctrine is traditional.) Rebelling against the strictures of common law provocation, the drafters sought to give juries broad powers to exercise their moral judgment based on a wide range of factors, including, to some extent, the particular psychology of the defendant.

In a case where the defendant acted with a mens rea sufficient for murder, the homicide will nevertheless be classified as manslaughter under the MPC if the defendant suffered from "an extreme emotional disturbance for which there was a reasonable explanation or excuse."[13] The rule further provides that the

---

10. Judging Evil, supra at 151–55.
11. Id. at 142–46, 159–60.
12. E.g., People v. Cassassa, 404 N.E.2d. 1310, 1317 (New York 1980) where the state's highest court found that the finder of fact had "concluded that the murder in this case was the result of defendant's malevolence rather than an understandable human response deserving of mercy. We cannot say, as a matter of law, that the court erred in so concluding."
13. Sec. 210.3

"reasonableness of such explanation or excuse shall be determined from the viewpoint of the person in the actor's situation under the circumstances as he believes them to be." This rule encompasses all cases that would fit the common law discretionary approach to provocation—and more.

The rule does not restrict the kind of emotion involved. It may be rage, or grief, jealousy or any other strong feeling.

The rule does not require a provoking event as does the common law. A person may become extremely emotionally disturbed because of psychological processes internal to herself or himself, not prompted by the victim's conduct.

The rule says nothing about timing. There is no cooling off period here.

For all this, the practical differences between EED and common law provocation can be exaggerated. The defendant's emotional disturbance still must be reasonably explained or excused. Triers of fact may interpret the requirement of reasonableness according to their own norms, and these may prove more similar to traditional concepts of provocation than the wording of the rule might suggest.

Extreme Emotional Disturbance

As with other forms of provocation, the first element of EED is easily established in most cases. It is the requirement that the defendant have acted under the influence of a strong emotion. As we have seen, the rule appears agnostic about the kind of emotion. What matters is that the emotion be strong enough (i.e. extreme) to disturb the individual's normal decision process. This will not usually involve irrationality.[14] Instead, we look for indications in appearance, speech, conduct and surrounding events that the defendant experienced great emotion at the time of the homicide.

For Which There is a Reasonable Explanation/Excuse

At the heart of the doctrine, as with common law provocation, is the requirement that the emotion be, in some sense, reasonable. Here we find the central controversy, and I believe incoherence, of EED. The language of the rule explicitly demands both a subjective and an objective analysis, an individualized and a universalized standard *in the same element*. The subjec-

---

14. To put this in terms of neurobiology, we are looking for indications that decision-making is coming from the more primitive, limbic portion of the brain which handles instinctive reactions rather than the prefrontal cortex which handles deliberative assessments. See Elkhonon Goldberg, *The Executive Brain* 21–36 (2001).

tive/individualized analysis comes from the requirement that the fact finder should determine the reasonableness of explanation or excuse "from the viewpoint of a person in the actor's situation under the circumstances as he believes them to be."[15] The objective/universalized analysis comes from the requirement that there must be a reasonable explanation or excuse for the defendant's emotional state.

Analysis begins with the defendant's "situation," taking "the viewpoint of a person in the actor's [defendant's] situation under the circumstances as he believes them to be." Taking this information into account, we then ask whether the defendant's emotional state was reasonably explained or excused. The great analytic challenge is deciding how much the reasonable standard depends on the average ordinary person and how much it is informed by the particular traits and experiences of the defendant.

The drafters of EED clearly meant to create a more individualized reasonableness standard than the common law. Here the reasonable person likely shares the defendant's physical characteristics and at least some of his or her psychological makeup. From the drafters' commentary to the rule, it is clear that defendants should not be able to use their own idiosyncratic moral or political values to establish reasonableness. A defendant may not, for example, claim that his own beliefs about the wrongs of illegal immigration make reasonable his homicidal rage at illegal workers. The decision maker must decide whether it believes the defendant's rage was reasonably explained or justified. On the other hand, it appears that a defendant's extreme grief or psychological trauma might be considered reasonable even if such grief or trauma was not connected to anything the victim said or did. The drafters of the rule left most questions of individualization to decision maker discretion.[16]

> Ann is a successful insurance broker in her thirties who has been married for five years. She is excited when she learns she is pregnant. The pregnancy is difficult, but when she gives birth to a healthy baby girl, both she and her husband are delighted. After several days her mood changes however, and she refuses to see anyone or answer the phone. A week after the birth, Ann's husband leaves on a business trip over her strong objections. He returns three days later to find Ann staring at a wall and their baby dead in her crib. Ann states that she smothered it because it was "crying too much."

---

15. Sec. 210.3 (b).

16. As the commentary notes, the reference to the defendant's situation is "designedly ambiguous." *Model Penal Code and Commentaries* Comment to 210.3, at 62–63 (1980).

Ann is diagnosed with postpartum depression, a condition that can be quite severe and occur without much notice. Her psychiatrist states that she never suffered a break with reality (psychosis) but did experience a fundamental alteration of mood that profoundly disturbed her judgment. With treatment, Ann's mood improves and she expresses deep regret for her actions. Is she guilty of murder or manslaughter?

This is an appealing case for the EED rule because it may permit mitigation for a defendant with whom many may find sympathize, but who would be convicted of murder under the common law. Under the common law there is no provoking event that would cause a reasonable person to be extremely upset with the baby victim.

Under the EED rule, Ann does seem to have been extremely emotionally disturbed. Postpartum depression describes a severe form of emotional disturbance. And the psychiatrist's findings could be taken as a reasonable explanation for this disturbance. Beginning with the defendant's perspective, which would include her experience of postpartum depression, her sadness and despair seem reasonably explained. A significant advantage for Ann here is that postpartum depression stems from an observable physical condition not usually associated with criminality. While this is not a formal part of the rule, it may be may be important to a jury's sense of justice. Returning a manslaughter verdict in this case will not lead to a stream of killers seeking to escape murder charges based on birth-related depression.

The prosecution though will question whether anyone with postpartum depression could be described as "reasonably" disturbed. As with any mental health related defense, the prosecution would try to argue moral fault rather than illness. The prosecution may assert that while a mother being upset following birth and the departure of a husband on a trip are common enough, it does not usually come in the extreme form experienced by Ann. The ordinary new mother may become sad or angry for little reason, and certainly may become annoyed at a fussy baby, but not to the extent that she would be passionately inclined to infanticide. Ann's emotional reaction was unreasonable.

Bottom line? My money would be on the defense here because the EED rule is designedly hospitable to a mental/emotional disorder argument, and for a homicide defendant, Ann is a relatively sympathetic figure. A decision maker who understands EED as an opportunity for the exercise of unusual compassion or mercy may well see this case as appropriate for mitigation.

Martin, 16, has no friends. He spends most of his time listening to heavy metal music on his portable music player and playing violent video games on his computer. He will often go days without speaking to anyone. Some of his problems may be traced to the death of his father, who committed suicide when Martin was 10. Martin is sometimes teased by other students at school. He generally has a hard time reading other people's thoughts or feelings. One day a teacher makes an innocuous comment about Martin's clothes—he always wears black— and the class laughs. Martin becomes extremely upset and obsesses about pay back. He returns to school two days later with his father's gun and fatally shoots the teacher. His plan is to kill himself afterwards, but is restrained before he can.

Martin is examined by a psychologist who determines that he suffers from a severe personality disorder that causes him to be socially isolated and extremely sensitive to certain kinds of insults. The psychologist says that Martin interpreted the teacher's comment as a profound threat to his (Martin's) well-being. Could Martin be convicted only of manslaughter or is this clearly a murder case?

The legal analysis of EED here will be similar to that in Ann's case. Again there are clear indicators in both behavior and the psychologist's account that Martin suffered from an extreme emotional disturbance. The opinion of the mental-health professional will also support the defense argument that there was a reasonable explanation for the emotional disturbance—here a personality disorder rather than postpartum depression. Martin's youth might be an additional factor in his behalf. The defense may assert that Martin's emotional state should be compared to that of the ordinary teenager in his situation, not that of an ordinary adult. Youth, after all, is both a physical characteristic and an important psychological feature. Certainly adolescence is a time of life characterized by volatile and strong emotions.

Again the prosecution will try to emphasize the objective dimension of reasonableness, arguing that there is nothing reasonable about emotions stemming from a major personality disorder. No matter how much Martin actually understood the teacher's comment as threatening, it was not, and no reasonable person would understand it that way. Not even a reasonable teen (an admittedly challenging concept) would experience powerful homicide-inciting emotions because of a minor social taunt.

In the end, despite the analytic similarities between the two cases, I suspect that Martin would have a considerably harder time winning mitigation than Ann. His conduct is more socially threatening and his emotional problems appear more persistent and deep-rooted, despite his youth. There is no physical event to which to tie his emotional disturbance. Overall, his personality and conduct come closer to our expectations for a disturbed killer—a frightening murderer—than someone whose situation merits a significant degree of mercy. As a result, I suspect most juries and judges would favor the prosecution position. The important analytic point, though, is that, on its face, the EED rule applies as well to Martin as to Ann. Any difference in case outcomes depends more on our intuitive evaluations of defendants and their conduct than the dictate of the rule itself. This is a rule designed to give fact finders considerable discretion.

CHAPTER 11

Unintentional Killings: Depraved Heart Murder and Involuntary Manslaughter

We normally assume that brutality tracks intentionality. We think that the more intentional the harm, the worse the wrong. Depictions of crime in movies and on television generally follow this model, with the bad guy engaging in particularly deliberate malevolence. In some respects the criminal law does the same. Many offenses require purposeful wrongdoing, and when offenses are distinguished by degrees, intentionality often makes the distinction. Yet purposeful wrongdoing is not the only serious form of wrongdoing either in criminal law or morality. So it is that brutal, callous, and careless conduct—or sometimes omissions to act—that cause death may support serious criminal liability, even without a clear purpose to take life.

In this chapter we focus primarily on forms of murder and manslaughter that require proof of extreme recklessness (for depraved heart murder) or criminal negligence (for involuntary manslaughter). Some jurisdictions also have a third unintentional homicide offense located between these two, based on simple recklessness.

The common denominator of all these homicides is a judgment that the individual caused death through dangerous, antisocial conduct, thus demonstrating disrespect for others' basic welfare. Some homicides here, especially in the depraved heart murder category, may involve vicious attacks that would constitute significant crimes even without the result of death. Others involve lawful conduct performed in a dangerous and careless fashion. Most homicides considered involve affirmative acts, but the doctrines covered here also provide prime candidates for liability based on omissions to act.

Given that the distinctions between offenses here depend on mens rea, precision in mens rea language is especially important. Unfortunately, the ambiguities of traditional mens rea language can sometimes lead to confusion here. Nothing new there, unfortunately.

Depraved Heart Murder

This offense answers to a number of different names: extreme indifference murder, implied malice murder, and depraved mind or depraved heart murder. Despite the different names, the basic content of doctrine here is the same in most jurisdictions, involving two basic components: recklessness and indifference. Such murders are usually, but not always, classified as a form of second-degree murder.[1]

From the early common law to the present day, this offense has been seen as the moral and legal equivalent of basic purpose to kill murder: the defendant demonstrates the same level of culpability and merits the same punishment as if he intended to kill. This may serve as a general guiding principle: we should look for those instances of reckless conduct causing death that represent as serious a wrong as a purposeful killing done without premeditation or provocation.

The common law terminology for this offense constitutes some of the most colorful and morally evocative mens rea language found in our criminal law. William Blackstone spoke of the "dictate of a wicked, depraved and malignant heart."[2] An early Pennsylvania court described this offense as a killing that demonstrates "wickedness of disposition, hardness of heart, cruelty, recklessness of consequences, and a mind regardless of social duty."[3] Other common law adjectives for this kind of homicide include "wanton," "wicked," and "vicious."

For all of the richness of this language, however, it does not provide the kind of guidance needed in contemporary criminal law. A better model is the MPC definition of murder "committed recklessly under circumstances manifesting extreme indifference to the value of human life."[4] Here we see the two basic components of culpability: (1) recklessness and (2) extreme indifference. Most of the action in depraved heart murder analysis involves the first of these.

As with any offense, we may begin our study with paradigm examples of the crime: descriptions of conduct that are considered classic instances of the offense. Traditional examples of depraved heart murder include throwing heavy timbers off the roof of a building in a city or town without care for or warn-

---

1. Such murder can be classified otherwise, however, and may even support the death penalty. Arizona v. Tison, 481 U.S. 137 (1987).

2. 4 Commentaries 199.

3. Commonwealth v. Drum, 58 Penn. 9, 15 (1868).

4. Section 210.2 (1)(b).

ing to those walking in the street below; setting fire to or shooting into an occupied dwelling; riding a wild horse into a crowd.[5]

Contemporary cases include instances of extended, brutal beatings of another person by fists or hands or the use of severe and repeated violence against young children. Games of Russian roulette and cases in which an extremely drunk driver kills one or more in an accident after driving in an especially dangerous manner satisfy the doctrine.[6] All of these instances involve highly dangerous conduct, undertaken without justification, where the danger to others is readily apparent to one in the defendant's situation. All are redolent of a basic disregard for the welfare of the victim and the value of his or her life.

Depraved Heart Murder and Other Homicide Doctrines

Before we plunge into the details of depraved heart murder, we should situate the offense within the larger family of homicide crimes in American law.

Felony Murder

There is a significant factual overlap between felony murder and depraved heart murder. The proof the prosecution needs for felony murder will, in most cases, also satisfy depraved heart murder. For example, in most robbery, burglary or rape cases where the felon unintentionally causes death, the accused will have acted in a way that demonstrates recklessness toward the risk of death and indifference toward the value of another's life. Recognizing this, some courts and legislatures have effectively combined the two offenses. The drafters of the MPC sought to encompass felony murder within depraved heart murder by providing that the commission of certain designated felonies raises a presumption of the recklessness and indifference needed for depraved heart murder.[7] Some jurisdictions also recognize a doctrine called the provocative act doctrine, which extends felon liability for death caused by non-felons, using by a standard of recklessness similar to that of depraved heart murder. This doctrine is discussed in Chapter 12.

---

5. E.g., Blackstone, supra at 192; Wharton, *The Law of Homicide* 189–90 (3d. ed. 1907)

6. See Wayne R. Lafave, *Criminal Law* 741–42 (4th ed. 2003).

7. Sec.210.2(b). The great English jurist Sir James Fitzjames Stephen murder held that felony murder was limited to acts by the felon that were "knowingly dangerous" to human life. Proving that the act was knowingly dangerous is similar to proving recklessness and indifference toward the victim's death. See Reg. v. Serne, 16 Cox Crim. Cas. 311 (1887) (England).

Purpose to Do Great Bodily Harm

As noted in Chapter 9, in many U.S. jurisdictions, an act done with purpose to commit great bodily harm that causes the victim's death will constitute murder, absent legal provocation. In some jurisdictions, the mens rea of purpose to do great bodily harm is itself sufficient for murder. Otherwise, an act done with purpose to do great bodily harm will usually satisfy the extreme recklessness required for depraved heart murder.

Provocation/Voluntary Manslaughter

As we saw in Chapter 10, legal provocation is usually associated with purpose to kill homicides. A reckless killing that might otherwise meet the standards of depraved heart murder can also be mitigated to voluntary manslaughter, however. If the defendant acted with extreme recklessness, but while actually and reasonably provoked, then the verdict will be voluntary manslaughter rather than murder in many jurisdictions.[8]

Reckless Manslaughter and Involuntary Manslaughter

If the prosecution fails to prove the mens rea needed for depraved heart murder, conviction may still be had on several forms of manslaughter based on a lesser form of recklessness or criminal negligence. These will be covered in the second part of this chapter.

Depraved Heart Murder Mens Rea: Recklessness

As we saw in Chapter 6, the mens rea of recklessness has three components: (1) degree of risk; (2) lack of justification for risk and (3) awareness of risk.

Assessments of degree of risk feature prominently in appellate decisions on depraved heart murder. As we will see, for some courts the degree of risk posed by defendant's conduct is important to distinguishing between murder and manslaughter with respect to unintentional killings.

---

8. Note that the conviction here is for *voluntary* manslaughter, not involuntary manslaughter. The latter offense is a logically tempting option because, like depraved heart murder, it is a form of unintentional homicide. Provocation, however, mitigates murder to voluntary manslaughter. The distinction is important because voluntary manslaughter is usually punished more severely than involuntary manslaughter. The practical result is that defense attorneys will generally seek to defeat a depraved heart murder charge by arguing lack of recklessness or indifference rather than asserting provocation, preferring an involuntary to a voluntary manslaughter verdict.

Less emphasized, but still an important part of the overall analysis, is the lack of justification for defendant's risk taking. This element may excuse some dangerous conduct undertaken for a greater social purpose. The law does not condemn a doctor who performs a dangerous but potentially life-saving medical procedure that ends up causing the death of a critically ill patient. Nor will it condemn a hazardous, and ultimately fatal, police or military action needed to safeguard the public. Statistically speaking, the risks involved here may be high, but they are justified. The reverse is also true. Especially bad reasons for risk taking will heighten our judgment of recklessness. A person is more likely to be found reckless if he engages in dangerous conduct as part of other criminality, or for entirely selfish and trivial reasons. Engaging in risky behavior for the fun of it is a classic example.

Most controversies concerning the recklessness required for depraved heart murder involve the third component of recklessness: awareness. Was the defendant actually aware of the risk?

Jerry and Simon are neighbors who have a long-standing dispute over parking in the shared driveway between their homes. Jerry is a large, burly man in his early 30s with a short temper. Simon is a small man in his early 60s, who compensates for his lack of stature with a wicked tongue.

Jerry comes home after a long day to find Simon's car blocking the drive. He gets out of his truck and yells at Simon who is watering his lawn. Jerry becomes truly furious when Simon impugns Jerry's masculinity and his mother's femininity. Jerry picks up a heavy steel pipe from the back of his pickup. He swings it like a baseball bat at Simon. He lands a glancing blow on Simon's side, then, with a full swing, lands a powerful, direct blow on Simon's chest. Simon staggers and falls to the ground and does not move again. Paramedics are called but he is pronounced dead on arrival at the hospital. An autopsy shows that the blow to the chest caused traumatic injury to the heart which led to a fatal heart attack.

Jerry states that he had no purpose to kill or even seriously hurt Simon. He adds that, if he really wanted to hurt Simon, "I'd have clocked him in the head." Jerry states that he had no idea that hitting someone in the chest could be so dangerous.

What are the chances that the prosecution can prove that Jerry acted with the recklessness needed for depraved heart murder?

The prosecution may begin with the degree of risk element, arguing that Jerry's conduct was outrageously dangerous. For a burly young man to take a heavy steel pipe, and, using a full baseball style swing, deliver a crushing blow to the chest of a much smaller, older man, presents an imminent risk of death to the victim. This blow was not in the service of any larger social good, nor was it in any sense justified as self-defense. As to Jerry's awareness of risk, he was fully aware of the weapon that he had chosen, aware of the size and age of his victim, and must have been aware of his own force, and therefore we may infer that he was aware of a deadly risk of his conduct.

The defense will contest all three aspects of recklessness. In terms of actual danger, the defense will seek any medical facts to establish the relative rarity of heart attacks induced by chest trauma.

The defense will point out that the attack was prompted by Simon's conduct and especially his insulting words. Assuming that these were not sufficient to constitute legal provocation—and they almost certainly were not—they nevertheless may be relevant to the justification factor. Imagine if Simon had reacted to Jerry's initial complaint with a respectful refusal to move his car rather than with personal insults. In this scenario, Jerry's subsequent resort to violence would appear significantly more culpable and less justified because less "provoked." The same point may be important to indifference analysis, discussed later.

Finally, and probably most importantly, the defense would argue that Jerry's knowledge of Simon's physique and use of the pipe does not demonstrate that Jerry acted with awareness of a deadly risk. Like most individuals, Jerry was not aware that a blow to the chest could lead to a heart attack; probably he thought that the worst injury might be bruises or broken ribs. Therefore, the defense would contend, Jerry lacked awareness of a significant and unjustified risk; he was not reckless.

In sum, this will be a case where recklessness may be contested. This is not to say that the prosecution's burden of proof might not be met, but that compared to many depraved heart murder scenarios, proof of recklessness will be a challenge here. If recklessness is proven, the indifference element, discussed further below, may also be important.

> Arnie, TJ and Chuck are longtime drinking buddies going back to their college fraternity days. The men are in their late 20s. Arnie obtains a hunting license, and they all decide that it would be great fun to go hunting for wild turkeys. Each claims to be an experienced hunter, but in fact none know much about the sport. They gather what they believe are essential materials—a gallon of Wild Turkey whiskey, take-out food, ammunition and three firearms: a shotgun, a military style assault rifle, and a pistol. They travel into the country

and spend the day drinking and eating. By late afternoon all are drunk and violate basic rules of hunting safety with respect to dress, positioning, communication and handling of firearms. Arnie dozes off and is awakened by a rustling in the nearby brush. He immediately fires off five rounds from his military style rifle in the direction of the sound. It takes several minutes for him to realize that he has shot and killed Chuck while Chuck was relieving himself in the underbrush.

Arnie has never been in trouble with the law before, but now finds himself charged with the depraved heart murder of Chuck. What are the chances that the prosecution can prove he acted recklessly with respect to Chuck's death?

Again it makes sense to begin with assessment of dangerousness. Arnie's conduct was clearly very dangerous to anyone in the vicinity, and especially to Chuck. He used a deadly weapon, in fact an extremely dangerous deadly weapon, against an unknown target, without taking basic precautions to determine that it was not human. His failure to follow basic hunting safety rules and his intoxication increased the dangerousness of his conduct.

There was no justification for this risk. This was not a military or police operation, but a recreational activity. Even assuming significant social value to hunting, there is no need to conduct it so dangerously.

The big issue here will be awareness of risk. Arnie will argue that he had absolutely no idea that Chuck was in the brush and he would never have fired had he known. He thought he was firing at a turkey or other animal.

Arnie would like to argue that he lacked awareness because of intoxication. He would like to say that he was not aware of his surroundings or the danger involved as he if he had been sober. But this is not an argument he can make. As we will see in Chapter 19, Arnie will *not* be able to use his intoxication to negate recklessness here. Under both common law principles and the MPC, voluntary intoxication evidence cannot be used to negate the required mens rea for this offense. Any diminution in perceptive abilities is deemed his own fault. As a result, we assess Arnie's awareness of risk as if he were sober.

The prosecution will argue that Arnie's decision to fire his weapon five times into a location where he could not see his actual target, knowing that there were at least two other people in the general vicinity, represents awareness of a significant risk that he might be firing at a human being. The defense will argue to the contrary, that having just woken up, he instinctively fired, without any conscious awareness of danger to another human being.

Here, as elsewhere, we confront practical problems with assessing awareness. Absent a defendant admission, how can the prosecution prove beyond a reasonable doubt that the defendant was *actually* aware of the risks involved? Decision makers often resort here to what may be called must-have-been-aware analysis. This is a form of analysis that requires considerable care or it will dilute the recklessness requirement, effectively converting it into negligence. Here's how it works, at least in theory.

The decision maker notes the warning facts which were readily apparent to anyone in the defendant's position. These are the facts, inherent in the situation or of which the defendant was directly apprised, that put the defendant on notice concerning the risk involved. These facts would lead any person with concern for others to a recognize that death or serious bodily injury was being threatened. Arnie had a deadly weapon and understood its deadly nature. He was aware that other human beings were in the vicinity. He could not see clearly what he was shooting at. Any reasonable person in Arnie's position would understand that there was a significant risk that shooting at movement in the bush might end up killing or wounding a human being. From this the decision maker may infer that Simon, not suffering any incapacity of which the law takes account, also must have been aware of a deadly risk.

An important caution: this style of analysis can easily go wrong and effectively reduce recklessness to a form of negligence. The final determination must always be that the facts indicate that the defendant *was aware* of a significant risk, not just that any reasonable person would have been aware. For more on this distinction, see the sidebar on The Art of Reasonableness.

In the end, as in many cases of this sort, the fact finder will have considerable discretion in determining whether the prosecution proved that Simon acted recklessly. In addition to the factors already delineated, the decision maker's view of the defendant, victim, and hunting generally may be significant. Also important to the resolution of the depraved heart murder charge, will be assessment of indifference, discussed below.

The Indifference Requirement

Recklessness is not, by itself, enough to satisfy the mens rea requirements of depraved heart murder; the fact finder must also determine that the defendant manifested "depraved indifference" or "extreme indifference to the value of human life." What does this mean? What work does this element do?

The indifference requirement comes directly from common law formulations of murder and serves primarily to give decision-makers a qualitative marker to distinguish between murder and manslaughter. It invites the decision-maker to decide whether the defendant demonstrated the kind of callousness and cruelty characteristic of murder or whether the accused's conduct should be classified as a lesser offense. This can be done in several ways.

Appellate courts frequently treat the indifference element as establishing a requirement of extreme dangerousness. Thus unintentional murder is distinguished from unintentional manslaughter by the sheer dangerousness of defendant's conduct. As one court has held, for murder, a defendant's conduct must be "imminently dangerous and present … a grave risk of death," where the lesser offense of manslaughter involves only a "substantial" risk of death.[9] From the appellate perspective, a dangerousness standard has the advantage of providing objective criteria for assessing verdicts. This makes recklessness the subjective element and indifference the objective element of depraved heart mens rea. But that is only one way of understanding the indifference requirement.

Indifference may also be understood as a quantitative reassessment of all three elements of recklessness. In addition to measuring the relative risk of the defendant's conduct, the decision maker assesses justification and awareness. The less justification for the risk-taking, and the more evidence of awareness of risk, the more likely is a finding of indifference. Along these lines, many commentators describe the overall mens rea of depraved heart murder as extreme recklessness, with indifference providing the adjective of extreme.

Alternatively, indifference may encompass factors not directly addressed by recklessness, including demonstrations of particular cruelty by the defendant, and assessment of the relative innocence or vulnerability of the victim. These can be important to an intuitive determination about whether the crime merits categorization as a murder or a manslaughter.

The multiplicity of views of indifference can be frustrating for students, but in practice this is an element largely committed to the discretion of the initial decision maker. It's a jury question.

To illustrate indifference analysis in practice, we return to our earlier cases on recklessness.

Jerry's Killing of Simon

Here the level of risk in Jerry's single pipe blow is not as high as in most paradigm instances of depraved heart murder. Death by heart attack is not a common result of a hard blow to the chest. As a general matter, the risk of death from such conduct may be significant but probably not "imminent." This assessment would be different had the strike been to Simon's head, a more vulnerable part of the body.

---

9. People v. Roe, 542 N.E.2d 610, 611 (N.Y. 1989).

Awareness of risk assessment follows a similar track. Fact finders are more likely to believe Jerry was aware of a substantial risk of death with a head blow than a body blow.

Finally, the fact that Jerry is responding to Simon's conduct (parking in the drive) and personal insults, makes his reaction less indicative of a general callousness toward the value of the victim's life, and more a spontaneous expression of anger. A jury could find extreme indifference to the value of human life here, but the element would also give the jury an invitation to decline a murder conviction in favor of a lesser offense.

Arnie's Shooting of Chuck

This case provides a useful example of indifference considerations potentially independent of recklessness. Although the law considers all victims equally worthy, victim identity may pay a role in assessment of indifference. In this case the victim, Chuck, was a full participant in this misbegotten hunting expedition. The death of someone who also chose to drink and pay no attention to basic safety precautions, indeed whose carelessness may also have contributed to the result, means that this offense may appear less weighty on the relative scales of moral and legal wrong. As a result, decision makers may be less inclined to deem it murder. By contrast, if the victim were a birdwatcher, or a young boy out for a walk with his dog, the same reckless conduct by Arnie might appear in a different light. Now a decision maker may be inclined to say that the defendant manifested indifference to the value of human life.

An important caveat. The law does *not* mandate or even suggest that this kind of victim valuation is relevant to indifference. Nevertheless, when fact finders are given an essentially discretionary decision like this about offense severity, such considerations may be influential.

Omissions to Act

So far we have focused on killings resulting from affirmative acts. Depraved heart murder may also be, and frequently is, based on an omission to act, however. For example, there are a number of depraved heart murder cases based on failure to care for the young, the sick, or the elderly. A caretaker who fails to provide basic nutrition and health care for a vulnerable person, leading to that person's death is a prime subject for a depraved heart murder prosecution. Here the prosecution needs to show that the defendant had a duty to act and omitted to act; that the omission was reckless and demonstrated indifference to the value of human life; and finally that it caused the victim's death. The basic analysis is illustrated by the following.

Mary Jo owns several pit bull dogs, which she keeps in her fenced backyard. Mary Jo knows that the dogs have been specially bred for fighting, and are capable of doing serious harm to other animals and human beings. She hopes to breed the dogs and sell their offspring for a large profit. In the surrounding community such dogs are popular among drug dealers and can command a large sum. One of these dogs is named Brutus. The person who sold Brutus to Mary Jo told her that he needs extensive training and regular exercise, but Mary Jo ignores this advice. Her care for Brutus is limited to regular shots and feeding.

The backyard fence where Brutus and the other dogs are kept is poorly maintained, and twice in the last month the dogs have escaped and threatened others in the neighborhood. In one incident, the dogs surrounded two small children and appeared about to attack, before an adult intervened. Several persons, including a police officer, have warned Mary Jo that she needs to take greater precautions with her animals or someone will be seriously hurt or killed. She says the dogs are perfectly safe "as long as no one bothers them."

While Mary Jo is away from the house, Brutus escapes and attacks and kills a five-year-old boy walking home from kindergarten. Mary Jo is arrested. Can she be successfully prosecuted for depraved heart murder?[10]

Although normally Mary Jo would not owe any duty of care to an unrelated child in the neighborhood, as the owner of Brutus she is responsible for any harm to neighbors that it causes or threat that it poses. It is her responsibility to keep this potentially dangerous animal secure. Therefore her failure to secure Brutus can be an omission to act on which liability is based. This omission would certainly include inadequate fencing and the failure to properly train Brutus.

Causation also is apparent here. (For causation generally see Chapter 13.) Mary Jo's failure to secure the dogs led to Brutus's escape and the fatal attack on the boy. Her omission to act represents the actual and proximate cause of the boy's death. The real question is mens rea: recklessness and indifference.

The prosecution will argue that leaving this untrained, aggressive dog in a poorly fenced backyard, given his recognized propensity for violence, represented a large risk to many in the neighborhood, especially children. There was no justification for this risk; the dog could have been better trained and kept more

---

10. E.g., People v. Davidson, 987 P.2d 335 (Kan. 1999). There are also a number of reported cases upholding verdicts of involuntary manslaughter for fatal dog attacks.

securely. Mary Jo's lack of attention to these matters has no larger social justification, and on its face indicates her lack of concern about risk to others.

As is often the case, awareness of risk will be the main battleground for litigation. The prosecution will argue that she was aware of the risk by virtue of knowing of the dog's breeding and reputation, the warnings she had received from the police and others, and from prior escapes. She must have known that any number of people in the neighborhood would be vulnerable to a serious attack, including small children.

The defense will argue that Mary Jo was not at all aware of a major risk of death or great bodily harm posed by Brutus. Dogs may bite and scratch people; they almost never kill. This dog had never seriously hurt anyone, and while it frightened people enough for them to express their concern, this by no means conveyed to Mary Jo a realization of deadly threat. Notice once more that the final decision depends on how the fact finder reads the evidence. There is often no absolutely determinative proof or disproof of recklessness.

Finally, assuming that recklessness is shown, what about indifference? In those jurisdictions that emphasize assessment of dangerousness, there will be major controversy concerning exactly how dangerous this dog was. A relative assessment of justification and awareness probably tilts in the prosecution's favor. Most important to the prosecution's showing here, however, is the vulnerability of this five-year-old boy. If recklessness is proven, the jury might well find that Mary Jo's keeping Brutus under these conditions demonstrated extreme indifference to the value of the lives of children and perhaps others in the neighborhood.

Spotting Omission to Act Liability

Sometimes omission to act cases hide in plain sight, in that liability *follows from* an initial affirmative act. For example, in the case of Jerry and Simon, assume that we determine Jerry did not act with the mens rea required for murder in striking Simon. Nevertheless, assume that Jerry's blow did injure Simon, leaving him moaning and disoriented on the ground. Because he caused Simon's injury, at this point Jerry has a duty to seek care for Simon. At a minimum he should call for assistance. If Jerry simply laughs at Simon in his misery and walks away, murder liability might result *if* Jerry's failure to give or seek aid led to Simon's death, that is, if making the call for assistance would have saved Simon's life. Such liability would also require a determination that when he walked away, Jerry was aware of a significant risk that Simon would die without care, and his disregard manifested extreme indifference to the value of human life.

Omission liability following affirmative wrongful acts adds an additional dimension to many homicide cases. Any person who causes a significant injury may thereafter be subject to depraved heart murder liability—or depending on mens rea, a lesser form of manslaughter—simply for failure to render care.

How to Talk About Reasonableness: Distinguishing Legal Standards and Credibility Arguments

One of the hardest distinctions for law students to maintain, and sometimes even for courts, is that between awareness and should have been aware, between recklessness and negligence. As we have seen, recklessness requires that the defendant have been actually aware of certain facts; negligence rests on whether a reasonable person would have been aware of these facts. Law professors love to catch law students making mistakes here, as in arguing for recklessness based on what a reasonable person would perceive, or what the defendant should have realized. Demonstrating just how slippery this distinction can be, appellate court opinions sometimes manifest similar imprecision in discussing the mens rea requirements of unintentional murder and manslaughter.

One way to keep the lines clear is never to mention reasonableness when the mens rea is recklessness. But actually this goes too far. There is one way that reasonableness might be relevant to recklessness. It involves an argument about defendant credibility.

Assume that defendant claims no awareness of risk based on a particularly bizarre story. Defendant states, for example, that he had no idea that slashing someone with a sword was dangerous because he was so used to playing video games where injuries and deaths are not real. This is an unreasonable explanation and, by itself, might satisfy the requirements of criminal negligence—a reasonable person would have understood. Note that if the defendant stands charged with a reckless offense, however, this account tends to negate the required mens rea. If the defendant was not aware of any substantial risks from his conduct, if he truly believed that he operated in a video game reality, then he did not act recklessly. But should we believe the defendant?

The prosecution may use the very unreasonableness of defendant's account to cast doubt on his credibility. The prosecution may argue that no reasonable person would ever confuse a real sword and its dangers with a video game. The prosecution would maintain that this story is unreasonable and therefore implausible. Far more likely is that the defendant is lying, and has come up with this unlikely story to avoid guilt. Thus from its very unreasonableness, its very incredibility, the fact finder may infer that the defendant is lying about the risks he perceived. The de-

cision maker may conclude that the defendant was, in fact, aware of the risks involved. Again, note that we cannot move directly from the unreasonableness of defendant's story to proof of recklessness, but can use the unreasonableness of his account to argue against his credibility, an argument that is consistent with and may support an inference of recklessness.[11]

Reckless Manslaughter

The next category of offenses down the homicide ladder from depraved heart murder is manslaughter. There are several varieties that need to be distinguished.

Some jurisdictions have adopted the MPC, which provides for two lesser offenses of unintentional homicide: a form of manslaughter based on simple recklessness, and a lesser offense based on gross negligence. The Model Penal Code calls these manslaughter and negligent homicide respectively. I will denominate them somewhat differently. The first will be called reckless manslaughter, according to its distinctive mens rea. The second will be called involuntary manslaughter, because this is the most common name in American law for unintentional homicide based on gross negligence.

Where recognized, reckless manslaughter is defined primarily by its relationship to those offenses above and below it on the homicide hierarchy. It is distinguished from depraved heart murder in that here recklessness alone will suffice for conviction; there need be no showing of extreme indifference to the value of human life. Reckless manslaughter is distinguished from the offense below it on the homicide ladder—involuntary manslaughter—because the former requires recklessness rather than negligence.

To illustrate crimes that might fall into the category of reckless manslaughter, recall both the Jerry-Simon driveway dispute and the Arnie-Chuck hunting debacle. In both cases a fact finder might determine that the defendant was aware of a significant and unjustified risk of causing deadly harm. A full-strength blow to the torso of a 60-year-old with a heavy pipe, and multiple shots from an assault rifle at an unknown target in the brush, both involve obviously dangerous conduct where the perpetrator disregards the risk of death.

---

11. For example, in Davidson, 987 P.2d at 683, in a case involving depraved heart murder based on recklessness and indifference, affirming a conviction where subjective awareness was clearly required, the court stated concerning defendant's awareness that her dog might pose a fatal risk to the victim: "It was sufficient ... that she could have reasonably foreseen that the dogs could attack or injure someone ..."

Yet a fact finder may balk at calling these deeds murder. They do not necessarily rise to the same level of dangerousness, cruelty, or callousness as do classic forms of depraved heart murder. Therefore the jury might convict for reckless manslaughter: recklessness without extreme indifference.

Involuntary Manslaughter

Involuntary manslaughter is generally defined as an unintentional killing based on grossly negligent conduct. The defendant caused the death of another by disregard of a significant and unjustifiable risk of which a reasonable person would have been aware. The key language in analysis here (as always with negligence) is: "should have been aware." While recklessness requires that the offender be *actually aware* of risk; *should have been* aware is sufficient for criminal negligence. Should-have been-aware does not tell us all we need to know about negligent culpability, however. We still need to differentiate criminal negligence, also known as gross negligence, from the "ordinary" negligence required for most civil liability.

As we've seen, appellate courts also sometimes distinguish murder and manslaughter according to degree of risk. Courts state that depraved heart murder involves conduct that poses great and imminent risks of death while involuntary manslaughter involves only a significant risk of death.

Involuntary manslaughter cases involve an enormous variety of fact patterns. They are less likely to involve brutal attacks than are depraved heart murder cases and more likely to involve lawful activities that are undertaken in a dangerous manner. Quite a few cases involve care for children or the elderly.

Criminal Negligence

As discussed in Chapter 6, a person's perceptions and conduct are criminally negligent when they constitute a "gross deviation from the standard of care of a reasonable person."[12] Such negligence involves more risky conduct, more notice of risk, and less justification for the risk than does ordinary civil negligence.

Maurice was a devoted father, mentor and coach of his tennis playing daughter Claudette. At the age of 15, Claudette was a top-ranked

---

12. MPC sec. 2.02(2)(d). On occasion, ordinary negligence has been the basis for involuntary manslaughter. See State v. Williams, 484 P.2d 1167, 1171 (Wash. Ct. App. 1971) but here the legislature later changed the law to require either recklessness or gross negligence for manslaughter. Wash. Rev. Code secs. 9A.32.060, 9A.32.070.

amateur player, preparing to move into professional competition. Maurice was determined that she make it in the big-time. He had sacrificed his career and personal life to advancing his daughter's prospects. This summer, he knew, would determine the course of her future.

As a coach, Maurice sits at courtside and has access to the players' water bottles. He dumps the contents of two sleeping pill capsules in the water of Claudette's competitor. It seems to have little effect, but Claudette does win the match. In two succeeding matches, Maurice does the same, except on these occasions he uses the contents of three capsules to ensure the desired effect on Claudette's competitors. On the last occasion, Claudette's opponent, Sara, collapses following the match at her hotel room. She is taken to hospital where, despite intensive treatment, she dies. Blood tests and an autopsy reveal that she was drugged and investigation soon leads back to Maurice. He admits everything, tearfully saying, "I just thought it was harmless, everybody takes those pills. And these kids are in great shape. I know I was cheating, but I never wanted this."

Medical experts say that the effects of the chemicals in the sleeping pills are highly variable depending on the individual. In general, young persons are much more susceptible to ill effects than adults, and negative effects are exacerbated by dehydration and stress, including the stress of athletic competition. They agree that the unconsenting administration of such substances presented a significant risk of serious harm to a highly stressed teenage athlete.

Maurice is charged with the involuntary manslaughter of Sara. Will he be convicted?[13]

As given here, the facts indicate a degree of danger sufficient for involuntary manslaughter, but perhaps not for depraved heart murder. Similarly, there is insufficient proof that Maurice was aware of a deadly risk as would be needed for a murder charge. There is no doubt, however, that a reasonable person would have been aware that Maurice's conduct was potentially dangerous to the health of the unwitting recipients. The only question is whether Maurice acted in a way that represents a *gross* deviation from the standard of care for reasonable person. Here the fact that Maurice acted in his own self-interest, that he violated the bodily autonomy of a young person and flouted basic rules of

---

13. See Molly Moore, For Tennis Dad, Deadly Obsession to Win, Washington Post, March 4, 2006.

competition will contribute to a judgment that this was a gross deviation from the standard of care of a reasonable person.

Punishing Negligence: Awareness and Criminal Responsibility

Since the mid-20th century, some Anglo-American legal scholars have argued that awareness of wrongdoing is a prerequisite for criminal punishment. They ask: How can a person choose to do wrong, if unaware aware of what makes it wrong? How can failure to perceive be the basis for criminal condemnation and incarceration? Therefore recklessness should be the minimum mens rea for any serious criminal offense, these scholars argue.[14]

Yet there are many instances where modern criminal law imposes significant liability without subjective awareness. There are many strict liability offenses, offenses based on negligence; we might also point to the situation of intoxicated individuals charged with reckless offenses, where intoxication is excluded from considerations of awareness. How can these forms of liability be justified if awareness is critical? Some possible answers may be found in new work on consciousness and perception.

As the saying goes, some information goes in one ear and out the other. Why? Because it is not of personal interest. It does not matter to us, or worse, represents information we do not want to hear. By contrast, we immediately grasp information that matters to us. You can hear some-one say your name across a crowded, noisy room because your name has such significance for you. This illustrates that perception is something we do; it's not just a passive process. We take in information from the world through all of our senses—or not—according to our efforts and our per-ception priorities. We pay much more attention to some things than oth-ers, according to long-standing interests and attitudes.

What this means for criminal responsibility is that there are times when our failures to perceive may be attributed to insufficient effort or bad per-ception priorities. Failures to perceive critical information may reflect morally responsible choices. When failures to perceive involve deadly and unjustified risks to others, they constitute wrongful choices which can jus-tify criminal conviction. The person who does not see the clearly appar-ent dangers of his own driving, or the dangers of unsafe handling of firearms, who is oblivious to the hazards of certain chemicals or other dan-

---

14. E.g., Glanville Williams, Criminal Law: The General Part 122–23 (1961). See also, Larry Alexander, Foreword: Coleman and Corrective Justice, 15 Harvard J. L. & Pub. Pol'y 621, 631–36 (1992).

> *gerous workplace conditions, generally does not care enough to see these hazards. He or she has other priorities. Under this view, punishing for careless conduct does not so much track a lack of intellectual ability or sensory fault as a morally culpable lack of concern. Or so I have argued.*[15]

Individualization Problems

As with any reasonable person standard, we confront problems of individualization in involuntary manslaughter. Exactly who is the reasonable person for purposes of defendant's liability? What characteristics of the defendant might be attributed to the reasonable person? Generally physical characteristics are included, but these are rarely the source of controversy in criminal homicide. Physical disabilities do not often play a role in critical failures to perceive risk, and when they do they will provide an excuse as long as there was no fault in failing to anticipate the dangerous situation. A blind person will not be faulted for failing to see, assuming the person has not chosen to put himself in a situation where that disability might threaten others.

The most serious individualization issues involve the mental, emotional, or cultural characteristics of the particular defendant. For example, should a retarded teenager who gives birth to a child unaided and mistakenly causes the infant to die, be held to the standard of an ordinarily reasonable person, or should the standard reflect her disability?[16] Should cultural or religious beliefs or practices ever be taken into account in assessing reasonableness? Standard definitions of negligence suggest a negative answer to these questions, but there may be exceptions.

Normally, conduct that represents a gross deviation from the standard of care of a reasonable person and that causes death will indicate moral culpability. It will demonstrate that the person lacked basic concern for the welfare of others, not just a lack of intelligence or skill. But there are cases that raise questions about the connection between negligence and moral fault.

> Terri and Bart are parents of four children. They are extremely loving and concerned parents. They are committed to natural health care, which means that they eschew any vaccines or drugs for their children. In 15 years of child-rearing, this has not caused any major health

---

15. Samuel H. Pillsbury, Crimes of Indifference, 49 Rutgers L.Rev. 105 (1996).

16. State v. Everhart, 231 S.E. 2d 604 (N.C. 1977) (holding that low intelligence is relevant to determining involuntary manslaughter of a newborn infant).

problems. Indeed, their children appear to be much healthier than average.

Eight-year-old Jenna comes down with a fever. Terri treats her with an herbal remedy that has often proven effective in the past. The fever, however, persists. After four days, Jenna becomes extremely lethargic. She stops eating. Terri and Bart seek the help of others in their natural health community, and try other organic remedies at their suggestion. Jenna's fever reaches 105. Extremely worried about her health, the parents take Jenna to a doctor, who suggests a course of antibiotics. After much agonizing, Jenna and Bart decide not to administer the antibiotics, however, believing that antibiotics can do serious harm to young people. Jenna dies three days later. Medical experts contend that she would have lived if she had received the antibiotics when they were prescribed.

Terri and Bart are charged with the involuntary manslaughter of Jenna. What relevance, if any, is their sincere belief that antibiotics are dangerous to the young?

Putting aside for the moment the defendants' beliefs about antibiotics, all the basics of involuntary manslaughter appear here. Given the indications of serious illness and the advice of a medical professional that antibiotics would provide a cure, the failure to provide those antibiotics appears a gross deviation from the standard of care for reasonable person. This omission, by persons that owed the victim a duty of care, led to death. Chances are it will also lead to conviction.

Terri and Bart's personal beliefs about antibiotics are not relevant to what the reasonable person would think or do in this situation. Unlike most persons guilty of involuntary manslaughter, they have not demonstrated any lack of concern for the victim, but that may not matter. The current legal standard is reasonableness, not lack of concern. Courts in the U.S. generally have refused to individualize according to religious beliefs, and are unlikely to do so for personal or cultural beliefs or traditions.[17]

Other Forms of Manslaughter

There are at least two other forms of manslaughter recognized in many jurisdictions that require a brief mention: unlawful act manslaughter and vehicular manslaughter.

---

17. E.g., Walker v. Superior Court, 763 P.2d 852 (Cal. 1988).

Unlawful act manslaughter, also known as misdemeanor manslaughter, parallels the basic structure of felony murder, but is based on a lesser predicate offense and results in a lesser homicide conviction. In many jurisdictions, a finding that the defendant's commission of a misdemeanor caused death will be sufficient to produce a verdict of involuntary manslaughter. There are, however, many jurisdictional variations in the kinds of offenses that will suffice for the predicate "misdemeanor." These may actually be felonies that do not qualify for felony murder, or certain kinds of misdemeanors, or virtually any criminal violations, including traffic violations.

Finally, many jurisdictions also recognize a separate offense of vehicular manslaughter. This is a lesser form of homicide offense where defendant's negligence causes a traffic death. The existence of this offense does not, however, preclude the state from seeking a conviction for depraved heart murder or involuntary manslaughter for deaths caused in a vehicular accident, if the culpability standards of these greater offenses are met.

CHAPTER 12

FELONY MURDER

To many legal commentators, felony murder is the shark of contemporary homicide law: a throwback to an earlier age. Like the shark (and the cockroach among other change-resistant species), most creatures of its era died out long ago. Felony murder is said to date back to pre-modern English law when liability was based primarily on the harm done by defendant and concepts of mens rea were primitive. While most other crimes subsequently developed sophisticated concepts of mens rea, felony murder persisted—and persists—in determining liability primarily by result.[1]

The truth, though, is more complex. Current American felony murder law is the product of modern U.S. legislation and judicial interpretation. Reflecting public sentiment, it dramatically increases punishment for certain felonies that result in death. Even if its structure is archaic, the policy choices behind felony murder are modern—and very American.[2]

Still the shark analogy holds in at least one respect: this doctrine presents problems coexisting with others. In particular, how do we recognize both felony murder *and* the other forms of murder and manslaughter that require mens rea for killing? How can we preserve the significance of premeditation, provocation, purpose to kill, recklessness and negligence in homicide law, yet still recognize felony murder? How can we set limits for this rule with a potentially insatiable appetite for doctrinal territory? Answering this challenge has produced many of the complexities of current felony murder.

The essential structure of felony murder is simple. A person who: (1) commits a felony, and (2) in so doing causes death, should be convicted of felony murder. This simple structure masks many details and jurisdictional differences, however. As we will see, not all felonies will qualify as the basis for felony murder and special rules may apply to its causal requirement.

---

1. This is the thrust of People v Aaron, 299 N.W.2d 304 (Mich. 1980) in which the Michigan Supreme Court eliminated felony murder in that state.

2. For this perspective on felony murder law, I am indebted to Guyora Binder, The Origins of American Felony Murder Rules, 57 Stan. L. Rev. 59 (2004).

Felony murder law is particularly sensitive to statutory variation. Because different jurisdictions have different felony murder statutes, this chapter cannot provide a complete review of relevant doctrine, but will only seek to introduce critical concepts. Before beginning that task, however, we need to situate this doctrine in criminal law generally.

Heightened Culpability and the Politics of Felony Murder

Felony murder represents a particularly dramatic example of a principle that may be called heightened culpability. This holds that when a person chooses to commit a lesser wrong, but in so doing causes a greater harm, then the actor should be punished as if he or she had chosen to commit the greater harm. That is, the person should be punished as if the individual acted with full mens rea as to the greater harm.

The principle of heightened culpability may be found in many offenses, explaining why some elements important to offense severity are nevertheless strict liability. For example, in many jurisdictions the offense of assault on a police officer is a significantly more serious crime than simple assault. One might expect that the distinction would be tracked by mens rea: that a defendant would have to know that the victim was a peace officer in order to be guilty of the greater offense. And in some jurisdictions this is true, but in others the peace officer element is strict liability. As long as the defendant acted with the required mens rea for the lesser crime of assault, and the victim turned out to be a peace officer, the defendant may be guilty of the greater offense without any notice of the victim's law enforcement status. Such heightened culpability provisions may be controversial, but they are also common.

Considered in this light, felony murder does not represent a fundamental break with the rest of criminal law, but rather an extreme and therefore controversial example of a principle (heightened culpability) recognized in other parts of the law. Under its rule, a defendant may be convicted of murder, often first-degree murder, when the only mens rea proven is that required for the underlying felony (as in, the mens rea for the underlying felony of robbery or arson). The defendant need not have acted with any mens rea as to the victim's death. For example:

> Alfred is furious when he sees his Neighbor allowing his dog to defecate on Alfred's pristine front lawn. Alfred has put up big signs warning against this. Alfred decides that burning the Neighbor's dog-

house would teach the Neighbor a good lesson. That night, after ensuring that the dog is not present, Alfred sets the doghouse alight with a small amount of gasoline. Because there are other flammable materials in the Neighbor's yard, of which Alfred is unaware, the fire rapidly spreads to an adjacent home where an elderly man lives by himself. Inside, the homeowner has stacked on the floor every magazine, newspaper and piece of mail received in the last 30 years. Needless to say, this is a serious fire hazard. When some of these materials catch fire, the rest of the house rapidly goes up in flames, killing the man.

Alfred tells police that he had absolutely no idea that the fire would spread and had no intent to hurt anyone, not even the Neighbor's dog. Can Alfred be convicted of felony murder?

The main question here is whether Alfred is guilty of arson. Assuming that he did commit arson by purposefully and unlawfully burning a structure (the doghouse), that arson is a qualifying felony for felony murder in the jurisdiction (it usually is), and the arson caused the fire that killed the victim, Alfred may be convicted of felony murder. In most jurisdictions this will be first-degree murder, subject to some of the highest penalties available.

The fact that Alfred acted with no purpose to kill any human being, did not know that his actions would kill, and probably was not even reckless with respect to killing another human under these facts, does not matter. It is even possible that a fact finder would not find Alfred criminally negligent with respect to risks to human life from setting a doghouse on fire. No matter. Alfred may be found guilty of felony murder without any mens rea with respect to causing death.

In this example we see that felony murder can transform conduct of lesser culpability into criminal liability of the highest order based on happenstance. Whether Alfred faces conviction for a relatively minor offense centering on burning the doghouse, or the most serious category of murder, depends on factors largely beyond his knowledge or control: flammable materials in the neighbor's backyard and in the victim's house. How can this be justified?

Felony murder, at least as it functions in many jurisdictions today, stands in significant tension with both deterrence and retribution theories of punishment.[3] Both theories seek to proportion severity of punishment according

---

3. E.g., George P. Fletcher, Reflections on Felony-Murder 12 Sw. L. Rev. 413 (1981); James J. Tomkovicz, The Endurance of the Felony-Murder Rule, 51 Wash. & Lee L. Rev..1429 (1994). For efforts to justify at least some increased liability for killings during the commission of felonies, see Kenneth W. Simons, When Is Strict Criminal Liability Just? 87 J. Crim. L. & Criminol. 1075, 1121–25 (1997); Guyora Binder, The Culpability of Felony Murder, 83 Notre Dame L. Rev. 965 (2008).

to the defendant's choice to do wrong. By contrast, at least in some cases, felony murder establishes the punishment level according to fortuity of result rather than an individualized assessment of the defendant's choice to do wrong.

The modern felony murder rule may not match up that well with punishment theory, but it definitely has popular appeal. A robber or a rapist or a burglar who kills in the course of his crime demonstrates significant culpability and a high degree of dangerousness. By virtue of its fatal outcome, the crime generates public outrage. A person is dead who would be alive had the defendant not committed the felony. This conduct merits significant punishment and the confluence of felony and death make murder an appealing verdict.

Notice that the real controversy here is not whether the felon should be punished, but how much. The argument against the doctrine is that felony murder punishes too much: in excess of the offender's culpability. While convincing to those who are moved by general principles of justice, this argument is a tough sale in an American political market that is skeptical, to say the least, of arguments for lesser punishment of persons who cause serious harms.

In practice, felony murder usually produces less controversial verdicts than its structure, or our initial example, might suggest. In most cases, the felon who causes death will have acted with at least recklessness toward the death of the victim, demonstrating culpability equivalent to that of depraved heart murder. And if recklessness is not clear, then criminal negligence usually is. While legally possible, there are almost no felony murders involving purely accidental, non-negligent deaths.[4]

Truth be told, many convictions for felony murder come in cases where the killer likely acted with purpose to kill. In these instances, the prosecution charges felony murder because the doctrine eliminates the need to prove purpose to kill beyond a reasonable doubt, and because it ensures that the homicide will be punished severely, usually as first-degree murder. In this fashion felony murder doctrine may correct for one of the potential weaknesses of premeditation analysis, ensuring that highly culpable but arguably non-calculated purpose to kill homicides will be classified as first-degree murder.

As an example, imagine an armed robber who kills a store clerk because the clerk took too long to empty the cash register. Here there may not be proof beyond a reasonable doubt of a calculated (i.e. premeditated) killing, but many

---

4. And yet the possibility remains. See, e.g. Ford v. State, 423 S.E.2d 255 (Ga. 1992) (overturning conviction of felony murder based on accidental shooting while cleaning a gun, because underlying felony of felon in possession of a firearm was held not an inherently dangerous offense.)

would agree that it should rank among the most serious of crimes. Felony murder ensures that it is a first-degree murder regardless of premeditation.

The real world harshness of felony murder rules often appears with respect to accomplices. Assume that in the robbery case mentioned above, the robber was assisted by a young man, Paul, who served as a lookout. Paul had been assured by Robber that there would be no shooting or physical violence. Nevertheless, Paul would be liable for first-degree murder based on the Robber's conduct. It's true that prosecutors could charge Paul with a lesser crime, for example simple robbery, but it is hard for prosecutors to decline charging on an offense as serious as felony murder.[5]

A few jurisdictions in the United States have eliminated felony murder, either by legislation or judicial abrogation. In these jurisdictions, killings that occur in the course of a felony are often handled under depraved heart murder, with the defendant's commission of a felony contributing to a determination of recklessness and extreme indifference.[6]

Is It Really about Dangerousness or about Culpability?

The standard justification for felony murder is that certain felonies present special dangers to human life and therefore require special efforts to deter. The idea is that an offense like robbery or rape is significantly more likely to cause death than other crimes. As a result, added punishment for any death that occurs is needed dissuade individuals from attempting these felonies.

As critics have noted, however, there is no solid empirical data showing that certain felonies are especially dangerous. Even robberies, the most dangerous of all of the felonies supporting felony murder, rarely cause death when considered in their statistical entirety. Instead, the judgment of dangerousness seems to be the result of questionable inductive logic: because we know of particular robberies or rapes that cause death, we believe that such offenses are commonly dangerous to human life.[7]

There is another explanation for felony murder which avoids this critique, though it remains open to another. Perhaps felony murder is based on

---

5. Which is primarily to charge offenses at the highest level supported by law. Also, charging accomplices with first-degree murder gives prosecutors the ability to encourage their cooperation in the prosecution of others.

6. See MPC sec. 210.2 (1) (b).

7. Without doubt, some robbers are extraordinarily dangerous. But felony murder rules generally do not distinguish between robbers who commit their crimes in an especially dangerous way and those who do not.

the judgment that most killings in the course of a felony represent especially heinous offenses. Felons who participate in felonies that cause death generally act with the culpability of murderers, by virtue of the confluence of a felonious scheme and a killing. When most people imagine a scenario of felony murder, they think of crimes—robberies or rapes in particular—like those depicted in Hollywood movies, in which cold-blooded felons kill innocent persons for cash, to eliminate witnesses, or for the sheer fun of wielding ultimate power.[8] Recent work in criminology documents that some perpetrators of violent crimes, especially robbery, do commit the offense for the thrill of exerting raw power over others.[9] From this we gain a picture of extreme wrongdoing and great culpability that may not be covered by the doctrine of premeditation. It suggests that we might need felony murder to ensure that such offenses are punished as the highly culpable crimes they are.

Still current felony murder law goes well beyond this rationale. It generally does not require proof of purposeful violence or an especially culpable motive, but encompasses all instances of death in the commission of a qualifying felony.

Qualifying Felonies

The first question in felony murder analysis is whether the particular felony charged qualifies as a lawful basis for felony murder. Not every felony will support a felony murder conviction. As part of this process, we also need to distinguish between felonies that support first and second-degree murder charges.

Determining whether a felony qualifies involves a two-step process of determining (1) initial eligibility and (2) satisfaction of the so-called merger rule.

Rules for determining initial eligibility of a felony for felony murder fall into three categories: (1) statutory designation, (2) inherently dangerous as committed, and (3) inherently dangerous by definition. If the felony is eligible under one of these rules, then the felony will support felony murder *as long as it is not disqualified* by the merger rule. As this brief introduction suggests, the law of felony murder can get very complicated, very quickly.

A few preliminary notes on language before plunging into doctrinal detail. In those jurisdictions that still define murder as a killing with malice afore-

---

8. As an example, see Michael Mann's 1995 movie Heat.

9. See Jack Katz, *Seductions of Crime: Moral and Sensual Attractions in Doing Evil* 80–113 (1998); *In Their Own Words: Criminals on Crime* 71–78 (Paul Cromwell ed. 2006).

thought, courts standardly speak of qualifying felonies as imputing the malice needed for murder. As is often true with malice discourse, this statement serves primarily to reconcile archaic language with modern murder law. It does not provide concrete guidance.

More useful is the principle that a qualifying felony must be inherently dangerous. Only those felonies that present special dangers to human life merit the punishment boost that the felony murder doctrine supplies. To the extent that the felony is inherently dangerous, we can presume significant culpability toward fatal harms simply by its commission.

Often the determination of inherent dangerousness is made legislatively, as when a legislature designates that the commission of certain specific felonies may support a first-degree felony murder conviction. As a result, where felonies are statutorily designated (as supporting felony murder), courts rarely have much to say about dangerousness.

Judicial determinations of inherent dangerousness normally occur when the prosecution seeks felony murder based on a felony that has *not* been specifically named in a felony murder statute. Often such charges will represent a form of second-degree murder.

Statutory Designation

As just noted, many jurisdictions have murder statutes which list by name the felonies that will support first-degree murder.[10] A typical statutory list of felonies for first-degree felony murder includes robbery, arson, rape, kidnapping, and burglary, and attempts at any of these offenses. If the commission of any such felonies causes death, then conviction for first-degree murder should follow.[11]

When felony murder is charged under a statutorily designated felony, the only major issues for determination are: (1) Did the defendant commit the charged felony, and (2) Was death caused by the commission of the felony?

Avoiding a Language Trap — Attempts and Felony Murder

A caution here about a linguistic trap concerning attempts and felony murder: we must distinguish between felony murders based on attempt felonies and felonies whose commission endanger life, but do not cause death.

---

10. E.g., 18 U.S.C. sec. 1111.

11. As discussed later, most legislatively designated felonies, by definition include conduct inherently dangerous to human life and have independent elements sufficient to survive the merger rule.

> *Attempts at designated felonies that cause death will support felony murder in all jurisdictions that recognize the doctrine. Thus, a defendant who commits an attempted robbery which causes death will be guilty of felony murder. Similarly, an attempted rape that causes death will support a felony murder conviction. In each case, while the underlying offense is an attempt felony, the final verdict is felony murder.*
>
> *In most jurisdictions, there is no offense of attempted felony murder.*[12] *Where a defendant in the commission of a felony comes close to killing another, but does not, this cannot be felony murder, because no death has been caused. Nor could this be attempted (felony) murder because as we will see in Chapter 15, attempted murder requires purpose to kill.*

Inherently Dangerous Felonies

Where felony murder is based on a non-designated (by murder statute) felony, courts must develop their own criteria for inherent dangerousness. There are two basic approaches: (1) inherently dangerous according to the statutory definition of the felony and (2) inherently dangerous according to how the felony was committed by the defendant.

Inherently Dangerous by Definition

In a few jurisdictions, for a felony to be inherently dangerous, it must, *by definition*, involve danger to human life.[13] The statutory definition of the felony must specify acts that necessarily endanger human life. If the felony can be committed in a way that does not threaten human life, then the felony will not be eligible for felony murder. This will be so even if the defendant actually committed the felony in a particularly dangerous fashion. Thus the analysis here is sometimes described as *in the abstract* because it focuses on the abstract statutory definition rather than the particular facts of a case.

The definitional approach to inherent dangerousness has the benefit—for those skeptical of felony murder—of significantly limiting the number of qualifying felonies. This is especially true when we see how its requirements combine with the strictures the merger rule. The rule is also highly formalistic and often counterintuitive in its application, however.

---

12. E.g., State v. Gray, 654 So.2d 552 (Fla. 1995).
13. People v. Phillips, 414 P.2d 553 (Cal. 1966).

Miriam has always liked caring for others. After taking several courses in basic health care, she finds herself asked to give medical advice to those in her neighborhood without medical insurance. Soon she is calling herself "Dr. Miriam" and providing basic medical care, including prescription drugs, for a modest fee. A young mother comes to see her with an infant who has a bad earache. Miriam does not inquire about the child's history with medication. She simply gives the mother antibiotics for the child. The child has an allergic reaction to the medication and dies within two hours.

Miriam is charged with practicing medicine without a license, which requires proof that she: "knowingly represented herself to be, and acted as, a licensed physician, without having a license to practice medicine." Assuming that she is guilty of this felony, can she also be found guilty of felony murder in a jurisdiction that follows the inherently dangerous by definition approach to qualifying felonies?

The answer is no. Analysis here begins *not* with the facts of the case, but with the definition of the felony. The felony of practicing medicine without a license centers on unlicensed practice and has no requirement of actually endangering human life. While the purpose of the statute is to prevent untrained persons from endangering health by just the kind of conduct described here, such danger is not specified by the statute. A person could be convicted of this felony even if he or she provided superb medical care. This is not a felony which, *by its definition*, requires acts of inherent danger to human life.[14]

Sometimes it is difficult to determine exactly what crime is charged under a particular statute. Many criminal statutes describe a number of different ways of committing an offense; some of these may be inherently dangerous and others may not be. Appellate courts vary in their handling of this problem. Some include all of the offense possibilities in their analysis, with the usual result that dangerousness is not met because some ways of committing the offense are not inherently dangerous. Alternatively, the court may choose to define the offense in a more limited fashion, selecting only the statutory language that would cover the defendant's case, in which case inherent dangerousness may be shown.

Another difficulty is simply determining how much danger is sufficient to constitute inherent dangerousness. For example, when the illegal distribution of drugs leads to death by overdose, is the illegal distribution of cer-

---

14. See State v. Burroughs, 678 P.2d 894 (Cal. 1984).

tain drugs an inherently dangerous felony? The offense of distributing heroin has been found inherently dangerous; distribution of some other drugs has not.[15]

Inherently Dangerous as Committed

Most jurisdictions determine the dangerousness of non-designated felonies according to an assessment of *both* the statute defining the felony and the facts of the case. The court initially looks at the statutory definition for requirements of dangerousness, as in the abstract approach, but the key issue is usually whether the prosecution has proven that this particular defendant committed the felony in a way that posed a significant threat to human life. This is sometimes called the factual approach to inherent dangerousness. Unlike the definitional approach, which is determined solely by judicial decision, the *as committed* approach involves questions of both law and fact, meaning that the trial jury has a critical role to play in determining dangerousness.[16]

Recall Miriam's case of practicing medicine without a license. Could this felony qualify for felony murder under the as committed approach to inherent dangerousness?

Focusing now on Miriam's actual conduct, we might find that her misrepresentation about, and lack of, medical licensing created dangers that caused the child's death. There would likely be sufficient evidence for a jury to determine that, as committed by Miriam, this felony was especially dangerous to life and therefore would support a felony murder verdict.

The major difficulty that arises in assessing factual dangerousness (as opposed to statutory dangerousness) is the need to distinguish between the result of death and its likelihood. All cases prosecuted as felony murder involve a death. If simply causing death establishes dangerousness, then all cases in which a felony causes death become felony murders. This sweeps too broadly. Instead, we must look at the situation at the time of the felony's commission to determine whether the defendant's acts, assessed at that point, created a significant risk of death. Thus, a felon's illegal possession of a firearm might be inherently dangerous where used to enforce a drug deal, leading to a fatal shootout,

---

15. See People v. Taylor, 11 Cal. App. 3d 57 (1970) (furnishing heroin an inherently dangerous felony); People v. Williams, 406 P.2d 647 (Cal. 1965) (conspiracy to possess methedrine not inherently dangerous).

16. E.g., State v. Stewart, 663 A.2d 912 (R.I. 1995).

but not where the conduct is the cleaning of a firearm, and death results from the gun's accidental discharge.[17]

The Merger Rule

To qualify for felony murder, the felony must not only be dangerous, but it must clear the merger rule, also known as the independent felony requirement. In nearly all instances, this is a problem only for non-designated felonies.[18]

The merger rule addresses the threat previewed at the beginning of the chapter that, if not restricted, felony murder may effectively wipe out all forms of murder and manslaughter offenses based on mens rea. The merger rule ensures that only a distinct subset of homicides may be eligible for felony murder treatment—and so helps keep felony murder in its place.

To understand the merger rule, it helps to begin with the central problem that it seeks to address. Consider the felony of assault with a deadly weapon. On its face, this felony seems a most promising candidate for felony murder because, by definition, it seems to involve danger to human life. To deliberately threaten or attack a person with a deadly weapon would seem to involve endangering that person's life, meeting any test for inherent dangerousness. But consider the consequences if this felony qualifies for felony murder.

> Fredi decides that he has had enough. The manager of the apartment building, Ollie, has for weeks been making salacious remarks and lewd gestures toward Fredi's girlfriend and on two occasions rubbed up against her in the hallway in a sexual manner. Ollie believes he can get away with this because he knows that Fredi is undocumented (an illegal immigrant). Fredi borrows a shotgun from a

---

17. E.g., *Commonwealth v. Garner*, 795 N.E.2d 1202 (Mass. 2003) (unlawful possession of firearm offense committed in a dangerous manner); *Ford v. State*, 423 S.E.2d 255 (Ga. 1992) (accidental discharge of firearm by felon in possession.). Status offenses such as the prohibition on a felon possessing a firearm generally will not meet dangerous by definition requirements, because there are many instances of the offense that will not pose a significant danger to others. But there are many other instances in which a particular felon's possession of a weapon *may* significantly endanger others, thus meeting the requirements of the as committed approach. See *Hines v. State* 578 S.E.2d 868 (Ga. 2003) (felon in possession offense found dangerous as committed in shooting death by hunter who was drinking and violated hunting safety norms).

18. This is because most of the statutorily designated felonies include a so-called independent purpose in their definitions. The only statutorily designated felony that has raised problems in this regard, in some jurisdictions, is burglary, depending on the crime to be committed therein. See *People v. Wilson*, 462 P.2d 22 (Cal. 1969).

friend and confronts Ollie in his apartment. Pointing the gun at Ollie, Fredi threatens to kill him if he does not get down on his knees and apologize. Ollie laughs. Fredi shoots. Ollie dies.

Felony murder?

This would definitely be felony murder if the felony of assault with a deadly weapon qualifies. Fredi's pointing and then shooting the gun would satisfy the assault with a deadly weapon felony, and this conduct obviously caused death. And as we have already seen, assault with a deadly weapon is likely to be an inherently dangerous felony both under the abstract and as applied approaches.

But notice the consequences if this felony qualifies: virtually all homicides by gun, knife or other deadly weapon—the great majority of homicides—now become felony murders. In any case where the defendant used a deadly weapon to commit homicide we would not bother with analyzing premeditation, provocation, purpose to kill, recklessness or even negligence, because none would be required under the rule of felony murder. Just prove the elements of assault with a deadly weapon and that a death resulted and we would have felony murder. Courts have assumed that legislatures in enacting felony murder statutes have not meant to perform such radical surgery on the rest of the law of homicide. The judicial challenge has been to develop a rule that prevents this result, and yet preserves space for felony murder.

Courts have tried to devise a test that would distinguish between felonies that should be considered subparts of standard mens rea homicide offenses, and therefore *merge into* those homicide offenses, from felonies with qualities that make them stand *independent* of homicide and therefore should support felony murder. If the felony merges, as assault with a deadly weapon does, then homicide liability must be based on standard mens rea analysis for murder or manslaughter; there can be no felony murder. Fredi may still be charged with murder, but the prosecution must prove his mens rea with respect to Ollie's death under the rules of murder discussed in earlier chapters.

As with other aspects of felony murder, while the merger rule is recognized in most jurisdictions, its wording and coverage varies considerably, a variation that often reflects differing—and sometimes changing—judicial attitudes toward felony murder. As a result, the discussion of merger doctrine here will be brief and introductory. The details will depend on the jurisdiction.

In essence, the merger rule seeks to identify elements of the underlying felony that require proof of something different than the straight violence inherent in homicide. Courts ask, in effect: Is the offense essentially about violence, or does it involve a wrong independent of violence? If, as with assault with a deadly weapon, the felony is entirely violence-focused, then it will merge into standard homicide analysis. In such a case, the prosecution must prove mens rea with respect to the victim's death according to the standard requirements of murder or manslaughter. If the felony involves a wrong distinct from straight physical violence, then it may qualify for felony murder.

Some of the best examples of felonies that do not merge comes from the standard list of statutorily designated felonies. For example, the offense of rape has a sexual element that stands independent of and distinct from the basic violence inherent in homicide. In robbery, the independent element is the taking of personal property; in arson, fire provides the independent element that precludes merger.

Hard cases for courts under the merger doctrine involve felonies that specify certain kinds of violence, such as child abuse, or drive-by shootings. By their specification, such felonies arguably provide some restriction on felony murder, but they still seem to be about violence and nothing else. As a result, courts in different jurisdictions see them differently. Courts also differ concerning whether the merger analysis should focus exclusively on statutory offense definition, or on the way that the charged felony is actually committed.[19] The bottom line? Consult your local jurisdiction.

Causing Death: Variations in Shooters, Victims and Timing

Assuming that the defendant committed a qualifying felony, we must determine whether the felony caused the victim's death. In most cases this is straightforward and noncontroversial. The robber shoots the store clerk, actually and proximately causing the clerk's death. End of story. There are, however, many variations involving the identity of the shooter (almost all of the difficult cases here are shooting cases), the victim, and sometimes the timing of the fatal events.

Timing Issues

In order for a killing to fall under felony murder, the felony must cause the death. This makes the chronologic relationship between the felony and death important. For example, if the defendant shoots the victim, then takes his wal-

---

19. People v. Robertson, 95 P.3d 873 (Cal. 2004) (no merger for grossly negligent discharge of a firearm because defendant shot only with purpose to scare).

let, there will be an important question of whether this represents a homicide followed by larceny, or a robbery accomplished by homicide. For felony murder, the prosecution must prove beyond a reasonable doubt that the qualifying felony—here robbery—was committed or was in process before the death.

There are also important issues concerning when a felony ends. Generally an escape from the crime scene is included within the commission of a felony. Escape is said to end when felon reaches a place of at least temporary safety.[20]

Identity of Shooter and Victim

Problem cases in felony murder causation mostly fall into two categories: where a co-felon is fatally shot by an innocent party responding to the felony and where an innocent person is killed by another innocent responding to the felony. The first of these arises with some frequency; the second much less often. Although these situations are distinguishable according to our sympathy for the deceased, it can be difficult to devise a principled means of distinguishing between them in law. In some jurisdictions, co-felon deaths are expressly excluded from felony murder coverage.[21] In other jurisdictions, courts have chosen to handle both types of cases with either the so-called proximate cause rule or the agency rule.

The Proximate Cause Rule for Felon Liability

Some jurisdictions, probably a minority, hold that felony murder liability may be imposed for any death that is the foreseeable result of the commission of a qualifying felony. Thus a surviving felon may be guilty of felony murder if a co-felon dies from a police bullet fired in response to the felony. This approach will also sustain felony murder liability if an innocent party kills another innocent in response to a felony, as when a police officer attempting to use lawful force against an armed robber, accidentally shoots and kills another police officer at the scene. Most problem cases that arise under this rule involve the deaths of co-felons, however.

> At the age of 25, Jessie has an extensive criminal record, including a prior conviction for robbery for which he served time in state prison. Unable to find a good paying job, he needs fast money. He decides to hold up the local liquor store. He recruits his 17-year-old cousin Antwon, who has always looked up to Jessie and will do anything he

20. See generally, 58 A.L.R.3d 851.
21. E.g., Colo. Rev. Stat. sec. 18-3-102(b); N.Y. Pen. Law sec. 125.25(3).

says. Antwon has been arrested for minor offenses, mostly tagging (vandalism) but has never spent more than a day in juvenile detention. Jessie carries a gun for the robbery. He instructs Antwon, who is unarmed, to wait in the car outside and act as lookout, warning of any trouble.

Jessie holds up the liquor store owner at gunpoint and takes approximately $300 from the cash register. He is about to leave when Eddie, an off-duty security guard enters to buy some cigarettes. Eddie has always wanted to be a police officer, and dreams about shooting it out with a criminal. His favorite movie scene is the "make my day" scene in Clint Eastwood's fourth Dirty Harry picture, "Sudden Impact." Seeing the robbery in progress, Eddie pulls his licensed revolver. Jessie responds by raising his gun as if to fire but Eddie shoots first, killing Jessie.

Throughout, Antwon sits in the car outside, not knowing what is going on inside. When he hears shots, he gets out of the car and runs, but is arrested two blocks away.

Assuming that Eddie was legally justified in shooting Jessie, can Antwon be charged, in a proximate cause jurisdiction, with the first-degree felony murder of Jessie?

The answer is yes. The robbery in which Antwon took part appears to have been the factual and proximate cause of Jessie's death. Under the rules of accomplice liability (Chapter 16), Antwon aided and abetted Jessie's robbery, making him guilty of robbery as well. The robbery foreseeably caused a death. Although the sequence of events following from the robbery was hardly standard, it is a scenario that has occurred many times. Causation is likely proven.

That the fatal shooting was done by a wannabe cop, Eddie, who was not a partner or agent of Antwon and that Eddie shot to thwart the robbery rather than to further it does not matter. Courts in proximate cause jurisdictions have held in similar situations that felony murder is justified by the added dangerousness of certain felonies (a danger evident here) and therefore the heightened liability and punishment is appropriate. The 17-year-old Antwon, who never carried a weapon or did anything but serve as getaway driver/lookout (and not very well at that) could face a life sentence for first-degree murder.

The Agency Approach to Felon Liability

Many jurisdictions hold that for a killing to be felony murder, it must be committed by a felon. Often this rule is taken directly from the statutory definition of felony murder, as in the requirement in many jurisdictions that the killing be committed "in furtherance" of a felony. The central concept here is that felony murder provides additional punishment for the particularly dangerous and wrongful acts of felons, and should have no application to the lawful acts of other persons, whose conduct is not within the direct control of offenders.

Under this rule, Antwon could not be prosecuted for the felony murder of his cousin and co-felon Jessie. The killing was committed by a legally innocent party (Eddie), and was committed to stop a crime and not further it. Notice that this rule would also preclude felony murder liability if Eddie had accidentally shot the store clerk rather than just Jessie. Although here the robbery would have foreseeably led to the death of an innocent party, the killing would not have been committed by a felon in furtherance of the criminal scheme.

The agency rule does not preclude all murder liability for killings by innocent parties, however. Such liability may be constructed based on a defendant's recklessness in committing a felony under a doctrine known as the provocative act rule.

Provocative Act Doctrine and Felon Liability

This doctrine is best understood as a hybrid form of liability which combines depraved heart murder mens rea with felony murder. It works as follows. If, in committing a qualifying felony, a felon acts in an *especially* dangerous and threatening fashion, inspiring a violent response from those threatened, any surviving felon may be held responsible for deaths caused by that response.

This doctrine *does* require mens rea toward death. A felon in the commission of the felony must have acted with awareness of a substantial risk that his conduct would lead to fatal violence, including the use of responsive deadly force by victims.[22] By committing a felony and instigating a confrontation likely to involve deadly violence he has acted recklessly as to the risk of death.[23] As a result, if a victim responds to the felon's conduct with deadly force and kills another human being, any surviving felon may be held liable for the murder of the deceased. This is true if the person killed is an innocent party, for example if the victim's shot goes astray and kills an innocent bystander. It is also true if the deceased is a co-felon.

---

22. The focus of analysis may be on the acts of a single felon because, via accomplice liability, other participants (co-felons) may be vicariously liable for those acts. For accomplice liability generally, see Chapter 16.

23. Analysis here normally focuses on awareness of risk. The lack of justification for the risk (which stems from the commission of a felony and not the victim's right to use responsive violence) as well as indifference to the value of human life are not usually mentioned. This may be because both are effectively satisfied by defendant's use of force or threat of force in the commission of a serious felony.

One note on felon identity. Any or all of the felons involved in the felony may be responsible for committing the so-called provocative act. Regardless of who actually committed it, any felon survivors may be responsible for the provocative act through the doctrine of accomplice liability. This means that it is possible that the one who committed the provocative act will be the deceased felon, and that the surviving felon charged with felony murder will not have been personally involved in the especially dangerous conduct that triggers murder liability.

Although this doctrine requires subjective awareness on the part of a felon—proof of actual awareness of a substantial risk that the felon's conduct will inspire a violent response—in practice, analysis turns on a largely objective assessment of the dangerousness of felon conduct. Decision makers must decide whether the felony is committed with the "standard" amount of threat, in which case the doctrine should not apply, or whether the felon's conduct involves such a heightened level of threat that responsive violence is especially likely, making any surviving felons criminally responsible for the fatal consequences.

The classic example of this form of murder liability is when a felon starts a shootout by firing the first shot during the commission of a crime. For example:

> Joey and Tuna are down on their luck car thieves who decide to go for a big score by robbing a money laundering operation in their neighborhood. They break into the warehouse where they know a drug syndicate stores its cash. Both men are armed with loaded handguns. As expected, they find two men with assault rifles standing guard over the van that contains the cash. Joey shines a flashlight in the guards' faces and yells: "Get down on the floor. You're getting jacked (held up)." When the guards hesitate, Joey shoots just above their heads. In response, one of the guards raises his rifle, opens fire and kills Tuna.
>
> Can Joey be held for murder in the killing of his co-felon, Tuna?

In a jurisdiction that follows the agency approach to felony murder liability, straight felony murder is not a possibility. The killing was done by one of the robbery victims, someone who, despite being involved in an illegal activity, would still have a right of self-defense as against persons using unlawful deadly force—as Joey and Tuna were. But what about this provocative act doctrine?

The major issue here is mens rea. Did Joey act with awareness of a substantial risk that his conduct would produce a violent response by their victims? The answer is almost certainly yes. Not only do we have the robbery threat but Joey fired the first shot, an act very likely to produce responsive violence from any threatened person who had the means to respond. Therefore we may say that Joey acted with awareness of a high risk that his conduct would produce a deadly force response, meeting the requirements of mens rea. Causation is satisfied because Joey's conduct led, in short order, to the fatal shooting of Tuna.

Not all cases are so straightforward, of course.

> Don and Margie are drug addicts who are starting to go through withdrawal. Desperate for cash, they decide to rob a liquor store. Margie will stand guard at the door. Don is to make the threats and take the money.
>
> Don enters the store and immediately pulls out a large .44 caliber revolver which he points in the face of the Clerk behind the counter. Don is sweaty, smelly and agitated. In a loud, harsh voice, replete with obscenities, Don orders Clerk to give him all the cash. Clerk, who has closed the cash register for the evening, has a hard time unlocking the register. Don becomes increasingly angry, waves his gun around, and describes in graphic detail how "this 44 gun could blow off your miserable motherf— head." The Owner of the liquor store now comes out of the back, armed with a shotgun and fires at Don's head, ending his life in sudden and horrific fashion.
>
> Margie is arrested as she tries to run from the scene.
>
> Assuming that Margie acted as an accomplice to Don's robbery, in a jurisdiction that follows the agency approach to felony murder liability, can Margie nevertheless be found guilty of Don's murder under the provocative act doctrine?

Again we might describe the major issue as mens rea—the requirement that Don have acted with awareness of a substantial risk that his conduct might inspire a violent response.[24] As a practical matter, however, analysis turns on the dangerousness of Don's conduct and therefore the likelihood that Clerk or anyone else present might respond with deadly force.

The prosecution would argue that the way in which Don committed this armed robbery was particularly frightening and therefore likely to provoke a violent response. By his words, his manner and his gestures with a gun, Don appeared to be on the edge of using fatal violence himself, meaning that Clerk or Owner would likely resort to responsive violence, if possible.

---

24. The reason that analysis here focuses on Don's mens rea is that he is the principal actor for purposes of the provocative act doctrine. Margie's liability is based on being an accomplice to Don's commission of the felony. For more on accomplice liability, see Chapter 16.

The defense will argue that the case involves nothing more than a standard armed robbery. By definition, armed robbery requires a threat of force with a weapon. That threat may be expressed by verbal or physical means, or both. Don's threats were not unusual therefore. Because Don did not fire the first shot and his mannerisms, tone of voice, and gestures are not meaningfully distinguishable from those of a basic armed robbery, the defense would argue that this would not fall under the requirements of a provocative act.

Outcomes here are hard to predict, meaning that the decision of the original fact finder will likely receive considerable deference on appellate review. [25]

---

25. See Taylor v. Superior Court, 477 P.2d 131 (Cal. 1970) (where divided court found the evidence sufficient for provocative act liability on similar facts).

CHAPTER 13

CAUSATION

The doctrine of causation illustrates the limits of rules in criminal law.

We need clear legal rules to inform the public and law enforcement about what is and is not criminal. But we also want the law to produce criminal *justice*, meaning that we want law to be sensitive to the justice considerations of each individual case. Unfortunately, sometimes human interactions are too varied and unpredictable to be regulated by a precisely stated, predetermined rule. So it is with causation.

The concept of causation is simple and unproblematic in most cases. To be guilty of murder or manslaughter, a defendant must have *caused* the victim's death.[1] The defendant's act, or omission to act, must lead to another's death. In most cases the connection between act and result is clear: deadly acts lead directly to death. There are other cases where natural forces or the actions of a victim or third parties make a major contribution to the result, however. These are the cases where extended causation analysis is required. We ask: Should the defendant be blamed, not just for his initial wrongful act, but also for the death that followed?

The challenge for students is to recognize what the rules of causation do — and what they do not. The rules structure the analysis; they are not always sufficient in themselves to direct legal outcomes, however. That may depend on considerations not explicit in the rules. Despite a wealth of sophisticated-sounding norms concerning intervening and supervening, dependent and independent causes, there are no clear, universal rules for the hardest part of causation: proximate cause. Decisions are tough to predict with any accuracy. Often the best we can do is to identify factors that may influence decision makers and then engage in *analogic reasoning*, a fancy term for comparing the facts of the present case to those of past decided cases.

In this chapter we will discuss two different types of problem cases involving causation: (1) those involving a different manner of harm than anticipated

---

1. As a matter of law, the doctrine applies to any crime requiring that the defendant cause a particular kind of property loss, physical injury, or death. Virtually all of the reported causation cases involve homicide, however.

or culpably risked by the defendant and (2) those involving a different victim than anticipated or culpably risked by the defendant. The second of these will be discussed at the end of the chapter under the heading of transferred intent. The first is our immediate and primary concern.

Act, Mens Rea and Causation

Before laying out the rules of causation, we need to establish the relationship between causation and other essential elements of the offense, namely the act and mens rea requirements. In all homicide cases, the defendant must have acted with the necessary mens rea for the particular homicide offense toward the victim's death. For example, in purpose to kill murder, the defendant must with the conscious object to end the particular victim's life.[2] Causation concerns what happens next chronologically: the actual, real-world consequences of defendant's act.

Easy and Hard Cases of Causation

It makes sense to begin with easy cases of causation. These are cases where there is no serious issue with respect to this element of the offense. Such cases are easy because death occurred *in exactly the way that the defendant originally intended, anticipated, or culpably risked.*[3] There are no causal surprises and therefore no real causation issues. Although there is no requirement that the prosecution prove that death occurred in the manner that the defendant intended or anticipated, if such proof is evident, causation automatically follows. The following illustrates.

Casey is a longtime, highly skilled employee of an automotive parts manufacturer. He is devastated when the company decides to move the plant overseas and lay off all domestic workers. Casey blames this decision on the greed and mismanagement of the company's Chief Executive Officer (CEO). Casey resolves that since his life has been ruined, he will end the life of the CEO. Using parts taken from the job and homemade explosive materials, Casey constructs a small bomb which he places in a package that he mails to the CEO. The CEO opens the

---

2. The only exception to this requirement of mens rea with respect to the particular victim is the doctrine of transferred intent, discussed later, which permits a transfer of mens rea from an intended victim to an unintended one.

3. See MPC sec. 2.03(2),(3).

package, setting off the bomb. Shrapnel from the bomb tears into several vital organs. The CEO is dead by the time that paramedics arrive, minutes later.

How does act, mens rea and causation analysis work here?

Here Casey voluntarily built and sent the bomb to the CEO, actions which he took in order to kill the victim. His conduct meets the voluntary act requirement and indicates both purpose to kill the CEO and premeditation about the killing. As for causation, this is an easy case because death occurred in exactly the way that Casey intended. He planned to kill the CEO by a bomb blast and he did so. There were no causal surprises.

Causation analysis really kicks in when there is some surprise in what occurs following the defendant's conduct. The death occurs in a manner different than what the defendant anticipated or culpably risked. Slightly altering the facts concerning what happens after Casey mails the bomb, converts the case into one where there are real causation issues.

> Casey builds and sends the bomb as previously described. This time the CEO opens the package while seated behind his desk and as a result, suffers only one significant injury, a wound to the arm that causes major bleeding. This bleeding could be stopped by basic first aid. But the CEO panics at the sight of his own blood, hits his head on a doorway and collapses to the floor, where he lies moaning. He is working by himself late at night and the only other person in the building is a security guard who does not hear the CEO's moans because he is listening to music on headphones. The guard finally finds the CEO when doing his rounds an hour later. At this point the paramedics are called but their arrival is delayed because they initially come to the wrong building due to a dispatcher's mistake. The CEO dies minutes after arriving at the hospital. Doctors say that if he had gotten to the hospital even 10 minutes sooner, he would have survived.

> How is causation analyzed here?

Here the defendant's act and mens rea are the same as before. And as before, the CEO dies of injuries inflicted by the bomb, just as defendant desired. Differences in how the death occurs raise some causation problems, however. The bomb blast proves less immediately harmful than in the first instance and the victim and two others make significant post-blast contributions to the victim's death. We have the CEO who panicked at the sight of his own blood leading to his own disablement. We have the security guard who because of his headphones didn't hear the CEO's moans. Finally we have the dispatcher who sent the paramedics to the wrong location. Casey had nothing to do, directly, with any of these actions or inactions. Casey did not plan or have the purpose for the CEO to die from this particular sequence of events. As a result, Casey's defense counsel may argue that, regardless of defendant's guilt in making and sending the bomb, others are truly to blame for the CEO's death. In other words, proof of causation is lacking.[4]

In fact, chances are good that causation for murder will still be found. The variation between what Casey thought would happen and what did is not so great as to break the connection between Casey's conduct and the CEO's death. Or, to put this another way, the post-explosion contributions to death are neither so bizarre nor so disconnected from the original wrong that they should relieve Casey of responsibility for the fatal consequences of his bomb. But all this is to jump to the bottom line, always a dangerous move in the law. Having provided an overview of causation, we now need to slow down and move methodically through the essential steps of factual and proximate cause.

Basic Elements of Causation: Factual and Proximate Cause

Causation has two elements: factual cause and proximate cause. Factual cause, also known as but for cause, rarely requires much legal analysis. It simply mandates that the defendant's action be a critical link in the chain of events resulting in death. In most cases, this is obvious.

The rule for proximate cause can be stated in a number of different ways, most often that the result must occur in a way that is foreseeable given the defendant's action. It involves a moral and legal assessment of the connection between the defendant's action, the actions of others, and the victim's death. When causation is at issue, the issue is usually proximate cause.

Factual Cause

But for the defendant's action, would the victim have died when she did? This is the basic way of framing factual cause. It seeks to determine if the defendant's actions can be linked to the victim's death. In the prosecution of a homicide case, but for causation is often an important issue, but usually because of questions about factual proof. For example, the prosecution will have to show

---

4. If proof of causation for homicide fails, the charge will become attempted murder here.

that it was the defendant who fired the critical shots or delivered the fatal blow.[5] Also included is proof that the victim was alive at the time of the critical events and now is dead. It is one of the reasons that the *corpus delicti*—the evidence of the body—can be critical to a homicide prosecution. Without proof of these matters, we cannot say that the defendant's action was the but for cause of death.

To illustrate how straightforward factual cause normally is, return to Casey the bomber. In both of the scenarios set out above, Casey is clearly the factual cause of the CEO's death. In both instances, the CEO would not have died but for Casey's bomb. Casey's bomb-related actions were critical links in the chain of events (whether long or short) leading to the CEO's death.

The only legally difficult cases involving factual cause are those where there are at least two equal and simultaneous contributors to the victim's death. In scenarios that test the creativity of law professors, we encounter simultaneous assailants with a variety of deadly weapons, each of whom acts with the required mens rea and directly hastens the victim's death, but neither of whom is necessarily *the* "but for" cause of death. Such scenarios give rise to the awkwardly named simultaneous equally sufficient causes exception, also known as the substantial factor test. Here we ask whether each defendant made a significant contribution to death, and if so, factual cause is met.

There is one common mistake to avoid with respect to factual cause. Analysis here focuses entirely on the defendant's action. *It does not matter if others also make but for contributions to death.* For example, in the second bombing scenario, the CEO's panic, the security guard's negligence, and the dispatcher's mistake each were important contributors to his demise. Each contributed to the fatal delay in medical treatment and so might be called a but for cause. Yet none of these contributions is relevant to the legal question of whether the *defendant's* act was the factual cause of death. They are relevant, however, to the next stage of the analysis: determining proximate cause.

Proximate Cause[6]

Under the common law, a defendant's act is the proximate cause of death if the result occurs in a way that is reasonably foreseeable, given defendant's chosen action or omission. Under the Model Penal Code, proximate cause is shown

---

5. Eg, Oxenidine v. State, 528 A.2d 870 (Del. 1987); People v. Dlugash, 363 N.E.2d 1155 (NY Ct. App. 1977).

6. Sometimes this also goes under the name of legal cause.

if the result "is not too accidental or remote in its occurrence to have a [just] bearing on the actor's liability or on the gravity of his offense."[7] Unusually for the criminal law, the actual wording of the proximate cause rule is not particularly significant. The action lies in the factual details of each case.

Regardless of the actual language used to describe proximate cause, the basic task is the same: to determine whether there is a close enough relationship between the defendant's act, mens rea and result to make the defendant criminally responsible for the result. In homicide, it means deciding whether a defendant's wrongful action is so closely connected to the victim's death that the defendant should be criminally responsible for homicide. As alluded to before, proximate cause analysis depends as much on decision maker intuition as on rule requirements. In fact, one often gets the impression that decision makers first make an intuitive decision about proximate cause, and then come up with legal reasons to justify the decision, rather than reach the decision through purely legal reasoning.

We can categorize proximate cause cases in a number of ways. One distinction is between human and nonhuman contributors. Speaking very generally, the contributions of animals or nature or mechanical failures tend to be viewed as somewhat more foreseeable than those of other humans. Nevertheless, generalizations remain unreliable here. It all depends on the facts.

> It is early autumn in a western wilderness area and the fire danger is very high (one level short of the highest rating of extreme). Christy and her college friends want to go camping over the weekend. Christy obtains a camping permit from the park ranger, who gives her an explicit warning about fire hazard. He states that open camp fires are absolutely prohibited. There are many warnings posted in the wilderness about fire dangers as well. After a day of hiking, Christy and her friends have a meal and then sit around talking, laughing and drinking wine. The atmosphere seems lacking without a fire though, and they decide that they can have one in the dirt area of the campground as long as they are careful. Christy prepares and starts the fire; before they go to sleep she smothers it with dirt. All believe that the fire has been extinguished. Unfortunately, after they have left the camp site, coals from the fire remain and when hot dry winds suddenly come up, the coals start a small fire in nearby underbrush. Because of understaffing, park rangers do not spot the fire for almost eight hours,

---

7. Secs. 2.03 (2) (b), (3) (b).

giving it time to grow. It moves quickly and threatens Herman, who is in the wilderness hunting.

Herman the hunter panics at the sight of wind driven flames coming his way. He runs to his four-wheel-drive vehicle and drives away at great speed, not wearing a seatbelt. He loses control on a curve, is thrown from the vehicle and strikes his head against a tree, causing a fatal injury.

May Christy be held criminally liable for the death of Herman?

Liability here would be based on Christy's voluntary act of setting the campfire and her omission to extinguish it (plus her duty to do so because she set the fire originally). Her mens rea could easily be reckless. She was explicitly warned of the dangers of a wildfire from an open campfire, and we presume that she would be aware that among the risks of a wildfire would be death to humans. There was no necessity for a campfire. Nevertheless, she disregarded these risks in setting the fire.[8]

Assuming proof of act and mens rea, the issue becomes causation.

Christy's conduct was a but for cause of the wildfire and Herman's fatal accident. But for Christy's lighting and then inadequately dousing the campfire, the wildfire would not have occurred as it did and Herman would not have panicked and suffered a fatal accident. (Note that the fact that a wildfire could have started from another source and had a similar effect upon Herman is not important; all we need to decide for but for cause is that *Christy's* actions were a vital link in the chain of events that led to his death.)

Finally we reach the real issue in the case: proximate cause. Was the result reasonably foreseeable given the defendant's action?

The prosecution will argue foreseeability by emphasizing the dangerousness of Christy's handling of fire in the wilderness and the manifold ways in which such conduct could endanger others, including persons like Herman. The defense will emphasize all of the unusual events that occurred after Christy left the scene, ranging from the sudden winds to the understaffing of firefighters to Herman's panic, all to support the conclusion that, while tragic, Herman's death cannot justly be attributed to Christy's campfire and therefore was not foreseeable.

---

8. If she was not actually aware of substantial and unjustified risks due to her precautions, we might say that her conduct here was criminally negligent, that it was a gross deviation from the standard of care that a reasonable person would take toward others who might be in or near the wilderness area. Note, if Christy acted with gross negligence toward persons like Herman, then her conduct also likely represented the cause of his death because such a death would be, by definition (of gross negligence), reasonably foreseeable.

So how do we resolve this debate? While strategic framing of the question is important (see sidebar), surely there must be some more specific rule that will decide the question. Unfortunately there is not. But we can find guidance in patterns found in previously decided cases.

Strategizing Causation: Framing the Causal Issue

In all areas of law, how the issue is framed affects how it is resolved. Few areas of law are quite as sensitive to different ways of framing issues than proximate cause, however.

The prosecution generally seeks to frame the proximate cause issue in broad, simple terms in order to emphasize the defendant's contribution. (Indeed, the prosecution may sometimes state the proximate cause issue so simply that it may sound indistinguishable from but for cause.) In Christy's case, I suspect the prosecution would see the issue as follows:

> *Is it foreseeable that setting an open campfire in the wilderness, despite explicit warnings and a prohibition on such fires, at a time when the fire danger is very high, might lead to a wildfire that would endanger others in the forest, leading to desperate efforts to escape in which persons take deadly risks and are killed?*

Such a question seems to lead naturally to an affirmative answer: a fatal result seems quite foreseeable given Christy's conduct in the situation.

Generally the defense will prefer a more detailed statement of the issue, setting out all the events that followed the defendant's action. Such a detailed statement will highlight the unlikelihood of death due to defendant's actions, and emphasize the contributions of others to the victim's death. The defense would prefer this statement of the issue:

> *Is it foreseeable that defendant's setting of an illegal but carefully monitored campfire, which was then apparently extinguished, would by virtue of sudden winds the next day after the campers leave, give rise to a small fire, that due to park understaffing would become a general conflagration and that this blaze would cause a hunter to panic and drive his vehicle recklessly, without a seat belt, and lose control and be thrown from the vehicle, strike his head against a tree and be killed?*

Again the strategy should be obvious. The more details are included, the less directly connected defendant's act and the final result appear to be.

Arguing by Case Analogy

Where, as with proximate cause, formal rules do not provide complete guides to decision making, holdings of previous cases often fill the gap. The challenge is learning to use them effectively.

We might imagine a map that sets out prior decisions, depicting a legal landscape of proximate cause. The challenge is how to situate the new case in the landscape. Where should it go on the map? We decide by legal analogy, identifying the ways in which the new case is similar to or different from past cases that found, or did not, proximate cause.

In arguing by case analogy we compare fact patterns and holdings rather than focus on judicial rhetoric. It's not so much what past courts *say* about proximate cause that matters legally, as what they *do*: what they hold based on the facts presented.

In looking at the facts and holdings of proximate cause decisions we can discern two general considerations or themes that influence decision makers. These may be explicit in the decisions or wholly implicit. Identifying their influence is important regardless, because they provide insight into how decision makers do and should reach judgments of proximate cause.

Predictability

All proximate cause rules consider the predictability of the result given defendant's conduct. The common law examines "foreseeability;" the MPC inquires whether the result is "not too accidental or remote." Both seem to establish a rule of statistical probability, or improbability. We judge the defendant's conduct and subsequent events according to what we would statistically expect to occur, the extent to which these events were likely or unlikely. Of course, being lawyers, this assessment is not actually statistical. (If we were good with numbers we would have gone to medical or business school, right?) Instead it is a common sense judgment, based on life experience, of what is usual and unusual.[9]

In Christy's case, predictability would seem to work in the prosecution's favor. Campfires were banned just because of the likelihood that they would start dangerous wildfires. That the fire appeared to be out and was reignited by sudden winds, does not seem unexpected. Indeed, these are likely the sort

---

9. An assessment, of course, that is done in retrospect, with knowledge of what actually did occur. The worse the final result, the more emotional pressure there is to find a wrongdoer responsible for it.

of risks that motivated the decision to ban open campfires. Nor does it seem unusual that there would be others present in the wilderness, or that someone threatened by a raging fire would react in a dangerous fashion, such as driving too fast and without a seatbelt. Thus the fatal accident, which is itself the predictable result of risky driving, seems to be part of a predictable chain of events beginning with the original campfire.

The defense will seek to rebut this reasoning by emphasizing the time lapse between campfire and fatal accident, and the many contributors post-campfire, in hopes that this will make the entire chain of events look unpredictable. Exactly how likely is it that an apparently extinguished campfire will cause a hunter to kill himself by dangerous driving?

We can perhaps hazard a few very general observations about assessment of predictability. Usually, legal decision makers view natural forces as somewhat more predictable than human contributions. In contemporary American society, there is a background assumption that while nature and physical events may be predicted, the free willed actions of individual human beings are less predictable and therefore more subject to individual responsibility.[10] Thus, in Christy's case, the sudden winds would likely be judged predictable and so would not break the causal chain that began with the campfire. Herman's panicked driving would be a relatively more promising candidate for breaking the causal chain.

When assessing the contributions of other human actors, ordinary negligence on the part of other contributors will often be seen as predictable, while gross negligence and more egregious wrongdoing may not be. The clearest example involves persons who provide medical attention. Generally, ordinary medical malpractice (civil negligence) does not break the causal chain but at least in some circumstances, gross negligence may.[11] We might say that ordinary negligence is a standard feature of life and thus predictable, as compared with more severe, and therefore unusual, forms of misfeasance or malfeasance.

Despite its importance, predictability can be over-emphasized in proximate cause analysis. Especially when other persons contribute to the result besides the defendant, our normative view of each person's contribution may be more

---

10. The interesting counterexample in ordinary language is the comparison to the chance of being struck by lightning. This is commonly viewed as the quintessentially unpredictable event, even though we can predict that a significant number of people will suffer it annually.

11. Grossly negligent treatment by itself may not be sufficient, however. See State v. Jacobs, 479 A.2d 226 (Connecticut 1984) (where defendant inflicts a dangerous wound, gross negligence in treatment must be the sole cause of death to break the causal chain).

important. For example, it is often said that gross negligence may break the causal chain in proximate cause, but ordinary medical negligence will not. Perhaps this is because ordinary negligence is more predictable, meaning more likely, than gross negligence. But the distinction may also track our distinctive view of the negligent actors. The grossly negligent actor appears more culpable than the ordinarily negligent one. This introduces a second aspect of proximate cause, what I call normative assessment.

Normative Assessment

The standard language of proximate cause rules do not immediately suggest the importance of normative analysis. As we have seen, talk about foreseeability suggests concerns about prediction rather than moral assessment of the parties involved. But when we consider the larger task of proximate cause, we see that normative assessment is an inherent part of any proximate cause decision.[12]

The essential task of proximate cause is to assess the defendant's responsibility for the ultimate result, taking into account the contribution of other persons and forces. In deciding whether we believe the defendant should be held responsible for the death, we necessarily judge—normatively—the contribution of the defendant and others to that fatal result. Whether this is articulated or not, we make a comparative assessment of blameworthiness—who should be blamed for the death that occurred.

The importance of normative assessment to proximate cause is most apparent in cases of other human contributors to the result. Here we will often find that even when death is a highly predictable result of defendant's action, proximate cause may be denied because some other contributor to the result is *more* responsible.

For example, there have been cases in which prosecutors have sought to charge murder where an individual provides direct aid to another's suicide. A highly depressed person talks about suicide and a "friend" offers a loaded gun, saying: "Go ahead. I think you should do it." And the victim does. Although it is highly predictable that the would-be suicide will turn the gun on himself, proximate cause is almost never found in the situation. Normatively, this looks like a suicide and not a murder. The primary person responsible for death is the one who fired the shot, not the one who provided the gun or encouragement.

---

12. Note the alternative language in the MPC requiring that the result be "not too remote or accidental in its occurrence to have a [*just*] bearing on the actor's liability or on the gravity of his offense.". Sec. 2.03 (2) (b), (3) (c) (emphasis added).

Normative analysis can also push in the opposite direction. For example, consider those cases in which the acts of a criminal wrongdoer leads to the death of a public servant: defendant's arson fire leads to the death of a responding firefighter; a police officer is killed chasing a suspect.[13] Here, even if the connection between the defendant's original wrong and the public servant's death is not especially close (i.e. not very predictable), decision makers tend to find proximate cause. The moral fault of the defendant, combined with the social value of the victim's efforts will convince many that the defendant should be held responsible for the fatal result.

To illustrate with Christy's case, imagine our assessment of proximate cause if the victim was not Herman the hunter, but a park ranger who heroically responded to the fire and led efforts to put it out. Even if these efforts involved foolhardy risk taking, many decision makers are likely to blame Christy for endangering a park ranger and so hold her responsible for the ranger's death.

By contrast, when the victim or other contributors are also engaged in wrongdoing, normative sympathies tend to favor breaking the causal chain. Two men decide to race their cars on a public highway, and one is killed during a risky passing maneuver—the jury or court may decide that the racer's death is better deemed a type of suicide rather than homicide.[14] Similarly, in Christy's case, we might view causation differently if the deceased was the member of Christy's party who suggested the campfire in the first place—or if we learned that Herman the hunter was drunk at the time and hunting out of season.

Many reported cases seem to turn on an assessment of the relative badness of the defendant's conduct. Survivors of a game of Russian roulette, which involves a raw daring of death, are more likely to be held fully responsible for the death of a competitor than when the competition is less outrageous in its hazards, as perhaps with street racing.[15]

Similarly, the relative innocence of a victim may weigh in favor of causation. What if in Christy's case, the person killed was a child who was accompany-

---

13. People. v. Arzon, 401 N.Y.S. 2d 156 (1978); People v. Matos, 83 N.Y.S.2d 509 (1994).

14. Commonwealth v. Root, 170 A.2d 310 (Pa. 1961); c.f. State v. McFadden, 320 N.W.2d 608 (Iowa 1982) (surviving racer found responsible for death of both an innocent six-year-old in another vehicle and a co-racer).

15. E.g., Commonwealth v. Atencio, 189 N.E.2d 323 (Mass. 1963). Similarly, fatalities caused by an explosion in a chewing gum factory might be distinguished from a devastating fire in a nightclub based on decision maker views of defendant conduct, where both cases involve pre-existing dangerous conditions attributable to defendant neglect. C.f., People v. Warner-Lambert Co., 414 N.E.2d 660 (NY 1980); Commonwealth v. Welansky, 55 N.E.2d 102 (Mass. 1944). This is speculative, however. There are also other grounds on which these cases might be distinguished. See also People v. Deitsch, 470 N.Y.S.2d 158 (1983).

ing her father on a hike? In this situation, although Christy's conduct is unchanged, and the predictability of the manner of death is virtually identical, we may be more inclined to blame the defendant for the result because of our sympathy for the victim, especially as compared to the defendant.

One last caution about normative analysis. What has been described here is no more than a set of tendencies. They do not represent rules. While we may discern trends in cases that give us some general guidance, in the end, decisions are fact sensitive and therefore case specific. Ultimately we must decide how a particular fact situation matches—or does not—the facts and holdings of previously decided cases.

When Causation Fails: Attempt and Other Criminal Liability

What happens if proof of causation fails? For example, what happens if we decide that Christy's campfire was not the proximate cause of hunter Herman's death? We look for alternative forms of criminal liability. In many cases, the defendant's original conduct constitutes an offense by itself. For example, individuals who engage in illegal road races violate the jurisdiction's traffic laws. Similarly, Christy would likely face penalties for having an illegal campfire. The problem is that the penalties for such offenses often seem trivial compared to the ultimate harm done. When someone dies as a result of wrongdoing, the urge to bring some form of homicide charge will always be strong. And so we may turn to attempted homicide.

When causation fails, the prosecution may seek conviction for attempted murder or manslaughter. The idea is that even though the defendant did not actually cause the death, he or she came close enough in choice and deed that it should be considered an attempt at homicide. There is a significant obstacle to conviction here, however: any attempt at homicide requires that the defendant have acted with *purpose to kill* the victim. As will be discussed in the chapter on attempt, purpose to kill is normally required for any attempted homicide charge. In Christy's case this will preclude such a charge. Christy had no desire to kill Herman, nor any desire to kill anyone in the forest when she lit the campfire.[16]

---

16. By contrast, recall the earlier example of Casey the bomb maker who acted with purpose to kill his victim, the CEO. If proof of causation failed in that case, an attempted murder conviction would be likely.

Transferred Intent: The Different Victim Problem

As mentioned at the beginning of the chapter, there is another kind of problem case often treated under causation: the problem of the different victim.[17] This occurs when the physical person actually hurt or killed is different from the one that the defendant meant to hurt or kill. When the only difference between intended and actual harm is the identity of the victim, the legal fiction of transferred intent "transfers" the defendant's mens rea from intended to actual victim. The defendant is convicted of an offense based on his or her mens rea toward the intended victim.

Transferred intent is a rule that looks good at first sight. Built on a simple legal fiction, it seems easy to apply and, in its core application, provides intuitively appealing results. Like some good looking people though, serious flaws are revealed on closer acquaintance. Indeed, the doctrine raises so many problems that the discussion here must be abbreviated. Our work will be confined to: (1) explaining the rule in its classic application and (2) describing the most common problems in applying the rule to other situations.

The Classic Application: Bad Aim

Transferred intent is always explained by the example of an attacker with poor aim.

> Despite considerable evidence to the contrary, Serena believes that she is a talented singer. She is offended by the conduct of Celebrity, the host of a talent contest show who ridiculed Serena's vocal efforts at an open audition. After thinking about it for several days, Serena decides to take action. She learns that Celebrity is scheduled to appear at an event in a nearby city. Serena borrows a revolver from a friend and stakes out a position in front of Celebrity's hotel. When Celebrity emerges to sign autographs, Serena aims her revolver at Celebrity and fires. Her shot misses Celebrity, but strikes and kills Tonya, a teenager standing nearby. Of what form of homicide might Serena be convicted for Tonya's death?

If we stick with our usual mens rea analysis—and some commentators believe we should—Serena's liability depends on her mens rea toward Tonya.

---

17. There is some controversy about whether this should be considered a problem in mens rea or sentencing, rather than causation. The way the doctrine is described by courts generally supports its treatment as a causal problem, however. It extends liability beyond what defendant originally intended or culpably risked in a manner similar to proximate cause.

This means that she could not be convicted for any purpose to kill homicide, but would likely be guilty of an offense based on recklessness. She shot with awareness of a significant risk that others nearby, like Tonya, might be killed. Without transferred intent, the most serious charge that Serena would face for Tonya's death would be depraved heart murder. Independent of liability for Tonya's death, Serena would also be guilty of the attempted murder of Celebrity.

Transferred intent increases Serena's liability for Tonya's death. Because Serena acted with the premeditated purpose to kill Celebrity, and the only difference between what she wanted to accomplish and what she did was the identity of her victim, transferred intent carries her mens rea from her intended victim (Celebrity) to her actual victim (Tonya). Serena should be convicted of the premeditated, purpose to kill murder of Tonya, a more serious offense than either depraved heart murder or involuntary manslaughter.

In this situation, the appeal of transferred intent doctrine is obvious. It ensures full punishment of Serena according to her original wrongful choice *and* the actual harm that she did. Her mens rea is the same and she ended up killing a human being as she desired, so why should she receive less punishment just because she missed her target? There is rough justice in holding her guilty of premeditated purpose to kill murder with respect to Tonya.

General Applications and Limitations

Before taking up some problems concerning the doctrine, a few general notes about its application.

Non-result Offenses

Although usually treated as a causation doctrine, transferred intent does apply to nonresult offenses. The most common example is the crime of assault.

Assume that in this jurisdiction assault requires a purpose to either threaten or physically harm another. Defendant tries to slug a supporter of a rival team in a sports bar in response to that supporter's over-vigorous celebration of his team's victory. In throwing his punch, Defendant loses his balance and accidentally strikes a waitress standing nearby. Defendant had no purpose to strike or threaten the waitress, but by virtue of transferred intent may be guilty of an assault on her. The man's purpose to assault the rival fan will transfer to the actual victim, the waitress. As required for transferred intent, there is no difference between the deed that Defendant meant to do and that which he did, *except* the identity of the victim.

A Different Kind of Mistake about Victim Identity

As we have seen, transferred intent applies when the defendant strikes or kills a different physical person than intended. It should be distinguished from cases where the defendant struck or killed the intended target but was mistaken as to who that person was. Transferred intent has no application here. For example, if Serena spotted a man in a red shirt that she believed was the Celebrity, and then shot and killed the red-shirted man, it would not matter if he proved to be someone else. Here Serena would be said to have acted with the premeditated, purpose to kill the actual victim. In the law's view, she meant to kill the man in the red shirt and that was the person killed.

Different Kind of Harm

Another important limitation on transferred intent is that it only applies when the defendant accomplishes the same kind of harm as originally contemplated. For example, what happens if a farmer unlawfully shoots at a wolf, with purpose to kill, but misses and kills a human being? Could transferred intent to operate here? No. The death of an animal is a different kind of harm under law than the death of a human being. Or, to put this another way, the farmer acted with purpose to kill an animal and not purpose to kill a human being. There is no sufficient mens rea (intent) for homicide to transfer.

Manner of Harm

Finally, transferred intent should not apply when the *manner* of harm is unanticipated. The MPC makes this limitation clear by its language that the actual result "differs only" in the identity of the person or property harmed.[18]

An Introduction to Problem Cases in Transferred Intent

As one commentator has noted, unlike most rules, transferred intent does not have a widely accepted definition or theoretical justification.[19] Instead it is a legal fiction designed to resolve a very particular kind of case—that of bad aim. Thus it is not surprising that difficult questions arise about its application to similar, but distinct types of cases.

---

18. Sec. 2.03(2) (a), (3) (a).

19. Douglas Husak, Transferred Intent, 10 Notre Dame J.L. Ethics & Public Policy 65 (1996).

For example, the classic case of transferred intent involves a purposeful attack. The doctrine is usually described as applying to intentional wrongs, by which courts usually mean crimes that require proof of either purpose or knowledge. But what happens when the offense charged may be satisfied by proof of defendant recklessness or negligence? Do these mens reas also transfer? Here, most of the time it doesn't matter because standard mens rea doctrine will produce the same result. The defendant will have acted with recklessness or negligence towards the actual victim and therefore there is no need to transfer mens rea from an original victim to another. We can imagine some cases, however, where transferred intent might be needed to reach the actual victim, and here authorities as to whether it should apply, are mixed. The MPC says yes; some respected legal commentators say no.[20]

A more significant issue—because it arises more often—is whether transferred intent should be limited to a single unintended victim, or whether it extends to multiple unintended victims. For example, if Serena shot a bullet that traveled through Tonya and struck a second bystander, Mark, killing them both, how would transferred intent work? Some jurisdictions say that Serena's original intent transfers to victim Tonya and then is "used up," so that liability for the second victim, Mark, will depend on her actual mens rea toward Tonya's death (recklessness or negligence). Other jurisdictions hold that the defendant's original mens rea transfers to all unintended victims.[21] And then there is the problem of whether transferred intent creates attempt liability with respect to persons in the vicinity who were threatened by the defendant's actions but not killed.[22] This illustrates the problems caused when we depend on legal fictions rather than real rules to do our analytic work.

---

20. MPC sec. 203 (3) (a). E.g., Wayne LaFave, *Criminal Law* 342 (4th ed. 2003).

21. See People v. Bland, 48 P.2d 1107, 1115 (Cal. 2002) (no using up of transferred intent for any person killed in addition to the intended victim).

22. Compare Bland, supra (no transferred intent for attempted murder of unintended victims) and State v. Rodriguez-González, 790 P.2d 287 (Ariz. App. 1990) (transferred intent does support attempted murder for bystander victims).

CHAPTER 14

Rape

No major crime in the United States has seen as much change in its legal treatment in the last 30 years as has rape. Definitions of the crime have changed along with evidentiary rules specific to the offense. What had been the most patriarchal of all offenses has been reconceived according to values of gender equality and autonomy.

And yet the extent of change can be exaggerated. Few crimes are as closely tied to cultural understandings as is rape, meaning that changes in formal law may not equal change in practice. It also means that change does not occur uniformly. It can vary according to jurisdiction, courthouse, and the particulars of the case.

Because the law of rape varies significantly from jurisdiction to jurisdiction within the United States, it will be impossible to give an account of the crime here that is both general and accurate. Instead the aim must be more modest, to introduce essential concepts and basic variations in doctrinal structure and analysis.

The word rape conjures up for many an act of intentional violence, of deliberate sexual predation. So it can be, and so it often is. As conceived by contemporary lawmakers and courts, however, rape is more than this; it is an offense of disregard for sexual autonomy, a crime of not caring about another's sexual choices. As a result, the modern offense covers conduct that traditional concepts and rules did not.

This chapter focuses exclusively on the crime of rape, or as it is known in some jurisdictions, sexual assault. Although this offense bears an important relationship to other sex offenses, including statutory rape and child sexual abuse, these will not be covered here.

A (Very) Brief History of Rape Law

History casts a long shadow on contemporary rape law. Modern legislative reforms and judicial interpretations reflect a determined effort to break with patriarchal views of gender, sexuality and individual responsibility found in earlier law. This means that to understand modern rules, we need to know how they differ from their predecessors.

By looking at three different aspects of this offense—conceptions of its essential wrong, paradigm examples of the offense, and views of the credibility of rape complainants—we can gain an overview of historic change here.

First as to the wrong itself. In feudal England, rape was fundamentally a violation of family honor by the taking of a female's chastity. The wrong was suffered not just by the female victim (and the victim was always female), but by her male protector (father, husband, brother or other male relative), who was the keeper of family honor. In the 19th century and into the 20th in the United States, the wrong became personal to the female victim, but still centered on chastity. Rape was seen as a violation of feminine virtue. As a result, attacks on the complainant's prior sexual virtue—or rather its lack—were permitted in the defense of rape charges. Today the essential wrong of rape is its violation of individual sexual autonomy. At the heart of contemporary rape is a disregard for another person's freedom to choose whether, when, and how to engage in intimate relations.

Paradigm cases of rape have also changed over the centuries. Traditionally this was a crime of dramatic and brutal violence by a man, usually a stranger, on a woman. The offense was characterized by objective signs of violence such as the use of weapons and the infliction of visible injuries to the victim's person. These characteristics are reflected in traditional rules requiring proof of overwhelming force by the defendant or physical resistance by the victim. Over the last generation, our understanding of sexual violence has changed as social scientists and others have documented the prevalence of sexual coercion between persons with a pre-existing social relationship, coercion that often occurs without deadly weapons or the infliction of obvious physical injury, yet which can be psychologically devastating. Modern changes in rape doctrine concerning force and resistance have been particularly aimed at such cases.

Accompanying these changes have been changes in the law's view of the credibility of complainants. Traditionally the law treated accusations of rape with skepticism. Suspicions that female accusers might lie found formal expression in legal requirements of prompt complaint, corroboration and resistance requirements. A major goal of rape reformers has been to eliminate the traditional rules of victim distrust in rape law. This has led to the elimination of the prompt complaint, corroboration and resistance requirements, and the enactment of rape shield laws which bar most inquiry into the complainant's prior sexual history.

Change in the law of rape has occurred as part of larger changes in gender relations. Because of its concern with sexual conduct, rape is a crime that implicates concepts of masculinity and femininity, romance, and power, all of which were subject to unprecedented change in the United States in the late 20th century. This fascinating and important story unfortunately cannot detain us further here. We have too much law to cover.

Basic Elements of Rape

The great 18th-century scholar of the English common law, William Blackstone, described rape as "the carnal knowledge of a woman forcibly and against her will."[1] In this compact definition we find the basic elements of the standard offense: (1) a particular sex act (2) done by force and (3) without consent. Many contemporary rape statutes follow a similar structure, though that similarity can be deceiving, for much depends on how we interpret these terms, especially force and nonconsent.

Modern definitions of rape also may be broken down into three basic requirements: (1) a specified sexual act or acts; (2) victim nonconsent; and (3) proof of defendant's culpable disregard for victim's nonconsent. The most controversy and doctrinal complexity involves the last of these requirements, for here different jurisdictions have devised different approaches. We will see that U.S. jurisdictions choose between two basic methods of proving defendant culpability re nonconsent. Jurisdictions require proof either that: (a) defendant used extrinsic force to accomplish the sexual act, *or* (b) proof that defendant proceeded with the sexual act under circumstances that demonstrate at least negligent disregard for the victim's nonconsent.

The Special Challenges of Element Analysis in Rape

As we have found with some other offenses—premeditated murder comes to mind—the same word or phrase in a statutory definition may be interpreted differently in different jurisdictions. This is also true in the law of rape with respect to the requirement of force, and to a lesser extent, nonconsent.

Element analysis in rape law also presents particular challenges because of the way that offense elements are interrelated. None stand alone. Proof of force, for example, may be critical to proving victim nonconsent *and* defendant awareness of that nonconsent. As a result, any change in the force requirement may affect the remaining elements. This means that even when the ostensible subject is force, the critical issue may actually be victim nonconsent or defen-

---

1. 4 *Commentaries on the Laws of England* 210 (1979)(1769).

dant's notice of nonconsent. Sometimes we must look beneath the surface of doctrinal discussion to see what is truly at issue.

Finally, this is an area of law where we must respect the potential difference between law as formally stated and as actually applied. For example, we will see that all jurisdictions have eliminated the formal requirement of victim resistance. Rape can be proven beyond a reasonable doubt without any showing that the victim physically resisted. Facts about physical resistance may still play an important role in rape cases, however. If the victim did physically resist, that conduct may help the prosecution prove both nonconsent and defendant culpability. And even when the law instructs otherwise, there may be times where decision makers find a lack of physical resistance important in evaluating those same elements.

The Sexual Act, Perpetrators and Victims

Analysis of rape begins with a particularly described sex act or acts. Sex act here does not mean an act of mutual sexual pleasure, but an act done by one person to, or with, another, for a sexual purpose. In this sense the act requirement of rape includes both a description of physical conduct and proof of the actor's sexual intent. A caution though: this sexual intent is a very minimal requirement, not usually contested in rape cases, and is distinct from the more central questions of victim nonconsent and defendant culpability with respect to nonconsent.

At common law, rape required an act of sexual intercourse, defined as any penile penetration of a vagina. As the quintessential act of heterosexual sex, this act presumes a sexual intent on the part of the male. Under this rule, the prosecution must prove beyond a reasonable doubt some degree of penetration (however slight) of the vagina by the male sexual organ. Traditionally, penetration of the vagina by fingers (digital penetration), by foreign objects and assaults upon mouth or anus fell outside the purview of rape, though they would constitute other, often lesser, offenses.

Recent reforms of rape have broadened the definition of the sexual act. Under modern legislation, rape often includes penetration of mouth or anus and the use of any body part (usually fingers) or physical objects to penetrate. Some statutes also include nonpenetrative assaults. The breadth of these definitions makes the sexual intent aspect of the act requirement potentially more significant. While it is nearly impossible to imagine penile penetration of a vagina that is nonsexual, there may be nonsexual touchings of breasts or buttocks or other intimate regions.

Under the common law, a rape could only be committed by a man upon a woman who was not his wife. Under the concept of feme covert, because a husband and wife were one legal entity, there could be no rape within the marriage. Meanwhile a man could not be a victim of rape, though he could be a victim of the common law offense of sodomy, a crime defined without regard to nonconsent. A woman could be an accomplice to a man's rape of another woman, but could not be the principal to the crime.

Modern reforms have ended the marital exclusion. Most jurisdictions today either permit a rape prosecution within the marital relationship, or recognize a separate offense of sexual assault on a marital partner. The offense is also gender-neutral, meaning that the perpetrator can be either male or female, as can the victim.

Male Victims of Rape

Originally the law required, and still our culture presumes, that rape is a crime committed by a man upon a woman. But men and boys can be victims of this offense, and girls and women can be perpetrators.[2]

The most underreported instances of this highly underreported crime of violence are probably rapes of men. The great majority of these, like the great majority of attacks on women, are committed by men.

The prevalence of rape in prison has received greater attention in recent years, along with some efforts at prevention and very occasional prosecutions. Such assaults remain common and almost entirely hidden from public view, however.

Outside prison, male on male rapes also occur with greater frequency than generally acknowledged, both in the form of so-called acquaintance rapes and stranger attacks. Unfortunately, both legal and support services for rape victims are often more geared toward female than male victims.

Finally, there have been documented cases of women forcing men to have sexual intercourse against their consent. The physiology of sexuality can be surprising here: fear can contribute to physical arousal against the will, including orgasm. This can be true for both male and female victims; one can be betrayed by one's own body.

It's also worth noting that surveys of young people concerning forced or unwanted sex document high percentages of young men who submit to unwanted sex with females as a result of female pressure. Usually these do not constitute sexual assault, as the pressure exerted is largely verbal,

---

2. See generally, *Male Victims of Sexual Assault* (Gillian C. Mezey & Michael B. King eds. 2d ed. 2000); Michael Scarce, *Male on Male Rape: The Hidden Toll of Stigma and Shame* (1997); Cindy Struckman-Johnson, "Male Victims of Acquaintance Rape," in *Acquaintance Rape: The Hidden Crime* (1991).

> but it does indicate that sexual aggression sufficient to override partner preferences is not an exclusively male trait.[3]
>
> Looking at the experience of male victims overall, it appears basically the same as for females. Males report an experience of violence and intimate domination that has profound emotional consequences for the individual and for future relations with others.

Victim Nonconsent

Central to the offense of rape is the requirement that the victim be unwilling, that she or he *not* consent to the sexual act. At common law, this was the requirement that intercourse be "against the will" of the woman. Victim nonconsent is always a critical part of the prosecution's proof. If there is a reasonable doubt about nonconsent, then the defendant must be acquitted.

Before delving into the doctrinal details of nonconsent, we need to be clear that initially our only concern is whether the complainant actually consented; we are not concerned here with what the defendant believed or should have realized about the complainant's sexual willingness. Often these two issues—complainant nonconsent and defendant culpability as to nonconsent—are intertwined. Sometimes nonconsent and culpability are intertwined as a matter of fact; sometimes they are interrelated as a matter of law, but for the moment we will focus only on the complainant's state of consent or nonconsent.[4]

A useful way to begin is with clear examples of nonconsent under the law. In all jurisdictions, age sets one important limit on sexual consent. Any person under the jurisdiction's legal age of consent is legally incapable of consenting to certain sexual acts, making any person who performs such acts with an underage minor liable for a sexual offense.[5]

Some persons above the age of consent will by virtue of mental disability also be held to lack the mental capacity to consent. In some jurisdictions extortionate threats or fraudulent representations may represent additional grounds to vitiate a victim's apparent consent to sexual conduct.

Here we will focus on two universal examples of nonconsent: unconsciousness and coercion.

---

3. See Struckman-Johnson, Male Victims of Acquaintance Rape, supra at 194–98.

4. It is true, however, that in practice, issues of victim nonconsent and defendant mens rea concerning nonconsent are often closely intertwined.

5. For sexual intercourse, the age of consent in many jurisdictions is 18. See Cal. Pen. Code sec. 289(h).

Unconsciousness

An unconscious person cannot consent to any sexual act. Proof of unconsciousness therefore proves nonconsent, without any need for proof that the victim expressed unwillingness.

> Chris, a socially inexperienced college freshman, goes to a fraternity party hoping to meet someone special. He has a great deal to drink. Toward the end of the night, he meets a very attractive college senior who seems interested in him. They dance, kiss passionately, caress each other and then go back to the senior's off-campus apartment. There Chris passes out. He wakes up naked in bed, to discover that the college senior, Mike, has just completed an act of anal intercourse on him. Chris protests: "I didn't want that at all." Chris hurriedly dresses and leaves, extremely upset.
>
> Is there evidence of nonconsent to sexual intercourse here?

Even though there was prior consensual romantic/sexual activity between Chris and Mike, and no verbal or physical resistance by Chris prior to intercourse, Chris's nonconsent to intercourse is clear on these facts. At the time of the act of intercourse, Chris was unconscious and therefore unable to consent.

Just to point out the obvious, this case is exactly the same if we change Chris's name to Christine. Regardless of analysis of force or mens rea with respect to nonconsent, one party to this sexual act was unconscious at the time of intercourse and therefore could not, and did not, consent.

Coercion

Nonconsent may also be proven by coercion: sexual compliance obtained by physical force or threat.

> T., a heavily built truck driver of 47 offers to give A., a slightly built waitress, 19, a ride home from the restaurant where she works the late shift. Ignoring A.'s directions, he drives to a deserted park where she has never been before, and stops the car. She starts crying and says that she wants to go home. He unbuckles his belt and says: "You do what I say, and you won't get hurt. Then you can go home." A. is physically repulsed by T., and has no desire for contact with him, but is very scared. At T.'s direction, she undresses and submits to intercourse. A. does not verbally protest or physically resist his sexual acts. He then takes her home.
>
> Is there proof of nonconsent here sufficient to support a rape charge?

Again this is a clear case. Here there was an explicit threat in defendant's statement: "do what I say and you won't get hurt." This statement is particularly threatening given the context. An older, much larger man who she hardly knows has taken her, against her express wishes, to a deserted place where she is effectively at his physical mercy. She is obviously upset, crying, and asking to be taken home. These provide strong indications of nonconsent to any succeeding sexual act.

Although the facts here strongly suggest that the defendant was aware of the victim's nonconsent, at this stage of our analysis that does not matter. Initially we just want to establish victim nonconsent.

Timing of Nonconsent

Nonconsent is assessed at the time of the sexual act. This includes the entire time from initiation of the sexual encounter to its end. If during that time the victim does not consent and defendant proceeds with the sexual act, then legally the nonconsent requirement is met.

Two Views of Nonconsent: What Do We Presume from Silence?

An important question in rape law is how to handle situations where individuals are relatively inarticulate concerning their sexual desires. Does the law presume sexual consent from silence or lack of protest, or should we presume nonconsent without an affirmative expression of desire? This is a fundamentally normative question about responsibility and criminality. But it is often intertwined with some difficult questions of fact.[6]

The traditional view of rape effectively placed the burden of proof of nonconsent—meaning the obligation of expressing nonconsent verbally *and* physically—on the victim. Nineteenth and early 20th century courts required that the victim indicate by dramatic physical resistance that sexual intercourse was unwanted. The formal requirement of physical resistance has since been abolished in most jurisdictions, but in many the victim still must verbally or otherwise express nonconsent. Whether by words, deeds or both, the complainant must have communicated unwillingness to the defendant. Nonconsent cannot be proven from silence in such jurisdictions.

---

6. Because sexuality is an aspect of human interaction where communication is usually nonverbal, signals of personal desire are socially complex and often blurred by intoxication, because communication can be confused by ambivalence concerning the situation and relationship, and is often affected by gender differences, fact finding on consent can be difficult. Finally, notice that as is common in the criminal law, the options are binary: sex can be either consensual or nonconsensual. Degrees of desire or reluctance matter only as they inform the final conclusion.

Many rape reformers have argued against this approach, contending that to presume assent from silence is to reward sexual aggression, disregard the harms of unwanted sex and devalue bodily autonomy. Sex involves extraordinary intimacy, making the individual vulnerable to serious physical and emotional harms. Therefore sexual consent, like consent to any other potentially dangerous touching, such as surgery, must be clear and affirmative. The individual must indicate by words, deeds, or both that she or he wants to have sexual relations. Without such affirmative expressions, the law must presume no consent. This position has informed changes in the law of consent in a minority of jurisdictions, which have defined consent as "an affirmative and freely willed agreement."[7]

The differences between these approaches may be illustrated by the following case.

> Eric is a junior in college, a business major who serves as manager of the college marching band. He is a pleasant young man, but does not have the most scintillating personality. He makes up for what he lacks in charm with a clear understanding of what he wants and great perseverance. As a result, he usually gets what he wants.
>
> From the moment he laid eyes on Madeline, a freshman flautist in the band, Eric was smitten. She is a musician and artist, who has a model's face and figure, along with a winning smile. She is always surrounded by others, especially interested young men. She is also moody and highly impulsive. She thinks that Eric is "cute in a bizarrely dull sort of way." She finds his interest in her ridiculous, but thinks him harmless.
>
> The band travels to a distant city for an away game and stays overnight in a motel. Musicians sleep four to a room; Eric reserves a single room for himself. He invites Madeline to come by "anytime she wants." At two in the morning, Madeline knocks on Eric's door and asks if she can come in, "because I really have to get some sleep and those idiots in my room won't shut up." She looks disheveled and has been drinking. She asks for a shirt to wear to bed and he gives her a large T-shirt of his. She undresses in front of him, puts on the shirt and gets in the king size bed (the only bed in the room). She kisses Eric

---

7. In California, for purposes of a rape prosecution, consent means "positive cooperation in act or attitude pursuant to an exercise of free will. The person must act freely and voluntarily and have knowledge of the nature of the act or transaction involved ..."Cal. Pen. Code sec. 261.6.

on the cheek and thanks him for letting her stay. She lies on her stomach, on the other side of the bed from Eric.

Eric begins to give her a back massage. She does not protest. He becomes sexually aroused, moves her legs apart, and penetrates her, achieving orgasm soon thereafter.

Madeline says to him, sharply: "Are you done now? Can I sleep?" He starts to apologize, but she tells him to shut up. A minute later she gets up, takes a shower, dresses and leaves the room, slamming the door behind her.

A week later, prompted by Eric's persistent attempts to ask her out despite her clear disinterest, Madeline reports the incident to school authorities, who call in the police and it becomes a criminal case.

Madeline says that she never consented to what Eric did, but he just "did it because he wanted to and couldn't get it any other way." Eric tells police that he never would have done anything that she didn't want, but that he thought based on everything that had happened, that "that's why she was there. I guess she had second thoughts after."

How would the analysis of nonconsent go in this case?

In jurisdictions where proof of nonconsent requires verbal or physical protest, the defense has a good argument for acquittal on this element. Madeleine did not by words or by deeds expressly indicate her disinterest in sex and Eric did not use violence or threats that would have made such resistance futile or dangerous. In jurisdictions where consent is left essentially undefined, the answer will depend upon the gender views of the decision maker. Traditionally minded decision makers, both men and women, are likely to read sexual acquiescence as assent: that because Madeleine went along with it, she agreed to it.

But what happens under the reform view of consent? Did Madeleine affirmatively express her willingness to have sex with Eric?

The prosecution will argue that she did not. By her words and her conduct, Madeline expressed an interest in sleep and nothing more. She had no prior physical or romantic relationship with Eric. Nothing she said or did in Eric's motel room signaled a dramatic change in their relationship, such that she would welcome the ultimate form of physical intimacy. The kiss on the cheek and expression of thanks were entirely consistent with a need for rest. The prosecution would argue that we no longer live in a time when a woman coming to a man's domicile at night should be deemed consent to sexual relations.

The defense will emphasize all of the indications of Madeline's sexual willingness: her appearance at two in the morning in the room of a young man that she knew was attracted to her, undressing in front of him, getting in bed with

him, and permitting him to massage her back. Prior to the point of intercourse, she never indicated that she wanted to be left alone. Throughout the
sexual act she made no physical or verbal protest. An affirmative expression
of willingness might be shown by her entire course of conduct, from the moment she knocked on the door through the act of intercourse. Her apparent
lack of enthusiasm during the sexual act does not indicate a lack of consent;
enthusiasm is not a requirement for lawful sex.

The verdict? The reform view of consent favors the prosecution here, but pre-
dictions are difficult where cultural attitudes can be so influential. In other
words, cultural values about gender may trump formal law here. The other
potentially critical factor, impossible to evaluate on a cold record, is how the
witnesses come across in court. Unconscious emotional identification with or
antipathy for a party by a decision maker can make all the difference.

The Force Requirement and Defendant
Culpability re Nonconsent

We have left to last the most important element of rape: the requirement usually known as the force requirement. For a rape conviction, it is not enough
that the defendant commit a sexual act without the victim's consent; he or she
must also have demonstrated culpable disregard for the victim's sexual autonomy. As mentioned earlier, there are basically two different approaches in current American law to proof of this culpability, what will be called the extrinsic
force and notice of nonconsent approaches.

Traditionally, and in most jurisdictions today, defendant's culpability depends
on proof that the defendant used extrinsic force or threats of such force to accomplish
the sexual act. Extrinsic force means acts of violence, threats of such violence, or
direct physical force to coerce the sexual act *beyond* any physical movement needed
to accomplish sexual intercourse or other statutorily defined sex act.

Not all jurisdictions read force this way, however. A number of appellate
courts today interpret force to mean *no more than* the movements needed to
accomplish the sexual act. In such jurisdictions, defendant culpability must
be proven by some means other than just the defendant's verbal or physical
conduct.[8] This is also true of the few jurisdictions that have eliminated the

---

8. Jurisdictions that have eliminated extrinsic force also usually have eliminated the requirement of evidence of express protest or physical resistance to show nonconsent. Therefore proof of nonconsent does not, by itself, necessarily establish defendant's culpability
toward nonconsent.

word force from their statutory definition of rape. In all these jurisdictions, the prosecution must prove that the defendant had sufficient notice of victim nonconsent that his or her proceeding with the sexual act demonstrates disregard for victim autonomy. Although not always stated in this fashion, such jurisdictions effectively require proof of defendant's *negligence* with respect to victim nonconsent.

A caveat must be added concerning this division of current law into two approaches. American law here remains very much in a state of flux and a complete account would detail many more distinctions between jurisdictions and even between decisions in the same jurisdiction than will be done here. Describing only two basic approaches oversimplifies the law, but it will serve to introduce basic themes in law concerning defendant culpability.

The Extrinsic Force Requirement

In jurisdictions retaining the extrinsic force requirement, rape requires proof that the defendant accomplished the sexual act either through violence, physical coercion or threat. This element stands legally independent of the nonconsent requirement. Even if the victim expressed nonconsent, the prosecution will fail without proof of extrinsic force.

The most obvious form of force is violence. Attacks upon the victim's body by weapon, hands or feet, or other methods provide classic examples of extrinsic force.

Another form of extrinsic force is physical coercion, meaning the use of direct force against the individual. If a man employs his superior strength or weight to wrestle a woman into sexual compliance, this constitutes extrinsic force regardless of whether physical injury results.

Finally, threats of harm, both express and implicit may satisfy the requirement *if* they are likely to induce reasonable fear of serious bodily harm. An express threat to kill or maim while wielding a knife would certainly demonstrate extrinsic force. The more difficult cases involve implicit threats, where the defendant's conduct in context may reasonably induce great fear of injury, even without any weapon or verbal threat. This will be the topic of further discussion below.

Note that so far the discussion of force has focused exclusively on the defendant's conduct. This is in keeping with the elimination of physical resistance as a formal requirement of rape and the importance of respecting sexual autonomy. Yet victim conduct in the form of resistance can still be important. Rape is by definition a relational crime, involving an interaction between persons. Determining whether the defendant used extrinsic force in some instances will depend on the reaction of the victim, because this affects what the defendant needed to do to achieve a sexual end. Even where legislatures and courts have eliminated any formal requirement of victim resistance, facts about whether, and how, the victim resisted *may* go to the proof of force.

Several previously mentioned examples will help illustrate analysis of extrinsic force.

> Return for a moment to the case of the truck driver, T., and the waitress A. Recall that T. offered her a ride home, but instead drove to a deserted area where he makes clear his desire for sex.

> Assume at this point that A. cries and asks to be taken home. T. undoes his belt and states: "You do what I say, and you won't get hurt. Then you can go home." She does as asked and sexual intercourse occurs. Is extrinsic force evident here?

T. did not display a weapon and did not commit any act of direct violence against A. except for the sexual act.[9] Nor did T. accomplish intercourse by the direct physical coercion of A. Proof of extrinsic force here depends on proof of a threat, express or implied. T. issues an express threat when he states that she will not get hurt *if* she does what he wants. This threat is given additional weight by circumstance: issued by a man much older, heavier and stronger than she, who has already taken advantage of her trust to isolate her from all possible help, in a premeditated scheme to achieve a personal sexual goal. Any reasonable person in A.'s situation would fear that a refusal to submit to T.'s demand would result in significant bodily harm.

But what about the fact that A. did not scream, kick or hit, did not try to run away, and did not expressly protest T.'s sexual advances? She just did what he wanted. Doesn't the lack of any victim resistance at the time of the actual sexual act indicate a lack of extrinsic force? Assuming that resistance is not legally required (that it is not an independent element of the offense), the answer should be no. In a situation where a reasonable person in A.'s situation would believe that escape is impossible and forced sex virtually inevitable, a lack of resistance does not indicate a lack of threat, only a prudential decision to avoid risking more serious injury. On these facts, the extrinsic force element should be satisfied.

Of course if A. *had* physically resisted, requiring T. to overcome her resistance with the application of direct physical coercion, violence or more express

---

9. Note that with the addition of a weapon to the scenario, this becomes a classic instance of rape by extrinsic force. If T. had pointed a handgun at A. when he made his sexual demand, the conclusion would be inescapable that he had issued a threat any reasonable person would find terrifying.

threat, then proof of extrinsic force would be more obvious. But modern law does not require such dramatics for this offense.

Inducing Reasonable Fear: The Gender of the Reasonable Person

Who is the reasonable person who sets the standard for whether words or conduct induce reasonable fear? In particular, is the reasonable person male or female? This is potentially important because, generally speaking, women fear violent sexual attack more than do men. A woman may see a serious threat of violence in a situation where a man may see only clumsy romance.

Closely related to the question of reasonable fear is that of reasonable reaction. The assumption of traditional rape law was that any woman threatened with sexual coercion would fight aggressively and without stint to resist. But this presumes that women respond to threat as men believe they would, an assumption that, among other problems, disregards the powerful effect of female socialization to nonaggression. Studies of sexual assaults indicate that many women are essentially frozen by fear when sexual assault appears imminent. Thus what might appear as acquiescence to sex is in fact a passivity caused by terror.

Finally, and more fundamentally, gender may affect understanding of the harm of coerced sex and therefore fear of it. Victims of sexual assault frequently describe the experience as life-threatening, even when no express threats to life are made. Why? Is this the result of socialization? Studies show that the great majority of sexual assaults in fact do not end in death or even serious physical injury. But something critical is missing from this assessment of harm. The sexual invasion of the body is a devastating experience that can change a person forever, doing permanent emotional and relational damage. On some level, everyone understands this. It's why the word rape carries such force, why many do not like even speaking the word. Yet it may be that more women than men "get it," contributing to a gender difference in assessing the threat inherent in acts of sexual aggression.[10]

As is usually true with the hardest questions about reasonableness, the answer is generally left to the original decision maker. Jurors are not instructed on the reasonable person's gender, leaving them to their own moral and social resources to decide the question of reasonable fear.

---

10. An important caution must be added here about gender generalization. In the trial of particular cases, assumptions about gender differences can be dangerous for attorneys who do not pay attend to distinctions relevant to the particular case. For example, in cases of acquaintance rape, female jurors may judge female complainants more harshly than do male jurors.

Return now to the case of Eric and Madeleine, fellow members of the band. Madeleine had came to Eric's room early one morning looking for a quiet place to sleep; Eric gave her a back massage, then engaged in sexual intercourse. Assuming that Madeleine did not consent to intercourse, in a jurisdiction that required extrinsic force, would the force element be satisfied by the facts presented here?

It would not. Even if Eric knew, or should have known that Madeleine did not consent to his acts of penetration, movement and ejaculation, he used no force above that needed to accomplish intercourse. He was not violent, did not directly coerce Madeleine in the sense of overcoming active physical resistance with superior force, and did not make an express or implied threat. He could not be convicted of rape in a jurisdiction with an extrinsic force requirement.[11]

Force Transformed: From Extrinsic Force to Notice of Nonconsent

Although force remains a formal requirement of rape in most jurisdictions, its meaning varies considerably according to jurisdiction. The trend in the last 30 years has been to reduce the requirements of extrinsic force. In a minority of jurisdictions it has been effectively eliminated. In these jurisdictions it is enough if the defendant used the "force necessary to accomplish the sexual act." This means just the physical force needed for the sexual act. This collapses the force requirement into that of the sex act, because once the sex act has been performed, then by definition "force necessary to accomplish the act" has been used.

Initially this change looks suspect because it seems to eliminate a critical feature of the offense. But it may be justified as part of the modern reconceptualization of rape as a crime against sexual autonomy. Under the traditional view of rape, extrinsic force was needed to prove a violent attack on female chastity, the crime's essential wrong. But if the essential wrong is disregard for victim autonomy, defendant's culpability may be proven in other ways. Proof that the defendant had clear notice of victim nonconsent and proceeded with the sexual act regardless will establish that the defendant culpably disregarded the victim's sexual autonomy. The following case illustrates.

On the night before her wedding, Elena stayed overnight at her aunt's house. Her aunt was to substitute for her deceased mother in

---

11. E.g., Commonwealth v. Berkowitz, 641 A.2d 1161 (Pa. 1994).

the ceremony the following day. Defendant, her aunt's boyfriend, who Elena had never met before, was to substitute for her deceased father at the ceremony.

Elena lay down on the living room floor on a sleeping bag and fell asleep. Between one and two a.m. she was woken by Defendant, who was naked. Elena knew that Defendant had been drinking heavily that night. Defendant pulled off Elena's pants and had sexual intercourse with her, then left the room. Elena dressed and left the house, extremely upset.

Describing the incident later, Elena said that she was paralyzed by fear of the Defendant which was why she did not make an explicit verbal protest against Defendant's actions and did not offer physical resistance. Defendant admits to police that he had sex with Elena and that Elena had not consented.[12]

Is there sufficient proof of force to convict of rape here?

Under a traditional reading of the force requirement, the prosecution would probably fail its burden of proof. Defendant used no extrinsic force: there was no weapon, no use of superior physical size or strength to overcome physical resistance. He did not even disregard a verbal protest. To put this another way, there is nothing in the purely physical interaction between defendant and victim to establish that defendant's conduct was unlawful.

This case shows why many believe the traditional force requirement to be overbroad, however. In this situation, the victim's nonconsent is clear, as is defendant's awareness of her nonconsent. Indeed, no person in Defendant's situation who had any concern with Elena's sexual autonomy, her right to make intimate choices for herself—recall, Elena was to be married following day and had no personal relationship with Defendant—would have thought that this crude sexual approach would be welcomed.

Question: A Crime of Sex or Violence?

Answer: Both
Rape reformers have long insisted that rape is a crime of violence and not sex. The victim's experience of rape is certainly an experience of violence, not sex. Reformers emphasize the crime's violence in order to combat the pernicious notion that unwanted sex is no big deal (the "just lay back and enjoy it" view), or that forcing sex on an acquaintance may be bad romance, but not a crime.

---

12. The facts of this example parallel those of People v. Iniguez, 872 P.2d 1183 (Cal. 1994)

> And yet rape is, by definition, a sex crime.
>   Rape is a worse crime than other assaults because of its sexual na-
> ture. The sexual dimension of the attack explains the soul-threatening
> aspects of the experience. Rape is also a more controversial crime than other
> crimes of violence because of its sexual dimension. By defining the most
> serious sexual wrong, rape necessarily implicates concepts of lawful sex
> and romance important to everyone. And while victims may not expe-
> rience the attack as sexual, perpetrators often do. Even offenders who
> thrill to the power and violence of rape do not see their own conduct as
> anything other than sex.
>   In short, rape is a crime of sexual violence; both aspects must be
> taken seriously.[13]

Negligence re Nonconsent, or, Mistake of Fact re Consent

The elimination of extrinsic force in some jurisdictions leaves a potentially
large gap in rape law. Without extrinsic force, how do we establish defendant
culpability with respect to victim nonconsent?

If extrinsic force is required for conviction, such force will also establish defendant's
culpability as to nonconsent. Anyone who uses extrinsic force to compel sex knows
that the sex is unconsented. A person who uses a gun, an express threat of harm
or direct application of physical force to compel sex clearly understands that his
or her partner is unwilling. But if the defendant only uses the force necessary to
commit the sexual act, then we can imagine situations where the defendant sincerely believed that the sex was consensual, even if it was not. In the realm of sex
and romance, extreme cluelessness is not uncommon. Throw in youthful inexperience, blurring of perception by intoxication, different gender perspectives,
and complex, often confusing forms of verbal and nonverbal communication in
the sexual arena, and the possibility of a reasonable mistake becomes plausible.
If we don't require extrinsic force, we need other proof of culpable disregard.

One possibility would be to require proof that the defendant had subjective awareness of the risk of nonconsent, i.e., acted recklessly as to nonconsent. For the most part this has not been the approach of U.S. jurisdictions.[14]

---

13. See Samuel H. Pillsbury, Crimes Against the Heart: Recognizing the Wrongs of
Forced Sex, 35 Loy. L.A. L. Rev. 845 (2002).

14. E.g., State v. Oliver, 627 A.2d 144, 152 (N.J. 1993); People v. Mayberry, 542 P.2d 1337,
1345 (Cal. 1975). For a jurisdiction that does require recklessness, see Hess v. State, 20 P.3d
1121, 1124 (Alaska 2001). See also Regina v. Morgan [1976] A.C. 182 [England].

The majority of states require some form of notice of nonconsent. Effectively they require proof of defendant's negligence as to nonconsent. A defendant will not be convicted if he honestly and *reasonably* believed that his partner consented to the sexual act. This is a notice of nonconsent standard because the key issue is whether the defendant had such notice of nonconsent, such warning signs, that any reasonable person would have realized the sexual act was without the partner's consent.

We now encounter a problem in categorization and labeling. Should we treat this requirement as an essential element of the offense, treating negligence as to nonconsent as a basic mens rea requirement, which the prosecution must prove beyond a reasonable doubt? Or should this be considered a defense of mistake as to which the defendant has at least the burden of production? I believe that the answer should be the former. Its judicial treatment often seems closer to the latter, however.

Courts generally speak of this requirement in terms of mistake and not negligence, thus suggesting an emphasis on defendant's proof rather than the prosecution's. Some appellate courts have ruled that the jury should not be instructed on reasonable mistake of fact as to consent unless the defendant or another witness has testified to support such a mistake. In effect, the burden of production on the issue is placed on the defendant.

There are pragmatic arguments in favor of this approach. Where the critical issue in a rape case is consent, the contest is almost always over witness credibility, not mistake. Generally the complainant testifies that she made her unwillingness very clear, while the defendant testifies that the sexual activity was clearly consensual. Neither party testifies that a mistake about consent was made or could have been made. Instead, the only question is who is telling the truth about what happened. In such cases appellate courts are understandably reluctant to overturn convictions for failure to instruct on a theory of the case—reasonable mistake—that no witness's testimony directly supported.

There is a problem with this approach, however. As we saw in Chapter 8, mistake of fact its best understood as a subset of mens rea doctrine. This means that, absent an extrinsic force requirement, notice of nonconsent, otherwise known as negligence, should be treated as an essential element of the offense which the prosecution must prove beyond a reasonable doubt. The defense should not have to produce particular facts to put the issue of negligence before a fact finder.[15]

---

15. Defense attorneys commonly argue for legal interpretations not directly supported by particular witness testimony. And as may be true in other criminal contexts, controversies about consent in rape may present situations where the truth is not captured by any

Putting aside questions of categorization, we must now consider the content of this requirement of notice of nonconsent and its reasonableness standard. We again confront the problem of gender identity. Is the reasonable person against whom we measure the defendant's conduct a man or a woman? The law's answer is the same as with the reasonable fear element considered earlier: this is a question left to the discretion of the fact finder.

Return one last time to the case of Eric and Madeleine. Assuming that she subjectively did not want to have intercourse with Eric, and the jurisdiction does not require extrinsic force, is there sufficient proof that Eric acted culpably, with reasonable notice of nonconsent?

Answering this question takes us back to the definition of nonconsent. If the jurisdiction defines consent as an affirmative expression of freely given agreement, then the prosecution can argue that the reasonable person would note its absence here. Madeleine never affirmatively expressed, by word or deed, her willingness to have intercourse. She only affirmatively expressed, by word and deed, that she wanted a quiet place to sleep.

In jurisdictions where consent and its negation is left undefined, Eric may prevail by arguing that a reasonable person might have mistaken Madeline's sexual willingness. In coming to his room late at night and asking, in effect, to sleep in his bed, in undressing before him, in not protesting his massage or his sexual acts, all given that she knew he was very attracted to her, a reasonable person in this situation might think that she agreed to sex. Her interest in him might not rise to the level displayed in a Hollywood romance, or even most pornography; still many men in Eric's position might believe she consented.

But notice the problem with respect to gender. This may be a particular instance where the reasonable man and reasonable woman disagree. If so, the gender of reasonableness may decide the case.[16]

---

single witness account. The accused may truly believe that the victim consented and so fail to see or admit any possibility of mistake. Yet a third party might decide that defendant was mistaken and perhaps reasonably so. It should be a legitimate part of the defense attorney role to suggest a legal interpretation of the facts favorable to the defendant, even if that does not exactly match the defendant's personal account.

16. The gender issue can be exaggerated. The prosecution's primary argument will be that Eric's ignorance about nonconsent, if any, stems from his desire for sex. It's not that a reasonable person would see the situation as he did, but that he was so interested in doing what he did that he disregarded signs of nonconsent. Finally, remember that reasonableness is a normative judgment, not a statistically accurate prediction of average behavior.

There is one other concern with respect to eliminating extrinsic force that requires mention: the issue of proportionality. Rape remains one of the most serious crimes that any person can be convicted of, based on one of the most serious harms that any person can suffer. Criminal law should match severity of punishment with severity of wrong. Some have argued that eliminating extrinsic force means that instances of unconsented sex, where the defendant was negligent as to nonconsent, are treated as severely as unconsented sex accomplished by extrinsic force. They argue that the extrinsic force offenses are worse, in part because they demonstrate a higher mens rea and therefore greater culpability on the part of the defendant. Others contend that both types of wrong merit punishment as rape.[17]

Telling the Truth about Rape: False Claims and Miscarriages of Justice

The most notorious quotation in the history of rape law is from the 17th century English Lord Chief Justice, Sir Matthew Hale, that "rape is an accusation easily to be made, hard to be proved, and harder yet to be defended by the party accused, tho' never so innocent."[18] Concern about convicting the innocent lay behind many features of traditional rape law and remains an important issue in contemporary reform. Without question, conviction of the innocent is a serious problem in rape. But miscarriage of justice cases in this area often present a different profile than we might expect.

Traditional rape law worried greatly about proof of nonconsent. How can we be sure that a sexual act claimed to be coerced and nonconsensual, was not in fact consensual? How can we be certain that the accusation was not made to hide illicit or now-regretted sexual activity? Heightened proof requirements with respect to force and resistance were designed to address these concerns. But the modern experience of this offense suggests that the real danger is elsewhere; most documented cases of innocent defendants convicted of rape have nothing to do with consent determinations.

The prevalence of false claims remains a matter of significant controversy today. In the 1970s and 1980s rape reformers argued that the percentage of false claims of rape was very low and certainly no higher

---

That many men would perceive and do as Eric did, does not render his perceptions and conduct reasonable as a matter of law.

17. For an overview of rape law and its contemporary controversies, including the significance of extrinsic force, see David P. Bryden, Redefining Rape, 3 Buff. Crim. L. Rev. 317 (2000).

18. 1 History of the Pleas of the Crown 635 (1971) (originally published 1736).

than other crimes of violence. Although police reported a relatively high rate of rape accusations later determined to be unfounded, reformers argued that this reflected the unjustified skepticism of law enforcement toward acquaintance rape rather than the actual rate of false claims. The real problem was that most rapes were never reported. Reformers argued that the disincentives to claiming rape, both legal and cultural, were so great that few if any women would make a false claim.

More recent studies suggest that the problem of false claims—at least at the initial investigative stage—is real. There are a significant number of claims that, on police investigation, appear to be false. Some of these claims may be made to avoid bad personal consequences from consensual sexual activity. Fortunately, the great majority of such claims never result in formal criminal charges. The greatest concern for the law must be with false accusations that reach the courtroom.

The majority of rape cases where clearly innocent persons have been convicted of this crime, or have faced extended investigation and prosecution, fall into two general categories: (1) stranger attacks where conviction depends significantly on a mistaken eyewitness identification; and (2) allegations made by complainants with mental disorders.

Some of the most dramatic recent cases of miscarriages of justice revealed by DNA evidence, where innocent persons have spent long years in prison, have involved rape defendants. In most of these cases, the victim misidentified the defendant. The accuracy of eyewitness identification of strangers, especially cross-racial identifications from highly stressful situations, is notoriously difficult for law enforcement and lay decision makers to assess. The sincerity of the victim, sympathy for her injury, and the persuasive power of eyewitness testimony have contributed to a number of false convictions—which obviously has nothing to do with the definition of rape. These are cases where a rape occurred, but the wrong person is identified as the rapist.

Less likely to produce wrongful convictions, but nevertheless troublesome, are instances of persons with mental illness making false, but initially credible allegations of very serious sexual attacks. The notorious Duke lacrosse team rape case apparently fits this model.[19] Linda Fairstein, a pioneering prosecutor of rape cases, documents a similar case that she handled in her memoir of prosecution.[20] These are cases that test the ability of police and prosecutors to both take seriously the allegations

---

19. See Robert P. Mosteller, The Duke Lacrosse Case, Innocence, and False Identifications: A Fundamental Failure to "Do Justice", 76 Ford. L. Rev. 1337, 1347, 1375–81 (2007).

20. Linda A. Fairstein, *Sexual Violence: Our War Against Rape* 217–30 (1993).

of persons who may have mental problems, but also to reconsider any initial assessment of a witness in the light of subsequently discovered evidence.

It is often said that rape cases are difficult because they involve a "he said, she said" contest over the facts. And it is true that in most rape cases there is no physical evidence to establish the criminality of the incident and no percipient witnesses beyond the parties. Yet similar credibility contests arise in other criminal cases, especially in robbery. (Where again, miscarriages of justice usually involve eyewitness misidentification.) The swearing contest aspect of many rape cases is undeniable, but is not as unique as often claimed.

None of this means that determinations of victim nonconsent and defendant culpability with respect to nonconsent are easy. Both false claims and mistaken memories may contribute to unjust verdicts here. And unfortunately, wrongful verdicts on these elements are not likely to be overturned, because there are no scientific tests for consent or mens rea.

Finally there are cases involving controversy about culpability and nonconsent where both parties appear to testify truthfully. Here justice turns on the decision maker's judgment about the moral and legal significance of the facts.[21]

---

21. See, e.g., State in the Interest of M.T.S., 609 A.2d 1626 (N.J. 1992); Commonwealth v. Berkowitz, 641 A.2d 1161 (Pa. 1994).

INTRODUCTION TO PART FOUR

INCHOATE LIABILITY

Part Four of this book concerns what is called, rather obscurely, inchoate liability. Inchoate means conduct that is incipient, or just begun. Inchoate liability therefore establishes criminal responsibility for an individual's participation in a criminal endeavor based on preliminary conduct that does not necessarily result in a concrete, physical harm. It includes attempts at crimes (Chapter 15) and liability for the criminal conduct of another in the form of accomplice liability (Chapter 16) and conspiracy (Chapter 17).[1] We should not confuse the requirements of inchoate liability with its actual reach, however. We will see that each of these forms of liability may also extend to conduct that produces very concrete, physical harms.

Each of the forms of liability covered involve individuals engaging in incipient criminal conduct, either individually or with others. This conduct is undertaken with sufficient awareness of or desire for harm doing and presents sufficient risks of harm that it warrants criminal punishment. Such conduct nevertheless requires special legal treatment, because the defendant's acts are in some important respect different from those required for standard criminal liability. Each doctrine emphasizes culpability based on mens rea. Each presents special analytic challenges and important questions concerning proof of wrongdoing and the necessity of harm for criminal punishment.

The Problem of Compound Crime Definitions

Perhaps the most important similarity between the doctrines of attempt, accomplice liability and conspiracy is an unfortunate one. All three involve compound crime definitions. In each case, a general rule of liability is provided to cover a nearly infinite variety of offenses. This means that, in each case, the relevant rule of inchoate liability must be matched up, somehow, with the rule of the particular offense to which it is now attached.

---

1. Except for a passing mention, the crime of solicitation will not be covered here.

For example, in ascertaining the requirements for an attempted robbery, we must determine the requirements of attempt, determine the requirements of robbery, and then determine how these interact to produce the requirements of attempted robbery. Complicity (accomplice liability) and conspiracy present similar challenges. The general rule of complicity or conspiracy must be matched up with the requirements of particular substantive offenses in order to produce the rule we need for the case at hand. The basic liability formula for inchoate offenses looks like this:

[inchoate liability rule] + [elements of underlying criminal offense]
= [inchoate liability for underlying offense]

This formulation by itself provides very little in the way of actual rules, however. It only illustrates the challenge. For example, each of our inchoate liability rules will have a mens rea component, as will the great majority of the underlying criminal offenses involved. And, as we have seen, mens rea terms never stand by themselves. They must always have partners, elements to which they apply. Thus, the big question is how the mens rea terms set out in the general inchoate liability rule interact with, or are distinguished from, the mens rea requirements of the underlying offense.

CHAPTER 15

ATTEMPT

The idea behind the law of attempts is simple enough. Persons who make significant efforts to commit crime should face punishment even if their criminal goals are not achieved. Such conduct demonstrates both culpability and danger to society. Unfortunately, generalities only take us so far. We need specific rules to define the requirements of act and mens rea in attempt. To a striking degree, however, the rules of attempt are stated only generally, meaning that a great deal of work must be done on a case by case, situation by situation, or offense by offense basis.

Major issues in attempt liability fall into three basic categories: act, mens rea, and so-called impossibility. Initially we must decide where to draw the line between conduct sufficient for an attempt, and preparatory conduct that falls short of an attempt. We must then resolve what mens rea is required for an attempt at a particular offense, as compared with the mens rea required for the completed offense. Finally, there is the issue of whether attempt liability should be prohibited because defendant's effort at crime could never be successful under the circumstances.

The Act Requirement for Attempt

Because a person charged with an attempt offense does not actually complete the act required for the underlying crime—does not actually possess the drugs, kill the victim, steal from the store—we need a special set of criteria to determine whether he or she has committed a sufficient act for an attempt at the offense. Here it will help to review what we previously learned about the act requirement.

We saw in Chapter 5 that the voluntary act requirement provides assurance that the offender will be punished for something he did and not just thought. We also need to prove that the defendant's bodily movements—or in some instances failures to move—were directed by a conscious mind. We have seen that proof of a criminal act often establishes defendant culpability and dangerousness, because it provides evidence of mens rea. All these considerations are implicated in the act requirement for attempt crimes.

Completed v. Attempt Crimes—The Act Requirement

To illustrate the difference between the act requirement for completed offenses and for criminal attempts, consider a simple case of shoplifting.

> Shopper passes by a display of expensive earrings three times within the space of five minutes. She removes a scarf from a nearby display, tries it on, and then replaces it. As she does so, with her other hand she takes a pair of earrings and places them in her large purse. Some minutes later she pays for several inexpensive items at the cash register and leaves the store. A security guard stops her in the parking lot and finds a $150 pair of earrings—which she did not pay for—in her purse.
>
> Can Shopper be convicted of petty theft: the "knowing unlawful taking of merchandise valued at less than $250, with the purpose to deprive the owner thereof permanently"?

This is not an especially hard case, but analysis will help show the importance of the act requirement to proof of mens rea in cases of a completed offense.

To prove theft, the prosecution must prove that the offender voluntarily did the act of taking the merchandise from the store. The prosecution must also show that the defendant stole—acted with awareness of the wrongfulness of the taking and with a purpose to deprive the owner permanently. Here the Shopper's conduct, going by the earring display several times, apparently using the scarf to disguise her taking of the earrings, going through the checkout line but not paying for the earrings and then exiting the store all tend to indicate a purpose to steal: taking with knowledge that it was unlawful (because the earrings were not paid for) and with a purpose to keep the item. Shopper may still contest this proof, arguing that the placement in her purse was accidental and she had no intent to steal. The point is that her physical conduct constitutes the prosecution's best proof of her criminal intention.

> Now assume that Shopper acted in the same fashion with respect to taking the earrings but was stopped by a security guard before she reached the cash register. Now what?

Although Shopper has clearly "taken" the earrings in the sense of reducing them to her (temporary) possession, because she has not actually left the store without paying for the jewelry, her conduct is harder to read. The argument that she put the earrings in her purse without any thought of theft now seems more plausible. Perhaps she put the earrings in her purse because it was a convenient place to keep them until she reached the cashier. Or, perhaps she *was* thinking about stealing the earrings, but had not decided whether to actually do it. Either way the evidence raises more doubts about whether she should be convicted of a crime.

Because with attempts at crime we often have less defendant conduct to assess, we have potentially less information about defendant's culpability and dangerousness. As a result, we need a special rule to establish the sufficiency of an act for attempt liability. We need a rule that distinguishes between non-criminal "preparation" and sufficiently culpable and dangerous conduct to establish attempt liability.

Basic Themes in Act Analysis

Before introducing the two most important rules for determining the act requirement in attempt, it will be help to set out some general themes in act analysis, considerations that regularly influence courts in their interpretation and application of act rules.

The Time (and Place) Continuum

One way of understanding the attempt act requirement is to imagine a time line extending from the most preliminary preparations relating to a crime to the last possible action taken to commit a crime. Usually paired with timing is a consideration of geography—the physical proximity of the defendant to final commission of the crime. For example, in the commission of a burglary, the last possible action taken towards its commission will place the defendant in close proximity to the location of the planned break-in. But because issues of geography usually pair with questions of timing, for purposes of simplicity, the focus here will be primarily on timing. Where on the time continuum should we locate the act requirement?

For illustrative purposes, we begin with a rule that no American jurisdiction currently follows: the so-called last step rule. This rule states that only the last possible act prior to completing the crime is sufficient. Putting aside the metaphysical difficulty of defining what the last step in any course of action might be, this rule has been rejected because it is too restrictive. An angry man, who has previously threatened the life of the victim, who approaches the victim with drawn gun, yelling: "I'm going to kill you", is suddenly tackled and disabled by a heroic intervener. Under last step analysis, this individual might not be convicted of attempted murder because he never actually aimed the gun—or, to interpret the rule even more strictly—squeezed the trigger of the gun. These latter acts might be deemed the last acts required for an attempt at homicide. Yet many would agree that this defendant has already done enough for attempted murder.

One thing we know for sure. *If* the defendant's conduct constitutes the last step prior to the completion of a crime, then it will satisfy any current test for test for the act requirement under attempt.

Objective Assessment of Danger v. Evidence of Culpability

As noted before, the act in attempt liability is important for establishing both dangerousness and culpability. In some jurisdictions— and cases—emphasis is placed on objective signs of the defendant's criminal dangerousness. Courts focus on how close the defendant came to actual crime commission. On other occasions, the most important factor seems to be evidence of the defendant's culpability, evidence in other words of his or her mens rea.

At least as they are stated on their face, we will see that the dangerous proximity rule tends to emphasize objective dangerousness while the substantial step rule tends to emphasize evidence of defendant's criminal intent.

Words v. Conduct: Equivocality Analysis

Another theme in act analysis involves the reliability of different kinds of proof. Courts sometimes prefer proof of defendant's physical conduct to proof based on words. This distinction is found in a rule sometimes cited, but less often followed (at least in its original form), the so-called equivocality rule.

As classically stated, the equivocality rule mandates that only nonverbal conduct may satisfy the act requirement. It is, in effect, a silent movie test. Imagine that we have a silent movie of the defendant's conduct, similar to what might appear on a surveillance camera recording: does the visual record strongly suggest criminal activity, or is the conduct depicted consistent with innocence? The rule strongly privileges proof of conduct over proof based on words.

Return to the example of our Shopper. If her movements in placing the earrings in her purse appear furtive, such as looking around to see that she is not being watched, or using the scarf to disguise her movements, then we might deem the evidence "unequivocal" concerning her criminality. If her physical movements are equally consistent with an unplanned placement of the earrings in her purse, her conduct would be deemed equivocal.

> At least in its original version, the equivocality test excludes from consideration otherwise highly probative verbal indicators of culpability. For example, statements by Shopper to an acquaintance prior to going into the store that she wanted to "rip off some stuff" or Shopper's admission to a security guard after being stopped that "I know it's wrong, I don't know why I did it" would not be considered for proof of the act requirement under attempt. The notion here is that with respect to the act requirement, we need more concrete evidence of dangerousness and culpability than can be provided by mere words. It is informed by the common notion that actions speak louder than words.
>
> Although the equivocality rule is not the rule for attempt liability in most jurisdictions, courts will sometimes use a kind of equivocality analysis to help decide whether the defendant's act was dangerously close to success, or represented a substantial step.

Rules for the Attempt Act Requirement: Dangerous Proximity and Substantial Step

There are two main rules on the sufficiency of an act for attempt liability: one often identified with the common law, the dangerous proximity rule; and another from the MPC, usually dubbed the substantial step rule.

On their face, these rules seem to embody different philosophies of liability. The dangerous proximity rule seems to establish a more robust act requirement, requiring acts close in time and place to the last act. It emphasizes objective dangerousness. Conversely, the substantial step rule seems to establish liability much earlier on the time continuum, thus including more conduct within the purview of criminal attempts. It tends to emphasize defendant's mens rea.

These apparent distinctions between rules do not always hold up in practice, however. Jurisdictions vary significantly in how they interpret act requirement rules, to the extent that interpretive variations may prove more significant than the actual choice of rule. This means that the explanations that follow, which largely rest on the wording of each rule, should be read cautiously. The most important guide to the law remains the relevant decisions of appellate courts in the jurisdiction.

Another important consideration that we cannot track here is that act analysis necessarily depends on the nature of the crime. Courts will develop guidelines for sufficient acts according to whether the crime involves robbery or theft, a sex offense, a drug offense and so on. Each have their own typical patterns of commission and present their own particular problems with the act requirement. Therefore the most important considerations in resolving a particular case may be previous decisions relating to that particular crime.

Dangerous Proximity to Success

In many jurisdictions, a defendant commits a sufficient act for attempt liability if his or her conduct is judged "dangerously close to success." This rule sets the act requirement relatively close to that of the completed criminal act, with the result that many commentators state that the critical question involves how much the defendant had left to do to accomplish a criminal end. The more unfinished business between what the defendant did and what the completed offense would require, the less likely that a sufficient act was committed. Another way to express the inquiry about dangerous proximity is to retrospectively observe the defendant's conduct and ask how much we fear that he or she was about to achieve criminal success. The more frightened we are of defendant's criminal efforts, the more likely that a sufficient act has been proven for attempt.

> On a cold winter day in a small western town Defendant enters a bank wearing a heavy winter coat and knit cap. The security guard immediately notices Defendant because he has never seen him before and because Defendant does not immediately approach either one of the tellers or the desk of a bank officer. Instead Defendant looks around the bank lobby, including at the walls and ceiling, as if to check for surveillance cameras.
>
> Defendant then pulls down his knit cap over his face, effectively hiding his identity, and places a hand in his coat pocket. At this point he is about 15 feet from the row of bank tellers. He takes two steps toward a bank teller. The security guard then tackles him. Defendant is found to have a large knife in his coat pocket. Has Defendant committed a sufficient act for attempted bank robbery under the dangerous proximity test?

The answer is likely affirmative. While Defendant has not taken the last step needed for such a robbery—making a forcible demand for money from the teller—in moving toward the teller with a weapon in his pocket and his face covered by a mask, Defendant is acting like a bank robber and not at all like a law-abiding citizen. There is no reasonable lawful explanation for his conduct at this point. Defendant has also reached the point where, taking all the facts into consideration, we are likely to be frightened that he is about to commit a robbery.

The defense may respond that the accused was still physically too far from the teller for there to be sufficient objective dangerousness. Additionally, without either a verbal or written demand, it is not clear that Defendant is about to commit a robbery. I suspect these arguments will be unavailing at least as to the act requirement. We still have a suspicious-acting (recall the casing-type activity), armed single male approaching a bank teller with a mask over his face. It looks like an armed robbery in progress.

> Same facts as above *except* that Defendant does not pull the knit cap over his face before taking two steps toward the row of bank tellers. Assume that his knife remains unseen in his pocket. Same result?

Now the case looks different. Even though there is no difference in timing or geography, and quite possibly no difference in actual dangerousness, Defendant's conduct now may be seen as potentially innocent. It was Defendant's converting his cap into a mask to hide his identity that provided the single most powerful indicator of his robbery intentions.

While Defendant's conduct on entering the bank is consistent with casing the location for robbery, and carrying a large knife in his pocket is suggestive of a criminal enterprise, there is nothing in his overt conduct that clearly distinguishes it from that of an innocent person. Looking around a bank lobby before approaching a bank teller is hardly unusual and can have many innocent explanations. Carrying a knife into a bank is more unusual, but is not, at least in the western United States, by itself indicative of bank robbery. On these facts the defense has a strong argument that the Defendant did not commit an act in "dangerous proximity to success" of bank robbery.

The examples considered so far track a common set of issues involving the need to distinguish between potentially innocent and criminal conduct. Another set of issues in the act requirement involve persons clearly interested in criminality, but whose willingness to actually commit a crime may be in question. The law seeks to distinguish here between the serious would-be criminal, who merits punishment, and the wannabe who, at least on the facts adduced, does not. The former are persons bent on committing a particular crime who are thwarted by circumstances or human intervention. The latter are persons whose commitment to criminality is uncertain. The following fact pattern illustrates.

> In response to a rash of bank robberies in a suburban community, a team of FBI agents sets up surveillance in the vicinity of a branch bank they believe may be the next target. At about midmorning, FBI agents spot a car that circles the block four times. Inside are a man and a woman, apparently engaged in a heated discussion. The man gestures with one arm twice in the general direction of the bank. Finally the car pulls into the parking lot belonging to the bank and several other

stores. The woman steps out of the car and a somewhat over-eager FBI agent declares over the radio "it's going down." Agents surround the two and take them into custody.

Found in a neat pile on the back seat of the car are a handgun, several plastic garbage bags and a demand note which reads: "put the money in the bags." Confronted with the demand note, the woman says that her boyfriend was going to rob the bank. The boyfriend maintains that he had just been joking about robbery with his girlfriend, that he would never have actually gone through with it. Do these facts satisfy the dangerous proximity test?

The prosecution argument is that there are strong indications that the two were headed toward the bank to commit a bank robbery. Their conduct is consistent with casing activity: the demand note, gun and garbage bags all indicate that their plan was a bank robbery. As a result, when the woman got out of the car, it was likely that the pair were only a minute or two away from committing bank robbery. It appears that the two had done most of what was necessary to set up the robbery. All they needed to do was walk into the bank and hand over the note.

The defense will argue that even if the evidence demonstrates a bank robbery *plan*, the defendants were so far in both time and place from an actual robbery, that there was no dangerous proximity to success. With one of the potential robbers still the car, one just outside of the car in a suburban parking used by several commercial establishments, and without a clear move toward the bank— let alone actually entering the bank—the pair were nowhere near the point at which we would be seriously frightened of them as bank robbers. Perhaps law enforcement had a reason to stop them for investigation, but the arrests occurred during what courts often call the *locus poenitentiae*, meaning the place of repentance. They still had not reached the point of no return. Even assuming that they were seriously contemplating bank robbery, that it was not all a joke, they still had not fully committed to the plan. They easily could have turned back.

In sum, the proof here does not establish the pair to be sufficiently determined in their criminal scheme or close enough to its commission to be convicted and punished as attempted bank robbers.

Substantial Step Strongly Corroborative of the Actor's Intent

The substantial step rule can be stated in several different ways, but its essence is that the defendant must have committed a substantial step in a course of criminal conduct, strongly corroborative of the actor's criminal purpose.[2] In some jurisdictions, courts add the adjective of "firmness," such that the substantial step must corroborate the "firmness of the actor's criminal purpose." This latter variation makes specific reference to the problem of criminal determination discussed previously. The issue of firmness, however, is a significant consideration even without its explicit mention in the rule, just as it is under the dangerous proximity test.

By contrast with the objective dangerousness emphasized by proximity analysis, the substantial step rule focuses primarily on proof of mens rea: the criminal purpose necessary for attempt. (Exactly what forms of mens rea are required for attempt will be discussed in a separate section below. For now, we will just focus on the defendant's intent to commit a crime as opposed to engage in lawful conduct.) Consistent with the MPC generally, what matters most is proof of the defendant's culpability via subjective forms of mens rea, here purpose. The attempt act requirement is explicitly linked to mens rea, with analysis designed to distinguish particular ways of proving mens rea through defendant's conduct.

The substantial step test is often said to depend on what the defendant has *already* done to commit a crime, in contrast with dangerous proximity that focuses on what is left to be done. Substantial step therefore seems to contemplate liability based on conduct that occurs earlier on the time continuum than does the dangerous proximity test. But as noted previously, how this rule *works* (decides cases) depends on how it is interpreted by the appellate courts of the jurisdiction.

> Return to the original examples of the potential lone bank robber. How does the substantial step rule analyze the act requirement in these instances?

In the first case, where the defendant headed towards a teller after having converted his knit cap into a mask that covered his face, the same considerations that argued for a sufficient act under dangerous proximity to success will probably satisfy the substantial step rule. The defendant's apparent casing activity, combined with moving towards a teller with a mask pulled over his face, while armed with a knife, all suggest a substantial step towards bank robbery, with the mask and knife especially being corroborative of a purpose to rob the teller.

---

2. MPC sec. 5.01(1) (c), (2): "an act or omission constituting a substantial step in a course of conduct planned to culminate in [his] commission of the crime ... strongly corroborative of the actor's criminal purpose".

By contrast, in the second case where the defendant does not pull the cap over his face, his conduct appears far more ambiguous. While he has still done a great deal toward bank robbery, assuming that is his plan, his conduct is not strongly corroborative of criminal purpose. Once all facts are taken into account, his conduct should make any law enforcement type suspicious of robbery, but we lack a sufficiently clear indication of a robbery plan to deem his conduct strongly corroborative of a purpose to rob.

What about proof of the act requirement under the substantial step test for attempted robbery in the case of the couple arrested in the suburban parking lot?

Here the substantial step rule potentially gives the prosecution a better argument than under the dangerous proximity test, again depending on how the jurisdiction reads the substantial step rule. The prosecution would argue that considering all that the couple did toward bank robbery—circling the bank, drafting a demand note, assembling gun and garbage bags, that they had made a very substantial step towards bank robbery. The defense would reiterate the same arguments made previously under dangerous proximity to argue for a less than substantial step, especially to argue that there was no firmness here. The accused were at most wannabe, in-their-fantasies-only, Bonnie and Clydes.

Even in jurisdictions that follow the substantial step test, courts often emphasize objective dangerousness in their analysis of the extent to which the defendant has made a final commitment to criminality.

Concerned about sex predators who establish contacts with minors online, a number of law enforcement agencies conduct Internet sting operations. The following describes one such operation.

An undercover police officer, who represents herself to be Tiffany, a 13-year-old girl, engages in conversations in a chat room for teenage girls. She converses online with Ralph, a 37-year-old insurance claims adjuster (who represents himself to be in his 20s). After several discussions about junior high and friends and music, Ralph inquires about boys and sexual matters. The discussion becomes more intimate. After almost three weeks of nearly daily Internet exchanges, Ralph proposes a meeting so that he can "get to know her better—much better." The conversation includes graphic descriptions of various sexual acts they may attempt. They make arrangements to meet at a particular time and place, with Ralph flashing his headlights three times to establish that the coast is clear. Both wish to keep the meeting secret from Tiffany's parents.

The police set up at the arranged location. A female police officer dressed as Tiffany had described she would, arrives at the scene. Ralph sees her but fails to signal. He is then arrested. In his possession is found a receipt for the rental of a nearby motel room. In the motel room are found condoms, lubricant, vibrator, and pornographic materials. Later he tells police that he was not going to do anything with "Tiffany" but just wanted to talk because he was lonely. The materials found in his motel room have nothing to do with her, he says.

Ralph is charged with attempted lewd and lascivious conduct with a minor under the age of 14. Has Ralph committed a sufficient act under the substantial step test?

From the prosecution's perspective, Ralph has done a great deal of activity toward sexual activity with a minor. There were weeks of seductive activity on the Internet, a meeting planned, the rental of a motel room, assembling of sexual materials. That Ralph did not follow through with the headlight signals says more about his fear of being caught than a lack of willingness to engage in criminal conduct. All of his actions indicate a serious desire to engage in sex with a girl under the age of 14, the prosecution will contend.

The defense will argue that Ralph's conduct may be morally reprehensible, but he never crossed the line into criminal conduct. The strongest point for the defense is that there never was a minor under the age of 14 who was put at risk. No such person conversed with Ralph on the Internet and no such person showed up at the meeting place.[3]

Putting aside the use of law enforcement to impersonate a minor, the defense can argue that defendant's Internet representations cannot be taken seriously. People misrepresent themselves on the Internet all the time and also say outrageous things that they would never actually do. Therefore all of the conversations on the Internet must be treated skeptically. The Internet is about talk, not action. Ralph's critical decision point, the line between talk and criminal action, was the headlights signals, which he never gave. The rental of a motel room and stocking up with sexual items does not say anything about a determination to have sex with a 13-year-old girl; it is equally consistent with other, lawful solitary (or mutually consensual adult) sexual conduct. In sum, the defense will contend that Ralph's conduct does not demonstrate the clarity or firmness of criminal purpose that the law requires here.

---

3. This was determinative in State v. Duke, 709 So.2d 580 (Fla. Ct. App. 1998). For a legislative effort to specifically criminalize such behavior, see Florida Statutes secs. 847.0135 (3), (4).

Abandonment

Closely related to the question of a sufficient act for attempt liability is the doctrine of abandonment. This is the rule, recognized in some jurisdictions, that a person may do more than is required for attempt liability and yet avoid conviction by proof that he or she subsequently abandoned the criminal scheme. There are essentially two different approaches to abandonment issues. In those jurisdictions where the act requirement is set very late in the time scheme— usually those following the dangerous proximity approach—no defense of abandonment is recognized. Those jurisdictions which follow the MPC substantial step test, usually do permit such a defense, albeit in very limited form.

Common Law/Dangerous Proximity—The No Abandonment Approach

The more traditional view of attempt liability under the common law generally treats the line between a sufficient and insufficient act for attempt purposes as irreversible. This approach can best be explained by reference to completed crimes.

> Defendant commits a bank robbery, leaves the premises and then returns home to inspect the proceeds. After considering the rather paltry sum that he has obtained, he comes to have second thoughts about the robbery, and indeed his entire course of life. He vows to change his ways. As a first step he drives back to the bank, goes up to the victimized teller, hands back the money and issues a deeply felt apology for his earlier action. "I hope that we can all just forget that this ever happened," he concludes. The bank manager proves less forgiving (as is so often true) and calls the police. Defendant is soon arrested and charged with bank robbery. Can the Defendant avoid conviction by virtue of his post-robbery actions?

The answer is no. Once Defendant has received money from the teller as a result of his threat, the crime of robbery is complete and cannot be undone. A prosecutor may decide not to prosecute or a judge may sentence leniently because of Defendant's subsequent actions, but under law, the original crime cannot be erased by subsequent acts of repentance.

Many jurisdictions view the commission of an act sufficient for attempt liability in the same fashion. Once the accused has gone beyond "mere preparation" and reached the point of "dangerous proximity to success," no subsequent change of heart will have any legal effect.

A no-abandonment rule usually pairs with a fairly late act requirement. In order to preserve a locus poenitentiae, and so provide a legal incentive for voluntary decisions to turn away from crime, courts in such jurisdictions usually require the attempt act to be close in time and space to the completed criminal act. The opposite can also be true: allowing an abandonment defense often pairs with a relatively early act requirement.

The MPC Voluntary Abandonment Approach

The Model Penal Code's substantial step test allows for a relatively early attempt act, but then compensates by providing for a separate affirmative defense of voluntary withdrawal.[4]

Under the heading of "renunciation of criminal purpose," the MPC declares that a defendant may avoid liability for attempt even after committing a "substantial step," if the defendant then voluntarily abandons or prevents the commission of the planned crime. The key to this doctrine is the notion of a *voluntary* withdrawal or renunciation. The circumstances must manifest "a complete and voluntary renunciation of his criminal purpose." A defendant's decision to give up—to abandon—a criminal plan is not voluntary if it is deterred by law enforcement or by the difficulty of its accomplishment at that time and place. Instead the defendant needs to present evidence that he or she experienced a true change of heart with respect to this form of criminality.

Mens Rea

There are few areas of criminal law where basic doctrine is stated in as simple and yet as unhelpful a fashion as the mens rea requirement for attempt. Most jurisdictions say something like: "An attempt requires that the defendant intend to commit the crime attempted."[5] From this statement we learn that the mens rea for attempt is intent, which here usually means purpose.[6] But the real question is: *purpose as to what?*

---

4. Sec. 5.01 (4).

5. "An attempt to commit a crime consists of two elements: a specific intent to commit the crime, and a direct but ineffectual act done towards its commission." Cal. Pen. Code sec. 21a.

6. In sec. 5.01 (1) the MPC also includes knowledge with respect to a result: "or with the belief that it will cause such results without further conduct on his part."

With respect to underlying crimes that themselves require purpose, attempts present few additional problems with mens rea. For example we had no difficulties with the mens rea required for attempts at shoplifting or bank robbery in our previous examples, because both crimes involve underlying purposeful criminality. Theft and robbery involve purposeful takings and/or use of force. The difficulty arises with attempts at offenses that normally require proof of knowledge, recklessness, negligence, or some form of strict liability. What does it mean to act with the purpose to commit a crime of unlawful possession? Or with purpose to engage in unlawful intercourse with a minor? The standard statement of the attempt mens rea rule does not tell us.

Recall that attempt offenses, like other forms of inchoate liability, are by their nature compound offenses, involving two sets of mens rea requirements. Here we have the purpose required for attempt and, usually, some further mens rea required for the underlying offense. The challenge is determining how these two sets of mens reas interact. The following formula sets out the problem.

attempt mens rea (purpose) + mens rea for underlying (i.e. completed) offense = ? mens rea for attempted offense

The answer, as we will see, depends on how we categorize the underlying offense, whether it is a result or conduct offense. We begin with an example of a result offense.

> Sara comes to the District Attorney's Office with a chilling story. She reports that her father nearly died the week before because his prescription heart medicine had been diluted by the dispensing pharmacist, Robert Hill. A preliminary investigation reveals that over several years, Hill diluted a number of pharmaceuticals in order to purchase expensive wines for his wine collection. Hill has confessed to the dilution but denied that he wanted to kill or injure anyone. Sara tells the Deputy District Attorney: "Because of this guy's greed, my father just about died. He should get some kind of murder charge, not just some rinky dink illegal prescription thing."
>
> The question is whether these facts support an attempted murder or attempted manslaughter charge against Hill.

Here we encounter a striking example of the power of ordinary language to shape criminal responsibility. Assume that the prosecution can prove that pharmacist Hill acted with recklessness sufficient to satisfy the requirements of depraved heart murder but did *not* act with purpose to kill. That is, he acted with recklessness demonstrating extreme indifference to the lives of his customers—but without any desire to hasten the end of any customer's life, which would be bad for business. Since death did not result from Hill's actions, but his actions were likely sufficient to meet the act requirement for attempt, and were committed with a form of mens rea sufficient for murder (extreme recklessness) we might expect that Hill would be convicted for attempted murder. But that's not the way attempt law works.

Attempted murder suggests an intentional killing. In ordinary language, to attempt something means to try to accomplish it, to have a purpose to achieve it. Thus, in ordinary language, to say that Hill attempted murder means that he acted with a purpose to kill. Which he did not have. Under the facts given, Hill did not dilute prescriptions with the purpose of killing anyone. Hence the conclusion that he did not *attempt* to kill Sara's father.

We can certainly imagine a different legal outcome. If we were to be guided just by principles of deterrence and retribution, we might conclude that Hill should be convicted of some form of inchoate homicide offense: he demonstrated sufficient dangerousness and culpability for such liability. The problem remains the connotations of ordinary language. What he did does not sound like *attempted* murder. In any event, under current law, Hill cannot be guilty of attempted murder because murder is a result offense and Hill did not act with the purpose to achieve that result, the death of the victim.[7]

Basic Mens Rea Requirements for Conduct and Result Offenses

For offenses that require proof of a particular result, the mens rea for attempt is purpose to accomplish that result, plus any other additional mens rea requirements for the underlying offense. This means that for result offenses such as homicide, the mens rea requirements for attempt are significantly different from those of completed offenses. All forms of homicide attempts—all attempted murders and all attempted manslaughters—must be based upon proof of purpose to kill. Although knowledge, recklessness and even negligence may suffice for murder or manslaughter convictions with completed homicides, purpose to kill is required for attempted murder and attempted manslaughter.

---

7. E.g., Jones v. State, 689 N.E.2d 722, 724–25 (Ind. 1997); Smallwood v. State 680 A.2d 512, 515 (Md. 1996). There are a few contrary precedents, among them: Brown v. State, 790 So.2d 389 (Fla. 2001) (attempted second-degree murder does not require specific intent); People v. Thomas, 729 P.2d 972 (Colo. 1986) (affirming conviction for attempted reckless manslaughter).

Relatively few offenses in our pantheon of criminality require the proof of particular results, however. Most are so-called conduct offenses. Crimes such as burglary, drunk driving, and drug possession are typical conduct offenses because they do not require proof of any physical harm to person or property. For an attempt at a conduct offense, the defendant must act with purpose to do the simple act on which criminal liability is based, plus any other mens rea required for the underlying (conduct) offense. This will be explained in much greater detail below. First, however, we need to better understand the distinction between a result and a conduct offense.

Distinguishing Result and Conduct Offenses

There is surprisingly little case law on the distinction between result and conduct offenses. Indeed, most cases do not even mention the distinction. For the most part courts have been content to resolve the mens rea requirements for the particular offense presented, without setting out a general rule applicable to all cases and offenses. As a result, we are left to distill from case holdings a more explicit rule about the distinction between result and conduct offenses. We begin with result offenses.

It appears that a result offense is a crime that *requires* proof of a particular *physical* harm to property or person. The harm must be physical and not merely psychological. The offense must require for conviction that the physical harm be accomplished and not merely threatened.

The most obvious and most common example of a result offense is homicide. All homicide crimes require, by definition, the death of a human being. Thus they require proof of the physical taking of life. Another example might be destruction of property, in which the offense requires proof that property be destroyed. A more subtle example would be arson, which involves the burning of property and thus its damage or destruction by fire.

The vast majority of criminal offenses, however, are conduct offenses. These crimes do not *require* proof of physical harm to person or property. Here we need to distinguish between statutory requirements and factual proof. Many victims of conduct crimes may be physically hurt or have their property damaged. But if the statute does not require such harm, then it should not be classified as a conduct offense for purposes of attempt mens rea. A good example of this potentially confusing distinction is the crime of rape.

Although rape involves physical conduct by the defendant that is profoundly damaging—psychologically—to the victim, most rape statutes do not require proof of any physical injury or property damage. Therefore, it is a conduct offense and not a result one. Even if the particular case involves serious physical injury to the victim—which injury is relevant to proof of essential elements of the rape offense—this does not change the categorization of the offense. It changes the way that the offense is proven in the particular case, but does not alter the statutory definition. Remember, the distinction between result and conduct is based entirely on the statute and not the evidence used in a particular case. One more example should help illustrate this sometimes elusive distinction.

> Dangerous driving in this jurisdiction is defined as criminally negligent driving that endangers the lives or property of others. Should this be categorized as a conduct or a result offense?

While the requirement that the driving endanger either lives or property seems to suggest a result focus, this is in fact a conduct offense. The statute requires only a threat to life or property; no physical harm to person or property need be accomplished. As we saw with rape, it might be true that in a particular case the prosecution may prove endangerment by actual harm to property or persons, this would not change the categorization because it would not alter the statutory definition. The statute does not require proof of physical harm to persons or property.

One final note on offense categorization: legislators could easily convert most conduct offenses into result offenses if they so desired. A legislature could define dangerous driving as negligent driving that causes property damage or physical harm. Similarly, rape could be redefined to include the causation of a particular kind of injury. But notice the consequence. The additional language would both limit the cases that could be brought as completed offenses *and* would heighten the mens rea requirements for attempt by requiring proof of purpose to harm. These are not changes that have much popular appeal.

Mens Rea for Attempts at Result Offenses

The mens rea required for an attempt at a result offense is as follows: in addition to any other mens rea that may be required for the offense, an attempt at a result offense always requires proof that the defendant acted with purpose to accomplish the result.

Again homicide provides the best illustration. As noted before, all homicide offenses are result offenses. Consequently, any attempted homicide offense requires proof that the defendant acted with purpose to achieve the result, the result being the victim's death. Therefore, *all attempted homicides require, at a minimum, purpose to kill.* As a practical matter this works a significant change in the mens rea possibilities for attempted homicide.

All of the non-purpose to kill forms of mens rea that suffice for completed homicide offenses (either murder or manslaughter) become insufficient to support attempted murder or attempted manslaughter. There will be no attempted depraved heart murder because depraved heart murder involves recklessness toward death and any attempted murder must be based on purpose to kill. Similarly, there will be no attempted involuntary manslaughter, because while negligence (usually) suffices for proof of that offense, any attempts at manslaughter must involve proof of purpose to kill. For a discussion of attempts and felony murder, see Chapter 12.

In many jurisdictions, attempted murder is limited to attempted premeditated murder (purpose to kill + premeditation) or attempted murder (purpose to kill without premeditation or provocation). Attempted manslaughter, meanwhile will usually be based on purpose to kill plus evidence of provocation or, where recognized, imperfect self-defense.

> In a city with a history of racial tension over police use of force, the acquittal of white police officers in a prosecution for beating a black motorist in a widely publicized incident leads to street protests and violence. Young African American men attack motorists stopped at an intersection who appear white or Hispanic. A tractor-trailer stops and the white driver is pulled out of the cab by an African American man who beats him with fists, kicks him on the ground and smashes his head with a brick, fracturing his skull. The attacker does a small dance of triumph, then leaves the driver, apparently unconscious, on the pavement. He is later rescued by several African Americans who risk their lives to drive him to a hospital. The truck driver suffers brain damage and facial disfigurement, but survives. Can his attacker, on these facts, be convicted of attempted murder?[8]

The answer would appear to be yes, assuming that the jury is convinced that the attacker's use of fists, kicks, and especially the brick demonstrate a purpose to kill. The prosecution would argue that anyone who uses such extreme violence, partially crushing the skull of the victim, and reacts with apparent delight to his victimization, must have had a purpose to kill.

The defense will respond that although the attacker's use of violence was purposeful, it was designed to hurt and injure, but not kill. There was no use

---

8. The facts here bear some resemblance to the beating of Reginald Denny in Los Angeles in 1992. See Lou Cannon, *Official Negligence: How Rodney King and the Riots Changed Los Angeles and the LAPD* 498–513 (1999).

of a deadly weapon such as a knife or gun, nothing to take this incident out of the realm of a bad beating. That the driver suffered life-threatening injuries was not the design of the attacker. Defendant might be guilty of an aggravated assault, but not an attempt at homicide.

Note that had the driver died, the prosecution could argue for murder based on either purpose to kill *or* recklessness demonstrating an extreme indifference to the value of human life. The latter option would make the defense's job considerably more difficult. However this option is not available in an attempted murder prosecution, because murder is a result offense, meaning that attempted murder requires purpose to kill.

Mens Rea for Attempts at Conduct Offenses

Unlike result offenses, the attempt mens rea for conduct offenses rarely changes the prosecution's proof requirements in any significant fashion. To be guilty of an attempt at a conduct offense, the defendant must have the mens rea required for the underlying offense (that is, the conduct offense mens rea) and also the purpose to commit the act on which criminal liability rests (the attempt mens rea). Although the latter mens rea can be important, it does not usually connect to any aspect of *wrongful* conduct.

To explain mens rea for attempts at conduct offenses, we will break down conduct offenses according to their own mens rea requirements, grouping them into purpose and knowledge offenses, reckless and negligence offenses, and those based on strict liability.

For Purpose and Knowledge Offenses

Burglary may be defined as acting with purpose to enter into or remain within a structure, knowing that such entering or remaining is unlawful, with purpose to commit a crime therein. The completed offense requires two forms of mens rea: (1) knowledge of unlawfulness of the entry or remaining and (2) purpose to commit a crime within the structure. An attempt at burglary involves a third mens rea: that the defendant have demonstrated the purpose to enter or remain in the structure. In terms of our usual mens rea analysis, this third requirement is unusual because there is nothing inherently wrongful about entering or remaining in a structure. (Recall the general rule that a mens rea term should modify a wrongful aspect of defendant's conduct.)

Theft provides a similar example. Theft may be defined as taking the property of another, knowing that the taking is unlawful and with purpose to deprive the owner thereof permanently. Again the underlying (conduct) offense has two mens rea requirements: (1) knowledge of the unlawfulness of the taking and (2) purpose to deprive the owner of the property permanently. Both describe aspects of wrongdoing inherent in stealing. To convict someone of attempted theft, the prosecution must prove these mens reas and a third as well: purpose to take the property in question.

With respect to conduct crimes that require purpose, the additional purpose required for an attempt rarely creates a major issue. If the prosecution can prove that defendant acted with the mens rea required for the underlying offense, then the purpose required for attempt is probably shown as well. For example, in attempted burglary, a person who demonstrates that she knows that entry into a location would be unlawful, and who had a purpose to commit a crime therein, will likely also be shown to have had a purpose to enter.

What about attempt mens rea when the underlying offense is based on knowledge?

> Elaine is suspected of dealing cocaine during the course of her job as a bartender at Club Naranja. An undercover officer gives Elaine $5,000 to buy cocaine. She says it will be delivered shortly by a woman she calls Justine. Ten minutes later the undercover officer observes Elaine take a phone call and walk out to the back of the bar. There in the alley a tall woman (Justine) approaches carrying a large handbag. She is about 20 feet from Elaine when a police patrol car—not involved in the undercover operation—appears at the far end of the alley. Justine runs away. She is quickly run down and arrested. A large quantity of cocaine is found in her handbag.
>
> Can Elaine be convicted of attempted possession of the cocaine found in Justine's handbag?

Assume here that possession of cocaine requires that the defendant exercise actual or constructive control over cocaine, with knowledge that the item is a controlled (illegal) substance. This is a conduct offense because it does not require proof of any physical harm—though of course use of cocaine can be physically harmful. Because it is a conduct offense, for an attempt, the prosecution needs to prove (1) the mens rea for cocaine possession: knowledge that the substance possessed is an illegal drug, and (2) mens rea for the attempt: purpose to do the prohibited act, which here would be to take possession of the critical item. Thus the prosecution would have to prove that Elaine, in taking a phone call, going out to the alley and waiting for Justine was acting with purpose to take possession of the cocaine in Justine's handbag, and that Elaine was aware that the item she was going to take possession of was an illegal drug.

Mens Rea for Attempts at Reckless or Negligent Conduct Offenses

Things get a little stickier when we consider attempt liability for conduct offenses that are based on recklessness or negligence. Initially there is a question about whether this is even possible. How can one be liable for an *attempt* at a reckless or negligence offense? Doesn't this raise the same problem that we saw with attempts at reckless and negligent homicides? In fact, it does not, because of the previously mentioned distinction between conduct and result offenses.

While there are cases that seem to rule out attempt liability for any reckless or negligence offense, the majority view—and I believe the better reasoning—is that attempt liability is possible as long as the underlying offense is a conduct rather than result offense. (In fact, most of the judicial language suggesting a blanket rule against attempt liability for reckless or negligence offenses involves cases where defendant is charged with a result offense.) As long as the prosecution can prove defendant's purpose to do the prohibited act and any recklessness or negligence required for the underlying offense, attempt liability may be sustained.[9]

As always, a specific example will provide a helpful guide. Consider the offense of dangerous driving, defined as driving in an unreasonably dangerous manner. The mens rea for this offense is negligence—the driving must be unreasonably dangerous, representing a gross deviation from the standard of conduct of the ordinary law-abiding driver. Can there be an attempt at this offense where the defendant's driving would have been negligent? Consider these facts.

> Ralph, a veteran truck driver, is about to get behind the wheel of a heavily-loaded tractor-trailer rig to go down a mountain road. An independent owner-operator, Ralph has had a hard time making ends meet, and has skimped on maintenance on his vehicle. He has been warned that the truck's brakes are suspect and on a previous trip he noticed that the brake pedal feels very soft, a dangerous sign. He still believes that the truck should be okay going down the mountain though. He starts the engine, puts the truck in gear and is about to let out the clutch when he is approached by a highway patrol officer. The officer tells Ralph to shut the rig down for an inspection.

---

9. See MPC secs. 5.01(1)(a),(b). Sec. (b) covers result crimes (purpose attaches to result); sec. (a) covers conduct crimes (purpose attaches to the "conduct which would constitute the crime").

Examination of the brakes reveal that they are almost entirely shot, and would have failed disastrously on the mountain road, risking an extremely serious accident. The truck also is missing any documentation of regular safety inspections. Can Ralph be charged with attempted dangerous driving?

Here Ralph cannot be charged with actual dangerous driving because, at least based on the police officer's direct observations, Ralph never actually drove out on the road. As for attempted dangerous driving, there are two mens rea elements to discuss: the mens rea of negligence for the underlying offense and the mens rea of purpose required for the attempt. (Remember from our previous discussion that dangerous driving is a conduct offense because, although it involves a threat of physical harm, it does not require proof of actual physical harm.)

Did Ralph demonstrate the negligence required for dangerous driving? Ralph was about to drive a truck that any reasonable person in Ralph's position would have known was at great risk of brake failure, which on a mountain highway, could lead to an extremely serious accident. Hence we would say that any reasonable person would understand that driving under these conditions was dangerous. The negligence element is established.

What about proof of the purpose for the attempt? Here the prohibited act is driving on the public road. Therefore the prosecution needs to prove for an attempt, that Ralph was acting with the purpose of driving on the road. As we saw before, there is no requirement that the attempt purpose go to any aspect of wrongfulness. All that's required here is that Ralph acted with a purpose to drive. It appears that he did. The facts indicate that Ralph started the engine and put the truck in gear in order to drive on the public highway. Therefore, the prosecution can likely prove that he acted with purpose to drive at the time that he was stopped.

Of course the defense would like to argue that because Ralph neither had purpose nor knowledge that his driving would be dangerous—despite warning signs, he apparently sincerely believed the rig was safe—he should not be guilty of any attempt offense here. In most jurisdictions, however, that is more than the law requires for conviction. As we have seen, the attempt purpose goes only to driving, leaving the negligence with respect to dangerousness requirement of the underlying offense unchanged—and doing all of the most important work to establish culpability. Ralph should be convicted of this offense.

For Strict Liability Offenses

The same analysis holds for offenses that include strict liability elements. For example, consider the offense of statutory rape: unlawful sexual intercourse with a minor.

> In this jurisdiction, it is a felony for any person over the age of 18 to engage in sexual intercourse with any person under the age of 18. The age element of this offense is strict liability. Michael meets Laura at the beach at a resort hotel and asks her to meet him that evening. Michael is 22 years old; Laura says that she is 18. In fact, she is 16. They go out for the evening, then Laura invites Michael back to her hotel room; the two drink wine from the minibar, partially undress and engage in sexually intimate conduct, though short of sexual intercourse. Michael tries to persuade Laura to have "real sex" that is, sexual intercourse with him. She says she wants to think about it. Her contemplation period is cut short when Laura's parents unexpectedly enter the hotel room. They discover the two young people in a state of undress and are very upset. Laura tearfully admits everything, which leads to Michael's arrest.
>
> Can Michael be convicted of attempted unlawful sexual intercourse with a minor?

The answer is yes. Although Michael would like to argue that he must have acted with the purpose or at least knowledge that Laura was under 18, such proof is not required here. Underage sex with a minor is a conduct offense. It may sometimes lead to physical harm, but such harm is not required for conviction. As noted above, the age element in this offense is strict liability (true in most jurisdictions) and that will not change for an attempt. The attempt mens rea—the purpose—attaches only to the prohibited act, which here is sexual intercourse. As long as Michael had the purpose to have sexual intercourse with Laura, and he was actually over 18 and Laura under 18, all the elements for an attempt at this offense are established.

Impossibility

There are occasions when the defendant's attempt at a crime was not merely unsuccessful, but hopeless. Given the circumstances, success was literally impossible; there was no way that the defendant could have committed the underlying offense. But does this matter? It depends on the doctrine of impossibility.

The doctrine of impossibility itself often appears impossible. Its frequently chimerical distinctions have frustrated generations of law students and courts, explaining why the majority of U.S. jurisdictions in recent years have eliminated the rule by either statute or judicial decision. In most jurisdictions impossibility is no longer a defense to attempt. But because impossibility remains a viable doctrine in some jurisdictions, and because understanding the current state of law in other jurisdictions requires a review of earlier doctrine, we must at least briefly touch on the mysteries of factual and legal impossibility.

The Traditional Rule: Factual v. Legal Impossibility

Courts traditionally held that legal impossibility excuses from a charge of attempt, but not factual impossibility. The distinction lies in whether the source of impossibility rests on a legal or a factual insufficiency.

If, under the circumstances of the case, what defendant wanted to do would not have been a crime—would not have satisfied the underlying offense— then this is legal impossibility and precludes guilt for attempt. By contrast, if the defendant could not have committed the offense because the *facts* were different than he believed them to be then this is factual impossibility, which is never a defense.

On first encounter, this distinction between fact and law appears sensible and workable. Certainly no one should be convicted of a crime when the defendant's intended conduct does not meet the definition of a crime. On the other hand, it seems wrong to exonerate the defendant for mere factual stupidity. For example, a person who shot at another with purpose to kill, but who did not realize that his target was already dead, should not avoid guilt for attempted murder because of his factual ignorance.

The problem is that the apparently common sense distinction between facts and law quickly breaks down when we examine particular cases. At some point *all* factual mistakes that prevent successful completion of the offense can also be characterized as legal deficiencies, because they demonstrate that the statutory requirements could never be satisfied.

A standard example of the problem is presented by cases of attempted larceny by pickpockets. A pickpocket reaches his hand into another's trouser pocket in order to steal, but the pocket is empty. Obviously this circumstance— the empty pocket—eliminates any chance of a successful theft. We might well characterize this as factual impossibility, because defendant is simply ignorant about the pocket's contents. On the other hand, the definition of larceny requires the taking of property, and if that property does not exist, then there is a fundamental mismatch between conduct and criminal definition. There is no crime of stealing imaginary property. Seen this way, the case appears to be one of legal impossibility. Although most courts categorized such cases as factual impossibility, some leading decisions held the opposite.

Equally problematic have been cases of receiving stolen property: taking possession of property that is stolen, knowing it to have been stolen. What happens in a police sting operation when the defendant takes possession of an item believing it to have been stolen, when it actually was and always has been in the lawful possession of the police? Many courts have held that because it is not a crime to take possession of a lawfully possessed item, even believing it to be stolen, that these circumstances constitute legal impossibility. But notice that here the defendant's mistake about the stolen status of the property looks very much like the would-be killer's mistake about his victim being alive. Both involve standard kinds of mistakes about the state of the world that we would not normally believe would excuse from culpability.

The bottom line for legal and factual impossibility? Where legal rules do not provide predictable, reliable results, the rules need to be changed. So it is that most jurisdictions have decided that legal impossibility needs to go. I quite agree.[10]

Eliminating Impossibility: The MPC

Highly influential in the elimination of impossibility has been Section 5.01(1)(a) of the Model Penal Code. Under this section, there are three basic components to proof for attempt in so-called impossibility cases: (1) a sufficient act for attempt; (2) mens rea for the underlying offense; and (3) hypothetical reasoning with respect to any missing element.

Analysis here always begins with the statute defining the underlying offense. From this we should be able to deduce what is required for a sufficient act (almost never an issue in so-called impossibility cases) and what is required for mens rea. Assuming that there is sufficient proof of both, then we move to the missing element: that part of the crime that defendant could not meet because of particular circumstances. In homicide we have seen that this might be the

---

10. There are certainly dissenting views. See e.g., John Hasnas, Once More unto the Breach: The Inherent Liberalism of the Criminal Law and Liability for Attempting the Impossible, 54 Hastings L. J. 1 (2002). A number of commentators support the elimination of the fact versus law distinction but argue there should be some limitation on attempt liability according to a lack of real-world dangerousness posed by the defendant's conduct. See, e.g., George P. Fletcher, Constructing a Theory of Impossible Attempts, 5 Crim. J. Ethics 53 (1986).

requirement that the victim be alive, or in receiving stolen property, the requirement that the property actually be stolen. As to this missing element, we apply what may be called hypothetical reasoning. We ask: *If* what the defendant believed with respect to the missing element were true, would the missing element be satisfied under the statute? If so, a defendant may be convicted for an attempt. The following example will illustrate.

> In this jurisdiction, whoever knowingly distributes a controlled substance, cocaine, is guilty of a felony. This offense requires: (1) knowledge that the individual is transferring to another person an illegal drug and (2) proof that the substance distributed is cocaine.
>
> Mitch, has long wanted to be a really cool person, and thinks that being a drug dealer might achieve this end. He makes contact with Little Joe, known to be a big dealer. Mitch purchases from Little Joe for $500 a quantity of what he believes to be high-quality cocaine. In fact, the white powder that he buys is a combination of baking soda and powdered laxative. Mitch sells a small quantity of this substance to a friend, representing it to be cocaine. Can Mitch be convicted of any criminal offense here?

Mitch cannot be convicted of distribution of cocaine because the substance he distributed was not actually cocaine; in fact it was not even an illegal drug of any form. What about attempt liability? Under the old rules we would have to decide whether this case was better categorized as involving factual or legal impossibility. Now we do the three-step act, mens rea and hypothetical reasoning analysis set out above.

Whether we use the dangerous proximity or substantial step tests for the act requirement, Mitch has certainly done enough of an act for attempt liability. He has in fact distributed a substance.

As to mens rea, the offense requires knowledge that the item being transferred is an illegal drug. Mitch's representations to his friend who bought the substance and his interactions with Little Joe, corroborated by the high price he paid, indicate that Mitch sincerely believed he was distributing cocaine.

But there is still an element required for the underlying offense that is missing here: the substance distributed was not cocaine. Here we go to hypothetical reasoning. We ask what Mitch believed with respect to the chemical makeup of the substance and whether that belief, *if true*, would satisfy the statutory requirement. Here Mitch believed that he was selling cocaine, and if that were true (i.e., that the powder was cocaine) then the cocaine element of the statute would be satisfied. Hence, under the MPC analysis, and that used by many jurisdictions, Mitch would be convicted of attempted distribution of cocaine.

A Cautionary Note: Always Begin with the Statute

With the elimination of impossibility, there is only one kind of case in which a mistake about the criminal law will still excuse from liability. It is where the crime exists only in the imagination of the defendant. Such cases rarely arise in the real world, but have been known to appear in the minds of law professors, and therefore may be worth the attention of their students. Such cases will never cause any difficulty as long as we remember that analysis always begins with the statute in question and not the facts as perceived by the defendant.

> Karen is stopped for speeding by a highway patrol officer who asks if he can search her car. She gives permission. He finds in the trunk of her vehicle a loaded rifle. Karen says: I know it's against the law, but I just didn't have time to unload the gun after target practice because I'm late to pick up my kid at daycare.
>
> Karen has recently moved from a state which prohibits carrying a loaded firearm in a vehicle by any person who is not licensed to do so, to a state that has no such prohibition. Can she be charged with attempted carrying a loaded firearm in a vehicle, with the missing element of the existence of the statute being supplied by hypothetical reasoning?

The answer should be obvious: no. Attempt analysis begins and ends with analysis of the underlying offense. Since there is no relevant underlying offense in the jurisdiction, there is no possibility of attempt liability. Neither Karen nor anyone else can create criminal law out of their own imaginations.

CHAPTER 16

ACCOMPLICE LIABILITY

For such a standard and familiar part of Anglo-American criminal law, accomplice liability is marked by difficulty and surprise. The difficulties and surprises stem largely from the same source: the notion that a single general rule can accommodate all the factual and legal complexities of accomplice liability, regardless of the type of offense involved.

The law here surprises by both by what it covers and what it does not. Here enormous legal consequences can turn on small acts, even on a single word or gesture. An individual can become a murderer under law by uttering simple words of encouragement. Once established, accomplice liability in many jurisdictions may extend beyond the originally anticipated crime to include any other committed by the principal, if that further offense was a reasonably foreseeable consequence of the original crime. Yet it is also true that an individual may provide significant aid to another's criminal enterprise without becoming an accomplice, if that aid is not purposeful.

The rules of accomplice liability may be simply stated, and appear straightforward initially. But perhaps more than any other form of inchoate crime, the interaction between the requirements of inchoate criminality and those of the underlying offense create difficulties. General rules are not well suited to resolving particular cases here.

As elsewhere, the key to clear analysis here is careful use of legal language and attention to analytic sequence. Asking the right questions, in the right order, will bring a measure of clarity to this often murky area.

Terminology

The law of accomplice liability features a number of specialized terms which require brief introduction to prevent confusion.

We begin with basic synonyms. Accomplice liability may also be termed complicity, vicarious liability or aider and abettor liability. In most cases these terms are synonymous.

Next we move to the important distinctions. In determining liability, the criminal law distinguishes between the *principal* of a crime and the *accomplice*. The principal is the party who, with the required mens rea for the offense, commits the criminal act. The principal in a homicide is the person who does the physical act of killing; in rape, the principal is the person who commits the act of sexual invasion. The accomplice meanwhile is the individual who, with the required mens rea for accomplice liability, encourages or promotes the principal's criminal act.

On occasion we will also refer to the *primary* actor and *secondary* actor in a criminal event. Similar to the principal and accomplice pairing, the primary actor is the one who performs the criminal act; the secondary actor is the one who assists or directs that act. The primary/secondary actor terminology is broader, however, as it encompasses not only accomplice liability but also liability for directing an innocent or non-responsible actor. This latter form of liability will be discussed further below.

Finally, Anglo-American criminal law traditionally distinguished between the liability of principals and various types of accessories to the crime. In modern law, however, these distinctions concerning accessories have been almost entirely been eliminated. As a result, reference to being an accessory to a crime usually is synonymous with being an accomplice to that offense—with a single exception. Persons who provide aid to a criminal actor *after the completion of a crime*, face liability as an *accessory after the fact*. Accessory after the fact liability is distinct from accomplice liability and generally carries lesser penalties. It will not be discussed in any detail here. As a result, for clarity's sake the discussion will refer only to accomplices rather than accessories.

Punishment

An accomplice faces the same punishment as does the principal to a crime. The crime of conviction is exactly the same for both; only the theory of liability, the *way* in which the person is proven guilty, is different. So, for example, the accomplice who provided the gun used in a murder, and the actual killer, may be convicted of the same offense and face the same maximum sentence. There is no legal distinction between being convicted as a principal and as an accomplice in U.S. law, and no distinction is made between the two in criminal records. Where the judge has sentencing discretion, the accomplice may be punished less than a principal, but the accomplice may also receive greater punishment in some cases.

Related Forms of Criminal Responsibility

Before exploring the basics of accomplice liability, we should briefly consider the other ways that a person may be criminally responsible for another's conduct. In total, there are four ways a person may be criminally liable for another's acts: (1) accomplice liability; (2) conspiracy liability; (3) liability via causation; and (4) direction of an innocent or non-responsible actor. Conspiracy liability is the subject of the next chapter. Causation and direction of an innocent or non-responsible person are treated below. We will also briefly consider the creation of new offenses to cover particular kinds of criminal encouragement or promotion.

Causation

As we saw in Chapter 13, in crimes requiring a result (usually homicide), causation doctrine may operate to make a defendant liable for acts done by another. Ready examples include death caused by participation in risky contests such as street racing or Russian roulette. Here a survivor may be convicted of the murder or manslaughter of another contestant, even though that contestant was the immediate cause of his or her own demise. Although the deceased may have been the one to pull the trigger, or to drive the car off the road, these actions may be reasonably foreseeable to the defendant because of the nature of the contest. Liability for another's actions via causation is hardly automatic, however. As detailed in Chapter 13, fact-specific considerations of predictability and normative analysis may well persuade a fact finder that the defendant should not be held liable for the actions of another via causation. Indeed, that is usually the presumption of the law.

Direction of the Innocent and Nonresponsible

Imagine the owner of a trained attack dog who commands his Rottweiler to assault a hated ex-girlfriend who he spots in a park. The victim receives serious injuries to the face, arms and hands. Surely this describes a criminal act—and it does. But notice that the attack was performed by an animal, and we do not hold animals criminally liable. We would like to blame the dog owner, who commanded the dog to attack, but it was the dog who performed the criminal deed. There seems to be no union of act and mens rea here. In terms of accomplice doctrine, the problem is that we lack a responsible principal actor. The solution to this problem comes in the doctrine of direction of a innocent or non-responsible actor.

The basic ingredients are: (1) the criminal act is done by an innocent or non-responsible actor; and (2) that act was directed by another, with the mens rea required for the offense.[1] Here the mauling was done by a non-responsible actor (the dog), who was directed by the owner with purpose to injure the victim, the mens rea required for this offense.

Another way of understanding this kind of liability is via the metaphor of a puppet and puppet master. The puppet master is responsible for the actions of the puppet. Although this is an unusual way of describing the interaction between human beings, it is legally accurate when applied to innocent or non-responsible actors.

Non-responsible actors include animals, young children, the seriously mentally ill and extremely intoxicated persons. Liability under this doctrine may also be based on the conduct of an innocent actor: one who is otherwise responsible (meaning generally subject to criminal law) but who is ignorant of those facts that make the act criminal.

> Ralph and Winston have known each other since they were small boys in the same neighborhood. Now they are in junior high. Ralph is a gullible sort, and definitely not the brightest bulb in the local array. Winston by contrast is an inveterate schemer. He is much sharper than his mate, though perhaps not as sharp as he thinks.
>
> Winston recruits Ralph to help him with what he says is a test of an electronic store's new security system. Winston explains that he is a special consultant for the security company, and needs Ralph to take a cell phone from the store at Winston's signal. Ralph is excited, and wants to know if he will get a reward for his participation. Winston assures him that he will.
>
> Winston asks to see a number of high-end cell phones, which a store salesman shows him. When the salesman turns to answer another customer's question, Winston gives the signal; Ralph pockets one of the phones on the counter and walks out of the store. He is soon confronted by a security guard, who is surprised by Ralph's ready admission that he took the phone. The full story quickly emerges.
>
> Could Winston be found guilty of theft here—the knowing unlawful taking of the personal property of another with the purpose to deprive the owner thereof permanently?

---

1. E.g., MPC sec. 2.06(2)(a).

To anticipate rules that will be covered later in the chapter, accomplice liability will not work here in most jurisdictions, because the primary actor, Ralph, did not act with theft mens rea. He believed that taking the phone was lawful—part of a security test. Nor did he have any purpose to deprive the store of the phone permanently. Meanwhile Winston could not be charged with theft because he did not do the act of taking the phone. This would appear to leave no one liable, despite evidence of both a wrongful act (by Ralph) and mens rea (by Winston).

The legal solution to this apparent conundrum is the doctrine of direction of an innocent. Ralph here is the innocent actor and Winston is the criminal director. Or to put it less humanely, Ralph is the puppet and Winston the puppet master. Winston's direction of Ralph, an innocent because of his lack of mens rea, is undertaken with full theft mens rea on Winston's part, making Winston liable for theft. He would be charged with and convicted of the offense as a principal under a direction of the innocent theory.

Note that in this situation Ralph is an innocent rather than a non-responsible actor. Although not terribly bright, he does not display the kind of severe mental deficit or irrationality that would be required for non-responsibility due to general mental condition. He is simply an innocent, a dupe, for purposes of this particular case.

The direction of the innocent/non-responsible theory does not apply to many situations, but it does provide an initial question in our analytic sequence. In determining liability for the conduct of another, after identifying the person who is the primary actor, we should determine whether that individual is personally responsible. If so, analysis should proceed under accomplice liability. If not, the possibilities of direction of the innocent or non-responsible should be pursued.

Special Crimes of Aid or Encouragement

Many problems in inchoate liability can be avoided through the creation of offenses that provide specific definitions of inchoate criminality in specific contexts. Legislatures may decide to prohibit certain forms of criminal aid or encouragement independent of accomplice liability. Solicitation of criminal activity is a common example. Liability here depends solely on the solicitor's act and mens rea.

One advantage of creating separate crimes of aid or encouragement is that the legislature can tailor the mens rea requirement according to the severity of the crime. Where the criminal conduct is especially serious, the legislature can establish that knowing or even reckless aid may be sufficient for liability, instead of the purpose mens rea usually required for accomplice liability. The legislature can also specifically designate the types of aid that should be criminalized. For example, many jurisdictions have specifically defined offenses for assisting an escape from custody. [2]

Accomplice Liability and Joint Trials

Defendants charged with crimes via accomplice liability, or conspiracy, often find themselves tried along with other defendants charged with the same or related crimes. Whether a defendant is tried individually or jointly can have important consequences for both prosecution and defense. Here we consider some of the strategic considerations for each side.[3]

In general, the prosecution favors joint trials, where all defendants accused of related criminality are tried together. This is a more efficient procedure, cutting down on the costs of multiple juries, multiple appearances by witnesses, and the other duplications of time and effort inherent in multiple trials. The prosecution also usually favors joint trials because they maximize the amount of damaging evidence relating to a crime that can be introduced before a single jury. Even if the judge instructs the jury to consider certain evidence only against certain defendants, or for very limited purposes, that evidence can affect a juror's perception of all of the defendants. Finally, a joint trial may encourage defendants to blame each other, to the point that they effectively become additional prosecutors in the courtroom.

Still there can be advantages for defendants in joint trials. Sometimes defense counsel can mount a joint defense of their clients, permitting the pooling resources, both investigative and legal. A large disparity in the degree of involvement between defendants may also encourage a jury to acquit the least involved.

Perhaps the worst situation for any individual accused of participating in group wrongs is to be the only one left to blame. Where other wrongdoers have pled guilty, are tried separately, or are otherwise unavailable for blame, and the jury only hears of the defendant's contribution to a very serious wrong, the urge to blame the accused becomes powerful. A particular example of this may be found in cases of mothers accused of fail-

---

2. See, e.g., Cal. Pen. Code sec. 4534 (willfully assisting another's escape); sec. 4535 (providing escape materials).

3. The focus here is on strategic considerations rather than the law of joinder and severance by which courts decide whether there will be a joint trial.

> *ing to protect their children from the homicidal violence of an abusive father. If the father is not also on trial, the mother's role may appear more egregious than it would otherwise.*

Basic Principles of Accomplice Liability

A basic assumption of accomplice liability is that group criminality poses special dangers. Disparate talents joined together can form a team capable of much more than any individual. Group efforts make larger criminal efforts feasible: more extensive drug trafficking, more ambitious robberies, and so on. Partnerships or groups also have their own psychological dynamics. Individuals may encourage each other to take greater risks and inflict more serious harms than any might undertake on their own. As a result, the criminal law seeks to establish major disincentives to collective criminality in the law of accomplice liability (and conspiracy).

Within the bounds of accomplice liability there may be a large variation in culpability between participants, a variation which substantive law does not attempt to measure. The accomplice may be someone who gives slight verbal or physical encouragement or promotion to a criminal actor who needs no assistance. Indeed, the accomplice often plays a small role in the criminal scheme, acting perhaps as a driver, lookout, or provider of temporary shelter or basic supplies. On the other hand, the accomplice may be the mastermind of the criminal scheme, the most culpable of all. The comic book criminal mastermind—the Joker or Riddler in the Batman comics, or the evil criminal geniuses of Ian Fleming's 007 (James Bond) novels—are examples of individuals who accomplish much of their criminality through an accomplice role.[4]

Traditionally, accomplice liability is conceived as a form of derivative liability. This means that the accomplice's liability depends on the crime committed by the principal. At common law this gave rise to a number of procedural and substantive rules, including the requirement that the principal be convicted before the accomplice could be tried. While accomplice liability is still largely derivative in theory, today there are no procedural requirements for separate trials and the modern trend is to establish each participant's liability individually.

---

4. To be completely accurate, these criminal masterminds act as accomplices, directing underlings to commit various crimes in the early stages, but in the melodrama's climax, they are forced by the hero's challenge to commit crimes personally, thereby becoming a principal.

Primary Actor Liability

Because an accomplice is generally responsible for encouraging or promoting the principal's crime, establishing the principal's guilt is an important first step in the analysis. If the principal is not guilty, then accomplice liability under traditional rules is generally not possible. There are, however, exceptions. In some unusual cases the primary actor may have a uniquely personal defense, such as diplomatic immunity, which would not preclude accomplice liability for another's assistance. The Model Penal Code also has a special provision for extended accomplice liability under its rules concerning attempts. This will be covered at the end of the chapter, because its analysis requires an understanding of both the act and the mens rea requirement for accomplice liability.

Secondary Actor Liability: The Accomplice Act Requirement

To be liable as an accomplice, the individual must voluntarily act to promote or encourage the principal's offense. Usually this will be through an affirmative act: words, gestures or deeds. In a few unusual situations where the individual had a legal duty to intervene, a failure to do so may constitute promotion or encouragement of the principal's offense. Whether by affirmative act or omission, we will see that the encouragement or promotion need not have made a difference to the principal's conduct; generally there must have been at least a possibility that it did, however.

We can describe the acts of an accomplice in a number of different ways. The law often references efforts to aid and abet, to procure, to counsel, or to facilitate. In essence there are only two types of acts which will support accomplice liability, however: to encourage or to promote. To promote is to provide the principal with concrete assistance in the criminal deed. It is synonymous with aiding or facilitating the principal's criminal conduct. To encourage is synonymous with instigating, provoking or abetting the principal's criminal act.

In this section we will focus exclusively on *acts* of encouragement or promotion. There is a potential language trap here. In ordinary language, to speak of encouragement or promotion implies the intention to encourage or promote. But for the moment our only concern is whether the defendant acted in a way that *might have the effect* of encouraging or promoting another's crime. Questions about the purpose to encourage or promote will be addressed later under mens rea.

Types of Promotion or Encouragement

The act of promotion or encouragement may take the form of verbal encouragement or providing concrete aid, prior to the actual crime. An accomplice might supply information critical to the criminal endeavor, such as the location of a target, or provide concrete assistance in the form of transportation, weapons, or money.

The act of promotion or encouragement may also occur at the crime scene itself. Again, the accomplice may provide verbal encouragement or direct assistance. A timely warning, a threat, or help with physical tasks all may suffice. Depending on the crime, actions taken after the central criminal act may still be included within the scope of assisting the crime. For example, with theft or robbery, the asportation element—taking and carrying away the ill-gotten goods—is part of the offense. This means that anyone who provides assistance in asportation, such as driving a getaway car, may commit a sufficient act of promotion or encouragement.

At-the-scene assistance of a criminal actor will usually be the product of prior arrangement. The principal and accomplice will have reached some prior agreement about planned criminality. This is not legally required, however. For example, assume an individual assaults another in a bar and throws the victim to the ground. A stranger, who has never met either the assailant or the victim, joins in the beating, holding the victim down so that the assailant may land more effective blows. The stranger has done a sufficient act of encouragement or promotion of the assault despite not having any prior communication or arrangement with the principal.

An accomplice may provide legally sufficient assistance by mere presence at the crime scene *if* there is a prior agreement between accomplice and principal concerning potential aid by the accomplice. An example will illustrate.

> A burglar asks his girlfriend to wait in his car while he breaks into a house. He tells her to honk the horn if she sees anyone approaching. Because no one does approach, the girlfriend just kicks back and listens to music in the car. The burglar soon returns with his loot. Both are arrested. Has the girlfriend done enough to satisfy the act requirement for accomplice liability here?

At first glance, the answer would seem to be no. She simply waited in the car. Nevertheless, her presence did provide some assistance, by virtue of her agreement to act as a lookout. Her waiting in the car, under instruction, provided the burglar with a measure of confidence that he would not be surprised by an unexpected arrival, and therefore constitutes a sufficient act for accomplice liability. In this case, her "mere presence" at the scene, subject to prior agreement, represents concrete encouragement or promotion of the burglary.

A variation on the same facts. Burglar tells his girlfriend that he's anxious about his upcoming break in. He's not sure if he really wants to go through with it. His girlfriend says that she's not going to do it for him, but if he wants, she will come along with him and wait in the car around the block. He thanks her profusely. "Just knowing you're out there, makes a difference." The girlfriend does as she promises. What about the act requirement for accomplice liability here?

In this instance, the girlfriend has not agreed to act as a lookout and does not do so. She waits around the block. But she has provided moral support. Going with the burglar helps him overcome his anxiety. It encourages or promotes his crime in an important, albeit psychological fashion. Assuming that mens rea is proven, the girlfriend's agreement to accompany the burglar to and from the scene would be a sufficient act.

A third variation. Summoned to the scene by a silent alarm, police capture Burglar as he comes out of the residence, heading for the car where his girlfriend awaits. She claims ignorance of what her boyfriend was doing. Will her presence in the car nevertheless be sufficient for the act requirement for accomplice liability?

No. The proof here suggests presence without any prior arrangement between the alleged accomplice and principal. There is no proof that the girlfriend was present to provide boyfriend with assistance, physical or psychological, and therefore this element fails. Perhaps she was present according to a prior arrangement related to the burglary, but that cannot be proven here.

Sufficiency of the Act

How much encouragement or promotion is required for accomplice liability? The answer is, not much. The law attempts no assessment of the actual effect of the encouragement or promotion. The accomplice's act is sufficient if it *might have* encouraged or promoted the principal's criminal act.

Henry is a college sophomore who hangs out with other guys who like to drink, play video games, and mess around on the computer. Late one Friday night, the most talented hacker in the group—Gruber— announces that he will hack into the state law enforcement site. Henry is part of a group that crowds around Gruber's computer, looking at the screen which clearly warns against unauthorized entry. Henry yells, along with others, that Gruber should "go for it." Gruber hacks into this site. This causes major damage and triggers an extensive investigation, which leads back to Gruber and Henry. Henry's participation is captured by a video cam on Gruber's computer. Assuming that Gruber committed the crime of unauthorized electronic entry, did Henry commit a sufficient act to be held as an accomplice?

In this case, Henry's counsel may be tempted to argue that Henry's contribution was too trivial to support criminal liability. Gruber had encouragement from many others; he may not even have heard Henry saying "go for it." Nor is there any indication that Gruber needed encouragement; certainly he received no concrete assistance from Henry or anyone else. The law, however, is clear. Henry did utter words of encouragement, which may have been heard by Gruber, and might have influenced his decision, however slightly. That is sufficient to satisfy the act requirement.

The case would be different if Henry simply stood by silently while these events unfolded. Without evidence of a prior agreement, or physical gestures indicating encouragement, his mere presence under these circumstances would constitute neither encouragement or promotion.

Omissions to Act as Promotion or Encouragement for Accomplice Liability

An omission to act can suffice for the act requirement in accomplice liability, if the person had a duty to act. For example, a security guard leaves his post, permitting thieves to enter a luxury apartment building and break into an unoccupied apartment. By contract, the guard has a duty to safeguard the building—to secure it against unauthorized entry—which he fails to do here. His omission significantly promotes the break in. The act requirement for accomplice liability is met.

To anticipate somewhat the mens rea discussions that follow, the hard questions in omission to act accomplice cases usually involve whether the omission was done with purpose to encourage the offense. So, for example, if the guard was in league with the thieves and had been, or expected to be, paid for his help, accomplice liability would be clear—both the act and mens rea requirements would be proven. If there was no prior arrangement between guard and thieves, however, and the guard simply neglected his duties and the thieves independently took advantage, there would be no accomplice liability for the guard, because no proof of the required mens rea.

For some especially challenging mens rea issues relating to omission to act, see the subsequent sidebar, Hard Cases: The Parent's Duty to Safeguard a Child.

The MPC Act Requirement for Accomplice Liability: Attempts to Assist Completed Crimes by the Principal

The Model Penal Code defines the act requirement for accomplice liability in the same fashion as traditional law, but adds an additional feature. An *attempt* to aid a principal, even if ineffective, will also be a sufficient act for accomplice liability, assuming the principal proceeds to commit the crime.

Return to Henry and Gruber's case above, with some critical facts changed. Under this scenario, Henry was not present in the room with Gruber. Henry knew that Gruber was attempting the illegal entry at the time, however, and decided to help by sending Gruber advice on how to hack into the site via e-mail. Because of a problem with his Internet service (and don't you hate it when this happens?), Henry's e-mails did not go through. As a result, Gruber had no knowledge of Henry's efforts. How do we analyze the act requirement for accomplice liability here?

Under traditional principles, Henry would not be liable as an accomplice. His only possible acts of encouragement or promotion were his e-mails and these did not reach Gruber prior to Gruber's entry into the site. As a result, Henry did not commit any acts of encouragement or promotion of the principal. Under the MPC, however, his e-mails constitute attempted promotion and therefore would be sufficient for accomplice liability, assuming sufficient mens rea and a crime committed by Gruber.

Secondary Actor Liability: Accomplice Mens Rea

In modern American law, to be an accomplice, the accomplice must act with the purpose to encourage or promote the principal's offense. Accomplice liability therefore always requires proof of purpose. Sounds simple enough. The apparent simplicity of this formulation, however, masks considerable complexity. What *exactly* does it mean to act with the "purpose to encourage or promote the offense"? As with other inchoate crimes, the challenge lies in determining how the new mens rea of purpose interacts with the existing mens rea requirements of the substantive offense—the principal's crime.

On closer examination, mens rea analysis for accomplice liability involves two stages. These are the *purpose to promote* the principal's criminal act, *while sharing the principal's mens rea*. The first of these requirements—and in many instances the only significant requirement, is that the accomplice act with purpose to promote the principal's criminal act. She must purposely encourage or promote the robber's use of force or threat, the thief's taking of the item, or the blow in an aggravated assault. This requirement is often the only one mentioned, because the only significant issue in the case is whether the aid was rendered with purpose to assist an obviously criminal act—there is no further controversy with respect to sharing the mens rea required for principal's crime.

The second requirement is that the accomplice must provide purposeful assistance with a full understanding of the principal's criminal plan, including the basic mens rea requirements of the principal's offense. Although often implicitly included within the first requirement of purpose to assist the criminal act, it should be separated to account for those cases—especially involving reckless or negligent crimes—where its analysis must be done independently. Putting these together, accomplice mens rea requires that the accomplice act with: (1) purpose to promote the principal's criminal act, while (2) sharing the mens rea required for the substantive offense. This analysis holds for all crimes that require purpose, knowledge, recklessness or negligence; we will see that strict liability offenses fall under a slightly different rule.

We begin with purpose to promote or encourage the principal's act.

Mens Rea (1)—Purpose to Promote or Encourage the Principal's Act

Perhaps the most famous lines in the American literature of accomplice liability were penned by Judge Learned Hand in 1938. He held that to be an accomplice, a defendant must "in some sort associate himself with the venture, that he participate in it as something that he wishes to bring about, that he seek by his action to make it succeed. All the words used—even the most colorless 'abet'—carry an implication of purposive attitude towards it."[5] Judge Hand's declaration is usually seen as resolving a long-standing debate about mens rea in accomplice liability: whether an accomplice's promotion or encouragement of the principal's criminality must be purposeful or whether it is

---

5. United States v. Peoni, 100 F.2d 401, 402 (2d Cir. 1938).

enough if it was knowing. Most U.S. jurisdictions today require purpose. That does not mean that the purpose versus knowledge debate is resolved, however. Legislatures sometimes create separate crimes of facilitation which depend on a mens rea of knowledge rather than purpose.[6] The seriousness of the crime committed by the principal can also affect accomplice mens rea analysis, encouraging fact finders to infer purpose from proof of knowledge. Consider the following examples.

> Caron, a college junior, tells her friends that she needs to buy some marijuana in preparation for a college party. She goes to a senior who lives in the dorm, Timmy, who is well known as the local dealer. Timmy tells her that, unfortunately, he is "totally out," though he expects a shipment within a week. Caron becomes quite upset, on the verge of tears, claiming that her party will be a total failure unless she can score. Timmy then tells her that he does know another guy who might have some weed, and that other people say he is righteous (i.e., trustworthy). Timmy gives Caron a cell phone number and says that the guy calls himself 4Real. Caron calls the number, speaks with 4Real and they arrange a meeting, which leads to a purchase of marijuana.
>
> Caron has been acting throughout these events as a confidential informant for the local police department, which is pursuing drug dealing on campus. 4Real is arrested, but because he promises to identify his supplier, he is not charged. The local prosecutor decides he wants to pursue charges against Timmy, however, believing that his arrest and conviction will have a chilling effect on campus drug sales.
>
> Assume that 4Real is guilty of marijuana distribution, defined as: knowing distribution of a controlled substance, marijuana. Can Timmy be convicted of acting as an accomplice to 4Real's sale of marijuana to Caron?

As always, we begin with the primary actor's liability. Here there are two potential primary actors to consider: Caron, the purchaser of marijuana, and 4Real, the seller. Caron is not personally liable for purchasing marijuana because her actions were legally authorized as an agent of law enforcement. As a result, her purchase of marijuana cannot support accomplice liability charges

---

6. E.g., N.Y. Pen. Law sec. 115 et seq.

against Timmy, at least under traditional rules. Nor was she an innocent or non-responsible actor; she was fully aware of all of the facts relevant to criminal responsibility here. Thus traditional accomplice liability for Timmy must be based on the actions of 4Real.

Timmy might be charged as an accomplice to 4Real's offense of distributing marijuana. Timmy certainly did a sufficient act of encouragement or promotion. He provided critical information linking purchaser to seller (4Real's name, background and cell phone number), and therefore meets the act requirement for accomplice liability. But did he provide this aid with the purpose of promoting *4Real's sale* of marijuana?

The facts make clear that Timmy was at least reckless (aware of a substantial risk) that 4Real would sell marijuana to Caron. A fact finder might even determine Timmy was aware of a substantial certainty that such a sale would occur, meaning that he had knowledge of it. The defense would attempt to hold the legal line at knowledge, however, arguing that purpose toward 4Real's sale cannot not be proven. There are no facts showing a financial or other relationship between these two individuals, who if both retail drug dealers in the same market, are competitors. While Timmy might, for reasons of personal sympathy or business goodwill (referrals to another business establish that a business person cares about customer satisfaction), want to help Caron with her purchase, we have no reason to believe he cares whether 4Real succeeds with his sale. Timmy must have acted with purpose to promote or encourage 4Real's sale; a purpose to assist Caron in her purchase is not sufficient. All this suggests that the prosecution's proof of accomplice mens rea may fail.

The prosecution is not without arguments to support the necessary purpose, however. A prosecutor will likely argue that purpose may be inferred from knowing assistance. Timmy provided concrete, significant aid in a criminal transaction and therefore must not only have been aware that this sale would take place, but wanted it to occur. No one would provide this much assistance to a potential criminal transaction without wanting it to be completed.

How will this come out? Reasonable people may differ, but the prosecutor will have some difficulty convincing many prospective jurors, and even some judges, that Timmy clearly (i.e., beyond a reasonable doubt) acted with purpose to assist 4Real's sale of marijuana. Timmy seemed to want to help Caron; the help provided to 4Real appears incidental.[7]

Now let's change the facts to make the subject of the sale a more serious criminal matter.

---

7. See State v. Gladstone, 474 P.2d 274 (Wash. 1970).

Assume the same sequence of events with the same players, except that the material to be purchased is a quantity of radioactive materials sufficient to make a dirty bomb, capable of killing large numbers. Timmy knows that Caron belongs to a radical political organization devoted to violent revolution. Assume that 4Real is guilty of the knowing unlawful distribution of radioactive materials. What are the chances that Caron may be convicted as an accomplice to 4Real's crime?

Exactly the same arguments may be made as with the marijuana transaction, but the reading of mens rea may be different here. Because the illegal distribution of radioactive materials is extremely dangerous, defense arguments that Timmy acted only out of personal sympathy for Caron, or to promote goodwill for future transactions, will not carry much weight. These arguments presume that Timmy might want to help Caron with her purchase but remain entirely neutral as to 4Real's sale. Given that the consequences of the transaction are so serious to human life and that criminal liability here brings more severe penalties than with the sale of marijuana, we are much more likely to infer a purpose to aid from proof that the aid was knowing. It also seems much more likely, given the risks involved, that Timmy would not provide a referral to another potential seller unless he had a business arrangement or other close relationship with the seller.

Does this mean that the radioactive materials case necessarily comes out differently? No. But the arguments will be framed differently and will carry different emotional weight because of the difference in the nature of the principal's offense.[8]

Mens Rea (2)—Sharing the Mens Rea for the Principal's Offense

In addition to proving that a defendant purposely encouraged or promoted the principal's criminal act, the defendant must also share with the principal any additional mens rea requirements of the offense the principal commits. This additional mens rea requirement is well established in law, but can be hard to articulate.[9] I will speak of it as the requirement of shared mens rea.

---

8. It's also true that in a case like this, many may believe that knowledge should be sufficient for accomplice liability, a position that may incline some to read the facts as demonstrating the legally required purpose to aid.

9. Sometimes courts speak of the requirement that the accomplice *know* that the principal will act with the mens rea required for the principal's crime. Thus to be an accomplice to a principal's burglary, the defendant must not only purposely promote or encourage the principal's act of breaking and entering (the essential act of burglary) but must do so know-

As an example of this additional mens rea requirement, to be an accomplice to assault with purpose to do great bodily injury, the accomplice must not only purposefully encourage or promote the principal's act of assault, but must do so understanding that the principal will seek to (act with purpose to) do great bodily injury.

One important caveat before we explore this shared mens rea requirement: we are concerned here only with crimes that both accomplice and principal anticipate being committed. We will see that in some jurisdictions the accomplice may also be liable for unanticipated crimes by the principal, but this is a different problem that will be analyzed separately below.[10]

For Purpose and Knowledge Offenses

With respect to substantive crimes that require purpose or knowledge, we look to see whether the accomplice, in promoting or encouraging the principal's act, also shared the principal's mens rea with respect to his or her crime.

Dorothy White is a respected antiques dealer who faces a financial crisis because of her late husband's medical problems. She is approached by Walter Kimball, an individual with a questionable reputation in the antiques business, who asks for her help in selling what he says is a Chippendale high boy, a large piece of furniture, that he says dates back to the 18th century. White recognizes that the high boy is a modern reconstruction and therefore a fake, but also that it is very well done and will fool most buyers. Kimball admits that it is a fake, but says that he will pay White $5,000 cash if she will provide false provenance (a false history) for the item. White provides a document which indicates, falsely, that the high boy came from an estate that contained numerous items from the 18th century.

Kimball sells the high boy to a couple with a new mansion to furnish, using White's documentation to prove that it is an 18th century

ing that the principal planned to commit a crime therein, the mens rea (the "with purpose to commit a crime therein" element) that distinguishes burglary from other related offenses. The emphasis on knowledge can lead to some awkward locutions, though, as where we have to imagine what one person might know about another person's purpose or knowledge and so on. For this reason I prefer to speak of the accomplice sharing the principal's mens rea.

10. We will see that even in jurisdictions that recognize such extended liability, a threshold requirement is that the would-be accomplice meet the usual mens rea requirements to be an accomplice to the principal's anticipated offense.

antique. Kendall is later arrested. He immediately details White's participation in the scheme, hoping to lay some of the blame off on her.

Fraud in this jurisdiction is: making knowing false representations to another to obtain money or other material value. Can Dorothy White be convicted of fraud as an accomplice to Kimball's crime?

Kimball is clearly liable here as a principal for fraud because he represented to the sellers that the furniture was from the 18th century, when he knew that was not true, and he made this misrepresentation in order to obtain a higher price from the buyers than was warranted.

Now we move to White's potential liability as an accomplice to this offense. White must have acted both with the purpose to promote Kimball's criminal act—his representations concerning the furniture's value—and have done so with an understanding of Kimball's criminal mens rea, i.e., understanding that Kimball would make false representations about the furniture for material gain.

First, did White purposefully act to encourage or promote Kimball's criminal act of representing that the furniture hails from the 18th century? The answer is yes. In return for $5,000 cash, she provided documentation to support Kimball's representation of the high boy's age. She provided Kimball with the requested documentation in order to, i.e., with the purpose that, Kimball make the representation he did.

Next we must establish that White also acted with an understanding of Kimball's criminal mens rea, that is, that she understood that Kimball would be making a false representation about the furniture to obtain material gain. Did she share Kimball's mens rea with respect to the falsity of the representation? Again the facts are clear. White was fully aware of Kimball's misrepresentation because she knew the document that she provided was false. And, she was aware that Kimball would use this document in order to obtain money. She shares with Kimball the mens rea requirements of the underlying offense.

For Reckless and Negligence Offenses

Because accomplice liability requires a purposeful mens rea, it might seem incompatible with substantive crimes of recklessness or negligence. But here linguistic appearances deceive. As long as we clearly distinguish between the two stages of mens rea analysis—between the purpose to assist the principal's act and sharing of any other mens rea required for the principal's offense—we see that there is no bar to accomplice liability for reckless or negligence crimes. The accomplice must purposefully promote or encourage the principal's criminal deed while manifesting (sharing) the required recklessness or negligence toward the other aspects of wrongdoing required for the offense.[11]

> Barclay is desperate to get to the airport to catch a flight to London. If he misses the flight he will miss a chance at the biggest deal of his career. He rushes out of his downtown hotel, cuts in front of a line of people waiting for taxi cabs, and grabs one that has just dropped someone off. He tells the cabbie, Ereit, to "get me to the airport and step on it." (Barclay has heard people talk like this in the movies). Soon Barclay complains that Ereit is not going fast enough. Ereit points to the weather conditions and says that the road is very icy, and going any faster would be very dangerous. "It's not that bad," Barclay maintains. He flashes a $100 bill and says that if Ereit can get to the airport in 15 minutes, it will be his. Ereit is a recent immigrant to the country and could really use the money. The cabbie increases his speed to well above the speed limit. A mile away from the airport, an elderly pedestrian is crossing the street. When Ereit sees her he brakes but the car skids on the icy road and strikes her. Serious injuries result.
> Ereit is charged with dangerous driving: driving in a manner dangerous to others, being reckless as to the danger. Assuming that Ereit is guilty of this offense, can Barclay be found guilty as an accomplice?

In this case, the principal's critical action is his driving, particularly his fast driving on slick roads. This is the basis of the dangerous driving charge. Turning now to the accused accomplice, we see that Barclay promoted Ereit's fast driving by his words and offer of a $100 bonus. Barclay's purpose in doing so was to promote fast driving, thus proving the first of our mens rea requirements for accomplice liability.

Next we move to the requirement that the accomplice Barclay share any other mens rea required for the principal Ereit's offense. In this case, this is recklessness with respect to the dangerousness of the driving. Here, Barclay would like to argue that he did not want Ereit to drive dangerously, nor did he believe that driving faster would be dangerous—see his comment that "it's not that bad." In effect, he would argue that he was neither purposeful nor knowing with respect to the danger involved. But conviction of this offense may be based on recklessness—and that will be hard to negate here. The prosecution will contend that, considering the weather and Ereit's warning about road con-

---

11. E.g., State v. McVay, 132 A. 436 (R.I. 1926) (accomplice to involuntary manslaughter).

ditions, that Barclay was aware of a substantial and unjustified (business opportunities notwithstanding) risk of danger to others from speeding. As a result, there is a good chance he may be convicted as an accomplice. He had purpose to promote the cab driver's act of fast driving and shared the driver's recklessness as to its danger.

The analysis of accomplice liability for negligence offenses will be essentially the same, differing only according to what should be the now-familiar differences between recklessness or negligence themselves.

For Strict Liability Offenses

Accomplice liability is not often applied to substantive offenses that are strict liability, but in most jurisdictions there is no legal bar. There is, effectively, a different mens rea rule for this situation, however. Accomplice liability here requires not only purpose to promote the principal's act, but also requires awareness of those facts that make the conduct criminal. This means that, in this situation, accomplice liability actually requires a higher mens rea for the accomplice than the principal.

> Karlin, a native of Australia travels to the United States on vacation. She tells the customs agent on entry that she is visiting friends, which is true. She travels to a ski resort, where she meets some interesting people and applies for a job as a cook. Brad, the hotel manager, hires her because he is in desperate need of a cook and finds her very attractive. He does not ask to see any identification, and says that he is fine with paying her in cash. A week later, federal agents from Immigration and Customs Enforcement (ICE) do a workplace raid and arrest Karlin for violating the terms of her visa by taking paid work while in the country. Karlin was never specifically informed of this legal restriction. The offense, however, is strict liability. Assuming that Karlin is guilty, can Brad be convicted as an accomplice to her immigration violation?

Brad encouraged and promoted Karlin's illegal work by giving her a job. He did so with the purpose that she would work. Therefore he has satisfied both the act requirement and the first mens rea requirement, the purpose to promote that act. This would seem to be sufficient because there isn't a second mens rea requirement as the offense is strict liability. But most jurisdictions will nevertheless require some proof of mens rea on Brad's part with respect to the immigration violation. The prosecution must, at a minimum, prove that Brad was aware that Karlin was in the country as a tourist, because this is the factual predicate for her offense. Brad might also have to know that it was a violation of law for Karlin to obtain paying work while in the country.

Why the distinction in mens rea between the principal and accomplice here? Consider the particulars of this case. As an Australian citizen visiting the United States, Karlin is herself aware of the circumstances of her entry, and any failure to grasp the legal restrictions that come with her immigration status may be fairly attributed to her. Brad, however, was not involved in Karlin's entry into the United States and therefore would not have the same knowledge or responsibility that Karlin does, hence the need for additional proof of awareness of wrongdoing.[12]

Hard Cases in Accomplice Mens Rea: Parental Failure to Safeguard Children

Criminal law scholars and appellate judges necessarily have different priorities. Scholars place a high priority—often the highest priority—on intellectual coherence. They seek to develop a consistent scheme of rules and principles across all of criminal law. Appellate judges share this ambition, but balance it with the need to do justice in the case at hand. This difference in priorities is well illustrated by the problem of accomplice mens rea in cases involving parental failure to safeguard children from abuse.

The common pattern of these cases involves a serious child abuser— often, but not always the male partner of the child's mother—who inflicts serious violence or sexual violation on the child. The non-abusive parent, usually but not always the mother, has notice of this abuse and in many cases full knowledge of it, but does not intervene verbally or physically or report the abuse to authorities. Where possible, the abuser is prosecuted, but charges may also be brought against the passive partner as an accomplice to the abuser's crimes.

Many of the appellate decisions in such cases devote primary attention to the act requirement of accomplice liability. The court asks if the passive parent's omission to act is sufficient for accomplice liability. I believe this misstates the real issue, which is mens rea.[13] Unless we decide to change the act requirement for omissions—and there may be some reasons to do so here— possible encouragement of the principal would be sufficient. Because the si-

---

12. Of course, the prosecution may still argue that Brad had the required mens rea here, that his hiring of Karlin indicates his awareness of potential problems with her legal ability to work. He did not ask for any identification, very unusual for employers, and likely in violation of other laws, such as Social Security laws.

13. E.g., State v. Rundle, 500 N.W.2d 916 (Wisc. 1993); State Walden, 293 S.E.2d 780 (N.C.1982).

*lence of a parent in the face of obvious abuse sends a signal of condonation
or support for the abuse, such silence may suffice for accomplice act encouragement or promotion. And, of course, the parent had a legal duty to act on
the basis of parentage. But there is still an important question in these cases:
Did the parent fail to act* with the purpose *of promoting or encouraging the
principal's act of abuse, his or her punch, kick, or act of sexual invasion?*

*In some cases, courts go to great lengths to infer purpose from proof of
knowledge. The passive parent is said to have had the purpose to encourage or assist the act of abuse in order to maintain a relationship with the
perpetrator.*[14] *But it is hard to read such cases without reaching the conclusion that the facts speak much more clearly to the passive parent's knowledge or recklessness concerning the abusive act than they do to purpose to
encourage that act. We might believe that the passive parent is culpable for
his or her inaction, and should be blamed for lacking the courage to protect,
or at least attempt to protect, a helpless, brutalized child—but this is a different form of blameworthiness than basic accomplice liability demands.*

*The bottom line here? This is likely an instance where either the leg-
islature should create a new offense of parental failure to protect children, or there should be an explicit statutory change in mens rea with
respect to accomplice liability in certain cases, such as child abuse, where
the offense committed is particularly severe.*

Accomplice Mens Rea and Liability for Unplanned Offenses

Now we come to one of the most difficult and controversial aspects of accomplice liability: liability for crimes committed by the principal that were not
originally anticipated by the defendant, but should have been. As the vulgar phrase
goes: s— happens. The best laid plans (though admittedly few criminal schemes
are these) can go wrong. Different crimes end up being committed than were
originally planned. This creates no difficulties for the principal's liability, but
it does raise major issues with respect to an accomplice. Is the accomplice's
criminal responsibility limited to what he or she believed the principal would
do, or should liability also include criminal acts that reasonably might be expected to flow from the original criminal scheme?

---

14. E.g., Ex parte C.G., 841 So.2d 292, 298–301 (2002); People v. Stanciel, 606 N.E.2d
1201, 1209–11 (Ill. 1992).

Jurisdictions fall into two basic camps on this question. Some jurisdictions, including those that follow the MPC, adopt what may be called a strict mens rea approach. Accomplices here are liable only for those crimes as to which they share mens rea with the principal, meaning only those crimes that were jointly anticipated. Other jurisdictions follow the natural and probable consequences rule, holding that an accomplice who is liable for assisting an anticipated crime, will also be liable for unanticipated crimes, if these are deemed the natural and probable consequence of the anticipated crime.

To set the problem more concretely, we will speak of the distinction between crime A, the planned offense, and crime B, an additional, unplanned crime also committed by the principal. As we will see, even in extended liability jurisdictions, there must always be a crime A as to which the accomplice had both act and offense mens rea. A concrete example will help us see the problem and the analysis more clearly.

> Paul is a computer guy who does contract work for a home security company. Through this work he gains access to home security codes. He has heard that an older man whose home is protected by the security company keeps a large amount of gold in his house. He tells Edgar about this and proposes a deal. Paul will provide the combination to the home's security system in return for 50% of the proceeds from the house burglary. Paul drives Edgar to the house on a Sunday morning when he knows that the homeowner goes to church. He also knows that the homeowner lives alone.
>
> Edgar enters the house, ransacks it, but finds only some silverware which he stashes in a bag. Then he hears the back door open. A middle-aged woman who works as a domestic helper lets herself in to cook a Sunday meal. Edgar threatens the woman with a knife and orders her to go into the living room. At this point police burst in. (Edgar did not fully disable the alarm system when he entered.) Both Paul and Edgar are arrested. Both are charged with: burglary and kidnapping.
>
> Burglary is the knowing unlawful breaking and entering with the purpose of committing a crime therein. Kidnapping (as relevant to this case) is defined as the knowing, unlawful use of force to move a person from one location to another for purposes of committing or furthering a crime, including robbery or burglary. Of what crimes may Paul and Edgar be convicted?

In this scenario, burglary is crime A and kidnapping is crime B. Paul and Edgar have jointly schemed to commit a burglary. This is the crime that Edgar actually committed (breaking and entering with the purpose to commit theft therein) and that Paul clearly assisted. Paul promoted this offense with the purpose that Edgar break into the house and steal items inside. Thus Paul demonstrated both the purpose to promote actor's breaking into the house and shared with Edgar knowledge that the break in was unlawful and that it was committed with purpose to commit a theft therein. Paul meets all the requirements for straight accomplice liability for burglary, the crime A in this scenario.

Edgar is also clearly guilty as a principal of crime B, the kidnapping, because he forced the victim at knife point to move from one location to another, knowing that it is illegal, and for the purpose of either committing or furthering the offenses of burglary and possibly also robbery. The big question is whether Paul can held as an accomplice for crime B. To answer this question we must explore in more detail the two main approaches to this problem: the strict mens rea approach and the natural and probable consequences approach.

The Strict Mens Rea Approach

Under the strict mens rea approach, no major divergence is permitted between the crime the accomplice meant to assist, and the crime actually committed. The defendant must purposely aid or encourage the criminal act *and* must share whatever mens rea is required for the principal's offense. If the defendant gave the principal an automobile to do a drug deal, the principal's use of that automobile to kill a pursuing police officer would not be covered by accomplice liability.

Paul here is a full accomplice to Edgar's burglary—the crime they both planned. The kidnapping that Edgar committed, however, was entirely unplanned according to the facts given. Paul said nothing and did nothing to indicate awareness that anyone would be in the home, or that if someone was there, that person should be threatened or forcibly moved. Because Paul demonstrated no mens rea with respect to Edgar's kidnapping of the domestic helper, Paul cannot be convicted as an accomplice to this crime under the strict mens rea approach.

One additional caveat should be added with respect to the distinction between planned and unplanned crimes. Even in a strict mens rea jurisdiction, there will be some flexibility in determining what crimes were planned. Persons involved in crime rarely document their criminal plans, and discussions of future criminality may be vague, with many important aspects left unspoken but understood. Proof of what was anticipated, therefore, may depend on context and inference.

Liability for Unplanned Crimes: The Natural and Probable Consequences Rule

In many jurisdictions, an accomplice is liable not only for any planned crimes by the principal (assuming that standard accomplice act and mens rea requirements are met) but also for any unplanned crime *if* that crime is deemed a natural and probable consequence of the originally planned crime. An accomplice is liable not only for the crime A which was planned, but crime B, which was not—if crime B appears to have been a natural and probable consequence of the commission of crime A.

The point often missed by students of accomplice liability here is that even under the extended liability rule there is a threshold requirement of full accomplice liability proof, including full mens rea, for crime A *before* we can consider any liability for crime B. Here, Paul must have promoted or encouraged, with full accomplice mens rea with respect to crime A, Edgar's burglary, before we can undertake natural and probable consequences analysis of crime B, the kidnapping. Once standard accomplice liability for crime A is established, then, and only then, can we talk about natural and probable consequences and crime B.

The natural and probable consequences rule is controversial in both concept and application. Arguments in its favor are that it is needed to meet the inherent difficulty of proving planning between criminal associates. Criminal offenders often do not plan ahead. They do not consider the full consequences of their actions. Should that absolve from liability one who helped set the criminality in motion? The accomplice's culpable promotion or encouragement of crime A may be seen as starting a criminal process that should include all related, subsequent offenses.

On the other hand, the possibilities for overreaching here are enormous. Many individuals involved in group criminality are followers who make only a small contribution to the criminal enterprise and have little or no idea of the crimes that others might commit. Retrospective bias is a real danger here: that subsequent crimes, especially if serious, will be seen as prefigured by the planned crime, both because this is how it did transpire (at least in a chronological sense) and because of the natural urge to blame all who contribute, even tangentially, to serious wrongs.

Now to applications.

> Can Paul be held as an accomplice to the kidnapping committed by Edgar under the natural and probable consequences rule?

As we have seen, Paul had the necessary act and mens rea to be an accomplice to Edgar's burglary, crime A. To put this another way, Paul met all the requirements of the strict mens rea rule for accomplice liability for the burglary. As a result, the threshold requirement of the natural and probable consequences rule is met. The question now becomes: was the unplanned kidnapping in fact a natural and probable consequence of the planned burglary? Analysis here tends to be fact specific and highly discretionary. Which is another way of saying that it can be hard to predict.

The prosecution would argue that any burglary of a house includes the risk of crimes being committed against persons found in the residence. This would include the risk of committing kidnapping, because any person found in a residence might need to be moved for security purposes (security of the burglar that is). Although the defendants apparently sought to avoid any personal confrontation here, these can always occur in a house break-in, and therefore the kidnapping should be considered a natural and probable consequence of a burglary.

The defense will emphasize that, on the facts given, Paul had no idea that Edgar would act in this fashion. There are no facts indicating that Paul was aware that Edgar was armed or was likely to use a weapon, or that there was any significant likelihood of a person being in the house. As a result, the kidnapping represents a major deviation from the original criminal plan and liability should fall exclusively on Edgar.

The Individualization Problem: Mens Rea Variations Between Accomplice and Principal

Confusingly similar to the problem of different crimes, is a distinct legal problem, that of different degrees of liability between accomplice and principal for the same crime. This individualization problem arises when the accomplice and principal have agreed on the commission of a particular type of crime and the principal commits that type of crime, but the accomplice and principal demonstrate different levels of mens rea with respect to a critical element of the offense. In this situation we ask: To what extent can we individualize the liability of accomplice and principal, if they differ in terms of level of mens rea and therefore the *degree* of offense committed?

The answer, outside of homicide, depends largely on jurisdiction, and thus will receive only brief discussion here. Instead we will focus on homicide, where individualization of liability is the norm. For example:

> Sharon loathes her ex-husband, Fred. She knows that Fred is hot tempered, violent, and overprotective with respect to their 15-year-old

daughter, Tami. Sharon also greatly dislikes Tami's 25-year-old boyfriend, Ralph. She devises a plan to get rid of both Ralph and Fred.

Sharon tells Tami that she will have the house to herself, knowing that Tami will then invite boyfriend Ralph over. When she believes the time is right, Sharon places a frantic call to Fred: "I think Tami's being raped! Come over now—and bring your gun!" Her hope is that Fred will shoot and kill Ralph, which will eliminate Ralph as a boyfriend and lead to Fred's imprisonment.

Fred rushes over, barges into the house and finds Ralph and Tami having sex in the living room. Tami yells: "don't shoot, he's my boyfriend." Nevertheless, Fred shoots Ralph dead. Fred is subsequently arrested. Unfortunately for Sharon, her manipulations are documented in her diary and she is charged as an accomplice to Fred's killing. What result?

Fred here would likely be found guilty of purpose to kill murder (without premeditation) or possibly voluntary manslaughter based on provocation (based on a belief that either a forcible or statutory rape was underway). Sharon meanwhile would be guilty as an accomplice. She did significant acts of encouragement or promotion of the killing by setting up the entire scenario and especially with her phone call. She did these acts with the purpose to encourage Fred to shoot Ralph. In terms of her mens rea with respect to Ralph's death (the shared mens rea requirement), she clearly planned a homicide and therefore meets the mens rea of premeditated purpose to kill murder. Under the individualization rule, Sharon would be found guilty of premeditated murder of Ralph as an accomplice while Fred would be found guilty of non-premeditated purpose to kill murder or voluntary manslaughter of Ralph as a principal.

Individualization can also work in the other direction, with an accomplice being convicted of a lesser homicide offense than the principal. For example, we might imagine a situation in which the accomplice had an honest but unreasonable fear of the victim, limiting her liability to voluntary manslaughter under the rule of imperfect self-defense, while the actual killer was unafraid and therefore could be convicted of murder.

The individualization problem is less likely to arise outside of homicide, because most crimes do not have different degrees. Nevertheless, many offense types come in felony and misdemeanor variations, so the individualization problem is certainly possible. Here jurisdictions vary. Some limit accomplice liability to the offense actually committed by the principal, on the theory that accomplice liability is vicarious and one cannot be an accomplice to more than what was actually committed. Others permit individualization just as in the homicide context. Complicating matters considerably here is the possibility that courts will treat this problem as not one of individualization of degree of liability, but a problem in different crimes to be handled under the rules (strict mens rea v. natural and probable consequences) discussed previously.

MPC Attempt Liability—A New Possibility for the Wannabe Accomplice

Recall that under the traditional common law approach, there can be no accomplice liability without an actual crime being committed by the principal. As mentioned briefly before, however, there is a provision in the Model Penal Code that creates a form of attempt liability to cover some such situations. Where an individual meets all the requirements for an accomplice in terms of both act and mens rea, but the principal does not actually commit the anticipated crime, Section 5.01(3) of the Code makes the would-be accomplice liable for an *attempt* at the anticipated crime. Described in the abstract this sounds rather complicated. It is less so in practice.

> In an old industrial city, the Union is waging a long and bitter battle with the local Plant. The strike has gone into a critical phase, where the Plant owner has started hiring replacement, nonunion workers, called scabs by Union members. Warren is a veteran of many union battles and in charge of "unofficial" strike discipline. He instructs Mike, a younger Union member, in an effort to "send a message" to a newly-identified scab. Warren tells Mike where the scab customarily hangs out. He gives Mike a heavily taped baseball bat and shows him how to break the man's legs with it. Mike seems to go along with the scheme, but rather than carrying it out, reports it to police. Can Warren be charged with any crime for his efforts to promote the aggravated assault on the scab? Aggravated assault is defined as an unlawful attack done with purpose to cause great bodily injury.

Under the traditional common law approach, because the principal, Mike, did not commit a crime of aggravated assault, Warren cannot be charged as an accomplice. The only possibility is that Warren might be charged with solicitation to commit aggravated assault.[15]

---

15. Conspiracy would be a possibility *if* the prosecution can prove that Mike and Warren had agreed to the assault, then Mike changed his mind. Proving such an agreement will

Under the MPC, the lack of a completed offense does not preclude accomplice-type liability, but does change its label and punishment. Instead of working under the provisions for accomplice, we look under the special provision for attempt in Section 5.01 (3). We need to determine if Warren met all the individual requirements—act and mens rea—for an accomplice. In his detailed instructions and provision of the baseball bat, Warren certainly did the act of encouraging and promoting an assault. He spoke and provided the bat with the purpose of encouraging the assault on the scab, and with an understanding that Mike would act with purpose to inflict great bodily harm, satisfying accomplice mens rea. The fact that no such crime actually was committed by the principal means that Warren would be convicted for attempted aggravated assault under the provisions of 5.01 (3).

---

be difficult given that Mike never followed through, however. He can argue he never truly committed to the plan. For more on conspiracy, see Chapter 17.

CHAPTER 17

CONSPIRACY

No doctrine in criminal law better illustrates the power of a purely legal concept than conspiracy. The idea that persons who cooperate in criminal conduct may implicitly form a criminal group, a conspiracy, thereby fundamentally changing the rules of proof, liability and punishment, is not one found outside the law. The idea that a simple nod or offer of help may make a person part of a criminal organization and potentially responsible for future crimes committed by others, even persons entirely unknown to the individual would strike most nonlawyers as strange. Yet this is but one of the unusual features of conspiracy law as it stands in many jurisdictions.

There is also no doctrine covered in this book as complex as conspiracy, and therefore no chapter where a reminder that coverage here is selective is more important. Many important issues involving conspiracy will not be covered here, or will be covered only briefly. Our focus will be on the most basic problems in determining the existence of a conspiracy, its nature and penal consequences.

Finally, there may be no more controversial basic rule of criminal liability than the law of conspiracy (though felony murder is definitely a contender). The doctrine has been subject to searching critique from a wide variety of academics, judges and practitioners, although to rather limited effect. For conspiracy also has powerful defenders. Though a doctrine subject to abuse, it has also been an important weapon against group criminality and organized crime. In short, it is a doctrine about which the best and the worst can be said, with some accuracy.

As is often the case in U.S. criminal law, there are many jurisdictional variations in the law of conspiracy, especially between federal and state law. Because conspiracy has long been an especially important part of federal prosecutions, a great deal of conspiracy law is federal; this is reflected in the chapter's coverage.

Basic Rule and Rationale

Conspiracy is a difficult form of liability to introduce because it does not easily break down into component parts. As we will see, the act and mens rea requirements of conspiracy are interrelated and difficult to disentangle. Another challenge for the student of this law is that much of the significance of the conspiracy charge involves legal consequences that lie, strictly speaking, outside of substantive criminal law in the realms of evidence law and criminal procedure. To appreciate the significance of a conspiracy charge requires an understanding of non-substantive concepts such as hearsay and venue and joinder. As a result, the crime will be introduced in stages, with the offense described initially in fairly general terms, with a more detailed examination of each essential part of the doctrine following.

Basic Definition

A conspiracy is usually defined as an agreement by two or more persons[1] to commit a crime or crimes.[2] The act of conspiracy is the agreement itself. Many jurisdictions also require proof of an overt physical act in furtherance of the conspiracy.

The mens rea of conspiracy is twofold; the prosecution must prove that the defendant demonstrated: (1) the purpose to join in a criminal endeavor; and (2) any mens rea required for the crime that is the object of the conspiracy.

One of the best ways to introduce conspiracy is to compare it with other inchoate liability doctrines: attempt and accomplice liability.

Conspiracy Compared with Attempt

In Chapter 16 we saw that attempt liability requires proof of a substantial act beyond "mere preparation." The requirement that a defendant take concrete action toward the commission of the underlying crime is an important

---

1. Some jurisdictions dispense with the plurality requirement, that two or more persons agree to pursue criminality. The MPC in particular takes a unilateral view of conspiracy, in which one person can become a conspirator even if the other purported conspirator lacks true criminal intent, perhaps because he or she acts on behalf of law enforcement. See MPC sec. 5.03(1)(a). Because most jurisdictions require plurality, and the great majority of cases involve at least two true co-conspirators, issues of unilateral conspiracy will not be discussed here.

2. The common law definition of conspiracy, which remains valid in some jurisdictions today, covers an agreement to commit an unlawful act, normally a criminal act, *or* a lawful act in an unlawful manner. The possibility of a conspiracy having a noncriminal aim raises many important issues, but because the great majority of contemporary conspiracy charges allege criminal objects, these will be the sole focus of attention here.

part of attempt doctrine. Conspiracy by contrast is complete when conspirators reach a criminal agreement. As a result, conspiracy liability potentially reaches much further back in time, into the realm of "mere preparation," providing for liability when attempt law would not. An example illustrates.

> Two young men notice a luxury SUV parked on the street and decide that they should steal it. They proceed to engage in an extended discussion of time and method for the theft. This discussion is overheard by an undercover police officer. If, prior to the two actually doing anything to steal the vehicle, an arrest is made, might they be convicted of an offense to related vehicle theft? In particular, might they be convicted of an attempted theft, or conspiracy to commit motor vehicle theft?

These young men have not done a sufficient act for an attempt. Their discussion would be classified as mere preparation and would not constitute conduct either dangerously close to criminal success or a substantial act strongly corroborative of their criminal intent. They are just talking, and talking, at least for this offense, will not be enough to constitute an attempt.

But talking may be sufficient for conspiracy. If we decide that these two young men have agreed to commit motor vehicle theft in the future, then they may be convicted of a conspiracy to commit motor vehicle theft.

Another important distinction between an attempt and conspiracy concerns the possibility of punishment for both the inchoate crime and the underlying offense.

> In this instance, the two young men ogle the SUV, talk about how much they want to steal it, and then finally act. They break into the vehicle, start the engine and begin to pull out into traffic. The vehicle comes to an abrupt stop, however, because of a struggle between them over how to change the radio channel presets. An alert police patrol officer notices, inquires, and finally arrests the two. What can they be charged with now, based on both the initial conversations witnessed by the undercover officer, and the taking of the vehicle, witnessed by the patrol officer?

Prosecutors here may be tempted to charge two offenses: an attempt to steal based on the initial conversations and theft based on the breaking into the vehicle and starting it up. The decision maker, however, will have to make a choice. Either the defendants committed *only* an attempt because they never actually took the vehicle, or their offense was a completed theft, in which case their conduct leading up to the vehicle taking, that would otherwise be an attempt, will *merge* into the completed offense. The bottom line is that under these facts, the defendants can only be punished for either an attempted theft of the SUV or (more likely on these facts) theft of the SUV. Conspiracy liability is not so limited.

In many jurisdictions, conspiracy is a separate offense from any substantive offense committed as part of the conspiracy, meaning that both the conspiracy and the substantive offense can be punished separately. With respect to our young thieves, their agreement to steal the SUV (the conspiracy) and the subsequent taking of the SUV (motor vehicle theft) are separate offenses and may be punished separately. They do not merge.[3] As a result, sentences imposed for (1) conspiracy to commit motor vehicle theft and (2) motor vehicle theft *may* be ordered to run consecutively. And you wonder why prosecutors love conspiracy?

Conspiracy Compared with Accomplice Liability

As we saw in Chapter 16, a person may be criminally liable for the conduct of another if the would-be accomplice encourages or promotes the other's criminal act, does so with the purpose to promote that act, and also shares the mens rea required for the underlying offense. Conspiracy law in many respects overlaps with accomplice liability. There will be many instances in which the facts satisfy both forms. Here we will focus on those aspects of conspiracy liability that provide prosecutorial advantages as compared with accomplice liability.

We saw previously that to be an accomplice, one must act to promote or encourage the principal's offense. This act need not be terribly significant to the principal's conduct, but there still must be provable physical action on the part of the accomplice, such as encouraging words, physical assistance, prior agreement and presence, to fulfill the act requirement. With conspiracy, however, words of agreement, or conduct that indicates agreement, will be sufficient for the act requirement. There need not be (though there often will be) conduct specifically directed toward another's criminal act. Also, depending on jurisdiction, a person who joins the conspiracy may be liable for a wide range of crimes subsequently committed by other co-conspirators, liability that may be considerably broader than under the rules of complicity.

---

3. See Iannelli v. United States 420 US 770, 790–91 (1975).

This is not to say that conspiracy is always a more promising route for the state than accomplice liability. The complexities of conspiracy present challenges for factfinders that maybe avoided with a more straightforward complicity presentation. There will also be cases where the proof better fits a defendant acting to encourage a particular offender and offense rather than entering into a larger agreement.

Evidentiary and Procedural Advantages of Conspiracy

This initial comparison of conspiracy with the law of attempt and accomplice liability suggests some of the advantages that prosecutors may enjoy in pursuing a conspiracy charge. But there's more—a lot more to favor prosecutors here.

Perhaps the single greatest advantage of a conspiracy charge for prosecutors is the co-conspirator exception to the hearsay rule. Providing a full explanation of this rule would unfortunately take us too far into the law of evidence, so a shorthand version must suffice here. Any statements made by a co-conspirator in furtherance of the conspiracy may be admitted in the case against a defendant charged with conspiracy.[4] This means that, subject to what is called "joining up" (establishing final proof of both the conspiracy and the defendant's membership in it) incriminating statements by a wide variety of charged and even uncharged conspirators can be used against the defendant. Acts of co-conspirators done prior to defendant joining the conspiracy can even be used to prove the existence of a conspiracy

Conspiracy also brings major advantages in determining where a criminal case can be brought, what is called venue. In most criminal cases, venue lies where the criminal act was committed. With conspiracy, venue lies not only where the agreement was reached but also where any overt act was done (which as we will see can be as little as the place where a telephone call was placed or received) or where any of the crimes done in furtherance of the conspiracy were committed.[5]

Current law standardly permits the prosecution to bring all co-conspirators to trial together.[6] As discussed in Chapter 16, such joint trials usually bring significant advantages for the prosecution. If all this were not enough, in the

---

4. See Bourjaily v. United States, 483 U.S. 171 (1987).

5. See Hyde v. United States, 225 U.S. 347 (1912).

6. See Fed. R. Crim. Proc. 8; United States v. Paolino, 935 F.2d 739, 751–52 (6th Cir. 1991).

federal area there are also special conspiracy laws, such as RICO, which bring further substantive and procedural advantages to the prosecution.[7]

Rationale

Why are the rules of conspiracy so different from those of other criminal offenses and why are so many of those differences to the advantage of the prosecution? What is the rationale for this crime whose proof can seem amorphous and yet whose penal consequences can be severe?

The basic rationale of conspiracy law is that group criminal activity presents special dangers to society and, perhaps, special difficulties in its prosecution. It represents the negative side of the common observation that we can accomplish more working together than as individuals.

Conspiracy is literally about *organized* crime, about those situations where individuals combine to break the most basic rules of society. It therefore addresses the dangers of collective, and potentially *intelligent* criminal endeavor.

Such organized criminality presents particular dangers to the rule of law because of the possibility that it may supplant democratic institutions and undercut law enforcement. For example, if ordinary business activity depends on the payment of protection money to a criminal organization, then the protections that law promises such businesses become illusory and respect for the law diminishes. But the problem is potentially larger than this. If sufficiently profitable, criminal organizations can corrupt law enforcement and indeed all of government.

Prosecutors often contend that only conspiracy law provides the necessary tools to effectively attack criminal organizations. If restricted to accomplice liability, police and prosecutors would have to focus on the lower levels of criminal organization, on the persons who actually commit the crimes and their immediate associates. Because the state must prove direct contact between accomplice and principal, it is difficult to reach the leadership of a large criminal organization. And it is true that conspiracy law has been effectively used to combat a wide range of organized criminality including that involved in narcotics trafficking, political corruption, white collar fraud and prison gangs.

The rationale of conspiracy is not necessarily coexistent with its rules, however. Conspiracy charges can be and often are brought against defendants who

---

7. 18 USC secs. 1961 et seq.; (conspiracy to conduct a racketeering enterprise). A similar statute is: 18 U.S.C. sec. 1959 (a) (Violence in Aid of a Racketeering Enterprise) (VICAR).

commit offenses jointly, but with very little organization or intelligence. Such offenders present no large-scale threat to democracy or the rule of law. Indeed, the law of conspiracy does not require a true criminal organization, only an agreement by two or more persons to commit a crime or crimes.

Even strong defenders of conspiracy recognize the need for prosecutorial discretion in its use. Conspiracy represents the heavy artillery of criminal law and should be deployed against only the most threatening targets.

The Agreement

At the heart of conspiracy law is the agreement of the co-conspirators to commit a crime or crimes. The agreement represents the act of conspiracy. Without proof of agreement, there is no conspiracy.

The requirement of an agreement is unlike any other act requirement in the criminal law. It seems to describe a criminal intent more than a physical action or event. And indeed we will see that the mens rea requirements of conspiracy are inextricably intertwined with the agreement.

Along these lines, some have complained that proof of agreement does not provide concrete evidence of wrong*doing* as opposed to *thinking* about wrongdoing, one of the basic tasks of the voluntary act requirement in criminal law. Is there any way to understand a criminal agreement as an act or event in the physical world as opposed to just a mental state? I think there is, but it requires shifting from a purely individual to a social perspective.

The joint commitment of at least two persons to undertake criminal activity changes the social relationship between those involved. In this respect it is like the formation of a contract, where individuals make personal commitments to each other according to mutually understood social norms, commitments that also have legal significance. When two or more persons agree to form a criminal enterprise, whether for a single crime or a whole host of offenses, they create a new and dangerous social relationship that arguably warrants legal recognition.

Before proceeding to further description of conspiratorial agreements and their proof, we need a brief mention of mens rea. As noted before, there can be no final separation of agreement from mens rea, because each aspect of the offense requires the other. There is no criminal agreement unless the conspirators demonstrate the *purpose to agree*. And, defining what a criminal agreement is, depends in significant measure on a second aspect of mens rea, the mens rea of individual co-conspirators toward the target offenses to be committed as part of the conspiracy.

Proof of Agreement

In any conspiracy case, prosecutors must prove the conspiratorial agreement beyond a reasonable doubt. This poses some obvious difficulties. As is commonly observed in conspiracy law, such commitments are rarely put in writing or otherwise documented. Narcotics traffickers do not ask new hires to sign contracts on joining the organization; would-be bank robbers do not undertake formal training before joining the assault.[8] As a result, proof of an agreement must be by inference. Prosecutors offer proof of actions and statements by co-conspirators that indicate their commitment to a joint criminal enterprise. In essence, fact finders are asked to take a retrospective look at patterns of action and statements of alleged conspirators to determine if the evidence clearly indicates they were engaged in a specific, collective criminal endeavor. As always, examples will illustrate.

> Police present prosecutors with the following evidence from surveillance cameras and witnesses to the crime. Carolyn enters the Easy Cash check cashing establishment on a Friday afternoon at 4 p.m. She appears to look through some promotional material, while she checks out the lobby area. The security guard soon leaves the lobby via a back door. Every hour he takes a short cigarette break in the rear parking lot. Almost immediately Carolyn takes off her large orange hat and stands in front of the front glass window to the business. A minute later Arlen enters. Arlen is Carolyn's boyfriend.
>
> Arlen pulls out a large handgun and holds up the cashier, taking large amounts of cash. While he is doing this, Carolyn stands directly in front of the back door which the security guard would use to reenter the lobby. Arlen runs out the front door with cash in a large bag. Carolyn follows. Almost immediately both are picked up at the curb by Bobby, Arlen's younger brother. They drive away in Bobby's car.
>
> Can all three be charged with conspiracy to rob?

Notice that in this case we have no documented verbal communication between any of the three before, during, or after the offense. All we have is evi-

---

8. As has been said: "a conspiracy is seldom born of open covenants openly arrived at." Lacaze v. United States, 391 F.2d 516, 520 (5th Cir. 1968). See also Direct Sales Co. v. United States, 319 US 703, 714 (1943).

dence of each of their actions and the possible pattern that they make together. This should be enough.

Proof of a robbery by Arlen is clear; the question is whether Carolyn and Bobby can be said to have reached an agreement with him to commit this robbery. Carolyn's conduct is entirely consistent with being part of a plan — she appears to signal Arlen that the security guard is gone when she goes to the front door without her hat. She then stands in front of the rear doorway in an apparent effort to block or delay the guard's reappearance. Her entire conduct is consistent with being part of a robbery and not especially consistent with being a customer. Her departure immediately following Arlen also indicates pre-arrangement.

Similar arguments can be made with respect to Bobby, who appears to have acted as the getaway driver. Of the three, though, he has the strongest claim against conspiracy membership. His attorney would argue that, at most, the facts show that he was supposed to pick up his brother and his brother's girlfriend at a particular time and place. How was he to know that they were involved in a robbery? The prosecution will respond that Bobby's conduct was totally consistent with being the getaway driver for a well planned robbery by persons with whom he had personal connections, indicating that he was part of the plan.

One more example.

> Judith is a real estate agent in a tough real estate market. Many of the people who come to her to buy houses have difficulty qualifying for mortgages. At a conference of real estate agents, mortgage brokers, and others associated with the local real estate market, Judith meets Kevin Smith, who tells her that he has access to foreign financing and can "make loans happen" when no one else can. He urges her to bring her more "financially strapped" buyers to him. She does and discovers Smith to be as good as his word. With his help, the weakest of her applicants receive mortgage approval. This means that all the sales go through and Judith receives her seller's commission. Judith later gets a copy of the loan documents for one of these transactions and sees that misrepresentations have been made about the buyer's income in the application for a federally guaranteed loan. Nevertheless she continues to refer clients to Smith.
>
> Smith is subsequently charged with federal loan fraud by submitting documents that misrepresent applicant income. Could Judith be successfully prosecuted for conspiracy to commit loan fraud?

The prosecution may contend that there is pattern evidence of a conspiracy to commit loan fraud involving Judith and Smith similar to the proof in the bank robbery example above. Each participant had a particular role to play. Judith supplied loan applicants; Smith produced the fraudulent loan applications. Judith was aware of misrepresentations in at least one loan application and had other warning signs of fraud based on Smith's representations and the universal success of even weak applicants. Each participant received financial benefits from the scheme from their respective commissions.

Unlike the bank robbery example, however, the defense here has a strong contrary argument. Judith herself did nothing illegal and had no personal arrangement with Smith. Even if she knew that Smith was submitting false loan documents, she did nothing apart from her ordinary work as a real estate agent to assist him. She provided no false information and received no additional benefit aside from the standard commission she received on a sale. To anticipate a discussion that we will take up again under the heading of mens rea, Judith's attorney can argue that, at worst, she knowingly assisted Smith in his fraud; she never acted with purpose to agree to join a fraud operation.

The bottom line is that, without more, the prosecution probably does not have sufficient proof that there was a conspiracy between Smith and Judith. Whatever might be said of Smith's individual liability, and Judith's morality, the evidence is consistent with the view that they acted independently, each taking advantage of the other's contributions without ever agreeing to work in concert.

Overt Acts

Under most, though not all, conspiracy statutes, in addition to proof of an agreement, the prosecution must also prove that at least one conspirator committed an overt act in furtherance of the conspiracy. An overt act is any form of observable physical conduct undertaken as part of the conspiracy.

At first glance, the overt act requirement might appear a significant additional burden for the prosecution. In light of what we have already seen as the essentially mental, and somewhat amorphous nature of the conspiratorial agreement, the overt act gives the offense a needed grounding in concrete action. In this respect it seems to do what a voluntary act normally does. And it is true that in some cases, the overt act requirement can make a difference to the ultimate outcome. But in most cases, there is less here than meets the eye.

For any conspiracy, there need only be a single overt act proven, by a single conspirator. Twenty individuals may be charged with participation in a conspiracy and yet only one need have committed an overt act for this requirement to be satisfied. Nor need the overt act be a criminal act. It may be in itself entirely innocent. The placing of a phone call, sending of an e-mail message, walking across the street, waving to another person are all examples of otherwise innocent acts that may constitute an overt act—if done in furtherance of the larger conspiracy. The act need not be especially important to the conspiracy as long as it is done in its furtherance.

Finally, some modern statutes eliminate any requirement of an overt act.[9]

The Agreement and the Extent of Liability for Co-Conspirator Crimes: The *Pinkerton* Rule

What happens, legally, when one becomes a conspirator? What liability follows from entering into a criminal agreement? At a minimum, one becomes guilty of the crime of conspiracy, which is normally a felony as long as the target offense is a felony. Even if no substantive crime is ever committed, the conspiracy can be charged, proven and punished.

But what if substantive crimes are committed as part of the conspiracy? How do we determine the individual liability of each conspirator? Here there are significant jurisdictional variations that to some extent mirror variations we saw with respect to the liability of accomplices.

Some jurisdictions limit co-conspirator liability to those crimes in which the defendant personally participated in some fashion. Similar to accomplice liability, the defendant must have acted to promote a co-conspirator's criminal act, with the purpose of promotion or encouragement, while sharing any further mens rea required for that offense. The only difference from accomplice liability here is that evidence relating to joining the conspiracy may assist in the proof of criminal purpose and promotion.

In federal law, and in a number of states, a conspirator's liability for a co-conspirator's crimes goes much further than this under the so-called *Pinkerton* rule. In such jurisdictions, all conspirators are liable for all substantive crimes committed by any co-conspirator in furtherance of the conspiracy after the individual's time of joining.[10] Under this rule the individual defendant need not have had any knowledge of the particular offense committed by another conspirator. Nor need the defendant have assisted this particular offense in any way. Nor is there any requirement of proof that the defendant sought the commission of this particular offense, beyond the defendant's assent to the

---

9. See 18 U.S.C. sec. 871 (narcotics distribution).
10. Pinkerton v. United States, 328 U.S. 640 (1946).

conspiracy as a whole, including its criminal aims. The following example illustrates the breadth of this doctrine.

Antonio Ramirez, is a shot caller (a leader) of the A Street gang, a powerful criminal organization in the southern part of the state. He is currently incarcerated in the west wing of the Hollow Hills Correctional Facility, where he is considered the most powerful inmate. Recently a rival gang from the northern part of the state, the Diablos Sagrados, has made a move to take over narcotics and protection rackets currently run by A Street members in the prison. Henry, a close associate of Ramirez is beaten in the yard and the sign of the Diablos carved into the skin of his chest, an obvious gang message.

Fearing that Ramirez will order retaliation, prison officials place Ramirez in administrative segregation, locked away from the rest of the prison population. While he is there, the shot caller of the Diablos, Pedro Bolda, is attacked by A Street members and killed. Statements by the attackers make clear that Bolda was killed to reestablish A Street primacy in the prison. Investigators believe that the attack was ordered by Ramirez but they cannot prove this because they cannot establish any communication between Ramirez and other prisoners after he was placed in administrative segregation. Is there any way, nevertheless, that he may be charged with murder?

Under these facts, Ramirez cannot be charged as a principal, because he did not commit a criminal act leading to the victim's death. He cannot be charged as an accomplice, because without proof of communication with other prisoners there is no evidence of encouragement or promotion of the homicidal act. But what about conspiracy?

Under the more restrictive approach to liability for co-conspirator crimes, Ramirez could not be charged, because as we have seen, the rules in this context essentially parallel those of accomplice liability and the personal connection needed for such liability is missing here. There are real possibilities under the Pinkerton doctrine, however.

We must first of course prove a conspiracy. The prosecution can allege that Ramirez was the leader of a criminal conspiracy in prison, going under the name of the A Street gang, which had criminal objectives in narcotics trafficking and violence to enforce its control of the inmate population. The prosecution will further allege that Bolda's murder was committed by members of the A Street gang in furtherance of the conspiracy: the murder was committed to reestablish A Street control of the prison in the face of a threat from a rival gang. Ramirez was a member of the conspiracy at the time of crime and therefore under Pinkerton may be held liable for the murder.

All of these points can be contested by the defense. The defense may contend that the A Street gang did not constitute or function as a criminal conspiracy; that the Bolda murder was not committed by members of any conspiracy of which Ramirez was a member, and that the murder was not in furtherance of any conspiracy that did exist. But if the prosecution meets its proof as set out above, Ramirez can be convicted of murder even if there is no evidence that he knew about the killing before it occurred or that he sought its occurrence.

Natural and Reasonable Consequences Extension of Liability

As generous as the Pinkerton rule is for prosecutors in its basic form, there's more! Mirroring a rule that extends liability for accomplices for unforeseen crimes by principals (see Chapter 16), in many jurisdictions conspirators may be held for crimes beyond the scope of the original conspiracy, if such crimes are reasonably foreseeable given the objects of the conspiracy.[11] This potentially expands liability enormously by including crimes designed to cover up the conspiracy and violence to thwart criminal rivals.

Now in his senior year at college, Mike has been involved in the sale and distribution of marijuana on campus for three years. He makes very good money and enjoys the work so much that he is planning to go to business school for a graduate degree. He believes that marijuana "doesn't hurt anybody" and even though it is against the law, isn't a "real" crime. He has contacts with a number of people off campus who supply him with marijuana and who, he knows, work with others in the drug trade. He is aware that the marijuana he sells comes primarily from growers out of state. Law enforcement has evidence that Mike is part of a marijuana distribution network providing almost 20% of the region's total supply.

Walt never finished high school and has an extensive criminal record. He is an impulsive man who is desperate to avoid a return to state prison because he has a wife and a new son. He drives a truck filled with a ton of marijuana that is stopped by a lone police officer

---

11. E.g., State v. Bridges, 628 A.2d 270 (N.J. 1993).

on a rural highway. The officer asks Walt for permission to search the truck. Walt says sure. When the officer turns back to his patrol car for a moment, Walt pulls out a gun and shoots the police officer in the head.

Now totally panicked, Walt runs from the scene.

Backup officers soon appear; the police officer is dead. Walt's cell phone, which he left at the scene, now rings. It is Mike, who leaves a message wondering when "the stuff will arrive."

Walt is captured and charged with the purpose to kill murder of a police officer in the course of official responsibilities, a form of first-degree murder in the jurisdiction. Could Mike also face such a charge via Pinkerton conspiracy liability?

We begin with the assumption that there is an ongoing conspiracy of which Mike and Walt were a part. The object of this conspiracy was to distribute marijuana, meaning that its target offenses would include the possession and distribution of the drug, but not murder. Mike therefore could not be charged with the murder in a jurisdiction that takes a strict mens rea approach to conspiracy; he never demonstrated a purpose to agree with others to kill a police officer, or to commit murder in any form. (He would also lack the purpose to encourage or promote an act of murder as is required under accomplice liability.) But what about under the *Pinkerton* rule and its reasonably foreseeable extension?

Now the question becomes whether the murder was a reasonably foreseeable crime given the nature of the marijuana distribution conspiracy. The prosecution, arguing in the affirmative, will contend that any drug distribution scheme involves the possibility of violence against those who might threaten its work, including law enforcement officers. What happened between Walt and the police officer is quite foreseeable in the course of drug trafficking.

The defense will argue that, at least here, the murder of a police officer was not reasonably foreseeable, because there was no other evidence indicating the use of violence to maintain the organization, or particular violent threats. In essence, the argument is that while some drug organizations may be violent, and commit violence against law enforcement, there is no evidence that this organization had such traits.

Without trying to predict an outcome here, the main point to recognize is that under the *Pinkerton* rule and its extension, Mike *could* be convicted of murder without any direct involvement or knowledge of the killing, because the fact finder might determine that it was a reasonably foreseeable crime given the nature of the conspiracy.

Abandonment and Withdrawal

Especially in a jurisdiction that follows the *Pinkerton* rule, determining when a conspiracy ends or when an individual conspirator withdraws from the conspiracy can be very important. Initially we must distinguish these two concepts.

Abandonment refers to the end of the conspiracy itself. Once the criminal collective is dissolved, no individuals may be found guilty as conspirators for subsequent crimes. Abandonment occurs when all members of a conspiracy cease conspiratorial efforts. It is when the criminal agreement no longer exists.

Withdrawal refers to the withdrawal of an individual member from an ongoing conspiracy. An individual may withdraw from a conspiracy by an affirmative act reasonably calculated to communicate to all conspirators, prior to the commission of any further crime, that the individual will no longer participate in the criminal agreement.[12] The key here is that the defendant must take affirmative action to break from the conspiracy and communicate that break with other members. Simply no longer participating in conspiracy activities is insufficient.

A defendant who has withdrawn will not be liable for crimes committed by other members of the conspiracy after the date of withdrawal. Traditionally, the law has *not* recognized withdrawal as a defense to a charge of conspiracy itself, however. The notion is that once one has entered a criminal conspiracy, the crime of conspiracy is complete. The MPC does recognize a very limited defense of withdrawal from conspiracy, however.[13]

Mens Rea

The mens rea requirements of conspiracy are two-fold, similar to what we have encountered with other forms of inchoate liability. The defendant must act with the purpose required for inchoate liability itself—here the purpose to agree—and must also demonstrate the purpose necessary to commit the target offense or offenses, which will include all of the mens rea requirements of those offenses.

Purpose to Join

The initial mens rea inquiry for conspiracy involves whether the defendant purposely agreed to join at least one other person to commit a crime or crimes.

---

12. See United States v. United States Gypsum Co., 438 U.S. 422, 464–65 (1978).
13. MPC sec. 5.03 (6) (affirmative defense of renunciation, which requires that defendant have "thwarted the success of the conspiracy").

As we have already seen, this requirement substantially overlaps with that of the act requirement. The only real distinction is that when we analyze the act of agreement, we are looking for a collective arrangement; when we analyze mens rea, we focus on a single individual's purpose with respect to the agreement. A good way to illustrate the distinction is where a conspiracy clearly exists, but there is an issue about whether the defendant demonstrated the purpose to join the conspiracy.

> Martha is the matriarch of a successful family business that manufactures and distributes methamphetamine throughout the Midwest. Her nephew Hank, who heads up manufacturing operations, approaches Joe Bob and makes him a proposition. Hank says that he will pay $1000 cash, with an initial deposit of $100, for use of a double wide house trailer on Joe Bob's property for one week. The price is a great deal more than the market value for rentals of similar property. Joe Bob is aware of Hank's business, and so knows that Hank is talking about methamphetamine manufacture when he talks about "cooking up some stuff." Joe Bob initially agrees. He takes the $100 and clears out some things from the trailer that he thinks might be harmed in the process. Two days before the operation is supposed to begin, however, Joe Bob changes his mind and pulls out of the deal. The manufacturing never occurs at the trailer.
> A week later federal authorities arrest Martha, Hank and others involved in the regional manufacture and distribution operation. Joe Bob now comes to you for advice. Is there any chance he could be charged with conspiracy here?[14]

Assuming there was an ongoing manufacture and distribution of methamphetamine conspiracy that included Martha and Hank, the question is whether Joe Bob joined that conspiracy by agreeing to rent his house trailer. Let's begin with what the prosecution might allege. The contention might be that Joe Bob, with knowledge that the trailer would be used for meth manufacture, agreed to take a sum of money far in excess of the usual rental value of the trailer. The prosecution would argue that from this knowledge and Joe Bob's willingness to share in the profits of the illegal operation, that he agreed to join the conspiracy. He said yes to the transaction and thereby showed a purpose to participate with Hank and others in the manufacture of methamphetamine.

---

14. The facts here are similar to United States v. Blankenship, 970 F.2d 283 (7th Cir. 1992). Note that if Joe Bob joined the conspiracy, his subsequent decision not to go through with the trailer rental will not constitute a defense, because the crime of conspiracy was complete with the establishment of an agreement.

The defense will strongly contest the inference of purpose from proof of knowledge. Assuming, as the facts state, that Joe Bob did know about the meth manufacture, that does not indicate a purpose to join. The defense will argue that Joe Bob was agnostic as to success of this particular manufacturing venture and had no interest in the larger manufacturing and distribution network. He would not receive a cut of the profits; this was just a one-off deal for the use of a house trailer for a week.

The defense will argue that finding conspiracy liability here would have dangerous implications for many lawful businesses. If knowledge of likely wrongdoing is sufficient, then sellers or renters of vehicles or physical premises or cell phones or other communication services, are among those who might become co-conspirators of their customers once they become aware that their customers may be engaged in an illegal enterprise of some sort. It should take more to join a criminal conspiracy.

And indeed, in cases like this, courts are often reluctant to infer purpose from knowledge. Fully aware of the larger consequences of a finding that the defendant joined a conspiracy, appellate courts will usually require more proof of a purpose to join than is shown in Joe Bob's case.[15]

Purpose to Commit the Target Offense

Proof of an individual's purpose to join the conspiracy will often effectively prove the second form of mens rea required, that the defendant demonstrate the mens rea required for the substantive offense(s) that are the aims of the conspiracy. For example, if a defendant demonstrates the purpose to agree with others to commit narcotics distribution offenses, that presumes the defendant had the required mens rea for narcotics distribution. For the most part, the target offenses for conspiracy are serious felonies that require purpose or knowledge; as a result, they are usually consistent with the purpose to agree mens rea element of conspiracy. Nevertheless, there are some hard cases with respect to offense mens rea here; they involve target offenses that can be committed with recklessness or negligence, or that have strict liability elements.

Can one conspire to commit a target offense when the defendant demonstrates less than purpose or knowledge as to critical elements of the offense? The answer is essentially the same as was given in accomplice liability with respect

---

15. E.g., People v. Lauria, 251 Cal. App. 2d 471 (1967). Notice that analysis of accomplice liability will be much the same. The prosecution here will also have difficulty inferring the purpose to encourage or promote the manufacture of methamphetamine needed for such liability from proof of knowledge that the manufacture would be assisted by the rental.

to mens rea for the underlying offense. If the target offense requires a result, then the conspirator must demonstrate a purpose as to that result. As with accomplice liability, this is a rule primarily for homicide. It means that—putting aside the reasonable foreseeability aspect of *Pinkerton*—conspiracy to commit homicide is limited to a conspiracy to commit a purposeful homicide, and usually means premeditated murder.[16]

With respect to so-called conduct offenses, which do not require proof of any physical harm to person or property, the mens rea for the target offense is the same under conspiracy as otherwise. For example, if assault on a federal law enforcement agent requires a purpose to do violence to another but is strict liability as to federal agent status, then a person may be guilty of a conspiracy to commit such an assault if he or she demonstrates a purpose to agree with another to commit a violent attack on an individual who subsequently turns out to be a federal agent, i.e., without any awareness that the victim is a federal agent.

The Agreement Redux: Identifying the Conspiracy

Some of the most complex issues in conspiracy law involve not whether there is a conspiracy but how the conspiracy—or conspiracies—should be conceptualized. Is there one conspiracy or are there multiple conspiracies? What is the object, or objects, of the conspiracy or conspiracies?

As a general rule, the prosecution will normally allege and seek to prove a single conspiracy, or at least will try to minimize the number of conspiracies. This will permit a joint trial of all (or at least most) defendants, a cumulation of evidence, and maximum penalties under the *Pinkerton* rule. The defense will often contend that if any conspiracy is proven, it had very limited objectives. The defense will often seek to differentiate between groups and activities to avoid defendants being lumped together in a single conspiracy.

To determine conspiratorial liability we must draw an organizational chart, or charts, of criminal groupings. Two different forms of conspiratorial organizations that recur frequently are chain conspiracies and wheel conspiracies.

---

16. But as we have seen, the reasonable foreseeability doctrine can expand liability dramatically. A conspirator with no awareness or direct involvement with a homicide committed by another member of the conspiracy might nevertheless be held liable for that homicide if it is a reasonably foreseeable consequence of the original conspiracy.

A chain conspiracy is one in which there is essentially a single line of criminal activity, in which individuals or groups in the conspiracy act sequentially to carry out the conspiracy's work. For example:

> Federal agents can establish a series of illegal arms exports that each follow the same pattern. A mid-level Officer in munitions supply at a military base creates fraudulent paperwork to divert antitank weapons to a Friend with a trucking business who acts as domestic shipper. The Friend transports the matériel to a port city. At that point an international Broker supervises the shipment of the arms overseas and its delivery to a Buyer. The Broker receives payment for the shipment, takes his share and wires the remainder of the sale proceeds to separate bank accounts controlled by the Officer and Friend. What kind of conspiracy is this?

This is a classic chain conspiracy, with three basic links in the chain: (1) the procurement of arms by the Officer; (2) its domestic shipment by Friend; and (3) its international shipment, delivery and sale by the Broker. Members of each link in this chain were either directly aware of, or would presume the necessity, of other persons in the chain, because each is vital to the success of the enterprise.

A wheel conspiracy is a more complex structure in which there is a central organizing individual or group (the hub of the wheel) which simultaneously deals with a number of other individuals or groups (spokes of the wheel), who also have some relationship to each other independent of the hub (the rim of the wheel). The biggest issue in many alleged wheel conspiracies is whether in fact there is a rim to the wheel, which unifies all into one conspiracy. If each individual or group connects only with the hub, then each spoke represents an independent conspiracy with the hub.

> From a small office in the nation's capital, Monique ran Your Perfect Night, an escort service providing high-priced male and female companionship and sexual services in 10 major cities in the country. (Its motto: "No questions asked. All dreams fulfilled.") In other words, it was a prostitution operation. Prosecutors can prove that Monique recruited, selected and trained escorts, handled the marketing of escort services, arranged liaisons between customers and escorts, and did basic problem-solving for the operation. Each escort was paid by Monique a flat rate according to hour and service provided and kept whatever tip the client provided. Generally the escorts worked alone, but sometimes they worked in pairs or in small groups for parties.

What additional evidence, if any, might be required for prosecutors
to show a single conspiracy between all escorts and Monique?

The issue here is whether there is a rim to this wheel. The evidence described here indicates that Monique and each of her escort workers conspired
to commit prostitution offenses. This suggests multiple conspiracies, depending on the number of escort workers. In order to make all this activity fall
within a single wheel conspiracy, the prosecution needs to develop the connections between escort workers.

How often do the escorts work together? Do they communicate with each
other as opposed to just with Monique? How much do they know about each
other's work? Proof of extensive escort-escort connections will help the prosecution establish that each escort worker understood that she or he was part
of a larger organization, and not just an independent contractor working for
Monique. Such connections increase the likelihood of a single conspiracy. Recall that if a single conspiracy can be established, then this will support a single trial of all charged conspirators and potential liability for all defendants for
all substantive prostitution crimes committed under the *Pinkerton* rule.

INTRODUCTION TO PART FIVE

DEFENSES

In this final section of the book we move from the essential elements of criminal offenses to what are commonly called affirmative defenses. As we saw in Chapter 3, such defenses function independently of the essential elements of the offense. All of the essential elements of the offense may be proven, and still an affirmative defense may produce acquittal. For example, a young woman charged with murder may have voluntarily fired a shot that actually and proximately caused the victim's death, may have done so with purpose to kill and without provocation, thus establishing all of the essential elements of murder, and yet still be found not guilty—if she acted in self-defense.

As we saw in Chapter 4, the defendant normally has the burden of producing evidence concerning an affirmative defense before it can be considered by the fact finder. So, for example, the defendant cannot argue self-defense to a fact finder unless she has produced sufficient evidence on the issue to meet the law's threshold requirement for evidence production. In some instances, the defendant may also bear the burden of persuasion on the affirmative defense.

What on paper appear to be clear distinctions between essential elements and affirmative defenses can blur in practice, however. While it is generally true that analysis of affirmative defenses is separate from analysis of essential elements, there are exceptions. For example, a person who killed because she feared for her life may argue that this fear not only supports her self-defense claim but means that she lacked the mens rea required for murder. She may say that, wanting only to protect herself she fired with purpose to scare or injure the victim, not to kill. Then there are doctrines, voluntary intoxication being the most obvious example, where the "defense" goes directly to the essential element of mens rea for the particular offense.

We are left with a set of doctrines that *usually* stand apart from essential element analysis, and usually involve exceptional circumstances that the defendant must establish to some degree in order to be considered.

Scholars often distinguish two general categories of affirmative defenses: justifications and excuses. A justification is a claim that an otherwise criminal act was both morally and legally justified by exceptional circumstances. Self-defense represents the classic contemporary example: a person may kill another in order to save his or her own life. Such an action is considered legally and morally justified. Similarly, a police officer's fatal shooting of a dangerous felon who poses a threat to others' lives, will be a justifiable homicide.

An excuse is a claim that although the defendant's conduct was legally and morally wrong, the defendant may not be held criminally responsible for it. A defendant who killed while insane does not contend that the killing was justified, but that by virtue of being crazy, he or she was not a responsible agent and therefore cannot be blamed in the way that the criminal law requires. Although the distinction between justifications and excuses is often emphasized in the academic literature, it will not be pursued here because it does not usually affect how courts or legislatures conceive of defenses.

Coverage of affirmative defenses in this Part is selective. We focus here on self-defense (Chapter 18) various doctrines of intoxication (Chapter 19) and insanity and related doctrines (Chapter 20). Some important matters relating to these doctrines, and a number of other affirmative defenses are not covered. For example, the exploration of self-defense concentrates on the use of deadly force, to the exclusion of other aspects including nondeadly self-defense and law enforcement. The defenses of necessity, duress, and entrapment are not covered. The rationale here is the same as elsewhere in this book: by taking sufficient time with a few representative defenses, students may build an understanding of concepts and skills that they can then apply to the study of other doctrines.

CHAPTER 18

SELF-DEFENSE

Self-defense is among the most intuitive of criminal doctrines. We can work out most of its rules just from the basic principle of necessity that lies behind it. This does not make self-defense law easy or noncontroversial, however. Rather, it means that the most difficult issues here tend to involve rule applications rather than definitions—though we will encounter some rule controversy as well.

Self-defense provides some of the great moral dramas of criminal law, because here the defendant asserts that the state's view of the case is exactly wrong. Under self-defense, the defendant claims that he did right and the victim did wrong. Self-defense recall, is a justification in modern law, not an excuse. Perhaps for this reason, claims of self-defense have a way of raising major value questions concerning honor and violence, as well as implicating cultural, gender and race differences. In self-defense cases, often more than the defendant's conduct is at issue.

The primary focus of this chapter will be on the use of deadly force in self-defense. This focus follows from our earlier attention to homicide (where such claims arise with some frequency) and permits coverage of some of the most important doctrinal issues, while also providing a needed limit to discussion. Unfortunately, it means that a number of significant self-defense doctrines will not be covered here, including defense of others, force to defend property rights and the use of force in law enforcement.[1]

---

1. On a related point, the chapter will not cover the MPC's proposed structure for self-defense, which makes the doctrine depend entirely on subjective perceptions (defendant's honest beliefs) and then provides for liability for reckless or negligent offenses if defendant's perceptions are found to meet reckless or negligent standards. Very few jurisdictions have adopted this structure. Other aspects of the Code on self-defense have been influential, however, and will be covered.

Self-Defense in the Liability Formula: Burden of Proof and Related Mens Rea Arguments

Self-defense is an affirmative defense, meaning that its analysis stands independent of any other part of the liability formula. In a homicide case the prosecution may satisfy the voluntary act, mens rea and causation requirements—and still the defendant may be acquitted due to the defense of self-defense.

As an affirmative defense, the burden of production for self-defense is normally on the defendant. This means that unless there is testimony indicating that defendant's use of force was justified, then no self-defense instruction will be given and its principles should not influence the verdict. Jurisdictions vary as to how much evidence is required to satisfy the burden of production, but often it is said to be enough evidence to raise a reasonable doubt concerning the issue.[2]

Once the burden of production has been satisfied, in most jurisdictions the burden of persuasion falls on the prosecution.[3] This means that to convict, the prosecution must disprove self-defense beyond a reasonable doubt. The fact finder must be convinced that the defendant *did not* honestly and reasonably believe in the necessity of defensive force.

Although self-defense doctrine operates independently from other elements of liability, in many cases the same facts that support self-defense will be relevant to mens rea as well. For example, in a purpose to kill murder case, a defendant may argue that he: (1) he shot with a purpose only to scare or wound, not to kill (a mens rea argument); and that (2) his use of deadly force was based on an honest and reasonable belief in its necessity (a self-defense claim). If successful, the first of these arguments negates proof of purpose to kill, a requirement of some (but certainly not all), homicide offenses. The second of these arguments will be sufficient to acquit regardless of mens rea. (For example, even if defendant acted with purpose to kill, self-defense may justify the killing.)

In murder cases, self-defense arguments frequently pair with provocation claims. The defendant's primary claim will be that he acted in full self-defense and therefore should be acquitted. If that argument fails, however, the defendant

---

2. E.g., Bolin v. State, 297 So.2d 317, 319 (Fla. Ct. App. 1974). See generally Chapter 4 on burdens of proof.

3. E.g., People v. Loggins, 100 Cal. Rptr. 528 (Cal. Ct. App. 1972) (burden of proof on prosecution; Martin v. Ohio, 480 U.S. 228 (1987) (constitutional for state to place the burden of persuasion on self-defense on the defense).

may contend that he acted while actually and reasonably provoked and so should be convicted only of voluntary manslaughter.[4]

Self-defense is a full defense to any crime of direct violence, including murder, manslaughter, any attempts at these offenses, and any form of assault. Some jurisdictions also recognize a doctrine known as imperfect self-defense, which can reduce a murder charge to voluntary manslaughter. This will receive separate attention at the end of the chapter.

The Values of Self-Defense

The essential value behind deadly force self-defense is the right to self-preservation. Whether considered an evolutionary dictate, a principle of natural law, a utilitarian concept, or a principle derived from some other moral source, its core precept is that no human being should have to sacrifice life or essential bodily integrity to an unlawful human threat.

The rules of self-defense are also shaped by another essential value: preserving human life. This means that deadly force should be limited to those situations where there appear to be no reasonable alternatives: the person must either suffer death or great bodily harm or inflict the same upon the threatener. The use of deadly violence in self-defense thus represents a limited exception to the general rule requiring the use of nonviolent, and especially non-deadly, means for resolving disputes.

These are the primary, but not the only values informing self-defense rules. We will see, particularly with respect to the retreat rule, that self-defense implicates notions of honor and courage. Some believe that honor, perhaps particularly male honor, demands the ability to stand one's ground against unlawful threat, even at the cost of deadly violence.

The rules of self-defense also implicate the value of courage, which here means the ability to keep one's head and assess threat rationally, even in emergency situations. These considerations inform the reasonableness requirement.

The requirement of reasonableness brings us to issues of emotional self-control reminiscent of those considered in provocation. We saw in Chapter 10 that provocation requires that defendant's passion, usually anger, be reason-

---

4. This discussion assumes a purpose to kill theory of either murder and manslaughter. Where the defendant is charged with an unintentional homicide, as in depraved heart murder or involuntary manslaughter, the line between mens rea analysis and self-defense may blur, because the justification aspect of recklessness and negligence will largely overlap with the reasonableness analysis of self-defense.

able to secure mitigation.[5] Self-defense requires that the defendant's perception of threat, or in emotional terms, defendant's fear, be reasonable in order to gain acquittal. Simply experiencing strong fear is insufficient.

Some have argued against requiring reasonable fear, contending that self-defense should be subjective, depending entirely on the individual's experience of threat. A very few courts have agreed, effectively eliminating any objective standard of reasonableness and threat assessment. But this position is very much a minority one, and appears primarily in cases where the defendant may have a special claim to sympathy.[6]

Basic Elements of Self-Defense

Self-defense generally is based on the principle that force (usually meaning violence) is lawful when used by a person who reasonably perceives it to be necessary to preserve life, bodily integrity or property rights. The force used must be proportional to the threat; as a result, deadly force is justified only in response to deadly threats.

The elements of self-defense may be broken down into two general parts which must then be further subdivided.

The defendant must:

(1) (a) honestly and
    (b) reasonably believe that he or she faces a threat that is
(2) (a) imminent and
    (b) unlawful, and that
    (c) the force used in response was necessary/proportionate to the threat.

The requirements of honest and reasonable belief apply to the three elements of imminence, unlawfulness, and necessity/proportionality.

---

5. Fear and anger of course have a close psychological relationship. Fear often converts into anger. Under law they are treated differently. Provocation usually concerns anger, though fear can contribute to the defendant's reasonable passion. See Chapter 10. Self-defense is quintessentially about threat and therefore involves fear.

6. E.g., State v. Leidholm, 334 N.W.2d 811 (ND 1983) (reasonableness includes defendant's psychological traits);. C.f. People v. Goetz, 497 N.E.2d 41, 47–50 (NY 1986) (rejecting defendant's "reasonable to him" reading of self-defense).

Honest and Reasonable Belief

Assessment of self-defense begins with its subjective element: the honesty of defendant's belief in a particular threat. Many self-defense cases turn on this element. Typically the prosecution argues that the defendant committed an act of violent aggression motivated by animosity toward the victim, rather than an action to defend against a perceived threat. The defense meanwhile emphasizes facts that indicate defendant used force only in response to a threat posed by the victim.

Although deciding this credibility question is often critical to self-defense — the claim will be denied if the jury believes defendant was acting out of aggression rather than fear — in law the hard cases turn on the second element: reasonableness. The fact finder must undertake an objective, retrospective assessment of the threat posed by the victim. Regardless of how the defendant perceived the situation, was it reasonable for a person in the defendant's situation to believe that the victim posed an imminent, unlawful, threat of deadly force?

Imminent Threat

Force may be used in self-defense only to thwart an imminent threat. As always in self-defense, the concept comes from necessity. Violence is not necessary except to deal with emergency situations, when there is no time to explore alternative solutions to conflict. Action must be taken *right away.*

The most common problems with imminence involve threats of future, but not immediate harm. The law distinguishes between a person who aims a gun at another, saying "I'm going to kill you," and the same person, presently unarmed, who says that "Real soon I'm going to get my gun and kill you." Both of these present threats of unlawful, deadly force, but only the first represents an imminent threat. As to the latter, self-defense law holds that the possibility of police intervention or other precautions mean that there are lawful, nonviolent means of preserving life. Deadly force is not necessary at that time.

The imminence requirement recognizes that many more threats are made than are carried out. The strict time limitation tends to confine the doctrine's application to the most dangerous threats, those that appear on the verge of execution. This limitation also helps prevent self-defense from becoming a general excuse for preemptive attacks on possibly threatening individuals. Without a strict imminence requirement, cases of self-defense might become indistinguishable from ordinary acts of aggression against persons with whom the individual has previously tangled.

The imminence requirement also limits self-defense in another sense, a sense more favorable to users of force. It only applies to the actual confrontation where force was used. It does not constitute a general requirement of conflict-avoidance. Individuals facing future (i.e. non-imminent) threats need not change their lives in order to avoid future conflicts. Prudence may dictate avoidance, but the law does not. If a bully warns that a reappearance in "his" neighborhood will be punished with death, the recipient of the threat need not avoid the neighborhood, assuming no other legal prohibition exists. Bullies do not make law.

We will see that the imminence requirement may raise particular problems in some domestic violence situations where future violence may be predicted with some accuracy but not its actual timing.

Unlawful Threat

To justify self-defense, the threatened force must appear unlawful. In the context of deadly force, this is rarely an issue because there are few instances where deadly force threats could be lawful. Nevertheless, they do exist. If a police officer, in the course of making an arrest for a violent felony threatens to shoot a suspect to effect capture, this use of force is lawful. The person being arrested has no right to respond with deadly force, even though the threat to his life may be both imminent and real.

Although the courts do not always make this clear, the lawfulness element is subject to reasonableness analysis. A person is entitled to self-defense to thwart a threat reasonably believed to be unlawful. In other words, mistakes are permitted—if reasonable. Therefore, if men break into a house in the early morning hours wearing dark clothes, brandishing guns and threatening to shoot—and do not identify themselves—an occupant may reasonably believe she faces imminent and unlawful deadly force and use deadly force in response. Self-defense provides a justification even if it turns out that the intruders were police officers executing a search warrant. (As is often true with self-defense, the main controversy will be fact-centered: on these facts, was the defendant truly mistaken about intruder identity? If so, would a reasonable person have been mistaken?)

The unlawfulness element requires analysis of aggression. The person at fault in starting the conflict is generally disqualified from claiming self-defense thereafter. Related issues will be explored in a subsequent section on aggressors.

Proportionality/Necessity of Responsive Force

Force used in self-defense must be proportionate to the threat faced. To be necessary, the user of deadly force must reasonably believe that he or she faces deadly force; a person who reasonably perceives a non-deadly force may only respond to that threat with non-deadly force.

Also falling under this element is the so-called retreat rule, which will receive separate discussion below. A minority of jurisdictions require that persons otherwise entitled to self-defense may not use deadly force in self-defense if they know of a clear, safe avenue of retreat.

Reckless or Negligent Direction of Defensive Force

The law of self-defense addresses violence used against a person making an unlawful threat, but what happens if this "defensive" violence claims an innocent victim? Facing a pointed gun in a crowded setting, a person entitled to use deadly force in self-defense may end up wounding or killing persons other than the would-be shooter. Real-life violence is not like in the movies; it tends to be messy, with third parties often caught in the crossfire. Does the authorized user of defensive force have any criminal liability for misdirected violence that injures or kills an innocent person?

Some courts have intimated that self-defense provides immunity from liability regardless of who is killed or wounded.[7] But this seems extreme. Instead we might ask whether, *considering the emergency situation*, the defendant's use of defensive force was reckless or negligent. If so, the individual should be convicted of a reckless or negligence offense. In practice, few will be convicted under this standard, because where an individual honestly and reasonably believes he or she faces a deadly threat, the individual experiences the highest possible degree of stress, and therefore, through no personal fault, is prone to make mistakes in response. As a result, most decision makers will judge incidents of misdirected defensive force to be the excusable result of extraordinary stress rather than manifestations of the kind of culpable carelessness that reckless or negligent offenses require.

Deadly Force v. Nondeadly Force

Deadly force is force that an individual uses with purpose to inflict death or serious bodily injury, or with awareness that it is likely to cause death or serious bodily injury.[8] This definition applies to both threats of force and to the force used in response.

---

7. Commonwealth v. Fowlin, 710 A.2d 1130 (Pa. 1998); People v. Adams, 291 N.E.2d 54, 55–6 (Ill. 1972) (although recognizing that the rule is not absolute).
8. MPC sec. 3.04 (2) (b) and sec 3.11(2) (defining deadly force aggression as "force which the actor uses with the purpose of causing or which he knows to create a substantial risk of causing death or serious bodily harm.").

In assessing deadly force, the threat must always be assessed in context. Consider the deadly weapon. Generally where a deadly weapon is used, deadly force is threatened. But its mere appearance on the crime scene may not be enough. A person who possesses a gun or knife but neither uses nor makes reference to it will probably not be found to have acted with purpose to inflict death or serious bodily injury. Similarly, the display of a gun or knife will be insufficient where the display is a defensive gesture, indicating only that deadly force might be deployed should the other party persist with the conflict. Conversely, words and actions that indicate the presence of a deadly weapon and intent to use it may be sufficient even if no weapon exists. A man who reaches into his jacket as if for a gun, while declaring his immediate intention to shoot, indicates an intent to cause death or serious bodily injury and therefore threatens deadly force.

Similar permutations arise with apparently non-deadly force. Normally a punch or kick will be categorized as non-deadly force. Punches or kicks delivered against a highly vulnerable person, such as an elderly man or woman, might be deadly force, however. Punches or kicks by a professional boxer or fighter delivered against one untrained in the martial arts might also constitute deadly force.

In assessing threats of deadly force for purposes of self-defense, serious bodily injury includes any threat to basic bodily integrity, including sexual assault or kidnapping and often other forcible felonies such as armed robbery. These crimes present great risks of harm to the person, both physical and psychological. As a result, they merit treatment at the same level of risk as other, more obviously deadly, threats.

Assessing Honesty and Reasonableness, Part One

Finally we are ready to get down to cases, to the analysis of facts that may or may not support self-defense.

> Jerome has modest ambitions. He just wants to graduate high school, find a girl and a job. But mostly he wants to graduate. To do that, he must survive his junior and senior years.
>
> Jerome recently moved in with his grandmother when a job transfer took his mother to another state. His grandmother lives in a part of the city that was once majority African American, but is now predominantly Latino. There are major crime problems in the neighborhood, and conflict between African American and Latino gangs.

Jerome is African American and has sometimes hung out with kids in an African American gang, but is not a gang member. He is tall (6 foot 2), but skinny and a poor fighter.

To get to school, Jerome must walk through territory controlled by the 4th Street gang. Avoiding their territory would take an additional 45 minutes each way. On several occasions Jerome is accosted by 4th Street gang members who shout racial epithets and promise to kill him if they find him in their neighborhood again. Jerome starts carrying a knife for protection.

Coming home one night in the winter when it is dark, Jerome walks down a narrow alley behind a fast food restaurant and is surprised by a young 4th Street gang member, Juan. Juan shoves him against a concrete block wall, causing Jerome to hit his head. Jerome pulls out his knife and swings it in Juan's direction. He inflicts several superficial wounds, but his final swing connects with Juan's neck. The knife blade severs Juan's carotid artery, a fatal injury.

Jerome is arrested and charged with murder. Forensic investigation of the scene indicates that the encounter was likely a surprise to each young man, and that Juan probably shoved Jerome to make his own escape. Jerome, age 16, was 6 inches taller and 30 pounds heavier than Juan, age 15. Juan, however, had a significant criminal record including crimes of violence, and went by the street name of Loco, or crazy, because of his reputation for violence.

Jerome tells police that he used the knife because "I knew the guy was 4th Street and I figured he was carrying [i.e., was armed] and probably there were others around. And these bangers [gang members], they don't care, they'll kill you for just looking at them wrong. I thought maybe he was going for something in his pants. Like a gun. I thought I was gonna die." In response to later questioning, Jerome admits that he was tired of being harassed, and had told a friend that he "wasn't going to take any more shit from anybody."

Despite Jerome's account, he is charged with Juan's murder. What are Jerome's chances for acquittal based on self-defense?

The first question is whether Jerome is telling the truth about fearing for his life. This is the honesty component of self-defense. Did he in fact believe that Juan was threatening him with deadly force? Here the prosecution will emphasize indications that Jerome acted aggressively and out of anger, rather than defensively, and out of fear. He was older, larger and heavier than the victim, never saw any weapon or received any specific threat on the occasion.

He was angry at his prior harassment, and may well have armed himself in order to take advantage of a situation just like this.

The defense will point to the prior threats against Jerome, his noninvolvement in gangs, and the inherent danger of encountering a member of a hostile gang in an isolated location, especially a gang member who immediately launched a violent attack. The defense will argue that anyone in Jerome's situation would have felt very fearful, making his account of great fear entirely credible.

Assuming that Jerome did fear for his life, then the major question is the reasonableness of that fear. Was it reasonable for him to believe that Juan threatened imminent, unlawful death or serious bodily injury? Unlawfulness will not be an issue here, because any threat posed by Juan was clearly unlawful. Jerome had done nothing to Juan. Nor is imminence likely to be a major issue. The fight happened suddenly and if Juan threatened deadly force following the shove in a dark alley, the threat was imminent. But there is a real question about whether Jerome reasonably perceived a threat of *deadly* force at that point.

The prosecution will return to many of the facts previously discussed with respect to honesty to argue that Jerome did not reasonably fear a deadly threat. There were no verbal threats, no clear evidence of a weapon, and although Juan did use violence against Jerome, the pushing against the wall was clearly non-deadly force. Jerome was entitled to use non-deadly force in response, but in fact used disproportionate deadly force (knife slashing) to combat a non-deadly threat. As an older, larger, heavier person, Jerome could not reasonably fear that Juan would threaten his life without the use of a deadly weapon and there was no indication that Juan possessed or was about to use such a weapon. So argues the prosecution.

The defense will also return to many of the facts cited previously, arguing that any reasonable person in Jerome's situation, having been previously threatened by members of the 4th Street gang, and now being suddenly attacked by a gang member, would believe that Juan might well be armed and about to launch a fatal attack. The defense will contend that Jerome's belief that Juan was moving for something at his waist, as if for a gun, makes reasonable his perception of deadly threat. It is unfair to require perfect threat assessment from someone in such a high stress, emergency situation.

Any history of conflict involving the defendant and victim will be important to self-defense assessments. In this case, we have no indication that Juan personally threatened Jerome previously, only that members of his gang had threatened Jerome. Although a history of direct personal conflict would be more salient on self-defense, the history of past gang threats does tend to bolster the reasonableness of his Jerome's belief that gang member Juan threatened deadly force in the alley.

A critical issue in the case will be the admissibility of evidence concerning Juan's personal history of and reputation for violence. There is no indication that Jerome was aware of this background. If he had been, then its significance would be clear, because it would give Jerome more reason to fear Juan. Even without such knowledge, though, courts often allow general reputation for violence evidence on the grounds that it provides some indications of propensity for violence relevant to self-defense issues. Therefore, it is possible that Juan's prior criminal record for violence and street reputation might be admissible here.[9]

As in many self-defense cases, resolution of self-defense issues may depend on character assessment. The prosecution and the defense will fight for juror hearts and minds over who is the good guy here and who the bad guy. (See accompanying sidebar) Although an inevitable part of self-defense, the emotionality of this contest raises the possibility that jurors might be influenced by nonlegal, unconscious influences such as race or appearance. Unfortunately these sometimes contribute to intuitive assessments of character and threat, independent of the facts of the case.

Finally, one practical point in the defense's favor here is the reluctance of juries to second-guess the use of force by otherwise law-abiding persons in emergency situations. If Jerome truly feared for his life, given that he had been threatened previously, many jurors will be hard-pressed to declare his fear unreasonable even if in retrospect it appears excessive. Or, to speak more precisely in terms of the burden of proof, assuming that the defense's burden of going forward has been met (almost certainly true here) and that the prosecution has the burden of persuasion, the prosecution will have real difficulty proving beyond a reasonable doubt that Jerome *did not* honestly and reasonably fear an imminent and unlawful threat of deadly force from Juan.

Good Guys and Bad Guys and Self Defense

All persons are equally worthy in the eyes of the criminal law. Whether the defendant is homeless or a chief executive officer, a drug dealer or a doctor, should not matter to the assertion of self-defense. Nor should the race, gender, or other status of the deceased change our valuation of the victim's life. But in the courtroom, especially in a jury trial, these matters can matter a great deal.

---

9. E.g., U.S. v. Emeron Taken Alive, 262 F.3d 711 (8th Cir. 2001). Meanwhile, Jerome might seek to admit reputational evidence on his own behalf in the form of character evidence. Witnesses may testify to his reputation in the community for truth telling and nonviolence, which may assist jurors in assessing his credibility and the likelihood that his use of violence against Juan was defensive rather than aggressive.

> *Assertions of self-defense in homicide cases often inspire an emotional contest over who should be considered the good guy and who the bad guy in the case. This emotional contest often appears to follow the law of self-defense, but not always. Sometimes legal conclusions just rationalize emotional reactions.*
>
> *As we have seen, self-defense claims require that decision makers assess the defendant's emotions and emotional control. In so doing, decision makers often ask themselves what they would have felt or done in the same situation. This makes the decision inevitably personal in some respect.*
>
> *Some commentators worry that the emotionality of self-defense issues may open the door to race and gender bias in decision making. Racial identity can contribute to exaggerated perceptions of threat. Ideas about gender can also affect assessment of threat and response to violence. Women are often perceived as essentially nonviolent, which means that in cases where a woman kills, her defense must confront a perception that she is unfeminine, which may place her beyond the understanding and sympathies of some decision makers, both male and female.*
>
> *Attorneys may also clash over the basic moral worth of the victim. A victim who is portrayed as a drug dealer, a drunk, or a bully may be found essentially unworthy of decision maker sympathy. As a result, the legal requirements of self-defense may be leniently applied.*
>
> *Just to be clear: the law does not condone bias, but if decision makers are subject to extra-legal emotional influences, trial lawyers need to take those influences seriously.[10]*

Assessing Honesty and Reasonableness, Part Two: Domestic Violence, Syndrome Evidence and Self-Defense Claims

The most controversial court decisions in the area of self-defense in the last 30 years have concerned its use in situations of domestic violence. The most

---

10. See Jody Armour, *Negrophobia and Reasonable Racism: The Hidden Costs of Being Black in America* (1997).

common scenarios involve persons abused by their intimate partners, usually women abused by boyfriends or husbands, who respond to that abuse with deadly force. Although prosecutors may decline to file charges based on evidence of self-defense, often such claims must be litigated in a criminal trial, especially if the partner was killed.

The law's treatment of such cases has raised a number of issues. Some argue that basic self-defense doctrine needs reform to accommodate the particular dynamics of these cases, both in the definition of reasonableness and with respect to the imminence requirement. Most legal controversies have centered on the use of expert testimony, especially testimony about battered woman's syndrome, or BWS.

Although recognition of domestic violence as a public policy problem in the United States goes back hundreds of years, current appreciation for the problem is fundamentally different in both depth and breadth. Some of this new appreciation may be traced to developments in social science. Social scientists have studied patterns of partner abuse to establish its prevalence, effects, standard features and dynamics. The best known of this work in the legal field is the formulation of the Battered Woman's Syndrome by Lenore Walker in the 1970s.[11] After initially skeptical treatment by courts, virtually all jurisdictions today accept the scientific validity of BWS and its potential use in resolving self-defense claims. As a result, testimony by experts on BWS in cases involving domestic violence has become common.

BWS is fundamentally an explanation of human behavior. It explains why persons persist in an intimate relationship with an abusive partner. In its original formulation, it held that some individuals experience a cycle of tension-building, violent abuse and reconciliation, that on repetition leads to a form of learned helplessness that helps explain the victim's inability to leave the abuser. Individuals may be predisposed to BWS by past experience, gender views and personality traits.

Testimony by an expert concerning BWS can assist fact finders by educating them concerning common patterns of violence in intimate relations. In particular, it explains why many persons who experience significant violence from a partner nevertheless remain in the relationship. This may cause the decision maker to view the defendant's testimony differently. For example, if she testifies that she suffered repeated, severe beatings from her husband (the homicide victim) in the past, many might question this, saying: Surely the relationship could not have been *that* bad, or she would have left him. The ordinary

---

11. *The Battered Woman* (1979).

presumption is that no modern, self-respecting woman would stay with a se-riously abusive mate. On learning that this pattern of violence in relationships is actually fairly common, decision makers may find the defendant's testimony about her partner's abuse more credible.

Expert testimony may also assist decision makers in assessing the reason-ableness of the threat faced by the defendant. The concept here is that abuse victims, by virtue of their past abuse experience, are better able to predict fu-ture violence than others might be in the same situation.[12] The difficulty here is to determine why the *syndrome* determination is important on this point. Clearly, prior incidents of violence between the parties are, and always have been, rel-evant to self-defense. In addition, testimony concerning common character-istics of abusers and their victims may give fact finders important insights into what happened in the case at hand. But the syndrome's mix of psychological and social explanation can make independent assessment of reasonableness difficult for legal decision makers.[13]

Because of these concerns, some courts permit BWS evidence to be con-sidered only on the subjective element of self-defense: whether the defendant actually feared imminent death or great bodily harm. In such jurisdictions ju-ries should not consider syndrome evidence with respect to the reasonable-ness of defendant's fear.[14]

In many jurisdictions, however, BWS may be considered not only with re-spect to honesty of belief in threat but also its reasonableness. While courts here maintain that the reasonableness standard itself does not change, and therefore the standard is *not* a reasonable person with BWS, the syndrome may nevertheless help in the assessment of reasonableness.[15] Courts specifically note that BWS evidence may support the accuracy of defendant's assessment of

---

12. Here, as elsewhere in self-defense, past experience evidence is admissible on the ground that experience may correlate with more accurate threat assessment. See People v. Goetz, 497 N.E.2d 41, 52–53 (NY 1986). With additional experience comes additional in-sight—we generally believe. Psychology teaches that experience can produce the opposite effect, however. Past traumatic experience can make a person hypersensitive, raising the question of whether such hypersensitivity violates the normative standard of reasonableness, or whether this trait should be accommodated on grounds of individual fairness—that heightened sensitivity was developed through no fault of the individual.

13. As originally presented, traits of the person with BWS include traditional gender views, passivity and learned helplessness. See State v. Kelly, 478 A.2d 364, 371–73 (N.J. 1984).

14. State v. Richardson, 525 N.W.2d 378, 382–83 (Wis. Ct. App.1994).

15. E.g., State v. Kelly, 478 A.2d 364 , 377 (NJ 1984); People v. Humphrey, 921 P.2d 1, 2 (Cal. 1996); Boykins v. State, 995 P.2d 474, 478–79 (Nev. 2000).

threat. Beyond this, the distinction between proper and improper use of the evidence with respect to reasonableness is hard to explain.[16]

Mildred and Alfred have been together for eight tumultuous years. On their first date, setting the tone for the relationship, Alfred pulled the barstool out from under Mildred, sending her crashing to the floor following a sharp remark she made. Somehow he made it up to her, though, and they were soon married. Alfred is an angry man, who demands total dedication and loyalty from his wife, and often finds her wanting. He dominates their relationship, controlling all economic assets and deciding all social engagements. He is often verbally abusive, and on occasion physically violent. Once, three years previously, he broke two of Mildred's ribs by pushing her down the stairs.

Mildred has left Alfred on three different occasions, but has always returned, largely as a result of heartfelt promises by Alfred to mend his ways. Following reconciliations, the couple gets along well for a period of time, but eventually Alfred resumes verbal and physical abuse.

Recently, relations between the couple have worsened. Alfred bitterly complains about Mildred's refusal to do housework, saying that the house is a "total pig pen." She tells him to pick up after himself. She complains bitterly about the money he spends on online gambling and pornography.

On a Saturday night after Alfred has been drinking most of the day, Alfred states that he is going to go online and "make a million dollars and be free of her forever." Mildred confronts Alfred in the bedroom where his computer is, demanding that he stop spending money online, that he is going to ruin them financially. Alfred becomes furious. He gets up and confronts her, fists clenched, stating that if she doesn't shut up, "I'll kick your fucking face in."

Mildred turns around and gets Alfred's revolver from the bedside table. She holds it at her side, the gun barrel pointing down. Alfred picks up a metal bedside lamp as if to use it as a weapon and says: "Better shoot me now, because otherwise you're dead." Mildred raises the gun, then hesitates. Alfred taunts her. "You'll never pull the trig-

---

16. Explanations in both appellate decisions and jury instructions about the limits of reasonableness are usually made in abstract terms, without concrete examples to illustrate. For example, CALJIC 9.35.1 seeks to guide jurors by making a distinction between what is reasonable and what is understandable. "An act which appears to be an understandable response is not necessarily an act that is reasonable under the circumstances."

ger. You don't have the guts." She proves him wrong with four shots to the chest, killing him. She calls 911 and reports that she has killed her husband.

Mildred is charged with the purpose to kill murder of Alfred. The defense retains an expert who is prepared to testify, based on an interview and examination of the police reports, that Mildred suffers from BWS. The defense plans to use this evidence to show that Mildred honestly and reasonably feared for her life in her final confrontation with Alfred.

Assuming that Mildred acted with purpose to kill, what are her chances of acquittal on a claim of self-defense?

On these facts, Mildred can argue self-defense regardless of BWS evidence. She will say that she faced a direct threat of imminent and unlawful deadly force based on Alfred's clenched fists and statement that he will "kick your ... face in", as well as his subsequent threat with the lamp and words: "Better shoot me now, because otherwise you're dead." These were issued by a man who had repeatedly inflicted serious violence upon her.

The prior history of violence by Alfred against Mildred will make more credible her claim that she believed that he was threatening her life with the lamp as opposed to lesser violence or just making verbal threats. This prior history with Alfred means that Mildred had particular experience with Alfred's threats and therefore may be more accurate in determining their severity than another person would. All this is based on their particular history, without reference to BWS testimony.

BWS testimony, in jurisdictions where it is admissible on both honesty and reasonableness of threat, would support self-defense along essentially identical lines. By relating Mildred's experience of abuse to that of many other persons, the expert may teach the fact finder that what otherwise could seem incredible about Mildred's account—that her longtime partner was also a longtime abuser—is in fact relatively common and therefore credible. Courts have also held that BWS may correlate with accuracy of violence prediction, a factor that could bolster the reasonableness of Mildred's judgment of threat.

Of course the prosecution will also have something to say about Mildred's claim of self-defense. At the time of the final confrontation, Alfred had only a bedside lamp in his hand. Mildred had the gun. Given that the gun was a far more powerful weapon, this suggests that he had more to fear from her than vice versa. The prosecution will also argue that the deadly shots came in response not to Alfred's threats to Mildred's life, but to Alfred's taunts that she lacked the guts to shoot. This might suggest a shooting in anger rather than in honest and reasonable fear as required for self-defense.

The bottom line here is that the jury's decision about Mildred's alleged honest and reasonable fear will likely to turn on its assessment of Mildred and Alfred and their relational history. This assessment may be influenced by expert BWS testimony, which may encourage a jury to take more seriously Mildred's account than it might otherwise. In this respect BWS testimony may assist the defense, but it is hard to say exactly what impact it will have, because it constitutes just one part of the evidence to be considered.

Science Meets Law, Again—But This Time Receives a Warm Welcome: The Curious Case of BWS

Outside of insanity, the law treats with great skepticism medical-scientific accounts of human behavior offered on questions of individual responsibility. Actually, that understates the point. Most such accounts are rejected entirely. Explanation for the dysfunctional behavior of otherwise rational persons simply does not provide any mitigation or excuse in law. Experts on psychopathy or addiction, on disorders such as pedophilia or kleptomania or compulsive gambling, as well as experts on many other syndromes that explain unusual behavior, are generally turned away when they appear to testify concerning criminal liability. Their testimony is rarely considered in sentencing. Except for Battered Woman Syndrome.

BWS, as it is commonly known, has won a special place in American criminal law. Both legislation and judicial decisions mandate its relevance to self-defense, at least where a factual predicate is laid, ensuring that social science experts may testify about this syndrome to assist juries in many self-defense cases. This testimony is relevant not just to the honesty of fear in many jurisdictions but also to the reasonableness of threat perception. Scientific experts provide behavioral insights relevant to a normative assessment of responsibility in reasonableness. Why? Why does BWS get such privileged treatment in the law?

One possibility is that the science here is especially strong, that the studies on BWS are more extensive and more scientifically persuasive than those for other disorders. That does not appear to be the case. Original accounts of BWS have come under serious scientific criticism, especially its originally central concept of learned helplessness.[17]

---

17. Donald L. Faigman, Note, The Battered Woman's Syndrome and Self-defense: A Legal and Empirical Dissent, 72 Va. L. Rev. 619 (1986); Robert F. Schopp, Barbara J. Sturgis & Megan Sullivan, Battered Woman's Syndrome, Expert Testimony, and the Distinction Between Justification and Excuse, [1994] U. Ill. L. Rev. 45.

> *Perhaps the courtroom success of BWS is due to the fact that, unlike other scientific accounts of human behavior, BWS speaks directly to responsibility issues. But this does not appear true either. The syndrome explains behavior rather than justifies or excuses it. Similar data and methods can be used to construct a batterer's syndrome that would explain why some individuals repeatedly engage in abusive conduct in intimate relations. Presumably few would believe such a syndrome would support a justification or excuse. The point is that while expert testimony on domestic violence may help factfinders understand common patterns of such violence, arguably relevant to factual issues in the case at hand, such testimony might be more helpful to legal decision makers if presented without the potential science v. morals problems inherent in the syndrome label.[18]*
>
> *The politics of criminal justice supply the best explanation for the warm welcome given BWS. As part of a fundamental reconsideration of gender relations, the prevalence of domestic violence, like rape, became a significant political issue. As with rape, this presented a crime issue on which liberals and conservatives could agree. And, as with rape, there was a serious problem in the courtroom. Women who lived with terrifying abuse and then killed their abusers were often sentenced to long prison terms for murder, with little appreciation for the threats they had faced. BWS testimony has contributed to a much better appreciation for the prevalence, viciousness and severity of domestic violence.*
>
> *The challenge for modern law here is that of universality. Can we devise rules that are truly universal, meaning applicable to all similar situations in the criminal law? Why consider syndrome evidence relevant to reasonableness here if we are not willing to do so elsewhere? Why rely on syndrome evidence that emphasizes the passivity of female victims—their inability to act for themselves—when all the rest of law and culture trends in the other direction?[19] Finally, if current law does not handle certain kinds of homicides arising out of domestic violence well—particularly those where there is not a clearly imminent threat—does the problem lie primarily in self-defense law, or in other doctrines, such as provocation?*

In cases where the use of force does not come in an immediately threatening situation, BWS testimony has the potential to change the outcome of the case.

---

18. See Alafair Burke, Rational Actors, Self-Defense and Duress: Making Sense, Not Syndromes Out of the Battered Woman, 81 N.C. L. Rev. 211 (2002); Robert P. Mosteller, Syndromes and Politics in Criminal Trials and Evidence Law, 46 Duke L. J. 461 (1996).

19. See Anne M. Coughlin, Excusing Women, 82 Cal. L. Rev. 1 (1994).

Evie, age 22 and Bud, age 35, have been boyfriend and girlfriend for three years, ever since Bud gave her her first hit of methamphetamine. Drugs are their main common interest. When they argue, each frequently resorts to hitting or other violence. Bud's violence is much more severe than Evie's, however. At different times he has threatened her with a knife, a gun, and on one occasion, sexually assaulted her.

The two live in a dilapidated, isolated farmhouse that Bud inherited from his grandfather. Once when Evie tried to run away, he tracked her down, dragged her back and after tying her to a chair, subjected her to prolonged torture by forcing soda up her nose with a straw, a technique that he learned on a cable television show about police use of torture in other countries. There is a phone in the house, but Evie knows that police response to the location can take hours, if they respond at all.

Bud becomes very angry when he learns that Evie has smoked the last of his meth. He slaps her and says that she is facing some "serious, serious shit." He has said many times that he will kill anyone who messes with his drugs. He lies down on a couch, drinks a beer and falls asleep.

Evie takes a fire iron (a long iron rod with a blunt hook at the end for moving logs in a fireplace) and strikes Bud with it in the head numerous times, then flees the house in Bud's car. Although severely injured, Bud manages to call 911 and is rushed to the hospital. He dies from his injuries two days later.

Evie is arrested in another state when she uses one of Bud's credit cards to buy herself a designer label dress. She says that she never reported what happened because she did not think anyone would believe her, and she thought that Bud was dead "so it didn't matter."

The prosecution believes that Evie killed Bud in an act of aggression, perhaps as retaliation for past wrongs, but also to steal Bud's car, credit cards and cash.

Evie will testify that based on her past experience with Bud and the "look in his eye," when he spoke his last words, that she was sure that he was going to kill her—and probably that very day—unless she did something to stop him. A defense expert will testify that Evie fits battered woman's syndrome.

In a jurisdiction that permits BWS syndrome evidence to be considered for both the honesty and reasonableness of defendant's fear, what are Evie's chances of a successful self-defense claim?

The central controversy in this case is Evie's motive for killing. Did Evie kill Bud for material benefit and retaliation for past wrongs, or did she truly act in defense of her own life? In this case particularly, BWS testimony may be important to Evie's credibility. What otherwise would look like a case of entirely self-interested venial conduct (that is, all about drugs and money) might instead be seen as a desperate defense against a lethal abuser. Although her subsequent conduct would not indicate this, expert testimony about the commonality of the kind of abuse that Evie suffered would tend to bolster her account of the violence that she says Bud inflicted on her.

Assuming we believe Evie's account of what happened between her and Bud, and we believe that she honestly feared for her life when she fatally attacked him, there is a major question with respect to the reasonableness of her fear, and especially reasonableness with respect to the imminence of a fatal attack. Did she honestly and reasonably believe that Bud posed an immediate threat to her life? The case appears to fall into a particularly difficult category of cases where the threat of violence is not literally imminent, but appears virtually inevitable *and* the individual's only effective response is immediate deadly force. If the would-be defender waits until the threat becomes imminent, the opportunity for an effective defense will be gone.

The prosecution would argue that the law's dictate is clear here: no reasonable person would believe that an unarmed man sleeping on a couch represents an imminent threat of deadly force regardless of what he may have said. There are too many other things that Evie could have done to avoid this attack for us to say, as a matter of law, that her use of violence was truly necessary. She did not *reasonably* believe in an imminent fatal attack.

The defense will argue that Evie reasonably believed that a fatal attack was imminent, relying especially on the notion that BWS testimony may bolster an individual's accuracy in violence prediction. Will this succeed? While a sleeping man would not appear to be an imminent threat, the relevance of syndrome evidence to the reasonableness of Evie's fear may give jurors the opportunity, should they be so inclined, to give Evie the benefit of the doubt on imminence.

When Self Defense Fails: Imperfect Self-Defense and Provocation

If self-defense does not succeed in Evie's case, she may have arguments for a conviction of voluntary manslaughter rather than murder. To preview the discussion that closes this chapter, if Evie honestly but unreasonably believed that she faced imminent deadly force from Bud, then in some jurisdictions the doctrine of imperfect self-defense would produce a voluntary manslaughter verdict.

Evie might also argue provocation to achieve the same result. Bud's past attacks, combined with his most recent threat arguably provoked in her great fear and anger, a state of passion representing actual and reasonable provocation. As a result she might be convicted of voluntary manslaughter, not murder.[20]

The Retreat Rule

In some U.S. jurisdictions, the use of deadly force in self-defense is limited by the so-called retreat rule. This holds that a person may not use deadly force to repel an unlawful threat of deadly force if that person is aware of a safe avenue of retreat from the threat. Retreat considerations come under the necessity/proportionate response element of the self-defense rule.[21]

It has three prerequisites, or trigger requirements. It applies only to:

(1) an innocent party facing a deadly threat;
(2) outside the home; and
(3) when the innocent party wishes to use deadly force in response.

The retreat rule does not apply to an individual who is at fault in starting the violent conflict. The rights of so-called aggressors to self-defense are treated in a separate section below.

The retreat rule generally does not apply within the home. Although some jurisdictions make an exception for co-dwellers of a residence, most hold that a resident need not retreat from a deadly threat in the home, even if aware of a completely safe avenue of retreat.

Finally, the retreat rule does not apply if the innocent party uses only non-deadly force. All jurisdictions maintain that a person can meet an unlawful threat of force with non-deadly force regardless of retreat opportunities. This means that if an individual faces a deadly threat and chooses, for whatever reason, to respond only with non-deadly force, the individual may wait for the clash to occur, regardless of retreat opportunity.

Even with all three preconditions met, the retreat rule will not apply in many situations because of its strict requirement of a safe retreat opportunity. A person need not retreat before using deadly force unless the individual *knows*

---

20. The cooling off period requirement of the traditional provocation rule can be an obstacle to such cases, however. See Chapter 10.

21. Retreat also could be considered relevant to the imminence requirement except for the general principle, previously considered, that one need not avoid lawful activities even if they may bring conflict with others.

of a *completely safe* avenue of retreat.[22] That such an avenue existed in fact does not matter if the defendant was not aware of it. Nor is awareness of a probably safe means of escape sufficient; the rule speaks of complete safety.

Despite all these restrictions, an increasing number of jurisdictions, perhaps the majority in the United States find the retreat rule too restrictive and have rejected it. Consistent with the idea that the "true man" (hence its sobriquet: the "true man" rule) does not back down from a confrontation with unlawful threat, here an individual may respond to unlawful deadly force with deadly force regardless of retreat opportunity.[23]

> Dan Marconi and Harold Baines are neighbors in a rural part of the state. Both have retired early to escape the pressures of city life. Marconi is a former firefighter; Baines is a former police officer. Both are very protective of their properties. And virtually upon first meeting, each suspects the other of misconduct. A series of accusations, miscommunications, and deliberate reprisals fan suspicions into hatred. Among their long-standing grievances is Marconi's suspicion that Baines's New Age compost heap is the source of a rodent infestation and Baines' conviction that Marconi is dumping oil and other toxics from his auto repair projects into the stream that runs between their properties. Their long-running personal conflict comes to a head over a dispute concerning a tree growing between their properties, whose branches overhang the public highway.
>
> Marconi wants to cut the tree back in a major way. Baines argues that it should be left exactly as is. The two argue fiercely, and engage in a shoving match. After a brief pause, Marconi punches Baines hard in the midsection. As Baines struggles for breath, Marconi goes to his garage where he retrieves a chainsaw. He comes out of the garage, walks out on to the highway and starts the chainsaw. He begins walking toward Baines and the tree in controversy. At this point Marconi is about 60 feet away from Baines who stands on the highway. Baines's house is approximately 25 feet to Baines's right; his car is 10 feet away. Baines does not move as Marconi slowly approaches. When Marconi is about 15 feet away from him, Baines pulls out his old service re-

---

22. MPC sec. 3.04(b)(ii).

23. "[A] true man who is without fault is not obliged to fly from an assailant." Erwin v. State, 29 Ohio St. 186, 199 (1876). In some jurisdictions, the retreat obligation is included within the reasonableness assessment of self-defense. E.g., Commonwealth v. Toon, 773 N. E.2d 993, 1004–05 (Mass. 2002).

volver (which he is never without) and shoots and kills Marconi. He tells the investigating officers that he believed Marconi was about to attack him with a chainsaw and "kill him like in some god-awful horror movie."

Assuming we believe Baines's account, if he is charged with Marconi's murder, may Baines claim self-defense?

The only significant issue in this case is retreat. Taking Baines at his word, he honestly believed that Marconi was about to attack him with a lethal weapon, to wit, a chainsaw, and if so, had a reasonable belief that when he shot, he faced an imminent and unlawful threat of deadly force. In a "true man" jurisdiction that would be the end of the legal story. In a retreat jurisdiction, however, Baines may face some real difficulty.

The three trigger requirements for the retreat rule may be met here. Baines may be deemed an innocent party with respect to this conflict, meaning that he had full rights of self-defense. This would be so either because, by throwing the first punch, Marconi would be deemed the aggressor throughout, or because the initial non-deadly force incident was complete by the time that Marconi went to get his chainsaw, and returning to the scene of conflict with a chainsaw made Marconi the aggressor in the final confrontation.[24] The incident took place outside the home, on a public highway. And, finally, Baines clearly employed deadly force.

All of which brings us to the critical question: prior to shooting, was Baines aware of a completely safe avenue of retreat from Marconi? Because one can walk or run away from a man on foot with a chainsaw in a way not usually possible from a gun, a retreat obligation might attach here. Certainly his car would seem to offer an entirely safe place of refuge and escape, assuming he was aware of its location. Absent the presence of the car, his house might also represent a completely safe avenue of retreat, though here details about distances between the two parties, their relative foot speeds, and ease of house entry would have to be ascertained.

Aggressors and Self-Defense

Self-defense presumes a moral necessity for the use of force, meaning it envisions an innocent party defending against unlawful threats. It may not

---

24. This is not meant to be a determinative judgment, but represents one possible way of reading the sequence of events under self-defense law.

be used by aggressors, those at fault for starting the violent affray. Aggressors are disqualified from self-defense rights because, considering the entire sequence of events, their use of force may be traced back to their own original wrong.

The main issues with respect to aggressors concern: (1) identifying aggressors; and (2) restoration of self-defense rights to aggressors.

Who is an aggressor? To use that age-old argument of children caught fighting: he or she is the one who started it. The aggressor wrongfully instigates the violent confrontation. Or, as one court put it, the aggressor commits an "affirmative unlawful act reasonably calculated to produce an affray foreboding injurious or fatal consequences."[25]

Often the aggressor is the first one to resort to violence in the dispute, but this is not required. A violent confrontation might be started by words alone, if they are sufficiently threatening or designedly provocative. We do need to distinguish between starting an argument and a fight, however. In most cases, to provoke *violence* requires an act of violence, or a direct and credible threat of violence.

Generally the aggressor is denied rights of self-defense unless he or she takes action to nullify the original aggression and defuse the confrontation. As described further below, restoration of defense rights usually involves both verbal and physical withdrawal from the confrontation.

The most difficult problem involving the aggressors occurs when *both* participants in a conflict are legal wrongdoers. This occurs in the following fashion. The original aggressor starts a non-deadly force fight with another; his opponent responds with deadly force. The original aggressor has done wrong in starting the conflict and the responder has done wrong by employing excessive force in self-defense.

A good example of a two-wrongdoer situation comes from our original case involving Jerome and Juan, the young men who briefly fought in the alley. In that case, Juan was the original aggressor by virtue of shoving Jerome against a concrete wall without any justification. This use of force against Jerome might well be considered non-deadly force, giving Jerome the right to respond in kind. Jerome, however, resorted to a deadly weapon, a knife, which he used to inflict a fatal injury. Assuming that a reasonable person would believe the original threat was not deadly, then Jerome's response is excessive. What then would occur, if Juan had a moment's time to decide on his own response to Jerome's deadly force? What would Juan's legal options be here? The answer, we will see, depends on the jurisdiction.

---

25. United States v. Peterson, 483 F.2d 1222, 1233 (D.C. Cir. 1973).

The Traditional Aggressor Rule

The traditional rule on aggression is that once a person becomes an aggressor by starting a violent conflict, that person remains an aggressor for purposes of self-defense analysis unless the individual takes some significant and usually dramatic action restore his or her self-defense rights. Restoration of rights requires a renunciation of aggression by both words and deeds, a requirement that may be called the obligation of withdrawal. The defendant must communicate a good faith desire to abandon the conflict with no further use of force, as by words and putting up his or her hands. Often critical to proof of a sincere renunciation, though, is physical withdrawal from the conflict. This involves pulling back from the place of confrontation, even at some risk to the individual. To avoid confusion with the retreat rule, we will speak of this as a *withdrawal* from the conflict. Among the critical differences between these rules is that the retreat obligation is predicated on knowledge of a completely safe retreat, where the withdrawal obligation may involve significant risks to the person withdrawing. (See also the sidebar, Avoiding a Language Trap)

Under the traditional rule, unless the aggressor withdraws from the conflict, he or she has no right to use self-defense *even* if the other party wrongfully escalates the fight from non-deadly to deadly force. Should this occur, however, and the original aggressor responds with deadly force, some jurisdictions will consider this offense to be voluntary manslaughter rather than murder. This will be further discussed in the section below on imperfect self-defense.

The basic idea behind the requirement of withdrawal is that because the aggressor is at fault for starting the violent affray, he or she may be required to take some risks, both physical and moral, to defuse the conflict.

The Last Wrongdoer Rule

To avoid the harshness of the aggressor rule in the two-wrongdoer situation, some jurisdictions follow what may be called the last wrongdoer rule.[26] Under this rule, we ask whether the defendant's use of force was an honest and reasonable defensive response to victim's wrongful escalation of the conflict to the level of deadly force. For example:

---

26. The MPC articulates one version in Sec. 3.04(2)(b)(i), excluding from deadly force self defense only those who "with the purpose of causing death or serious bodily harm, provoked the use of force against himself in the same encounter ..."

Angela and Debbie have lived together for three years as lovers. A persistent source of tension in the relationship has been Debbie's insistence that she can still see other people romantically. Debbie returns to the apartment late on the night of Angela's birthday. The two have a discussion in the kitchen that becomes heated when Debbie refuses to say where she has been. Angela starts throwing plates and glasses at Debbie. Debbie is struck in the face by a glass, and becomes very upset. She picks up a large kitchen knife and approaches Angela with the knife pointed at her. Angela takes the handgun that she customarily keeps in her purse and fatally shoots the knife-wielding Debbie.

Assuming that Angela was the aggressor in starting this violent conflict, can she nevertheless claim self-defense in a jurisdiction following the last wrongdoer rule? What about under the traditional common law rules concerning aggressors?

Angela probably can claim self-defense in a last wrongdoer jurisdiction. By throwing the plates and glasses she was likely the original aggressor (and the fact pattern asks us to assume this) which means that Debbie had the right to use proportionate force to protect herself. Since thrown plates and glasses likely constitutes non-deadly force, Debbie could use non-deadly force as necessary in response. Instead, Debbie wrongfully escalates the conflict to a deadly force level by resort to the large kitchen knife, with which she directly threatened Angela.

In the final confrontation between the two, Debbie represents the last wrongdoer, because of her use of excessive force. Angela therefore has the right to use deadly force in her own self-defense. Not that it is likely to be pursued here, but Angela would still be criminally liable for her initial plate and glass assault.

Under the traditional common law aggressor rule, this case looks quite different. As the original aggressor, Angela would have to take significant affirmative action by withdrawing from the conflict before she could regain any right to use force in self-defense. In this situation it means she would likely have to, at a minimum, declare that she no longer wanted to continue the conflict, and likely she would have to make some significant effort to physically withdraw from the confrontation, even if that withdrawal might be dangerous given Debbie's continuing knife threat. We would need to know more about the physical layout of the room and Debbie's proximity, but recall the basic idea that the aggressor's withdrawal may be required even at significant hazard.

Avoiding a Language Trap: Distinguishing Retreat and Withdrawal

The rules of retreat and aggression can be easily confused, because both involve obligations to pull back from violent confrontations. They need

> to be distinguished, however, because both their trigger requirements and the obligations themselves are quite different. One way to avoid linguistic confusion is to limit use of the word retreat to discussions of the retreat rule, and to speak of withdrawal to describe the aggressor's obligations for restoration of self-defense rights.
>
> To summarize: the obligation of retreat applies only to an innocent person's use of deadly force. The obligation of withdrawal applies to an aggressor's use of any force in alleged self-defense. The rule of retreat requires that the individual know of a completely safe avenue of retreat. The withdrawal obligation involves a potentially risky physical and/or verbal withdrawal from the conflict.

Imperfect Self-Defense: Mitigation from Murder to Voluntary Manslaughter

We have seen that self-defense operates as a complete defense. If successful, the defendant should be acquitted and face no penal consequences. If any part of self-defense fails, however, then defendant should be convicted, assuming that the essential elements of the offense are proven. Like most affirmative defenses, self-defense operates as an all or nothing doctrine. It either excuses from liability completely or has no effect. In homicide cases though, some jurisdictions have recognized a mitigation doctrine based on partial proof of self-defense elements, known as imperfect self-defense.

Imperfect self-defense holds that where the defendant honestly but unreasonably believes that he faces an imminent, unlawful threat of deadly force, conviction is merited for voluntary manslaughter rather than murder.[27] The doctrine potentially covers all aspects of reasonableness: imminence, unlawfulness, and proportionality/necessity. It is, however, limited to homicide cases.

A similar doctrine operates to mitigate the harshness of the traditional aggressor rule. If an original aggressor starts a non-deadly fight, and his opponent wrongfully escalates to deadly force, many jurisdictions hold that if the original aggressor, without withdrawing, responds with deadly force, (in a situation where withdrawal was possible) then any subsequent homicide should be treated as voluntary manslaughter and not murder.

---

27. E.g., Faulkner v. State, 458 A.2d 81 (Md. Ct. App. 1983); In re Christian S., 7 Cal.4th 768 (1994).

CHAPTER 19

INTOXICATION

"I was so smashed last night I don't know what I did."

"I've known her all my life, and I've never seen her act that way. Never. It was because she had so much to drink."

"I really wasn't thinking about anything. I was so blitzed I was just doing."

We know that people act differently when intoxicated. Indeed, that often seems to be the point of becoming high or drunk. And, as evidenced by the statements above, we often speak as if the intoxicated are less responsible for their actions than others. But when intoxicated individuals commit serious crimes, our view of responsibility changes. We are reluctant to support full or even partial excuses for those who commit harmful, wrongful acts while intoxicated. Yet the question remains: how culpable are those whose intoxication may have interfered with their understanding at the time of the offense?

The doctrine—really the doctrines—of intoxication involve different dimensions of culpability. Most intoxication arguments involve mens rea and therefore take us back to basic mens rea analysis. Intoxication doctrine in this respect reminds us of what mens rea involves, and especially what it does not. Other arguments, especially about involuntary intoxication, raise issues about individual responsibility. These will preview responsibility issues discussed in the next chapter on insanity.

Evidence that a defendant was intoxicated at the time of the offense raises two legal questions:

(1) Is an intoxication argument *legally available* to the defendant in the case? And—

(2) If available, *will the argument work*, given the facts of the case?

The first question deals with whether the jurisdiction permits defendants to use intoxication evidence to negate mens rea or otherwise excuse from liability. The second question arises only if the first question is answered in the affirmative. Then we must decide whether, considering the facts, defendant's intoxication either negates proof of mens rea or, if the intoxication was involuntary, negates the act requirement or satisfies the responsibility test specific to involuntary intoxication.

The bulk of this chapter, and most law concerning the subject, deals with voluntary intoxication, meaning instances where the person became intoxicated by choice. At the close we will deal with a distinct body of law involving intoxication from the unknowing or coerced ingestion of intoxicating material.

The importance of intoxication as a defense argument can be exaggerated. We will see that in many cases the argument is legally barred. Where it is available, it usually will not work, meaning that it will not persuade the fact finder to acquit based on the facts presented. Finally, even when successful, an intoxication argument normally reduces the level of conviction rather than excuses entirely. Despite these qualifications, intoxication remains a topic of importance, for defense arguments based on intoxication can raise the full range of culpability issues, from criminal intent to problems with rationality and self-control. Also, given the prevalence of intoxicated offenders, it is a potential factor in a wide range of criminal cases.

Generally, American criminal law does not distinguish between types of intoxicant. Law-makers have framed their rules with alcohol in mind, alcohol being the most prevalent and most criminogenic of current intoxicants. The assumption is that other forms of intoxication are susceptible to the same legal treatment.

Finally, a word about the status of intoxication as a "defense." Courts frequently declare that voluntary intoxication is not a defense to crime. And in the sense of being an affirmative defense, that is true. Voluntary intoxication doctrine is all about proof of mens rea. (We will see that some aspects of involuntary intoxication doctrine meet the criteria for an affirmative defense, however.)

In terms of burden of proof, all arguments about intoxication begin with evidence showing that the defendant was intoxicated. Usually this will be presented by defense witnesses. Then the prosecution bears the burden of persuading the decision maker that there is sufficient proof of mens rea and other essential elements, despite evidence of intoxication.[1]

Voluntary Intoxication: A Limited Mens Rea Argument

The law of voluntary intoxication may be structured around the following two questions:

---

1. See State v. Mash, 372 S.E.2d 532, 536–37 (N.C. 1988).

(1) Does the jurisdiction allow the defendant to argue that voluntary intoxication *might* negate a particular mens rea required for the offense? And,

(2) If the argument is allowed, will it work? *Did* the defendant lack the particular mens rea because of intoxication?

Intoxication is voluntary if the intoxication was knowing and uncoerced. The individual must have had a basic idea of the intoxicating qualities of the material ingested, and must have taken the substance of his or her own free will. The only exception is for certain individuals who may have an unusual, and heretofore unknown, susceptibility to the drug. This condition and other related problems with the voluntariness of intoxication will be discussed at the close of the chapter under the heading of involuntary intoxication.

Voluntary Intoxication and Identity: Rejecting Excuse Based on Altered Personality

Potentially the most persuasive argument about intoxication and criminal responsibility is one that the law uniformly rejects. As suggested by the quotes that opened this chapter, in social settings we are inclined to excuse or at least mitigate the wrongs of intoxicated persons because of the personality change that intoxication causes. The argument that, "It wasn't really me, that was the drink talking," may carry some social weight in the aftermath of heavy partying; it carries none in the criminal law.

Courts have long emphasized that evidence of voluntary intoxication goes only to the narrow issue of mens rea; any intoxication-induced personality change or associated loss of self control is irrelevant. The rationale is that the person who chooses to become intoxicated must take the consequences of that choice, especially if those consequences prove harmful to others. The criminal law's view here accords with its presumption of unitary personal identity. Every person is presumed to be a single responsible agent across time, regardless of personality changes caused by mood, including those induced by intoxication.

Drink, Drugs and Crime

So what, exactly, is the connection between intoxication and criminality?

We know that many criminal offenders, especially those who commit acts of violence, do so while intoxicated. We also know that many persons involved in the criminal justice system have substance abuse problems, *and that these problems contribute to criminal offending. Many property crime offenders, for example, have serious long-term substance abuse problems. We also know that the illegal drug trade often spurs homicidal violence. What are the implications for criminal responsibility?*

There are three big policy issues with respect to drink, drugs and crime: (1) the problem of addiction and free will; (2) the connection between the illegal drug trade and crime; and (3) criminogenic intoxication.

In the world of drug and alcohol treatment, addiction is considered a disease. It is a condition that requires treatment, not punishment. It is a basic truth of addiction that most addicts will not, and probably cannot, get clean without the help of others. Yet even in drug and alcohol treatment, personal responsibility is critical. Change only occurs when the addict accepts responsibility for his or her condition. Not surprisingly, criminal law also emphasizes individual responsibility here. The law presumes that even persons who are psychologically compelled to use intoxicants are personally responsible for their related conduct. Thus the addict is held responsible for crimes committed as part or in furtherance of addiction, just as the compulsive sex offender is for his or her crimes. In both situations, the law's commitment to free will is more a statement of value than an observation about human psychology or behavior.

What about the connection between illegal drugs and crime? The illegal drug trade fosters other criminality because addicts often commit crimes to raise money for drug purchases. Even more important, individuals involved in the drug trade have no lawful way of resolving disputes or regulating the marketplace. Violence is therefore a key business tool, often critical to establishing and maintaining distribution networks. These truths are frequently cited in favor of decriminalization. They do not make the individuals involved in such crimes any less responsible than any other offenders, however.

Finally, we need to consider the problem of criminogenic drugs. Does intoxication itself increase the risk or severity of criminal behavior? Are there substances that essentially turn people into criminal offenders a la Dr. Jekyll and Mr. Hyde?[2] In this respect there are potentially significant differences between different kinds of intoxicants. Many illegal drugs, while destructive to their consumers, do not directly motivate criminality. Heroin is one example. In fact our most criminogenic drug is legal for adult users: alcohol. There is a significant connection between alco-

---

2. Robert Louis Stevenson, *Dr. Jekyll and Mr. Hyde* (1886).

hol intoxication and violence. *The state of being drunk seems to increase the likelihood of doing violence, for at least some persons.*[3] *Alcohol's contribution to violence in the home and community was an important motivating force behind the temperance movement in the 19th and early 20th century. While the national experience with Prohibition means that we are not about to criminalize alcohol again, its criminogenic tendencies have not changed, and may help explain the recent move to eliminate voluntary intoxication arguments with respect to mens rea. For more on recent changes in the law, see the A New Trend sidebar below.*

The Availability of the Mens Rea Argument

There are two basic sets of rules concerning voluntary intoxication: those under the common law and those under the MPC. Although these often produce similar results, each employs a different analytic method.

Common Law: Specific v. General Intent

The basic principle of voluntary intoxication doctrine under the common law sounds simple. Any specific intent element of a crime *may be* negated by evidence of voluntary intoxication. General intent elements of a crime *may not* be negated by evidence of voluntary intoxication. In other words, a heavily intoxicated defendant may argue that, because of intoxication, he did not act with specific intent, if that is required for conviction. But if the mens rea for the offense involves only general intent, then intoxication is irrelevant to mens rea.

What seems simple in theory, however, becomes complicated in practice. Difficulties arise first in determining whether the offense requires general or specific intent and second, assuming specific intent is required, whether intoxication evidence in the case actually negates that intent.

The specific/general intent approach to intoxication has several immediately attractive features that may explain its durability in the face of extensive criticism. Dividing criminal offenses into two general classes of intent provides an apparently neat categorization of the many different forms of mens rea. Providing that intoxication may be argued only with respect to the higher forms of mens rea seems to accord with intoxication's effects on choice. We know that intoxication commonly interferes with higher levels of mental func-

---

3. See Montana v. Egelhoff, 518 US 37, 49–50 (1996).

tioning. This distinction also seems to provide public safety protection by limiting the excuse to specific intent crimes. In most cases, defendants acquitted of specific intent offenses by virtue of voluntary intoxication will nevertheless be convicted for a lesser, general intent offense. Unfortunately, appearances mislead here. None of these justifications withstand close scrutiny.

The distinction between general and specific intent forms of mens rea can be difficult to draw. The distinction often depends more on the form of words used in statutory or common law definitions rather than on principled distinctions between offenses. In different jurisdictions, or at different times within a jurisdiction, the same offenses can be oppositely characterized. For example, while depraved heart murder is usually labeled a general intent offense, it has sometimes been categorized as specific intent.[4]

The assumption that intoxication affects the capacity to have higher but not lower forms of mens rea is also questionable; this is further discussed under the heading of Capacity Talk in the section on the application of voluntary intoxication rules to facts.

Finally, the doctrine's public safety limitation is unreliable because in some areas of criminal law there is no general intent crime on which a conviction might be based in the event of voluntary intoxication. Nor does the specific versus general distinction necessarily track the severity of offense and punishment. One of the most serious criminal offenses, rape, is a general intent crime, while less serious offenses such as burglary and larceny are labeled specific intent.

Of course lamenting the law's imperfections will not, by itself, change the law. The general versus specific intent persists and must be taken seriously here.

Understanding the distinction begins with the basic idea behind the general and specific intent labels. A general intent crime is one that simply prohibits the commission of a wrongful act. Such offenses may have an explicit mens rea requirement, but if not, some form of mens rea is read into the offense by court interpretation.[5]

A specific intent offense is one in which, in addition to committing the basic wrongful act, the offender must act with a further mens rea, a mens rea usually—but not always—involving some variation of the phrase "with intent to."

A few standard examples of general and specific intent offenses will illustrate.

---

4. People v. Whitfield, 868 P.2d 272 (Cal. 1994)(specific intent). This decision was legislatively overturned one year later. Cal. Pen. Code sec. 22 (b.). C.f. People v. Langworthy, 331 N.W.2d 171, 177–79 (Mich. 1982)(general intent).

5. In MPC terms, the minimum mens rea for a general intent crime is *usually* recklessness; sometimes it is negligence. But this is more an observation of general likelihood rather than a reliable rule.

Breaking and entering: knowing unlawful entry into a structure.

This is a general intent offense because it describes only the wrongful act of entry. It has a mens rea, but only for the prohibited act of unlawful entry: that the offender know that entry into the structure is unlawful.

Burglary: knowing unlawful entry into a structure, with intent to commit a crime therein.

This is a specific intent offense because it condemns the wrongful act of entry *and* requires that the defendant act "with the intent to commit a crime therein." Breaking and entering and burglary represent a classic pairing of general and specific intent offenses because the general intent offense (breaking and entering) is a lesser included offense of the specific intent one (burglary).[6] Burglary is essentially breaking and entering plus an additional specific intent.

Larceny: knowing unlawful taking and carrying away the personal property of another, with intent to deprive the owener thereof permanently.

Here we have another classic specific intent offense, the specific intent element being: "with intent to deprive the owner thereof permanently."

Rape: Sexual intercourse by force and against the will of another.

This is a general intent offense because it describes only a wrongful act. As we saw in Chapter 14, its mens rea with respect to nonconsent ("against the will") is equivalent to negligence in many U.S. jurisdictions.

Attempted rape: an act done with intent to commit sexual intercourse by force and against the will of another.

Like all attempts, attempted rape is a specific intent offense because of the additional purpose mens rea (often described in terms of intent) required for attempt. Indeed all forms of inchoate liability—attempt, accomplice and conspiracy—are specific intent crimes because all require an additional purpose mens rea as part of inchoate liability.

In the realm of homicide, first-degree, purposeful premeditated murder is always classified as a specific intent offense, with both purpose to kill and premeditation being labeled as specific intent. Thus, voluntary intoxication evidence may be used to negate either premeditation or purpose to kill.

---

6. Determining greater and lesser offenses is critical for a number of other substantive and procedural issues, including what options a decision maker may have for conviction and the rules of double jeopardy.

As noted before, in most jurisdictions, depraved heart murder is a general intent offense and thus intoxication evidence cannot be used to negate either its recklessness or indifference elements. All forms of manslaughter are categorized as general intent offenses.

MPC: Purpose and Knowledge Only

The Model Penal Code also permits defendants to use evidence of voluntary intoxication to negate higher forms of mens rea, but it eschews the general/specific intent distinction in favor of its own mens rea categories. The MPC provides that voluntary intoxication evidence may be used to negate the mens reas of purpose and knowledge *but not* recklessness or negligence.

Intoxication is explicitly barred from consideration of recklessness under the MPC. Defendants may not argue a lack of awareness due to intoxication. Instead, decision makers are to assess recklessness as if the defendant were sober.[7]

Intoxication evidence is definitionally barred from negligence analysis because a judgment of negligence requires that the defendant have grossly deviated from the standard of care of a reasonable person in the situation. Needless to say, the reasonable person — the person whose standard of prudence sets the standard for all — is a sober one.[8]

The Model Penal Code's approach to voluntary intoxication has the advantage of clarity over that of the common law. It avoids the formalistic obscurity of specific and general intent but still prevents voluntary intoxication from undercutting responsibility for careless conduct while intoxicated that most persons would judge culpable.[9]

For the most part, offenses that would be deemed specific intent under the common law, and therefore eligible for a voluntary intoxication argument, would receive similar treatment under the MPC, because these offenses have a purpose or knowledge mens rea. For example, burglary using MPC terminology is a knowing unlawful entry into a structure for the purpose of committing a crime therein. Similarly, the inchoate crimes of attempt, accomplice, or conspiracy all require a form of purpose under the MPC.

Clear differences between the common law and MPC approach appear with offenses that require a knowing mens rea. Depending on their wording, these

---

7. Section 2.08(2).

8. Sections 2.08(2); 2.02(d).

9. The recklessness exclusion stands in tension with the MPC's general presumption that actual awareness of criminally significant facts is critical to culpability, however. See Section 2.02(3).(4).

might be determined general intent offenses under the common law, thus precluding a voluntary intoxication argument, but they will always permit an intoxication argument under the MPC.

> Clarence has been drinking all day, upset that his girlfriend just broke up with him. He is asked to leave a local restaurant because his loud cursing is bothering other customers. He replies that he "isn't going anywhere." Two police officers arrive to handle the situation. One lays a hand on Clarence's arm to move him outside; Clarence takes a swing at the officer and a violent struggle ensues.
>
> Clarence is charged with resisting arrest by a peace officer, an offense defined in this jurisdiction as: resisting arrest by a peace officer by force. Courts have interpreted the offense to require that the defendant know the person making the arrest is a peace officer engaged in public duties. Can Clarence argue voluntary intoxication to negate the required mens rea in this case?

Under the common law, Clarence probably cannot use voluntary intoxication to negate mens rea here, because the offense is likely to be deemed general intent. The statute simply prohibits the wrongful act of resisting arrest; no further mens rea is required. Here, the lack of any "with intent to" or "with knowledge that" language in the statute makes general intent categorization likely. Notice that the same offense could be stated as requiring forcible resistance to arrest "with knowledge that" the person making the arrest is a peace officer engaged in public duties, but as we have already seen, the general versus specific intent distinction often turns on just such formalism. That is, the form of words can matter more than their substance.

The MPC rule on voluntary intoxication is clear in this case: the intoxication argument is available. Because the mens rea required is knowledge, Clarence's attorney can argue to the jury that his intoxication prevented him from knowing that the person he fought with was a police officer. Of course arguing this and persuading a decision maker that it is true are separate tasks. It is to this second matter, the application of rules to facts, that we now turn.

Voluntary Intoxication: Application of Rules to Facts

Assuming the law allows the defendant to argue no mens rea based on evidence of voluntary intoxication, will the argument work? Will the judge or jury agree that the prosecution's proof of mens rea fails due to the defendant's intoxication?

Policy and Doctrine

Here we confront a deliberate irony of voluntary intoxication doctrine: defense arguments are most available where they are least likely to persuade. They are least available where they would be most persuasive.

Even where legally permitted, most arguments that an accused lacked mens rea will fail because the fact of voluntary intoxication will not change our view of why the defendant acted as he did. It does not change our understanding of defendant's mens rea. This is especially true with offenses that require purposeful wrongdoing. For example, two men after an afternoon's drinking fall into an argument and then engage in a fight. One pulls out a gun and shoots the other five times, killing him. How likely is it that the shooter here lacked the purpose to kill because of intoxication? The facts indicate that the defendant was angry and, acting on an angry impulse, used a deadly weapon in its most deadly fashion to kill the source of his anger. The facts indicate that the defendant wanted the victim dead.

In some cases, it's conceivable that the defendant's intoxication might *support* the prosecution's proof of a purposeful mens rea. The prosecution might argue that because alcohol intoxication often fuels exaggerated emotional reactions, especially anger, intoxication may make it likely that an intoxicated person will become highly enraged and retaliate for a real or perceived injury, intending to kill or do grave bodily injury. Thus, the prosecutor would say, the intoxicated defendant probably did act with the required mens rea.

Voluntary intoxication may serve the defense cause better in other situations, or with another form of mens rea. For example, premeditation, a specific intent mens rea, may well be affected by voluntary intoxication. The requirement for first-degree premeditated murder that the defendant have reflected on killing prior to actually committing the deed, might well be negated by evidence that the defendant's faculties were clouded by drink or drugs. Assuming that reflection did not occur prior to intoxication, a person who is intoxicated is less likely to weigh the consequences of homicide, to reflect on killing. The intoxicated person seems especially likely to act spontaneously and without reflection.

But despite its prevalence in law school discourse, premeditation is not an issue in many cases. So what about other forms of mens rea? Isn't there any other form likely to be negated by voluntary intoxication? The most promising candidate is recklessness—except that here the argument is prohibited. If it were allowed, evidence of voluntary intoxication might indicate that an individual was not aware of a significant risk, a key element of recklessness. People who are drunk or high are notoriously oblivious to risks to themselves and others. Yet both the MPC explicitly (with its recklessness exclusion) and the common law implicitly (because general intent offenses usually involve either a reckless or negligence mens rea), bar this use of intoxication evidence. The justification for this prohibition is that defendants who choose to obscure their faculties with intoxicants should not be able to claim an excuse based on such obscuration.[10]

Capacity Talk, Voluntary Intoxication and Proof of Mens Rea

Before any further exploration of how intoxication evidence might negate specific intent or purpose/knowledge mens reas, we must confront what I believe is a significant potential confusion in voluntary intoxication doctrine. It involves how we state the legal question.

Traditionally courts have spoken about the way that intoxication affects the defendant's *capacity* to have a certain mens rea.[11] The assumption is that if extreme enough, intoxication precludes the kind of mental functioning required for higher forms of mens rea. On first hearing, this seems to make sense. We know that intoxication degrades both physical and mental functioning. Just as we know that most intoxicated persons will not be able to perform certain physical tests, such as walking a straight line, we also know that an intoxicated person is not going to be able to engage in complicated mental activities. In an intellectual sense, many people become stupid when intoxicated — at least

---

10. This is not an entirely satisfactory answer, because a general awareness that one might act less carefully when intoxicated is not the same, morally or factually, as being aware of the particular risks required for the particular offense. E.g., United States v. Fleming, 739 F.2d 945 (4th Cir. 1984) (depraved heart murder conviction for highly intoxicated driver who drove at high speed down the wrong side of a divided highway, causing a head-on fatal collision).

Notice that even if intoxication evidence were available to negate proof of recklessness, the prosecution could argue that intoxication — especially alcohol intoxication — does not so much make the person unaware of risk as unconcerned about it. Nevertheless, American law makers have feared that jurors will not recognize this distinction.

11. For example, in Turrentine v. State, 965 P.2d 955, 968–69 (Okla. Crim. App. 1998) the court referred to a defendant becoming "so intoxicated that his mental abilities were totally overcome and that it therefore became impossible for him to form the requisite criminal intent" and that "appellant must show that the effects of the alcohol or drugs were such that he was rendered totally incapable of forming the requisite intent to commit murder."

when sufficiently intoxicated. If we arrange mens rea forms into higher and lower ranks according to the complexity of the mental functions they involve, then it makes sense for intoxication doctrine to track those distinctions.

So it is that traditionally some jurisdictions required proof that defendant's intoxication produced a "prostration of the faculties" before an instruction on voluntary intoxication could be given. So it is that litigation often focuses on the degree of intoxication and impairment, sometimes with expert testimony about the effect of particular intoxicants on mental functioning.

But there is a real problem here. In my view, this focus on mental capacity reflects a misunderstanding of basic mens rea, especially the mens rea of purpose. For a person to act with a "higher" mens rea (whether categorized as specific intent under the common law or purpose or knowledge under the MPC) normally does *not* require a high level of mental functioning. If a person has the desire and physical ability to take an item from a store without paying for it, she probably has the capacity to intend to take it permanently; a person with the desire and mental faculties needed to raise, aim and fire a gun at another human being probably also has the mental faculties to seek the victim's death. Remember, mens rea generally addresses the most basic reasons for the defendant's conduct, and even intoxicated conduct usually has some basic reason behind it.

Where the individual is truly incapacitated by intoxication, the person will not affirmatively "do" anything. The person will be passed out. The most obvious legal claim to make on behalf of such a person would be that he committed no voluntary act: he was unconscious at the time of the offense. No U.S. jurisdiction recognizes such a claim under voluntary intoxication however, holding that individuals are responsible for such loss of consciousness because they chose to become intoxicated.[12] (Again, the only claim that can be made on behalf of a voluntarily intoxicated defendant is a lack of mens rea.) The no-voluntary act argument is limited to involuntary intoxication, and will be discussed under that heading.

In fact, intoxication—especially alcohol intoxication—affects behavior more by disinhibition than by shutting down mental capacity. Intoxicated individuals say and do things they would not do or say if sober. When intoxicated, they act on impulses they would otherwise restrain.

The bottom line is that we would do better, in those cases where a voluntary intoxication argument is permitted, to ask why the defendant acted as he

---

12. This argument should be distinguished from the use of intoxication evidence to negate proof of the act itself. That is, the defendant might argue that he did not and could not have committed the act charged by the state because he was unconscious—comatose—at the time.

did, considering all of the evidence including intoxication, rather than ask whether the defendant had the "capacity" to act with a particular mens rea.[13] Our focus should be on whether the defendant's intoxication changes our view of why the defendant acted as he or she did. There are some instances where intoxication makes it less likely that the defendant acted with the required mens rea.

Applications

Tuesday is the day that Richard has worked for all his life. At midday he learns that he has been voted a partner of his law firm. Given the success of the firm, this means he will become a wealthy man. He goes out to celebrate with a number of his friends at the firm. They have drinks before lunch, a fine wine during the meal, and then after-dinner drinks. Leaving the restaurant, Richard is "feeling no pain." He decides to stop in an expensive jewelry store downtown to buy a special present for his wife, who faithfully supported him through long days and nights of law school and practice. He looks at a number of rings, some of them very expensive. He finally decides on one of the less expensive, for which he pays nearly $2000. Richard leaves the store, but as he does, the owner notices that one of the rings brought out to show Richard is missing. The store security guard stops Richard on the sidewalk outside the store and brings him back. The missing ring—worth nearly $20,000—is in Richard's pants pocket. Richard says he has no idea how it got there.

Richard is charged with theft of the ring: knowing unlawful taking of the personal property of another, with purpose to deprive the owner thereof permanently. Might Richard's intoxication lead to acquittal of this charge?

Under the common law, Richard can use evidence of his voluntary intoxication to argue that he lacked the specific intent required for this offense: the purpose to deprive the owner thereof permanently. Here Richard has a plausible argument, that by virtue of his intoxication, he may have accidentally put the ring in his pocket and walked out the door with it unawares. He left the store without any purpose to steal the ring, that is, without any purpose to deprive the store owner of it. He did not even know he had it in his pocket.

Notice how this reading of the case significantly depends on intoxication. An intoxicated person may misplace things and perform minor physical ac-

---

13. This is the analysis mandated by California law. See Cal. Pen. Code sec. 22.

tions with little or no conscious awareness, making it plausible that Richard did so even with a very expensive rang. If Richard were sober at the time, we would be much more skeptical that he could "accidentally" put a $20,000 ring in his pocket and innocently (without intent to steal) leave without paying for it.

Much the same analysis would follow under the MPC. Richard could argue that he lacked a purpose to permanently deprive, as detailed above. Under the MPC he could also argue that he lacked the knowledge that the taking was un-lawful, although this would not be especially plausible under these facts. He either knew that he was taking the ring from the store— and that the taking was unlawful—or he did not know that he was taking the ring at all.[14]

> Bill and Ted are serious football fans and equally serious drinkers. They conduct a day long tailgate party surrounding the game of their favorite team. Their team loses the game; the quarterback throws three interceptions and is sacked four times. Bill contends that the quar-terback's performance is convincing evidence of his total lack of abil-ity. Ted contends it's all the fault of his offensive line. In the evening, this dispute flares into fistfight. Ted gets the worst of it. He runs out to his car and returns with a gun. He aims it in Bill's direction and screams: "Don't ever insult my boy!" He shoots and kills Bill.
>
> Ted immediately is filled with remorse. Bill dies in Ted's arms, Ted declaring: "I didn't mean it, I didn't mean it. You have to believe me."
>
> Ted is charged with first-degree premeditated, purpose to kill mur-der. What are his chances of conviction, given his voluntary intoxication?

Ted may argue that because of inebriation he lacked the specific intent for this form of murder: both purpose to kill and premeditation. Of these the no-premeditation argument is the more promising.

Ted may argue that his intoxication tends to show that his conduct was spon-taneous, impassioned, and poorly considered. One of the effects of intoxication, especially alcohol intoxication, is to interfere with long-term calculation. There-fore evidence of intoxication tends to show that Ted did not consider the full con-sequences of killing, did not deliberate or reflect on it, before pulling the trigger.

He could also argue that he acted without purpose to kill. He might say that by virtue of drinking he became angry at Bill, and that he wished to scare him

---

14. Notice that Richard's best argument here is not that he lacked the mental capacity for intent to steal because of intoxication, but that because of intoxication, he did not re-alize the ring was in his pocket when he left the store and therefore he did knowingly take the ring unlawfully, nor did he act with purpose to deprive the store owner of the ring per-manently.

or possibly hurt him, that he did not have any desire to end his friend's life. Consider his reaction afterwards. That he killed Bill was a terrible unlucky consequence of admittedly dangerous conduct, but it was not Ted's conscious object. The prosecution, though, might retort that Ted's being drunk made him more likely to become extremely enraged and more likely to act violently on that rage. That means Ted did exactly what he intended at the time, though he probably did not consider the full consequences. Few offenders do.

If purpose to kill cannot be proven, the prosecution might attempt to prove depraved heart recklessness. Here Ted would *not* be able to use intoxication evidence to negate mens rea. In most jurisdictions that follow the general v. specific intent rule, depraved heart murder is general intent. Under the MPC, such murder is based on a mens rea of recklessness. In both instances, voluntary intoxication evidence is barred on mens rea.

This brings us to one last practical problem with intoxication and mens rea analysis. Exactly how do we assess proof of mens rea when we are not allowed to consider intoxication evidence, but the defendant was in fact intoxicated? In its recklessness exclusion, the MPC instructs that the decision maker must determine the facts which would be apparent to anyone in the defendant's position and then decide if such a person, when sober, would be aware of the risks involved.

In Ted's instance, we would ask whether a sober person in his situation would be aware that aiming a gun in the direction of another and pulling the trigger involved a significant risk to the other's life. Given that the effect of shooting would be obvious to anyone in Ted's situation, and also that the shooting was unjustified, done merely to end a personal dispute and retaliate for the loss of a fistfight, and was highly dangerous, the requirements of recklessness would be satisfied. The indifference element of depraved heart murder will likely also be met by virtue of the extreme danger of and lack of justification for Ted's action.

A New Trend: Eliminating Voluntary Intoxication Arguments Entirely

A number of states in recent years have passed legislation to prohibit all use of voluntary intoxication evidence to negate mens rea.[15] These efforts have raised issues of both constitutionality and justice. The constitutional issue is whether selectively eliminating voluntary intoxication evidence from consideration of mens rea effectively undercuts the prosecution's obligation under due process to prove all essential elements of an offense—

---

15. E.g., Ariz. Rev. Stat. Ann. sec. 13-503; Mont. Code Ann. sec. 45-2-203.

> *usually including mens rea—beyond a reasonable doubt. This question appears to have been largely resolved by the United States Supreme Court in Montana v. Egelhoff, in favor of constitutionality.*[16] *The badly divided Court did not, however, provide a clear rationale for why Montana's elimination of voluntary intoxication arguments was lawful.*
>
> *Putting aside the constitutional question for a moment, what about basic fairness? How can it be fair to bar from consideration a form of evidence that is potentially critical to mens rea and therefore legal guilt? One answer is that all jurisdictions bar voluntary intoxication evidence in some cases; this just makes the prohibition uniform. Proponents also argue that this prohibition eliminates the confusions of capacity-for-mens rea analysis discussed previously.*
>
> *In my view these arguments are not finally convincing, however, because as we have seen, there are cases in which intoxication is relevant to assessing defendant conduct. Intoxicated persons sometimes do act for different reasons than sober persons, which means that intoxication may give insight into why the defendant acted as he or she did, including whether the defendant acted with purpose or knowledge. Thus the elimination of all mens rea arguments based on voluntary intoxication appears a good example of the tendency of criminal law reforms to take extreme forms that manage to substitute new problems for old.*

Involuntary Intoxication

Most people who become drunk or high do so by choice; their intoxication is voluntary. Intoxication also can occur without choice, however, and in these cases we turn to the law of involuntary intoxication. An involuntarily intoxicated defendant may make three different legal claims: (1) no voluntary act due to unconsciousness; (2) insufficient proof of any subjective mens rea required (purpose, knowledge, or recklessness); or (3) assert that the intoxication induced a state of non-responsibility equivalent to insanity. All analysis begins with the definition of involuntary intoxication.

Defining Involuntary Intoxication

Intoxication is involuntary if the accused took the intoxicant without awareness of its intoxicating nature or if the consumption was coerced. Involuntary

---

16. 500 U.S. 37 (1996).

intoxication is most commonly claimed by individuals who take substances not knowing that they may be intoxicating. Such persons may have mistaken the nature of the substance or its likely effects.[17] An increasingly common claim of this sort is that the person took a prescription drug which had an intoxicating effect of which the individual had no notice.

Another form of involuntary intoxication involves extreme and unforeseen susceptibility to an intoxicant.[18] For example, some individuals are so sensitive to alcohol that even one or two drinks will induce extreme intoxication. If such an individual has an alcoholic drink without knowing of this condition, the resulting extreme intoxication may be treated as involuntary.

Finally, a person who was coerced into drinking or consuming an intoxicant, can claim that the resulting intoxication was involuntary.[19]

Involuntary Intoxication and the Act Requirement

A defendant who was involuntarily intoxicated may argue that intoxication rendered him unconscious, thus negating proof of a voluntary act. As we saw before, this argument is generally not available for voluntary intoxication, as most courts hold the individual responsible for choosing to become intoxicated. With involuntary intoxication the defendant made no such choice.

Involuntary Intoxication and Mens Rea

Similar to voluntary intoxication, a defendant may argue that evidence of involuntary intoxication negates the required mens rea for the offense. The significant difference with respect to involuntary intoxication is that the argument may be used for *any subjective form of mens rea*. In common law regimes, involuntary intoxication can be used to negate both general and specific intents; under the MPC it can be used to negate purpose, knowledge *and* recklessness.[20] It still may not be used for negligence, because the standard of care for negligence remains is that of a reasonable person—a reasonable sober person.

---

17. Carter v. State, 710 So.2d 110 (Fla. Ct. App. 1998) (mistaking anti-depression drug for over-the-counter pain killer); People v. Scott, 146 Cal.App.3d 823 (1983) (unknowing ingestion of hallucinogen in punch at a party causing a psychotic episode two days later); City of Minneapolis v. Altimus, 238 N.W.2d 851 (Minn. 1976) (ignorance of effect of prescription drug).

18. Model Penal Code § 2.08(5)(c) (1)

19. E.g., Burrows v. State, 297 P. 1029, 1035–36 (Ariz. 1931).

20. On occasion, courts give the offense a broad interpretation to find a form of mens rea relevant to involuntary intoxication. See Carter, supra (knowing intoxication required for driving under the influence where involuntary intoxication alleged).

Of course remember, as with voluntary intoxication, the availability of the argument does not mean that it will necessarily work on the facts. The fact finder must still determine the actual effect of intoxication on the defendant's alleged purpose or awareness.

Involuntary Intoxication as an Affirmative Defense

Finally, the defendant may use involuntary intoxication as an affirmative defense, similar to insanity. Even if the defendant acted with the required mens rea, the defendant may argue that the involuntary intoxication rendered him or her non-responsible. In most jurisdictions, the condition of involuntary intoxication effectively substitutes for the mental disease or disorder element of the insanity test. Then the accused must show a major deficit in rationality or in capacity for control, depending on the jurisdiction's test for insanity.[21] Discussion of this aspect of involuntary intoxication will be relatively brief in this chapter, because substantively it depends primarily on the rule of insanity, which is covered in Chapter 20.

Now to a fact pattern which will help illustrate the rules of involuntary intoxication.

Roslyn and her best friend decide to go out for a night of clubbing. They go to a new place that they've heard about, but find it dull, and decide to leave when a particularly persistent and creepy guy won't leave them alone. They drive home separately. Rosalyn has had three drinks over the course of three hours but does not feel intoxicated. She does start to feel poorly once on the road, however.

Roslyn is pulled over by a uniformed police officer in a patrol car who notices her vehicle weaving in and out of lanes. The officer smells alcohol on her breath. Her speech is slurred and she speaks angrily to the officer. When he orders her out of the car, she refuses. When the officer forcibly removes her, she grabs the officer's flashlight and strikes him in the head with it, yelling: "Get your hands off me you fucking pig!" Roslyn is then arrested.

Subsequent investigation by the defense indicates that someone at the bar slipped Rohypnol, the so-called date-rape drug, into Roslyn's

---

21. Torres v. State, 585 S.W.2d 746, 749 (Tex.Cr.App. 1979).

Conceptually distinct from involuntary intoxication is what has been called "settled insanity," a severe mental disorder which may result from heavy drinking over a long period and which may produce psychosis.

last drink at the club. This drug has a number of effects, including impaired motor controls, disorientation, and often unconsciousness.

Roslyn is charged with driving under the influence and resisting arrest with violence. Driving under the influence is: operating a motor vehicle while under the influence of an intoxicating substance. This is a strict liability offense. Resisting arrest with violence is: using violence against a police officer in the course of an arrest, knowing that the individual is a peace officer engaged in official duties.

What are the chances that Roslyn will be convicted as charged?

Initially we must determine whether Rosalyn became intoxicated voluntarily or involuntarily. She voluntarily consumed three alcoholic drinks; she involuntarily congested the drug Rohypnol. Because the facts as presented indicate that the impairment of her faculties stems from the Rohypnol rather than the alcohol, we can proceed on the assumption that this is a case of involuntary rather than voluntary intoxication.

The first defense argument we might consider is that Roslyn might not have committed the voluntary act necessary for the driving under the influence charge. She might contend that by virtue of her Rohypnol intoxication, her conscious mind was not in charge such that she did not commit the voluntary act of operating the car. We have seen that because the intoxication is involuntary, this argument is available. But will it work?

The prosecution will contend here that Roslyn managed to direct the car prior to being pulled over, and then pulled over in response to the police officer. Someone was driving the vehicle and that someone was Roslyn. Notice that if the police officer had come upon Roslyn when she was passed out behind the wheel of the car, her unconsciousness argument might be more persuasive. The prosecution would also emphasize her conduct after the stop, when she made insulting remarks and hit the officer with a flashlight, tending to indicate that she was making basic decisions about her body's movements.

There is another possible voluntary act argument to be made here, however. It turns on constructing a second voluntary act requirement for the driving under the influence offense. Roslyn might argue that driving under the influence presumes that the condition of being under the influence was arrived at voluntarily. Although it is not expressly stated in the statute, the assumption of legislators must have been that persons convicted had chosen to take intoxicants prior to driving. That is certainly the standard way in which this offense would be committed. Especially because this is a strict liability offense, it seems both unfair and beyond legislative intent, to convict a person for driving while impaired when that person did not choose to become impaired. If the court agrees, Roslyn will not be convicted of the impaired driving offense, because her state of impairment—her intoxication—was involuntary.[22]

What mens rea arguments might Roslyn make here? Recall that evidence of involuntary intoxication may be used to negate all subjective forms of mens rea. Roslyn is out of luck here with respect to the driving under the influence offense, because it is strict liability. But what about mens rea for the resisting offense charge? Here, the only question, under both the common law and the MPC, is whether her involuntary intoxication actually negated the subjective mens rea required for the offense: knowledge that the victim was a police officer engaged in official duties. To determine this, we turn to the particulars of the facts.

Did Rosalyn mean by her use of the word "pig," to employ a generic epithet for an obnoxious person, especially a sexually predatory male, or did she use this word as an epithet for police officer? If she meant the latter, that would indicate her awareness of his peace officer status and that he was in fact acting as a police officer. Supporting this interpretation is that the officer was in uniform and in a marked patrol car. Of course Roslyn might contend that even so, she believed the officer was engaged in some sort of sexual attack and therefore not engaged in official duties. Perhaps her intoxication might make that interpretation credible.

Finally, Roslyn might argue for an affirmative defense of non-responsibility. She would contend that by virtue of her involuntary intoxication, she was temporarily insane under the insanity test of the jurisdiction. Without going into the particulars of insanity (see Chapter 20) Roslyn would be arguing in most jurisdictions that she was either not aware of what she was doing or not aware of the wrongness of her conduct due to her involuntary intoxication. For the most part, these arguments would largely tracks the arguments detailed above with respect to mens rea. Her best prospect with regard to this quasi-insanity argument would be if the jurisdiction follows the MPC rule on insanity, and includes its volitional prong. Under such a rule, Roslyn could plausibly argue that she lost much of her ability to refrain from violence in this situation due to her involuntary ingestion of Rohypnol.

---

22. See People v. Koch, 294 N.Y.S. 987 (1937).

CHAPTER 20

INSANITY AND RELATED DOCTRINES

If there were an award for the Most Misunderstood Doctrine in U.S. criminal law, the defense of insanity would certainly be a contender. Indeed, there may be no set of rules more widely misunderstood—especially if we include the related doctrine of diminished capacity also covered in this chapter.

Contrary to popular belief, insanity is not a commonly asserted defense, nor when asserted is it usually successful. And even when it succeeds, the defense does not usually result in freedom for the accused. In fact, insanity is a relatively uncommon defense, does not usually work when attempted, and even when successful, the defendant often ends up being involuntarily committed to a mental institution for an extended period, sometimes for longer than the maximum sentence he would have received if convicted.

The doctrine is also subject to legal misunderstandings, especially concerning the relationship between insanity and mens rea. Many students of the law, and many legal reformers presume that proof of mental illness must affect mens rea. In truth, most criminally accused who suffer from mental illness may use evidence of their illness only to support an insanity claim. Major mental and emotional difficulties normally do not affect proof of mens rea.

Despite its relative rarity in the courtroom, the insanity defense has a central place in criminal law for it goes to the heart of the law's concept of individual responsibility. The doctrine demonstrates that culpability depends on rational choice making and not just mens rea. Which is not to say that determining such responsibility is easy. It is not.

In the historical ebb and flow of insanity law, the last 20 years have seen a major ebbing of support for the defense. Doubts concerning both the testimony of mental health experts and the judgment of decision makers have inspired a number of efforts to restrict the defense substantively and procedurally. In a few jurisdictions it has been eliminated. Related efforts have also restricted or eliminated the doctrine of diminished capacity, which permits the use of mental illness evidence to negate mens rea.

Why Excuse for Craziness?

In Europe in the Middle Ages, animals were sometimes tried for offenses against humans. A horse that had killed its owner with a kick might be put on trial, convicted and then executed. Today we think this crazy. It seems based on a fundamental misunderstanding of the nature of criminal responsibility. Animals (and very small children) simply do not choose in the way that is required for criminal responsibility. A similar notion lies behind the insanity defense. A person who is insane lacks some fundamental attribute or attributes necessary for individual human responsibility.

Some believe that an insane individual lacks the capacity for rational thought and self-directed action. The individual's choosing faculties have gone awry, making the person incapable of choosing otherwise and therefore undeterrable. A related, though not identical view, holds that a person who acts for fundamentally irrational reasons is not an appropriate subject for criminal responsibility. There is no possibility of a rational moral dialogue with a person who experiences a fundamentally different reality from the rest of us. This makes the process of their prosecution, conviction and punishment as nonsensical as trying and hanging a horse.

Distinguishing Insanity from Other Doctrines

Before introducing the basics of insanity, we need to distinguish the defense from several other legal doctrines that frequently arise in cases involving mentally ill defendants.

Competence to Stand Trial v. Insanity

The most litigated issue involving mental illness in criminal cases is not the insanity defense, but competence to stand trial. This is a procedural question that must be resolved prior to any substantive criminal proceedings, including a trial. The issue arises when a defendant, usually soon after charges have been filed, shows signs of a significant mental illness. The defense attorney, the judge, or even the prosecutor may raise the issue of mental competence and request a hearing. This contrasts with the insanity defense, which may be raised only with the defendant's consent.

Mental competence measures the defendant's basic understanding of the legal process. For the case to go forward, the defendant must demonstrate basic comprehension of who the defense attorney is, what the charges are, and the possible penalties. Judges ask *whether the defendant has "sufficient present ability to consult with his lawyer with a reasonable degree of rational understanding—and whether he has a rational as well as factual understanding of the proceedings against him."*[1]

Although this test aims at legal understanding, it is usually resolved based on testimony from mental health experts who have evaluated the defendant. If, based on such testimony, the defendant is found incompetent to stand trial, the court may order the defendant held for a period of time for mental treatment to restore competence. Usually this involves commitment to a locked facility, often a jail or prison, where mental treatment is provided, usually in the form of psychotropic medication. Defendants are then brought back to court periodically to reassess their competence. This process can take months and even years, but there is a constitutional limit. The court must dismiss criminal charges against the defendant once it reasonably appears that there is not "a substantial probability that he will attain [competence] in the foreseeable future."[2] At this point, if the criteria for involuntary civil commitment (explained below) are met, the defendant may be civilly committed; otherwise he must be released.

Civil Commitment v. Criminal Punishment

Standing in the shadows of the insanity defense is its civil law counterpart: involuntary civil commitment. In every jurisdiction, even without committing a criminal offense, individuals may be forcibly confined for mental treatment if determined to be a danger to self or others. The legal test for involuntary civil commitment, the length of that commitment, and the structure of civil commitment proceedings vary considerably between jurisdictions, however. For our purposes, it is sufficient to note that civil commitment usually requires proof of *present* threats to self or others. Improvement in mental condition during confinement will often require release from civil commitment, even if it is likely that the individual will suffer a relapse after release.

Ordinary civil commitment needs to be distinguished from special procedures for civil commitment following an insanity acquittal. Most jurisdictions have a different set of rules for involuntary commitment following an insanity determination. Post-insanity acquittal rules make involuntary commitment

---

1. Dusky v. United States, 362 U.S. 402, 402 (1960).
2. Jackson v. Indiana, 406 U.S. 715, 739 (1972).

much easier and subsequent release from commitment more difficult than under the ordinary civil commitment process.[3]

Mens Rea v. Insanity Defense

The distinction between mens rea arguments and the insanity defense is an important one. A familiar example from English law will provide a basic introduction. Further discussion of mens rea and mental illness will come at the close of the chapter when we take up the doctrine of diminished capacity, which focuses exclusively on mens rea.

> Daniel M'Naughton believed that the Tories—members of the Conservative political party in England—were out to get him. He believed the Tories would kill him if they could. Thinking that his only chance of survival was to kill the party's leader, M'Naughton traveled to London to assassinate the Tory prime minister, Sir Robert Peel. M'-Naughton waited by the road for the Prime Minister's carriage and when it appeared, he shot and killed the man sitting inside. The man killed was Robert Drummond, the Secretary to the Prime Minister, who was using the carriage that day.
>
> Mental health experts examined M'Naughton and found that he suffered from a serious mental illness, which included delusions of persecution, and that these provoked his attack.[4]
>
> Putting aside for the moment any question of insanity, did M'-Naughton act with the mens rea sufficient for murder?

As we saw in Chapter 9, one of the basic forms of mens rea for murder is purpose to kill. Here, M'Naughton demonstrated clear purpose to kill: his use of a deadly weapon in deadly fashion to carry out a plan of preemptive attack against a person perceived to be a deadly threat, indicates that his conscious object was to kill the man in the carriage. (That he actually killed the secretary rather than the Prime Minister is not a problem as it would be covered by the doctrine of transferred intent.) If premeditation were also required, this would likely be satisfied by the planning and calculation shown here. None of this changes the fact that M'Naughton acted for crazy reasons. The point is that M'Naughton acted with the necessary mens rea for murder. His mental illness might support the affirmative defense of insanity, but not lack of mens rea.

---

3. See Jones v. United States, 463 U.S. 354 (1983).

4. See M'Naughton's Case, 8 Eng. Rep. 718 (1843); Richard Moran, *Knowing Right From Wrong* (1981).

There are cases, however, in which mental illness may be relevant to mens rea. These will be considered at the end of the chapter under the heading of Diminished Capacity.

Burden of Proof

Insanity is an affirmative defense, meaning that the burden of production concerning insanity is on the defendant. Every case begins with a presumption of *sanity*. Thus the prosecution need not introduce evidence of the defendant's sanity in order to convict. Instead, the defendant must present some significant evidence of insanity, either through the state's witnesses, or through its own witnesses, to get the question of insanity before the decision maker. Once the defense meets the burden of production, then the question becomes which party has the burden of persuasion on insanity.

As a result of changes that followed the John Hinckley trial, many U.S. jurisdictions today put the burden of persuasion for insanity on the defendant.[5] This means the defense must affirmatively convince the fact finder, usually by either a preponderance of the evidence or by clear and convincing evidence, that the defendant was insane. In cases where the mental health experts conflict in their assessment of the defendant, the assignment of the burden of persuasion can be critical. As discussed in Chapter 4, the burden of persuasion can determine which side wins when there is significant uncertainty about a particular matter.[6]

Storytelling: Sickness v. Depravity

    The insanity defense puts special demands on trial counsel. The most obvious is the need to learn about mental health science. Trial counsel must learn enough about the field to interview, select, prepare and examine mental health experts. Counsel must learn enough to know what questions to ask, and how to explain and critique mental health evaluations. This is not the only special challenge that insanity cases present, however.

    Because the insanity defense often depends on technical medical terms, difficult for nonexperts to understand, attorneys must develop

---

5. 18 U.S.C. sec. 17 (b); People v. Skinner, 704 P.2d 752, 753 (Cal. 1985); Cal. Pen. Code sec. 25(b).

6. E.g., State v Green, 643 S.W.2d 902 (Tenn. Ct. App. 1982) (reversing verdict on grounds that the prosecution did not prove sanity beyond a reasonable doubt of a defendant who suffered from a long-term, serious mental illness.)

clear moral narratives as well. Each must develop a fact-based narrative that fits the expert testimony.

As in any case, each side in an insanity case attempts to construct from the facts a complete, compelling and concise story supporting the verdict sought. Toward this end, the defense tries to assemble the facts into a story of mental illness that will persuade the decision maker to find the defendant insane. Normally this means that the defense suggests a crazy motive for the defendant's action. Her actions were more sick than bad.

The prosecution must construct a counter narrative, an account of moral depravity rather than illness. The prosecution must argue for a sane, but immoral reason for the defendant's conduct, such as jealousy, resentment or rage. Prosecutors sometimes neglect this, instead focusing exclusively on the particulars of mens rea and insanity rules. They construct a fully sufficient legal argument, but one missing the moral and emotional force of a complete human narrative.

Essential Components of Insanity: (1) Mental Disease or Defect

The first requirement of insanity is that the defendant suffer from a mental disease or defect. Although this sounds like a question of medical diagnosis, and indeed its determination often turns on assessment by mental health experts, it is a legal question for the trier of fact. Unfortunately, this aspect of insanity law is relatively undeveloped. In many jurisdictions there is neither a general statutory nor a judicial definition of mental disease or defect. Instead the law tends to be quite ad hoc. Either legislatures make specific exclusions for particular disorders, or—more often—courts decide which mental problems will or will not qualify for mental disease or defect status according to what is presented in the case at hand.[7] Courts normally exclude mental disorders whose primary effects are on an individual's desires, judgment, and conduct rather than those characterized by significant distortions of reality perception and thought processes.[8]

---

7. E.g., Ariz. Rev. Stat. Ann. sec. 13-502 (A) (providing for a number of specific exclusions).

8. A mental illness that involves symptoms of psychosis—a break with reality—will meet any of the tests for mental disease or defect. Of these the most common is schizophrenia, but there are a number of other disorders, including depression and bipolar dis-

The best example of an excluded disorder is the condition of psychopathy. A psychopath is a person who appears incapable of empathy for others and therefore lacks an essential component of conscience. The condition is widely recognized in psychology, and many writers on legal responsibility have argued that the condition should disqualify a person from criminal responsibility. They ask, How can a person who lacks a conscience have the capacity to choose right?[9] Courts universally disagree. A psychopath does not have a mental disease or defect for purposes of insanity.[10] Courts have also excluded other mental disorders closely associated with criminality, such as compulsive gambling disorder[11] and various forms of substance abuse and addiction.[12]

Jurisdictions that have established a general definition of mental disease or defect have usually employed one of two tests: the *McDonald* rule or the APA test.

The *McDonald* rule defines a mental disease or defect as: "*any abnormal condition of the mind which substantially affects mental or emotional processes and substantially impairs behavior controls.*"[13] Although this test describes most persons who need treatment for mental problems, it does not provide clear criteria for identifying the kinds of mental problems associated with insanity. Most significant mental disorders will pass the test.[14]

---

orders that can — sometimes — be accompanied by psychosis. Much more problematic for insanity purposes are the major personality disorders. A broader range of mental disorders may satisfy the mental illness component of civil commitment schemes, especially for sexual predators and insanity acquitees.

9. For an introduction to the psychopathy literature in criminal law, see Charles Fischette (Note), Psychopathy and Responsibility, 90 Va. L. Rev. 1423 (2004).

10. See MPC sec. 4.01(2) (specifically excluding antisocial personality disorder (APD), a condition similar to psychopathy, from consideration as a mental disease or defect); Patton v. State, 878 S.2d 368, 374–76 (Fla. 2004) (affirming expert's opinion that APD is not a mental disease or defect for purposes of insanity.)

11. United States v. Torniero, 735 F.2d 725, 730–33 (2d Cir. 1984).

12. E.g., Commonwealth v. Sheehan, 383 N.E.2d 1115 (Mass. 1978). For the treatment of so-called "settled insanity" in which long-term alcohol use may lead to physical changes and a mental disease or defect, see the accompanying sidebar, Dual Diagnosis.

13. McDonald v. United States 312 F.2d 847, 850–51 (DC Cir. 1962). This definition appears as part of a definition of insanity that has been largely rejected since.

14. For example, a psychopath would appear to suffer from an abnormal condition of the mind (inability to feel empathy) that affects both thinking and especially feeling (lack of concern for others) and this condition substantially impairs behavior controls (by removing the most important internal check on immoral conduct). Yet psychopathy does not count as a mental disease or defect for insanity in any jurisdiction.

A stricter test for mental disease or defect is that proposed by the American Psychiatric Association (APA) and adopted by some jurisdictions.[15] This test distinguishes between severe mental problems that involve some form of psychosis—a break from reality—and other forms of mental illness that do not. Under this test, qualifying mental diseases or defects are: *"[t]hose severely abnormal mental conditions that grossly and demonstrably impair a person's perception or understanding of reality and that are not attributable primarily to the voluntary ingestion of alcohol or other psychoactive substances."* In contrast to *McDonald*, this test requires that the mental condition be *severely* abnormal and that it have a major impact on—*grossly and demonstrably impair*—the defendant's comprehension of reality.

Now for an example to see how these rules work.

> Bridget is a 50-year-old woman who has worked in the accounting department of Corporation for 17 years. She has never been arrested or suspected of any significant wrongdoing. She has been having a very tough time recently. Her recent divorce took a serious emotional toll, as has conflict with her teenage daughter. She also suffers from an undiagnosed thyroid problem which exacerbates a pre-existing tendency to depression. She develops a number of fears, including a concern that people at work are out to get her. She displays extreme anger on several occasions. When she receives a poor job review, the first in her career, she becomes deeply upset.
>
> The following day she is involved in a minor accident in the Corporation parking lot. However she refuses to get out of her car and share information with the other driver. A security guard, alerted to the situation, tries to stop Bridget as she drives away. He stands in the roadway as Bridget attempts to leave. Instead of slowing down, Bridget accelerates and her car strikes the security guard. The guard suffers a fractured pelvis, a broken arm, internal bleeding, and serious facial injuries.
>
> Bridget now stands charged with attempted murder and assault with a deadly weapon (a motor vehicle). A psychiatrist reports that Bridget was suffering from severe depression and paranoia (unfounded fear of others) at the time of the incident, brought on by her thyroid problem and "situational stress." The psychiatrist says that Bridget "perceived that the guard was part of those who were out to get her," but that she did not experience actual delusions.

---

15. See 140 Am. J. Psychiatry 6 (1980); People v. Vanrees, 125 P.3d 403, 408 (Colo. 2005).

Lay witnesses will report that both before and after the incident Bridget appeared rational and coherent, though she did seem very angry during the incident itself.

Does the evidence suggest that Bridget suffered from a mental disease or defect under either the *McDonald* or APA tests?

Bridget clearly suffered from a mental disease or defect under *McDonald*. Her depression and paranoia count as abnormal mental conditions that affect both thought processes and emotions. Depression is characterized by feelings of sadness and despair. Paranoia involves fear and thoughts about threat from others. Finally, these conditions seem to have affected her behavioral controls: witness her conduct in the parking lot. She is acting out her paranoia here.

Under the APA test, Bridget may not fare so well. Her depression and paranoia while abnormal, may not represent *severely* abnormal mental conditions. They certainly do not reach the level of severity of many individuals who claim insanity. Assuming they are sufficiently severe, however, the main question is whether her mental condition "grossly and demonstrably" impaired her perception of reality. Did she experience a break with reality?

The prosecution will argue that Bridget was not psychotic—see the expert's testimony on this—and that overall her disordered thoughts and feelings did not involve the kind of break with reality that the APA test contemplates. She did not hear voices, did not have visions, did not have delusions about alien conspirators or satanic forces. As many people do who suffer setbacks, she thought that others were out to get her and she angrily retaliated. Indeed, this is better understood as a case of road rage, the state will contend. Bridget may need mental health treatment, but under the APA rule, a prosecutor would argue that she did not suffer from a sufficient mental disease or disorder.

The defense would respond that Bridget's perception that the security guard was part of a larger conspiracy against her—for which there was little or no evidence—constitutes a major problem with reality testing. She did not comprehend what was actually going on here and therefore her condition did "grossly and demonstrably" compare her perception of reality. Why else would she try to run over the security guard?

The Politics of Insanity

Insanity is a notorious defense partly because it arises so often in high-profile cases. Fatal and near fatal attacks on famous leaders and celebrities are often committed by persons with serious mental illness.

Consider the two most influential cases in Anglo-American insanity law. The M'Naughton *rule comes from a case in which a Scotsman killed the Prime Minister's secretary in an effort to assassinate the Prime Minister; M'Naughton's acquittal upset many, including Queen Victoria and prompted a review of the defense at the highest level of the English judiciary in the House of Lords. More recently, the acquittal of John W. Hinckley Jr. for the attempted assassination of President Reagan provoked great controversy and led to significant changes in federal and state law in the United States.*[16]

Insanity also stirs controversy because of the nature of the offenses to which it is raised as a defense. Even when the victim is not famous, insanity cases often involve apparently senseless and unpredictable attacks, frequently deadly, upon persons with no previous connection to the defendant. This makes the crimes, and their perpetrators, especially frightening.

These factors combine with a third to stir great public feeling: there is rarely any doubt as to who committed the crime. Insanity cases are, virtually by definition, whydunit cases and not whodunits. There is no doubt that the defendant committed the criminal act, and as we have seen, there is usually little doubt about mens rea. This makes the defendant appear highly culpable under ordinary rules, and yet a candidate for a complete excuse, under insanity.

Finally, many question the value of testimony by mental health experts. For more on this, see the sidebar below on The Problem of Expertise.

The fact that insanity cases stir great controversy means that the law will always be under great political pressure here. Insanity serves to remind us that American criminal law not only has popular origins, but, in some important respects, must always respond to public demands.

Essential Components of Insanity: (2) Cognition

The next requirement of insanity involves the defendant's cognitive abilities. Cognitive ability refers to the individual's thought process. Cognitive tests for insanity assess the defendant's understanding of the wrongness of his or her own conduct.

---

16. Michael Perlin, *The Jurisprudence of the Insanity Defense* 335–40 (1994).

The *M'Naughton* Test for Insanity

Under the famous *M'Naughton* test, a defendant, *as a result of mental disease or defect, must either not know the nature and quality of his actions, or, must not know that his conduct was wrong* in order to be acquitted by insanity. The rule is cognitively focused, requiring either: (1) lack of knowledge of the nature or quality of actions; or (2) no knowledge of the wrongfulness of conduct. Note that these are disjunctive tests; satisfaction of either element (according to the applicable burden of proof) will produce an insanity acquittal.

Knowing the Nature and Quality of Actions

The first prong of *M'Naughton* assesses whether the defendant knew what he or she was doing. Even with seriously mentally ill defendants, it is rarely satisfied in practice. This prong has been eliminated in some recent reformulations of the *M'Naughton* test[17] but remains part of the law in many jurisdictions.

This prong of insanity describes a profound cognitive confusion that we might imagine is characteristic of the mentally ill but is rarely presented by those accused of crime. In order to commit the acts that comprise theft or assault or homicide, a person must have a basic grasp of material reality. One must know about such things as stores and guns and human bodies.[18]

In practice, analysis of this first prong of insanity proves very similar to mens rea analysis. For example, just as we saw that Daniel M'Naughton acted with murder mens rea in his attack on the prime minister's secretary, so it is clear that he understood that he was using a gun to kill another human being. Indeed the latter understanding is critical to the former. Another example will help illustrate.

Jake was a troubled young man who lived in a small town in Texas. He drank too much, had a quick and violent temper and expressed racially bigoted ideas, especially with respect to Mexicans. Everyone

---

17. See Clark v. Arizona, 548 US 735, 747–56 (2006).

18. The frequently used example in the legal literature comes from the Commentary to the Model Penal Code, which hypothesized a man squeezing his wife's neck, believing it to be a lemon. *Model Penal Code and Commentaries* Sec. 4.01 at 166 (1985). This example has been widely criticized as not representative of the kinds of delusions suffered by the seriously mentally ill accused of criminal acts. See Stephen J. Morse, Excusing the Crazy: The Insanity Defense Reconsidered, 58 S. Cal. L. Rev. 777, 802 (1985).

who knew Jake understood that he had mental problems, but Jake adamantly refused to seek treatment.

After being fired from his job, Jake stole a high-powered rifle and ammunition, dug himself a bunker on a hill above the town and began shooting migrant laborers of Mexican descent working in a lettuce field. He killed three and seriously wounded two others. Two hours later he was caught by police trying to board a bus leaving town. He was disguised—rather badly—as a woman. He initially gave a false identity. Soon, however, Jake admitted his identity and involvement. He told the police that he shot "the dirty Mexicans" because they were spreading a new antibiotic-resistant infection as part of a larger Al Qaeda conspiracy that had its origins in Hitler's Third Reich. Police find no evidence of such a conspiracy.

Jake is diagnosed by both defense and prosecution experts as severely schizophrenic. They agree that he suffers paranoid delusions concerning many persons, but especially those of Mexican heritage.

Assuming that Jake suffered from a mental disease or defect, did he understand the nature and quality of his actions?

Jake almost certainly does not meet the first cognitive prong of *M'-Naughton*: the facts indicate that he knew the nature and quality of his actions. He understood that he was firing a deadly weapon at human beings and that his actions, if successful, would kill. That was what he wanted. The major question will involve his understanding of wrongfulness— discussed further below.

There is one set of cases where "nature and quality" analysis may prove significant: where mental illness leads to a delusion about the victim's humanity. Mentally ill defendants charged with acts of violence often claim to have acted to defend themselves from malevolent others who are directed by supernatural forces. In previous centuries, the mad often claimed that their victims were agents of the devil. A more contemporary version is the belief that the victim was an extraterrestrial alien. Here we confront a question both metaphysical and pragmatic. Is it that the defendant truly did not understand that the victim was human, or is it that the defendant (like M'Naughton) saw the victim as human but believed him or her to be inspired or directed by malevolent forces? The former belief would tend to support the notion that Jake did not understand the quality of his actions. We will return to the problem of mental illness and recognizing humanity in the discussion of diminished capacity at the end of the chapter.

Knowing Right from Wrong

The last prong of *M'Naughton* is usually where the action is. It is also where most of the legal controversies lie. Every part of this prong is subject to potentially important interpretive questions.

When the rule speaks of "knowing," is this knowledge purely cognitive, that is, intellectual knowledge, or does it also include emotional understanding? The distinction could be critical. A person may know intellectually that conduct is wrong—know that she will get in trouble for doing it—and yet have little emotional understanding of wrongness. In practice, most jury instructions do not make a clear distinction between these rival views of knowledge, leaving the critical question to the trier of fact.

Moving on: What is it that the defendant must "know"? Depending on jurisdiction, the object of knowledge is variously described as the wrongfulness, illegality or criminality of defendant's conduct. These variations introduce an underlying philosophic and doctrinal question. Does knowledge here go to legal wrong or moral wrong? Does it defeat an insanity claim if the defendant understood that he or she was breaking the law and thus would be subject to arrest and prosecution? What if the defendant understood this but also believed that his conduct was morally justified? The *M'Naughton* case presents an illustrative example. Daniel M'Naughton likely understood that he was subject to arrest and conviction for shooting the Prime Minister, but he thought he had to do so because the Prime Minister and other Tories were out to kill him. Within his worldview, M'Naughton saw himself acting in self-defense. Again, most jurisdictions do not provide juries with an explicit instruction on legal versus moral wrong.[19]

One final, practical caution with respect to these interpretive nuances. Studies and experience suggest that most decision makers do not parse the legal rules of insanity the way that lawyers do. Most insanity cases turn on a complex emotional and moral assessment of the defendant, his conduct, and expert testimony, filtered through the personal experiences and philosophies of

---

19. Compare State v. Hollis, 731 P.2d 260, 269 (Kan. 1987) (legal wrong); People v. Skinner, 704 P.2d 752 (Cal. 1985) (moral wrong).

If knowledge does refer to legal wrong, this phrase should not be interpreted as meaning statutory knowledge. The defendant need not know the specific criminal law being violated. Requiring such knowledge would convert the cognitive prong of insanity into a kind of mistake of law claim and no court or legislature one wants that. What matters is that the defendant know his conduct will be socially condemned, that he risks prosecution and punishment.

the decision maker. Differences in these factors, rather than in rule interpretation, or even the rules themselves, generally have the most impact.

Return to the case of Jake noted earlier. Assuming that Jake suffered from a mental disease or disorder, do the facts indicate that he did not know the wrongness of his conduct?

The defense will argue here that Jake's shooting of the Mexican field workers is understandable only from Jake's delusional worldview. He has a bizarre and entirely unsupported belief that the workers were part of a Hitler-originated, Al Qaeda terrorism-by-infection scheme that would put the entire community, and perhaps the nation, at terrible risk. Therefore Jake believed that he was justified in his attack. What made his conduct actually wrongful—that his victims in fact posed no physical threat to himself or anyone else—was obscured by Jake's mental illness. The essence of this argument is that Jake's motive for killing was crazy.

The prosecution will retort that Jake acted not from illness but depravity, that his motive was not crazy but evil. Angry over the loss of his job, and filled with an ugly but common bigotry against people of another race and ethnicity, his rage motivated an attack on entirely innocent people. Jake's knowledge of the wrongness of his conduct is evident in the way he planned his attack and in his efforts to escape detection. If he had really thought his conduct was justified, he would not have tried to run away as he did, nor would he have tried to hide his identity or deny his involvement.

The MPC Test for Insanity

The Model Penal Code test[20] for insanity was designed to expand the defense beyond the *M'Naughton* rule in a number of respects. This means that whenever the facts would support an insanity defense under *M'Naughton*, they will also support insanity under the MPC test. The MPC may also provide for an insanity verdict in some situations where *M'Naughton* would not.

Section 4.01 of the Model Penal Code provides that "*[a] person is not responsible for criminal conduct if at the time of such conduct as a result of mental disease or defect he lacks substantial capacity either to appreciate the criminality [wrongfulness] of his conduct or to conform his conduct to the requirements of law.*" The MPC rule has three parts: (1) mental disease or defect and, either,

---

20. This test is sometimes called the ALI test, because it was originally proposed by the American Law Institute which authored the Model Penal Code.

(2) lacks substantial capacity to appreciate the criminality [wrongfulness] or (3) lacks substantial capacity to conform his conduct of the requirements of law.

The MPC has no definition for mental disease or defect, meaning that the previous discussion of that element applies equally here. The Code does have a specific exclusion for psychopathy, however.[21]

Cognitive analysis under the MPC largely parallels that under *M'Naughton*, with some differences noted below. It is the last prong of the MPC test, providing for a volitional test, which proves the most distinctive and controversial element of the rule.

Cognitive Analysis under the MPC

Although the cognitive prong of the MPC bears many similarities to *M'Naughton*, there are a number of potentially important distinctions. The *M'Naughton* rule asks whether the defendant knew the wrongness of conduct. This is an all or nothing question, seeking only a yes or no response. The MPC introduces a matter of degree with the adjective "substantial." Thus, a defendant could be found insane if the defendant had some ability to understand wrongness, but lacked a substantial ability to do so.

The MPC focuses explicitly on *capacity* to comprehend. While the *M'Naughton* rule asks whether the defendant did or did not understand wrongness, the MPC encourages inquiry into what the defendant *could* have comprehended—his or her capacity for understanding. The MPC rule provides for alternative language for the subject of understanding: either criminality or wrongness. This choice involves the same considerations discussed previously concerning legal versus moral wrong under *M'Naughton*.

Perhaps the most significant distinction is the MPC's substitution of "appreciation" for the *M'Naughton* rule's "knowledge." The word appreciation opens the door to arguments that the defendant's understanding must include the emotional, and not be restricted to the intellectual.

Application to Jake

Arguments concerning Jake's possible insanity under the MPC's cognitive prong are made in slightly different terms, but largely echo those under the *M'Naughton* rule.

Jake will argue that even if he knew that he would face arrest and prosecution for the shootings (hence his running away and crude disguise), because

---

21. MPC sec. 4.01 (2)(antisocial personality disorder exclusion).

of his delusions he lacked significant capacity to appreciate the wrongfulness of that conduct. He was not able to appreciate—could not comprehend in any meaningful way—the wrongness of what he was doing. He felt and believed that the field workers posed a deadly threat to the community. These feelings and beliefs so dominated his perspective that he could not and did not understand himself to be committing murder.

The prosecution will respond as before: that although Jake's manifestation of bigotry was extreme and might be connected to his mental illness, he nevertheless demonstrated basic understanding of his own wrongdoing. That he had the capacity to appreciate wrongfulness is indicated by the way in which he planned the attack and then sought to escape its consequences by flight from the jurisdiction. He understood that his conduct was wrong, but did not let that stop him. In sum, he did not shoot because he was crazy but because he hated Mexicans.

Essential Components of Insanity: (3) Volitional Analysis under the MPC

Unlike the *M'Naughton* rule, the Model Penal Code also includes a volitional prong to insanity. The MPC rule provides that a defendant is insane, regardless of cognition if, by virtue of mental disease or defect, he or she "*lacks substantial capacity ... to conform his conduct to the requirements of law.*"

This part of the MPC rule has been rejected by a number of jurisdictions in recent years. Its workability has been questioned. How can fact finders reliably tell whether a person *could not* conform to the requirements of law or simply *did not want to*?

The volitional prong also raises questions about the nature of individual responsibility. Is volition, as opposed to rationality, truly essential to a person being morally and legally responsible? After all, many persons, from psychopaths to kleptomaniacs to pedophiles to drug addicts, seem to lack the volitional capacity needed to refrain from criminality and yet they are held responsible.

Nevertheless, some jurisdictions retain the volitional prong of the MPC or have an insanity rule that includes similar considerations.

> Marguerite is a mother of three small children who has long suffered from depression and substance abuse. When her husband leaves her, she drinks more heavily. Her economic situation also becomes desperate. The center of Marguerite's life is her three children. But she starts to believe that her children are possessed, that

they are plotting to kill her. Marguerite calls the police to report her fears of her children; a police officer and a social worker come to her house in response. Marguerite repeats her fears of her children and says that she might have to "do something" to them, but adds: "I don't want to." The social worker suggests that she should commit herself for mental treatment, but Marguerite refuses, worried who would care for the children. She says that she keeps the television tuned to a religious channel and that will keep her and the children safe. Two days later, her eldest daughter calls 911 to say that her mother has drowned her two-year-old brother, Timmy, in the bathtub.

Police respond and find Timmy dead. Marguerite admits drowning her son. She says that she feels horrible about what she did, but "there was just this incredible pressure inside that was pushing and pushing me, like gravity and the tide and everything, to make me do it and I knew Timmy would get me if I didn't."

Assuming that Marguerite suffered from a qualifying mental disease or defect, might she be found insane under the volitional prong of the MPC?

Here, as in many cases, there may be considerable overlap between cognitive and volitional analysis. The defense may argue that Marguerite's delusions concerning her children show basic irrationality and therefore a lack of capacity to appreciate the wrongfulness of her conduct. There is no rational reason why she would consider a two-year-old a serious threat. The prosecution would point to a number of facts indicating Marguerite's appreciation of wrongfulness in statements that she made to the social worker before and the police after the killing. At both times she indicated some awareness that she should not harm her children. And she took measures to restrain herself, by calling the police originally and by leaving the television on a religious channel. These indicators of cognitive awareness mean that the availability of a volitional argument might make a difference in the case.

Marguerite's volitional argument is that even if she had substantial capacity to comprehend the wrongness of her action, she could not refrain from harming Timmy. The internal pressures generated by her mental illness were overwhelming. She remained a mother who loved her children; only the most overwhelming psychological pressure could force her to do what she did. As a result of that illness, she lacked substantial capacity to conform her conduct to the requirements of law.

The prosecution can question Marguerite's account of psychological in-capacity by pointing to the choices that she made. She was able to call the police before acting on her violent impulses. She was offered professional help, but she refused it. At the time of the killing she may have been overwhelmed by her need to "do something" to her apparently threatening child, but the prosecution may argue that in this experience she is no different than many persons who commit serious crimes. She acted while under the influence of a strong emotion. Subsequently she regretted her action and seeks to avoid responsibility by saying that the action was not characteristic of her, was not really "hers." The point is not that these arguments—or those of the defense—will necessarily prevail, but they should give some sense of the legal debate.

Dual Diagnosis: Substance Abuse, Mental Illness and Insanity

The phrase, dual diagnosis, signifies a person who suffers from both mental illness and substance abuse. Such individuals need treatment for both conditions; focusing on only one will not suffice. Dual diagnoses are fairly common, as individuals with mental illness often use alcohol and other drugs as a form of self-medication to relieve the most painful symptoms of their mental illness. Dual diagnosis is not a legal term, but it does raise the question of how we might distinguish intoxication and mental illness for purposes of criminal responsibility.

A defendant may not raise a claim of temporary insanity based on the effects of any voluntarily ingested intoxicant. Whether the intoxicant is alcohol, a narcotic or a hallucinogen, whether the consumption is the result of casual choice or an addiction, the resulting intoxication will not count as a mental disease or defect. This is true even if intoxication has a powerfully distorting effect on the individual's perceptions of reality. The only exception is when the intoxicating effect is profoundly different than anticipated, a condition known as pathological intoxication, which renders the intoxication involuntary in legal terms. For more on this, see Chapter 19.

In most jurisdictions, a condition known as "settled insanity," recognizes that long-term abuse of alcohol can produce lasting brain damage, manifested in irrationality. A long-term alcoholic may experience delusions and hallucinations similar to those caused by diseases such as schizophrenia, and these symptoms may occur even without the ingestion of alcohol.

Diminished Capacity

We close with an issue broached at the beginning of the chapter: the use of mental illness evidence to support not an affirmative defense, but as to negate mens rea.

Definition and Overview

As is often true in criminal law, clear understanding of diminished capacity requires a careful definition of terms.[22] As used here, diminished capacity refers to the argument that proof of the defendant's mens rea for an offense is lacking due to mental illness. For example, a defendant charged with stealing a car might argue that he lacked the purpose to deprive the car's owner of the vehicle permanently—a required mens rea—due to delusions he experienced as a result of his mental illness. Perhaps his mental delusions support his contention that he was only "borrowing" the car.

Understood in this way, diminished capacity should present few special problems. It involves nothing more than the use of a certain kind of evidence (defendant's mental illness) to negate proof of mens rea. The only question should be whether the argument works, that is, whether mental illness evidence changes our view of defendant's mens rea. But because mental health evidence raises special concerns for many, especially because it involves expert testimony, it receives special treatment in the law.

As we have seen before, complexity in criminal doctrine usually reflects a conflict in underlying values. Here the conflict is between the principle that conviction should depend on individual culpability (as measured by mens rea) and the fear that widespread use of mental illness evidence will result in the release of dangerous persons.

The principle that culpability depends on mens rea argues for no restrictions on mental illness evidence. The jury should be able to decide, based on the facts presented, whether the would-be thief experienced delusions and whether these delusions mean that he did not act with the required purpose to deprive permanently. Concerns about how this works in practice, however, have led many jurisdictions to impose restrictive rules, and some to prohibit diminished capacity arguments entirely. Understanding these concerns will be important to understanding the doctrine.

---

22. As is often true, unfortunately, in American criminal law, courts and legislatures do not always use the phrase in the same way.

Diminished capacity arguments potentially present greater public safety concerns than does the insanity defense. In theory, diminished capacity arguments could apply to any crime with a subjective mens rea requirement, meaning virtually all serious criminal cases. Moreover, if diminished capacity produces an acquittal, the special rules for involuntary commitment post-insanity acquittal will not apply.

Also troubling to many is that evidence of diminished capacity often comes from mental health experts who testify in abstract terms about a defendant's *capacity* to choose in a particular way. This can be very difficult evidence for lay fact finders to assess. Concerns about the testimony of mental health experts represent a major factor driving diminished capacity restrictions and prohibition. For more on this, see the accompanying sidebar on expertise.

Finally, the technique of shifting the burden of proof to the defense which has been used with the insanity defense, is not constitutionally possible here. Diminished capacity involves proof of mens rea; mens rea is an essential element of the offense and due process requires that the prosecution prove every essential element beyond a reasonable doubt. As a result, where diminished capacity is available, a defendant may gain acquittal by using mental illness evidence to raise a reasonable doubt about mens rea.

These concerns, and general anxiety about the difficulty of assessing the responsibility of mentally ill, have persuaded some courts and legislatures to restrict or bar entirely diminished capacity arguments.

The Elimination of Diminished Capacity

A recent case decided by the United States Supreme Court provides a good introduction to current controversies about diminished capacity and its elimination by some jurisdictions.[23]

> There was no question at trial that Eric Clark was seriously mentally disturbed. Both defense and prosecution experts agreed that he suffered from schizophrenia and had paranoid delusions.[24] Prior to the murder for which he was charged, Clark expressed the belief that a number of people he encountered were aliens and were out to get him. Among these aliens were government agents. He said that only bul-

---

23. Clark v. Arizona, 548 U.S. 735 (2006).

24. The severity of Clark's mental illness is also indicated by the fact that not only was he initially found incompetent to stand trial, it took two years of treatment to restore him to competence. Id. At 743.

lets would kill the aliens. Several weeks before the killing Clark remarked that he wanted to shoot police officers.

In the early morning hours, Clark drove his pickup truck around a residential neighborhood with music blaring. A uniformed police officer in a patrol car responded to a complaint about the noise, and, using the cruiser's lights and sirens, pulled over Clark's truck. Shortly after being pulled over, Clark fatally shot the police officer and ran away. He was subsequently arrested. The gun that killed the officer was found nearby, stuffed into a knit cap. Clark was charged with murder by "intentionally or knowingly killing a law enforcement officer in the line of duty."

Putting aside the question of insanity, how might Clark's mental illness affect proof of the required mens rea for murder in this case?

Absent consideration of mental illness evidence, the required mens rea may be inferred from defendant's statements and actions. Clark had previously expressed a desire to shoot and kill police. That is exactly what he did. By driving around a residential neighborhood with music blaring in the early morning hours, he acted in a way very likely to draw police attention. When he was pulled over, he fatally shot the uniformed officer who responded in a marked police car. These actions appear inexplicable except as actions designed to kill another human being, specifically an on-duty police officer.

When we take into account evidence of Clark's mental illness, however, an alternative interpretation appears. Schizophrenics often use loud music or other noise to try to drown out their own internal voices. This gives an alternative explanation of why Clark might have been playing his music loud.

Clark's delusions about humans-disguised-as-aliens raises the question of whether Clark believed that the victim was a human police officer or an alien in disguise. If Clark did not comprehend the human nature of his victim, then he did not intentionally or knowingly kill a (human) police officer.

This brings us to the legal question of diminished capacity: will expert testimony about Clark's mental illness be admissible on the question of whether he purposely killed a police officer? In the actual case, Arizona law prohibited such diminished capacity evidence, and the United States Supreme Court held that this prohibition did not violate the constitutional requirement of due process.[25]

---

25. Clark v. Arizona, 548 US 735 (2006). Justice Souter writing for the majority stated that Arizona law permitted what he termed "observational evidence" about defendant's mens rea but that expert testimony concerning diagnosis of mental disease and capacity for decision making were prohibited. Id. at 756–65. The Court also held that the state's elim-

The Problem of Expertise: Medical Science v. Law

A great deal of the legal controversy over insanity and diminished capacity centers on the testimony of mental health experts: usually psychologists or psychiatrists, who provide assessments of the defendant's past and present mental condition. Expert testimony is essential to sound decision making about many issues, especially insanity, but it nevertheless raises many challenges in criminal cases. How can mental health experts provide useful and reliable information to those who must actually decide cases—juries and judges?

The basic problem is that mental health experts and lawyers work in very different professional worlds. The mental health professions are primarily devoted to diagnosis and therapy, while legal professionals focus primarily on individual responsibility. Each field has its own language and essential concepts. Mental health experts speak the language of science, with its central concept of physical causation: what causes certain events in the physical world. Lawyers speak the language of morals, with a focus on the choices that individuals make. While each may deal with the same phenomenon—a person with a mental illness who undertakes certain behavior—each does so in a very different fashion. Moving between these worlds requires translating concepts and language from one to the other, and this is difficult at best. If not handled well, the differences in approach between law and mental health science lead to a turf battle, one that science normally loses because law necessarily controls the courtroom. The chart set out below provides a shorthand view of the different languages, aims and subjects of these two different worlds.

Medical/Scientific	Law/Morals
language of behavior	language of chosen action
primary aim is to treat	primary aim is to judge
concerned with genetic and environmental causes	concerned with reasons for action

Many recent reforms of insanity and diminished capacity have been based on criticism of expert testimony: that mental health experts do not know what they claim to, and that their expertise is of only weak relevance, if that, to legal questions. The fact remains, however, that mental health

---

ination of the "nature and quality" prong of the *M'Naughton* insanity test was constitutional. Id. at 746–55.

professionals know a great deal more about mental illness than do most lawyers or lay persons. For example, it takes significant experience with mental illness to recognize the symptoms of psychosis in some situations, or to distinguish between post-traumatic stress disorder and bipolar disorders. Unfortunately, the law has not devised reliable ways for experts to educate decision makers about common patterns of mental illness without also confusing medical and legal terms. To put this another way, the law has not done a good job of distinguishing between what experts can teach about mental illness and what decision makers must decide about the responsibility of the accused. Too often the law has veered between extremes: from allowing broad expert testimony with relatively little guidance to decision makers, to outright exclusion of potentially critical expert testimony.

In the author's view, mental health experts are most helpful in comparing the defendant's illness with general patterns of mental illness documented in the mental health literature. Mental health opinions on whether the defendant did or did not meet a particular legal standard, seem less useful. And, I would argue, experts do not have sufficient ability to assess psychological capacity—whether a defendant could have done differently in a particular situation—to permit expert opinions about capacity to choose.

Basic Diminished Capacity Doctrine—Where Recognized

With respect to diminished capacity analysis, we ask the same basic questions we did with voluntary intoxication: (1) Is the argument allowed? and (2) If allowed, will it work on the facts of the case?

For those jurisdictions that bar diminished capacity arguments, the answer to the first question is no in all criminal cases. A caution must be added here, however: it is important to look at the jurisdiction's definition of diminished capacity to know exactly what is prohibited. For example, in California, mental illness evidence cannot be used in any case to establish diminished *capacity*, meaning the *ability* to act with a particular mens rea, but such evidence may be used in some cases to determine whether the defendant actually *did* act with the required mens rea.[26]

---

26. In California, "diminished capacity" is statutorily prohibited, but mental illness evidence *may* be used to negate specific intent mens rea by proof that the defendant did not actually act with such mens rea. Thus the focus shifts from diminished capacity to what is called diminished actuality. Cal. Pen. Code sec. 28(a).

Specific v. General Intent, Again

In most jurisdictions where diminished capacity is allowed, we find a doctrinal structure similar to voluntary intoxication: mental illness evidence is available to negate specific intent forms of mens rea, but not general intent. Thus, initially we need to determine whether the particular offense has one or more specific intent elements.

As with voluntary intoxication doctrine, discovery of a specific intent element represents only the first step of analysis. Then we must determine whether the argument will work on the facts given. Consider the following example.

> A security camera records these events. Late at night, a salesman leaves an office building and walks through an alley to the parking lot where he left his car. Malcolm, a homeless person, is huddled in the alley. As the salesman approaches, Malcolm suddenly attacks him with a home-made knife, stabbing him 10 times in the chest and abdomen, killing him. Malcolm flees the scene, but is soon arrested because of the blood on his clothes.
>
> Malcolm is diagnosed as a schizophrenic, who suffers paranoid delusions. He maintains that he killed the salesman because the salesman was about to attack him. Malcolm could tell because the salesman wore his hair short, indicating that he was an Army commando. There is no objective evidence to indicate that the victim was a threat to Malcolm, however. Malcolm refuses to consider an insanity defense, because he believes he is not crazy. He says he just did what he had to.
>
> Malcolm is charged with the first-degree, premeditated purpose to kill murder of the salesman. Putting aside any question of insanity, can evidence of Malcolm's mental illness be used to negate proof of the required mens reas for this offense?

As we saw in the discussion of intoxication, the premeditation and purpose to kill needed for first-degree murder are specific intent mens reas. Therefore, at least in those jurisdictions that recognize the specific intent version of diminished capacity, Malcolm's defense counsel can introduce evidence of his mental illness to argue that he lacked one or both of these forms of mens rea.

> Assuming that the diminished capacity argument is legally available, did Malcolm lack the required mens rea for premeditated purpose to kill murder because of his mental illness?

Here we should begin with the more basic mens rea requirement: purpose to kill. There are strong indications of purpose to end a life in Malcolm's knife attack. Malcolm's repeated use of a deadly weapon on vital organs indicates that Malcolm sought the salesman's death. Nor are these indications undercut by Malcolm's paranoid delusions. Instead, these explain his motive for killing; why Malcolm wanted to kill. His mental illness might support an insanity defense, but probably does not negate purpose to kill.

The analysis of premeditation is more complex. The defense here has a plausible argument that because of mental illness, Malcolm was in a state of mental and emotional turmoil that precluded the kind of calculation about killing and consideration of its consequences required for premeditation. Instead the homicide was a spontaneous response to the sudden (apparent) threat posed by the salesman. If premeditation is defined in the jurisdiction as just a moment's thought about homicide prior to action, however (see Chapter 9), evidence of mental illness is less likely to undercut premeditation.

The MPC Approach to Diminished Capacity

The Model Penal Code does not provide any special rules for mental illness evidence. As a result, mental illness evidence may be used to negate all subjective forms of mens rea: purpose, knowledge, and recklessness. By definition, it cannot negate negligence, because negligence is an objective standard based on the standard of the reasonable person, a person presumed to be mentally sound.

Although in many instances the Model Penal Code rule will operate in similar fashion to the specific versus general intent distinction in other jurisdictions, there is one important difference. Under the MPC, mental illness evidence *may* be used to negate recklessness. Therefore, a defendant may argue that because of a mental illness he or she was not aware of the critical facts needed for conviction of a recklessness offense.[27]

Diminished Responsibility Distinguished

Often confused with diminished capacity is the concept of diminished responsibility. While diminished capacity involves negation of mens rea; diminished responsibility lowers the offense level due to lesser individual responsibility. In this respect it parallels insanity analysis. The great difference

---

27. This is also where the treatment of mental illness evidence diverges from that under voluntary intoxication. The MPC prohibits use of voluntary intoxication evidence to negate recklessness; there is no such prohibition for mental illness evidence.

between insanity and diminished responsibility is that a successful insanity defense leads to acquittal, where diminished responsibility reduces the severity of offense and therefore punishment.

Having said this, with a single partial exception, American law *does not recognize* any doctrine of diminished responsibility. Diminished responsibility arguments may be presented at sentencing, but in most instances such arguments cannot alter the actual offense of conviction.

The lone exception is a provision of the Model Penal Code discussed in Chapter 10, that murder may be reduced manslaughter based on *"extreme mental or emotional disturbance for which there is a reasonable explanation or excuse."* This rule goes beyond the traditional limits of provocation and, depending on how it is interpreted, may include a form of diminished responsibility. But because the rule requires reasonableness in explanation or excuse it is not a true diminished responsibility rule directly connecting mental disorder and reduced responsibility. [28]

---

28. By contrast English law provides for a manslaughter rather than murder verdict when the defendant suffered an abnormality of mind that substantially impairs mental responsibility. The English Homicide Act, 1957, 5 & 6 Eliz. II Ch. 11 sec. 2(1).

INDEX